EUROPE'S NEW FRONTIERS, VOLUME 1

In this book, leading commentators explore the new concept of 'crisis governance constitutionalism' in order to better understand how the EU is changed by times of crisis management.

European integration has become controversial due to the many crises: Brexit, the pandemic, migrations, energy crisis, the Ukraine war. Drawing on historical resources, the collection's expert essays show that rather than offer something completely new, crisis governance constitutionalism coexists with long-established constitutionalist narratives of EU integration.

Volume 143 in the Series Modern Studies in European Law

Modern Studies in European Law

RECENT TITLES IN THIS SERIES:

The Market Citizenship Illusion: Free Movement Rights for Atypical Workers
Alice Welsh

Actors and Roles in EU Disability Law
Edited by Delia Ferri and Eva S Krolla

The Impact of War (in Ukraine) on the EU
Edited by Inge Govaere, Sacha Garben and Eleanor Spaventa

The European Judiciary: A Community of Law and a Community of Judges
Edited by Alejandro Saiz Arnaiz and Joan Solanes Mullor

Dissensus over Liberal Democracy: Insights from European Judges
Edited by Ramona Coman, Viktor Kazai, Leonardo Puleo and Andrew Bradley

Structural Principles of EU Law
Marcus Klamert

Environmental NGOs and Access to Justice before the CJEU
Mario Pagano

Dealing with Rule of Law Crises in the European Union: Challenges from a Comparative Federalism Perspective
Niels F Kirst

EU Citizenship and Responsibility: The Evolving Roles of the Union, the Individual, and the Member States
Maria Haag

EU Cities Facilitating the Commons: Building Blocks of European Constitutional Law for Local Democracy
Chiara Salati

EU Competence and Power
Hannah Bogaert

Activating Human and Fundamental Rights Before the European Courts
Edited by Elise Muir, Sacha Garben and Inge Govaere

The Hidden Virtues of Discretionary Power in European Migration Law
Jonas Bornemann

Europe's New Frontiers: Law, Crisis, Governance, Constitutional Transformations, Volume 1
Edited by Leone Niglia

For the complete list of titles in this series see www.bloomsbury.com/uk/series/modern-studies-in-european-law/

Europe's New Frontiers, Volume 1

Law, Crisis, Governance, Constitutional Transformations

Edited by
Leone Niglia

•HART•
OXFORD • LONDON • NEW YORK • NEW DELHI • SYDNEY

HART PUBLISHING
Bloomsbury Publishing Plc
Kemp House, Chawley Park, Cumnor Hill, Oxford, OX2 9PH, UK
1385 Broadway, New York, NY 10018, USA
Bloomsbury Publishing Ireland Limited, 29 Earlsfort Terrace, Dublin 2, D02 AY28, Ireland

First published in Great Britain 2026

1

A catalogue record for this book is available from the British Library.

Library of Congress Control Number: 2026944329

ISBN: HB: 978-1-50999-001-6
ePDF: 978-1-50999-003-0
ePub: 978-1-50999-002-3

Typeset by Amnet

PREFACE AND ACKNOWLEDGEMENTS

LEONE NIGLIA

The scholarly discourse about law, crisis and governance presents us with a conundrum: as we gain knowledge about EU governance interventions, we face a new crisis that challenges the previously acquired knowledge. Yet this book submits to scrutinise the thesis that underneath the cycle of crises that have been affecting EU integration stand constitutional materials in transformation that underwrite them all, and that by directing our attention to these crisis-ridden structures we are able to unveil those *dureé moyenne* ways that equip us with the resources to map and govern the relevant constitutional conflicts. Understanding the design and impact of the EU crisis governance interventions, and among them of the groundbreaking Next Generation EU (NG-EU) programme, requires more than drawing on the immediate knowledges from bureaucracy, markets and expertise: it requires drawing on the deeper institutional and theoretical materials and their historical pedigree.

Exploring the constitutional qualities of the ongoing governance transformations is about embarking in this trajectory of becoming aware of the crisis ridden organisational principles not really considered in a literature that only approaches the theme in legalistic terms, as it is the case of the highly technical literature on the details of the NG-EU, and somehow glossed over in the salient critical literatures on constitutional imaginaries and on theoretical aspects of economic constitution materials. Once introduced as new view of the cathedral, *crisis governance constitutionalism* in its *reflexive* articulation becomes the third pillar of a triad of approaches that defines the perimeter of the critical debate over governing crisis in Europe.

We are still far from designing what I would call an 'intelligence of governance' as the possibility of agency (not system) that discerns and enables collective choices as needed towards crisis resolution — one that, I argue in the pages that follow, should be constitutionally reflexive as opposed to crisis interventions seen as the sheer management of the exercise of power pragmatically and apologetically accommodated by the legal discourse. To say it otherwise, the systemic steering problems need to be addressed through a renovated social integration discourse. One of the aims of the project, to which this book belongs, is to contribute to this fundamental task. The references to the works of Jurgen Habermas and of

Niklas Lhumann are about proposing further critical readings of them, without forgetting and consciously drawing on the lessons of the Kelsen-Schmitt dispute with regard to the aspects of emergency constitutionalism and of the safeguarding of the constitution. Key questions addressed in the light of this perspective include: whether and under which constitutional modalities crisis governance is under constitutional control; whether constitutionalism risks becoming about just managing crisis governance or whether the transformation of crisis governance as new constitutionalism can be combined with preserving the normative-constitutional heritage; whether we experience a normal or an exceptional mode of crisis governance constitutionalism.

The NGEU is the major EU crisis governance intervention that this book project analyses.

This book maps a range of constitutional positions, from legalism to democratic/social to ordoliberal constitutionalism, including introducing the new thesis of a *constitutionally reflexive governance* and, critically, of a context of a-constitutionality through crisis governance, discussing those governance theories characterised by the trait of *a-constitutionality* traceable less to an allegedly lack of democratic posture on the part of the 'experts' (as some argue) and more to historical developments, in my view, that is, a management culture insulated from the need for knowing and acting as part of a larger *constitutional* collective. The challenge of 'converting' a-constitutional narratives into constitutionally aware modes of reflexive governance is, in my view, ahead of us and this book provides arguments for the need to fill this gap.

This book adopts the comparative method of 'comparative juridical hermeneutics' as previously introduced by the editor in other publications, including two of them in this series – the monographic works *The Transformation of Contract in Europe*, *The Struggle for European Private Law. A Critique of Codification*, *The Structural Transformation of European Private Law. A Critique of Juridical Hermeneutics* – towards assessing the changing discourse of law crisis governance as juridical hermeneutical materials always subject to change and contestation and reflexively contributing to the ongoing transformation of integration and its constitutional characterisation.

The volumes in this series offer an interdisciplinary constitutional reading for understanding the work of the EU institutions, including considering the reviews of the NG-EU implementation process by the European Court of Auditors, and the work of the variety of organs of the member states in implementing the NG-EU national plans, including judicial decisions, also proposing ways for addressing *constitutionally* any reviewed mis- or lack of performance, as understood under the NG-EU.

This book is volume 1 of a series and it is part of the '*Transformations, Integration Through Law and Governance*' (L Niglia ©) multi-year interdisciplinary critical project led by Prof Leone Niglia and based on the following funding grants awarded to the editor as Principal Investigator since 2021: Jean Monnet Chair project n 101047903; Jean Monnet Centre of Excellence project n *101085488*; MUR, PRIN 2022 PNRR project n 2022P3Y2H2; Sapienza University research awards 2020-22.

Views and opinions expressed in this book are solely the responsibility of each author.

Acknowledgements

The editor would like to express acknowledgements: to the European Commission (Education, Audiovisual and Culture Executive Agency) for its support and co-funding as this edited volume is an output of the Jean Monnet Chair award (project no. 101047903) and of the Jean Monnet Centre of Excellence award (project no. 101085488); to the MUR, Italy, for its support and co-funding *('fondi dell'Unione Europea – Next Generation EU, componente M4C2, investimento 1.1. "finanziato dall'Unione europea – NextGenerationEU"*) (the PRIN 2022 PNRR project no. 2022P3Y2H2), and to Sapienza University for its support and co-funding the PRIN 2022, as this edited volume is an output of the PRIN 2022 PNRR; to Sapienza University for its support (research awards, 2020-22); to the Department of Scienze Giuridiche and to the Faculty of Giurisprudenza at Sapienza University, Rome.

Funded by the European Union NextGenerationEU

Co-funded by the European Union

Funded by the European Union. Views and opinions expressed are however those of the author(s) only and do not necessarily reflect those of the European Union or the European Education and Culture Executive Agency (EACEA). Neither the European Union nor EACEA can be held responsible for them.

Finanziato dall'Unione europea NextGenerationEU

MUR

Italiadomani PIANO NAZIONALE DI RIPRESA E RESILIENZA

SAPIENZA UNIVERSITÀ DI ROMA

CONTENTS

INTRODUCTION TO PART 3:
CRISIS GOVERNANCE CONSTITUTIONALISM AND THE PERSPECTIVES OF EXPERIMENTALIST AND OF PUBLIC GOODS' GOVERNANCE THEORIES (POLITICAL SCIENCE AND ECONOMICS)

LIST OF CONTRIBUTORS

Leone Niglia is Professor of Law and Jean Monnet Chair at Sapienza, University of Rome, Italy.

Ulrich Petersmann is Professor of Law at European University Institute, Italy.

Agustín José Menendez is Professor of Moral Philosophy at Universidad Complutense de Madrid, Spain.

Jiří Přibáň is Professor of Law at Cardiff University, UK, and judge at the Constitutional Court of the Czech Republic.

Ming-Sung Kuo is Reader at University of Warwick, UK.

Jonathan Zeitlin is Visiting Fellow at European University Institute, Italy.

David Jonas Bokhorst is Research Associate at European University Institute, Italy.

Edgars Eihmanis is Research Fellow at University of Tartu, Estonia.

Armin Steinbach is Professor of EU Law and Economics at HEC Paris, France.

1

Prologue: Between Constitutionalism and Crisis Governance: Three Perspectives

LEONE NIGLIA

1. Context: On Crisis and Knowledge

In a context of crisis, the three notions of crisis, governance and constitutionalism as referred to in the relevant literature descend from distinct sets of scholarly analysis that prioritize the addressing of each of them. Yet there is an urgent need to map their overall relationships in the institutional context of the European Union, towards identifying the knowledge that matters to understanding and acting, through choosing constitutionally what to do as a collective, in relation to the relevant EU crisis governance interventions.[1] A distinctive pattern of legal knowledge has been emerging that, implicitly or explicitly, brings together the three notions towards addressing crisis resolution, as this book aims to show through critically mapping that pattern.[2]

I see the formation of an EU-driven constitutional knowledge around crisis, governance and constitutionalism as complementing and mirroring, imperfectly and problematically, that kind of knowledge normally present in nation state democratic politics and that has been identified as the triad of knowledge from

[1] The use of 'EU crisis governance interventions' in this book is meant as the paradigmatic Next Generation EU (hereinafter NG-EU) but references to other EU crisis governance interventions such as the buying bonds' programme by the European Central Bank (ECB), the European Stability Mechanism (ESM) and Support to mitigate Unemployment Risks in an Emergency (SURE), are made in the narrative where relevant. Reference is here made to the NG-EU as proposed by the European Commission in May 2020 COM (2020) 456 final, *Europe's Moment: Repair and Prepare for the Next Generation* as approved by the European Council, see European Council Conclusions, 17-18-19-20-21 July 2020, EUCO 10/20; then in 2021 approved as the triad of the EU Recovery Instrument, see Council Regulation (EU) 2020/2094 [2020] OJ L433 I/23, of 14 December 2020, establishing a European Union Recovery Instrument to support the recovery in the aftermath of the COVID-19 crisis – and of the Own Resources Decision – see Council Decision (EU, Euratom) 2020/2053 [2020] OJ L424/1, of 14 December 2020, on the system of own resources of the European Union and repealing Decision 2014/335/EU, Euratom – and of the Recovery and Resilience Facility in Regulation (EU) 2021/241 [2021] OJ L57/17 of the European Parliament and of the Council of 12 February 2021 establishing the Recovery and Resilience Facility.

[2] This book is part of the '*Transformations, Integration Through Law and Governance*' (L Niglia ©) multi-year interdisciplinary critical project led by Prof Leone Niglia as indicated in the preface.

markets, from experts, and from deliberation.[3] It is a kind of constitutional knowledge that typically unfolds, as to both awareness and action, in relation to crisis situations in nation-state contexts and now, it is submitted, in the supranational context. It is knowledge that draws on institutional and theoretical materials, as the three parts of this book aim to show, and it enables insiders to ground crisis resolution in the context of Europe's plural heritage of constitutionalism.

Knowledge of governance of crisis is also related to the historically pathbreaking late-modernity phenomenon of the disappearance of the public sphere and of the crisis of meaning.[4] Yet there is evidence of a more complex reality that also includes counter-movements.[5] Seen in this light, this book considers the question of how the 'intelligence of governance'[6] has been changing as a result of the EU crisis governance interventions, and whether crisis governance has been producing conditions that enable new forms of inclusive governance 'deliberation' or whether it has restated forms of centralised intervention.[7]

I suggest that what I would like to call 'constitutional intelligence' (collective and autonomous intelligence, rather than just systemic intelligence)[8] needs to be looked at carefully as it pertains to governance as being able to shed light on the level of democratic governance that is unfolding in Europe at this moment. Under

[3] L Herzog, *Citizen Knowledge: Markets, Experts, and the Infrastructure of Democracy* (New York, NY: Oxford University Press, 2023). C Joerges 'Economic Constitutionalism and 'the Political' of the 'Economic'' in G Grégoire and X Miny (eds) *The Idea of Economic Constitution in Europe* at p. 189 discusses this in relation to the ECB crisis interventions (see later). I am arguing that a similar argument should apply to the NG-EU (see chapters 4 and 9): *'Following Lisa Herzog, economic ordering in a democratic polity needs to take three varieties of knowledge into account: the knowledge provided by the "discoveries" generated in market processes, the debates within expert communities, and the evaluation of deliberations. As a response to the financial crisis, European law has, instead, entrusted the ECB with – at best – loosely-controllable discretionary powers in the definition of exercise of monetary policy. To put it more drastically: epistemic infallibility has been complemented by the protection of political independence. This is anything but a promising future for the constitutionalization of Europe. It rather documents again the insufficiencies of macroeconomic constitutionalism and likewise microeconomic constitutionalism as advocated by the proponents of the private law society'.*

[4] See Habermas, Jürgen, *Ein Neuer Strukturwandel der Öffentlichkeit und die Deliberative Politik* (Berlin, Suhrkamp, 2022); B-C Han, *Infocracy: Digitilization and the Crisis of Democracy.* Trans. by Daniel Steuer. (Cambridge, Polity Press, 2022).

[5] K Polanyi, *The Great Transformation* (New York, Farrar & Rinehart, 1944). See also C Joerges and J Falke (eds), *Karl Polanyi, Globalisation and the Potential of Law in Transnational Markets* (Oxford, Hart Publishing, 2011); C Joerges, 'A New Type of Conflicts Law as the Legal Paradigm of the Postnational Constellation' in C Joerges and J Falke (eds), *Karl Polanyi, Globalisation and the Potential of Law in Transnational Markets* (Oxford, Hart Publishing, 2011) 465 et seq.

[6] See CE Lindblom, *The Intelligence of Democracy: Decision Making through Mutual Alignment* (New York, Free Press, 1965) (the intelligence of democracy) and D Innerarity, *A Theory of Complex Democracy: Governing in the Twenty-First Century* (London, Bloomsbury Academic, 2025) p. 206. However, I do not just see systems as in themselves intelligent (Innerarity at p. 206: 'the intelligence of the system itself' as 'emerging property of social systems') in that my own theory of comparative juridical hermeneutics rather suggests that constitutional actors radiate their 'intelligence' and choices as agents, in turn developing discursive structures that redesign constitutional orders (see L Niglia *The Structural Transformation of European Private Law. A Critique of Juridical Hermeneutics*, Hart Publishing, 2023).

[7] See below at chapters four, nine, ten.

[8] See and contrast DA Innerarity, *A Theory of Complex Democracy* (London, Bloomsbury Academic, 2025) at p. 206, see fn 6 above.

conditions of emergency interdependences as they unfold in crisis situations,[9] collective constitutional intelligence mutates the structure of hermeneutical struggles that see insiders repositioning themselves regarding the range of the integration objectives and goals.[10] They take up old concepts and notions and remake them, based on their own often conflicting interpretations, whilst eventually being subjected to those interpretations that become dominant and that happen to drive change – a change contingent on the background restructuring of notions and interpretations.[11] It is not just legalism or economic constitutionalism or constitutional imaginaries that matter but the juridical hermeneutics of the actual interpretative struggles.[12] In unveiling them all one can identify better the actual transformations as entailing changes in constitutional structures. Paraphrasing both Koselleck's work and Epictetus' fragments, we can say that in this emergency climate we get those constitutional words that, in re-describing, 'shock' humanity, here that emergency and shock belong to the same semantic condition.[13] This book directs its attention to these internal transformations with a view to mapping Europe's moving constitutional frontiers as crisis sees their redesigning around the rising governance of the relevant steering problems.

Identifying the re-characterisation of the collective 'intelligence of governance' means mobilising the overall constitutional resources towards addressing power asymmetries[14] as the 'difference'[15] that really matters. This is not about a 'system'[16] but about a living law that consists of a plurality of knowledges, as discursive,

[9] On crisis situations and emergency powers see the remainder of this chapter; in a vast literature see eg the political science debates on the definition of crisis, eg in Hanspeter Kriesi et al. *Coming To Terms with the European Refugee Crisis*, OUP. See also the Kelsen-Schmitt dispute: Kelsen, Hans, Wer Soll Der Hüter Der Verfassung Sein? Abhandlungen Zur Theorie Der Verfassungsgerichtsbarkeit in Der Pluralistischen, Parlamentarischen Demokratie, Hg. v. O Oyen, Robert Chr. van. Mohr *Zeitschrift der Savigny-Stiftung für Rechtsgeschichte. Germanistische Abteilung* 128.1 (2011): 904–907.

[10] On crisis and objectives, and on the crisis in social integration, see J Habermas, *Legitimation Crisis* (translated by Thomas McCarthy), (Frankfurt, Polity Press, 1973). On the crisis in systemic integration perspective, see D Innerarity, *A Theory of Complex Democracy* (London, Bloomsbury Academic, 2025); and N Luhmann, *Theory of Society* (Standford University Press, 2012). On hermeneutical struggles see, L Niglia, *The Structural Transformation of European Private Law. A Critique of Juridical Hermeneutics* (Hart Publishing, 2023), which relates to the thesis of *comparative juridical hermeneutics* as applied to the problem of crisis governance.

[11] R Koselleck, and K Tribe, *Futures Past: On the Semantics of Historical Time.* (Cambridge, Massachusetts: The MIT Press, 2018).

[12] L Niglia, *The Structural Transformation of European Private Law A Critique of Juridical Hermeneutics* (Hart Publishing, 2023).

[13] See notably R. Koselleck and K Tribe, *Futures Past: On the Semantics of Historical Time* (Cambridge, Massachusetts, The MIT Press, 2018) p 73 that quotes the 'well known saying of Epictetus' whereby "it is not deeds that shock humanity but the words describing them"', the original being – paraphrasing from the Enchiridion (Section XX) – 'Remember that it is not he who gives abuse or blows, who affronts, but the view we take of these things as insulting'. Taken from https://yourknow.com/uploads/books/5db48c35efecc.pdf

[14] See L Niglia, 'The New Transformation of Europe. Arcana Imperii' (2020) 68 *American Journal of Comparative Law* 151; A Menendez in Ch 3 in this book.

[15] See C Joerges, 'Economic Constitutionalism and "the political" of the "economic"' in G Grégoire and X Miny (eds), *The Idea of Economic Constitution in Europe. Genealogy and Overview* (Brill Nijhoff 2022), p. 789.

[16] See above fn 8.

irreducible to unity, and that need to be taken into account with a view to emphasise both its characteristics and its potential for crisis resolution.

* * *

As economic crisis problems translate into political crisis problems in a situation in which the state is ever more involved in governance,[17] the reflection on 'governance as constitutionalism' acquires a deep meaning in that it is about thinking how to regulate the newly found state role in governance as a legitimation resource while taking into account that a multilevel governance system is also at work and not just the state.[18] Reliance on the heritage of constitutionalism and crisis is all the more appropriate then. The state dimension as crisis experience has been somehow lost in the literature on the EU crisis governance interventions, which have been entirely focused on the supranational level and have represented the state as somehow passively assisting at the remarkable supranational *aggrandisement* of (fiscal) power.

* * *

The systemic steering problems emerging out of crisis need to be addressed through a renovated social integration discourse. The reference to the works of Habermas and Luhmann among others in my chapters are about undertaking re-readings towards this objective. Two aspects need be expressly pointed out, each of which I develop in the remainder, also as a way to propose my own rereading of the chapters' contributions: the argument that economic crisis problems translate in political crisis problems as a return of Habermas' thinking in his *Legitimation Crisis* regarding the dynamics of the steering problems and the need to address them in terms of social integration;[19] and the readings of the work of Luhmann that regard crisis conditions as systemic modes of governance and democracy, in this book project critically understood in terms not of just a system but of a collective mode of making conscious choices through actual actors.[20]

[17] On the return of the state in governance see chapters 4 and 9 in this book and, on the relevance of Habermas' thoughts in '*Legitimation Crisis*' as economic crises once again translate in political crises, see eg K Palmås and N Surber, . 'Legitimation crisis in contemporary technoscientific capitalism.'(2022) 15(3) *Journal of Cultural Economy* 373–379. https://doi.org/10.1080/17530350.2022.2065331 with the qualification that here at work is, as transpires from this book, governance as transnational in its relationship with the state, see eg, chapters 2, 3, 4 and 9 below.

[18] At one of the workshops on which this book is based a discussion took place on the relevance of multilevel governance as being different from the situation in Europe in the 1930s; in my view, the 1930s and the Weimar analogy are still relevant at least in the light of the argument in this volume on the continuing relevance of the state: on multilevel, and on multilevel and state, see L Niglia, 'A Genealogy of Constitutional Europe' in J Chaisse and O Stefan (eds.) *Advancing the Method and the Practice of Transnational Law* (Hart Publishing, 2023) and the chapters by Petersmann and by Menendez in this book.

[19] As discussed below at Chapter 4.

[20] See above, compare and contrast DA Innerarity, *A Theory of Complex Democracy*; earlier see N Luhmann *Theory of Society*, 2012.

2. Europe's New Frontiers: Constitutional Transformations

2.1 The Argument – changing discourses about crisis governance constitutionalism

I take the view that the NG-EU can be really understood not just through the theoretical frameworks of the extant European economic constitutional theses,[21] and of constitutional imaginaries understood as ideologies and as utopias[22] but, complementing these perspectives, through looking at EU transnational governance as a collective phenomenon, discursively framed,[23] that sets in motion a transformation in form and substance (state, EU governance, constitution) yet to be fully recounted.

This means, in no order of importance, first, directing our attention at implementation, that is, at how the system of governance as set in motion under emergency conditions that underlie the NG-EU has been actually working: at the process of implementation of the NG-EU through the national plans as it produces its ongoing outputs (funds' distribution, projects, reforms) through the thematic and nonthematic conditionalities under the Recovery and Resilience Facility (RRF); at what can be called an enhanced proceduralisation of budgetary funding under the RRF constituted by the compounding effect of its conditionalities, of the negotiations over the national plans, of their ongoing renegotiations, and of the overall EU Commission's oversight of the RRF.[24]

Second, it also means examining the changing discourses about crisis governance constitutionalism as a new rising legal consciousness. Both social and ordoliberal aspects are being rearranged towards making intelligible their deployment in the context of crisis governance.[25] Here one must also consider the relevance of broader

[21] See eg G Grégoire and X Miny (eds), The Idea of Economic Constitution in Europe. Genealogy and Overview (Brill Nijhoff 2022); Weber, Ruth, ed. *The Financial Constitution of European Integration: Follow the Money?* (1st ed. London, Hart Publishing, 202).

As to a definition of governance see the interpretation of governance' as meaning 'The structures, processes and actions through which private and public actors interact to address societal goals' on any scale from local to global' (IPCC report, 2023).

[22] See J Komárek, *European Constitutional Imaginaries: Between Ideology and Utopia* (Oxford, UK: Oxford University Press, 2023). Nor can it be understood in terms of legality as legalism, see on this below at Chapter 4.

[23] See above on comparative juridical hermeneutics.

[24] The 2020 Rule of Law Regulation is another aspect of what I am calling the enhanced proceduralisation of budgetary funding phenomenon. On the previous proceduralisation regarding the Euro crisis and related mechanisms for crisis resolution see, including, the European Financial Stabilisation Mechanism and then the European Financial Stability Facility and thereafter the European Stability Mechanism (ESM); and, the Memoranda of understanding, for the critical analysis of which see L Niglia The New Transformation of Europe. Arcana Imperii in (2020) 68(1)*The American Journal of Comparative Law* 151–185. Note that the RRF conditionalities are linked to digitisation and ecology, obliging states to arrange for the spending of a certain percentage of the funds in each of the two areas.

[25] See Part 1 of this volume. See C Joerges 'Economic Constitutionalism and "The Political" of "The Economic"' in G Grégoire and X Miny (eds) *The Idea of Economic Constitution in Europe* at https://brill.com/display/title/63005, at p 789 et seq.

aspects including populism and exceptionalism as they revitalise the plural tradition of constitutional thought that challenges us to rethink both the space and the time of governance.[26] From this vantage point, the conventional reduction to legalism in the literature on the NG-EU is both a way to understand an aspect of EU governance of crisis through constitutionalism and yet also a distraction from what is really needed.[27] Here, a contrast comes to mind: constitutional imaginaries[28] understood as ideology and as utopia must also interrogate us as to the actual discursive structures that make the rising EU governance intelligible, and it is to the latter that this book project directs its attention – towards complementing existing research on constitutional imaginaries and integration.

2.2 Discourses I[29]

The EU crisis governance interventions emerge out of a grammar that the EU Commission keeps framing as part of its regulatory power as reorganised around crisis governance, including the awareness regarding 'disenfranchisement, growing discontent, and the lack of a positive agenda' that 'combine into an erosion of trust in public institutions, polarisation, and an enhanced appeal of extremist, autocratic, or populist movements' so that in this view 'democracy is increasingly challenged as the governance model best suited to deal with growing socio-economic issues'.

This, then, concretely translates into actual measures imposed on the Member States through, for example,. the country specific recommendation of the European Commission for a Council Recommendation on the economic, social, employment, structural and budgetary policies of Italy of 4 June 2025 European Commission COM 212 2025 in which reference is made to the RRF.

This institutionalised crisis discourse is in turn the reference point of, and is coproduced by, academic contributions. It trespasses into scholarship and vice versa, as shown by the references made in the chapters that follow to EU

[26] See chapters 4, 5, 6, 9.

[27] On legalism, see below at Chapter 4.

[28] J Komárek, *European Constitutional Imaginaries*. See also Bartl *Prosperity*, 2024.

[29] Political Guidelines for the European Commission 2024–2029, 'Europe's future in a fractured world will depend on having a strong democracy and on defending the values that give us the freedoms and rights that we cherish'. Political Guidelines for the next European Commission 2024–2029, https://europa.eu/!wywg4P. p. 23. The Strategic Foresight Report, 2023 10 already recalled how 'disenfranchisement, growing discontent, and the lack of a positive agenda combine into an erosion of trust in public institutions, polarisation, and an enhanced appeal of extremist, autocratic, or populist movements' and how 'democracy is increasingly challenged as the governance model best suited to deal with growing socio-economic issues'. The report acknowledges that even 'in the EU, some of the core requirements for a functioning democracy are impaired'. A democratic impairment manifested in several phenomena like 'challenges to the rule of law, and an increasing silent citizenship, eg a consistent decrease of electoral turnout in many Member States in both national and European elections, or the growing lack of interest in general democratic life [. . .] the personalisation of politics, with political leaders considered more important than political parties, [. . .] polarisation of the political debate and the sense of isolation [. . .] amplified by mis- and disinformation, group dynamics in social media, or algorithmic bias'. https://commission.europa.eu/system/files/2023-07/SFR-23_en.pdf

Commission documents on crisis, lastly the so-called 'preparedness strategy'.[30] Policy reports participate in this. For example, in a report it has been held that closer cooperation in core areas and massive investment in shared objectives require that a 'choice between exit, paralysis or integration' be made.[31] And it has been added, on prosperity as key to the future, that 'If Europe cannot become more productive, we will be forced to choose. We will not be able to become, at once, a leader in new technologies, a beacon of climate responsibility and an independent player on the world stage. We will not be able to finance our social model. We will have to scale back some, if not all, of our ambitions. This is an existential challenge'.

We must acknowledge that the documents of the EU Commission are ambiguously relying on general constitutionalist materials and on new governance theories[32] yet paying poor attention to the aspects of autonomy and equality as considered in the remainder. This is an argument that I am proposing in this book.

2.3 Discourses II

Whilst opinions over political economic and political federal aspects are divided over the NG-EU as governance model - as demonstrated inter alia by the grand debate regarding whether the NG-EU should be seen as confirming or countering austerity and, if the latter, what new political economic directions are being taken, and regarding whether the NG-EU involves centralisation or deference[33] - this book gathers chapters that in my view point towards mapping the structural formation (as hermeneutics)[34] of '*crisis governance constitutionalism*', as the 'one thing' emerging out of crisis governance and of constitutionalism as applied to it, in the sense of a constitutionalism that changes itself through, and as a result of, crisis.[35]

[30] https://ec.europa.eu/commission/presscorner/detail/en/ip_25_856.

[31] M Draghi *https://www.europarl.europa.eu/news/en/press-room/20240913IPR23903/draghi-to-meps-europe-faces-a-choice-between-exit-paralysis-or-integration*; *The Future of European Competitiveness*, EU Commission September 2024.

[32] See below at part 3.

[33] For the opinion of the NG-EU as going beyond austerity see eg Zeitlin et al. in this book. For the opinion of confirming austerity see, eg, H Lokdam and MA Wilkinson, 'The European Economic Constitution in Crisis: A Conservative Transformation?', in G Grégoire and X Miny (eds), *The Idea of Economic Constitution in Europe. Genealogy and Overview* (Brill Nijhoff, 2022) 458. On centralisation see chapters 4 and 9.

[34] On juridical hermeneutics and EU law see L Niglia, *The Structural Transformation of European Private Law. A Critique of Juridical Hermeneutics* (Hart Publishing, 2023).

[35] For the argument whereby there would be no change (through the NG-EU, austerity policies would still be with us), see Menendez in this book at ch 3 and H Lokdam and MA Wilkinson, 'The European Economic Constitution in Crisis', in G Grégoire and X Miny (eds) *The Idea of Economic Constitution in Europe* (Brill, Nijhoff, 2022) pp. 458–486.

On centralisation vs deference see K Nicolaidis 'Once in a Lifetime'? An Immanent Critique of NextGenerationEU' at https://kalypsonicolaidis.com/wp-content/uploads/2022/06/FL-233-3-Nicolaidis.pdf

In my own understanding, the exceptionality of the NG-EU funding gives rise to an emergency regime that suspends the normal ways of understanding constitutionalism and its substance, which goes towards explaining the irresolutions that descend from the polarised opinions on the NG-EU read through the conflicting opinions of it being about austerity or Keynesianism and centralisation or deference.

What we see in operation as described in this book is, at once, exceptional centralisation, exceptional executive governance, a new mix ordo- and neo- liberalism, and of ordo and social liberalism, a-constitutional governance, reflexive constitutionalism, entrenched forms of legalism. In other words, in the exceptional conditions of crisis governance interventions everything is up for re-constitutionalisation: a shift from ordinary to exceptional constitutionalism is underway that calls for remedying any adverse impact on guarantees and rights as conceived of under ordinary constitutionalism, as it is the case whenever emergency measures are taken in crisis situations governed under *state* constitutionalism. We are therefore far from a 'complete decision' as in Franz Böhm's understanding of a *Gesamtentscheidung* qua '*complete decision of the type and form of the economic-social cooperation process*', re-elaborating Carl Schmitt's own understanding of the state constitutional as political unity,[36] in the sense that we are at a moment at which the dynamism of changes moves to the foreground.[37]

As we may be at a rupture point where what we can call the *doxa* of European constitutionalism is dramatically changing in that the range of 'taken-for-granted assumptions that undergird all explicit fights in a given area' are being transformed, mapping this transformation is one task of this book project.[38] Indeed mapping crisis governance constitutionalism is about gaining knowledge on the ways in which the forms of organising societal life known as democratic governance[39] are undertaking change through and under the vigilance of legal thought in its variety of modes of operation. This is evident both in what is the primary focus

Note the 'debt brake' changes through the amendment of the German Basic law, on which see A. Menendez Editorial in European Law Open 2025, as interrelated to the level of integration.

[36] F Böhm (ed), *Wettbewerb und Monopolkampf: Eine Untersuchung zur Frage des wirtschaftlichen Kampfrechts und zur Frage der rechtlichen Struktur der geltenden Wirtschaftsordnung* [1933](Baden-Baden, Nomos, 2010) (*Gesamtentscheidung* about the type and form of the economic-social cooperation process and notably referring to Schmitt's understanding of the state constitutional as to type and form of political unity, in C. Schmitt, *Verfassungslehre*, (München-Leipzig, Duncker & Humblot, 1928)).

[37] Bearing in mind, however, that to Böhm the revolutionary element in the Weimar Constitution is both acknowledged and yet criticised. On this aspect see now G Grégoire 'The Economic Constitution under Weimar: Doctrinal Controversies and Ideological Struggles' in G Grégoire and X Miny (eds) *The Idea of Economic Constitution in Europe*, above, at p 85.

[38] See P Bourdieu, *Distinction A Social Critique of the Judgment of Taste*, (Routledge, 1987) as discussed in S Rosenfeld *The Age of Choice: A History of Freedom in Modern Life*, (Princeton University Press, 2025) at p 2, 'doxa' being categorised as 'a form of common sense, a normative idea, or a meta concept' that 'typically. . . only becomes subject to scrutiny when a larger crisis undermines its self-evidence' ibid.

[39] See eg, Rosenfeld *The Age of Choice*, above, at p 260 referring to market-based consumer choice as the other ascendant and equally abstract systems of lives organisation. This parallelism emerges in this book at the points where democracy, governance and market intersect through integration.

of this book, that is the NG-EU[40] and as to the other kinds of EU crisis interventions as referred to in the reminder.

One must therefore come to terms with not just general constitutionalism as it changes under crisis conditions and as somehow (unreflectedly, as it were) keeping its key structures under legalism but, it is argued, as constitutionalism that now includes post-legalistic positions, which in this book is labelled 'crisis governance constitutionalism'. The analysis of 'crisis governance constitutionalism' enables moving towards posing and attempting to address a range of dilemmatic questions: does constitutionalism risk becoming about just managing crisis governance[41] or should we instead see crisis governance as new constitutionalism as 'good for being innovatively 'needed'?[42] Do we need a 'normal' or an 'exceptional' mode of crisis governance constitutionalism? How do the levels of regulation involved in the EU multi-level system of governance and their interaction change as a result of the rising crisis governance constitutionalism? Also, whether and to what extent and under which constitutional modalities crisis governance is under constitutional control; whether constitutionalism risks becoming about just managing crisis governance or whether we should encourage the transformation of crisis governance as new constitutionalism towards preserving the normative-constitutional heritage.

2.4 Discourses III

An aspect of the book, as I am arguing to read it in the light of the adopted perspective, consists of mapping change through crisis governance and framing it as constitutional change – and on the problematic character of such change.

[40] On previous studies of forms of crisis and constitutionalism see in a vast literature M Dawson, H Enderlein and C Joerges (eds), *Beyond the Crisis: The Governance of Europe's Economic, Political, and Legal Transformation*, (Oxford, Oxford University Press, 2015); C Joerges and C Glinski (eds), *The European Crisis and the Transformation of Transnational Governance: Authoritarian Managerialism versus Democratic Governance*, (Oxford, Hart Publishing, 2014); K Tuori and K Tuori. *The Eurozone Crisis: A Constitutional Analysis*, (Cambridge, Cambridge University Press, 2014); M Emerson and C Joerges. 'Reconfiguring the Politics-Law Relationship in the Integration Project through Conflicts-Law Constitutionalism' (2012) *European Law Journal: Review of European Law in Context*, 18 5: 644–666; C Joerges and C Kreuder-Sonnen. 'European Studies and the European Crisis: Legal and Political Science between Critique and Complacency' (2017) *European Law Journal: Review of European Law in Context*, 23 1–2: 118–139; C Joerges 'Pereat Iustitia, Fiat Mundus: What Is Left of the European Economic Constitution after the Gauweiler Litigation?' (2016) *Maastricht Journal of European and Comparative Law* 23 1: 99–118; C Joerges, 'Europe's Economic Constitution in Crisis and the Emergence of a New Constitutional Constellation' (2014) 15(5) *German Law Journal*: 985–1027; B De Witte, 'Euro Crisis Responses and the EU Legal Order: Increased Institutional Variation or Constitutional Mutation?' (2015) *European Constitutional Law Review* 434–457; and see B Ackerman, 'Three Paths to Constitutionalism – and the Crisis of the European Union' (2015) 45(4) *British Journal of Political Science* 705–714, which, in my view, is a conscious attempt to link crisis and constitutionalism in relation to regional redistribution in federal contexts from a comparative constitutional perspective.

[41] Note that Petersmann at a workshop leading to this publication has held that '*we run the risk of an emergency constitutionalism*'.

[42] In contrast to Petersmann's position are those who see governance 'good' given its innovative potential, as typically the behavioural economics literature tends to portray governance.

I sense that not even those who emphasise the power centralising connotation of the NG-EU, as in the view whereby we would be confronting a combination of *Schmitt* and *Hayek*,[43] acknowledge the extent to which the emergency characterisation of the NG-EU exposes us to an exceptional kind of governance that is politically remaking the EU and constitutional Europe, to be understood as relations of orders: where others see continuity I therefore also sense that a break is taking place. As a matter of fact, the states have consistently acted out of necessity in their decision to make the NG-EU programme, as have executives and their administrative organs acting in their capacity to implement the NG-EU, rather than as if executing a choice to adopt the continuation of a project of centralised governance, stretching back to the euro crisis. We have been assisting at a reconfiguration of the background relations of power among the coalitions of states in the context of the negotiations leading to the July 2020 decision that kickstarted the NG-EU program of funding, as well as in the ongoing exercise of power as to renegotiations of the NG-EU and as to the oversight of the relevant implementation activities through the national plans.[44]

Independently of the political economic substance of the changes – eg austerity vs Keynesianism – the constitutional change I am interested in is traceable to what I term 'debt constitutionalisation'.[45] From this vantage point, the writers who have been discussing aspects of emergency in relation to crisis governance[46] are right in pointing to the core development that we need to face, which I'd like to rephrase as the alteration of fiscal power, once the sovereignty of the state, as budgetary autonomy, due to its fundamental shift, as far as the NG-EU funding is concerned, from state to supranational.[47]

[43] H Lokdam and MA Wilkinson, 'The European Economic Constitution in Crisis: A Conservative Trasformation?', in G Grégoire and X Miny (eds), *The Idea of Economic Constitution in Europe. Genealogy and Overview* (Brill Nijhoff, 2022) 458, 4 on neo/ordo/liberalism.

[44] On renegotiation, see eg Italy's request of a fifth change of the national plan in 2025 and see the court of auditors review of 8 April 2025.

[45] See below at chapters 4 and 9.

[46] See Joerges, above, Nettesheim, above, and in this book Kuo at ch 6 and L Niglia at ch 9. On emergency and governance see L Niglia, 'The New Transformation of Europe. Arcana Imperii' (2020) 68 *American Journal of Comparative Law* 151 and in a vast literature, J-L Halpérin, S Hennette-Vauchez and E Millard (eds) *L'état d'urgence : de l'exception à la banalisation.* (Nanterre, Presses Universitaires de Paris, 2017).

[47] Necessity knows no bounds: even financially strong states are pushed under necessity to alter their own long-standing constitutional principles as with the debt brake amendment in Germany. On autonomous fiscal power as budgetary autonomy see C Wuertzer, 'When Size Matters: On the Legality of the Recovery Instrument 'Next Generation EU' in Light of its Unprecedented Volume' in R Weber, (ed), *The Financial Constitution of European Integration: Follow the Money?* (London, Hart Publishing, 2023): *'Without budgetary autonomy, it would seem, no effective and independent state power can come into being, because the exercise of any state power requires the authority to decide on the procurement and allocation of the resources required for this purpose'.*

And referring to M Schaper and M Philipp, 'Währungsstabilität und Staatsfinanzen bei Jean Bodin' in M Philipp (ed), *Debatten um die Souveränität* (Baden-Baden, Nomos, 2016) 99–122, 99 ('sovereign statehood is . . . not possible without sufficient and secure financial resources'). Note also C Joerges 'Economic Constitutionalism and 'the political' of the 'economic" in G Grégoire and X Miny (eds) *The Idea of Economic Constitution in Europe. Genealogy and Overview* (Brill Nijhoff, 2022) at p 793: *'the 'liberty to organise national life at will' is a democratic essential. Has this command been overruled by Europeanisation and globalisation? I suggest that we should care about its survival and that a survival is conceivable under a re-conceptualisation of European and international economic law as "conflicts law"'* and L Niglia Europe and Crisis https://www.europeanpapers.eu/e-journal/europe-and-crisis-introduction.

However, on the role of size, see Menendez in this book at ch 3.

Paradoxically the movement towards a new centralisation in governance as never seen since post-war times in Europe is accompanied by the disintegration of old certainties. The neo-liberal faith is vacillating, some hold, at the very moment that it triumphs, others tell us. Keynes returns in vogue and yet there are dissimilarities as to context against which Keynesianism must operate, with Hayek equally referred to in other accounts of opposite views; scholars identify a key tension between planning and democracy in the body of the NG-EU programme; a polarisation can also be noted between those who speak of a secure change towards a new political economy and those who see no change at all.[48] Even for those who reconstruct Europe's economic constitutionalism as neo-ordo-liberal, the recognition of the NG-EU as somehow different in inserting social elements has become a commonplace attitude.[49] I see this book's contributions as mapping the evolution of constitutionalism around these structural changes.

2.5 Of a constitutional, reflexively organised, governance

Whilst the book maps a variety of positions whose individual specificity is obviously open to interpretation, my own view and suggestion is, as one more key objective of this book, to landscape *a constitutionally reflexive mode of governance* understood as *constitutional guidance*[50] that reshapes the crisis interventions (as complexity) in the light of a range of legitimation requirements (autonomy, equality, proportionality) — as against the dominant mode of coercive governance and in support of the variety of plural counter-movements as they operate at the NG-EU implementation stage. This is so in two coextensive directions: by mapping the emerging crisis governance constitutionalism and by rethinking the role of the constitutional (and private law) heritage in that respect.[51] We can thus move towards recovering and taking back into the picture the role of the public sphere[52] as inevitably intertwined with the juridical hermeneutical heritage.[53]

[48] H Lokdam and MA Wilkinson, 'The European Economic Constitution in Crisis: A Conservative Trasformation?', in G Grégoire and X Miny (eds), The Idea of Economic Constitution in Europe. Genealogy and Overview (Brill Nijhoff, 2022) 458, at p. 485 and see below at ch 4. Note the German Constitutional Court judgment of 6 december 2022 - 2 bvr 547/21, 2 bvr 798/21, rejecting two constitutional complaints directed against the Act Ratifying the EU Own Resources Decision (*Eigenmittelbeschluss-Ratifizierungsgesetz – ERatG*).

[49] H Lokdam and MA Wilkinson, 'The European Economic Constitution in Crisis: A Conservative Trasformation?', in G Grégoire and X Miny (eds), The Idea of Economic Constitution in Europe. Genealogy and Overview (Brill Nijhoff, 2022) 458; Grégoire G. The EU's neoliberal constitutionalism(s). European Law Open. 2024 3(4) 705

[50] See for the thesis of 'constitutional guidance' below at chapters 4 and 9.

[51] See the next volumes in the series.

[52] J Habermas *Strukturwandel der Öffe ntlichkeit ; Untersuchungen zu einer Kategorie der bürgerlichen Gesellschaft Neuwied* (Luchterhand, 1976); J Habermas, *Ein neuer Strukturwandel der Öffentlichkeit und die deliberative Politik* (Berlin, Suhrkamp, 2022). J Habermas, *Between Facts and Norms: Contribution to a Discourse Theory of Law and Democracy* (W Rehg trs, Cambridge, MA, MIT Press, 1996).

[53] L Niglia, *The Structural Transformation of European Private Law. A Critique of Juridical Hermeneutics*, (Hart Publishing, 2023). It is helpful to refer to certain non-legal studies on crisis and critical analysis, that is, attempts by political economists to face crisis through studying critically the various factors as relevant and through arguing for the need to forge political alliances as needed – in my view legal principles (eg

In my own contributions in this book, I propose the argument that only a constitutional reflexively organised governance around a conscious just redistribution of the funding and of the burdens related to the reforms and the projects can ensure a change in substance in political economy towards inclusive decisions and redistributive justice, for no Keynesianism is possible without a state backing it up as legitimation force, thus turning upside down the legalistic arguments whereby one should identify a supposedly chosen political economic agenda just from the letter of the treaty articles such as Art 122 TFEU; instead, it is in the ways of implementation that we can identify the relevant changes: whether the NG-EU objectives are only lexicographically linked to the conditionalities or whether the NG-EU funding can and should be used towards respecting autonomy and equality objectives by balancing on that basis the conditionalities, as I argue in the remainder.

3. Three perspectives and eight declinations of crisis governance constitutionalism

3.1 The Context

'Crisis as emergency' is the condition that has given rise to the manifestation of an exceptional degree of power in executive form, as happened with the European

solidarity) must be about enacting this kind of critical study of social relations and distributive effects which in turn requires a critical approach, also interdisciplinary – eg see J Hernández Andreu, *¿Qué hemos aprendido de las crisis? Una perspectiva histórica* (Madrid, Delta Publicaciones, 2021) (at p 182 interpreting with critical realism (*realismo crítico*) '*eventuales debates, movidos para analizar en profundidad todas las variables en juego*', which facilitates the making of decisions in politico-social terms, knowing what gains and what one loses in politico-economic decisions; at p. 210 discussing ways to promote and negotiate the consensus of the majority of political forces, and to strengthen the cooperative action among the distinct zones of the EU; arguing for the introduction of humanist criteria in political economy, at p. 185–186); and, at p. 185, arguing that if he had to identify a univocal factorial explanation of the crisis 2008–2020 he would argue that it stands in the undermining of critical realist thinking, and defending Keynes against the theory of political economy as in neoliberalism; at pp 178-189 on the need for the 'rigorous optimization'(*el objective riguroso de optimizar los recursos provenientes de ayuda directa de la Union Europea, sin cobro de interes*) of the NG-EU funding (referring to the grants with no interests owed and yet seeing an obligation) which requires on the part of the central government and of the *autonomias* '*analisis continuo y contraste empirico permanente*' and adding that '*Los rapresentantes y autoridades politicas, a todos los niveles, tienen que informar y cambiar impresiones sobre sus proyectos con los agentes sociales de sus respectivas circumscripciones y en el ámbito institucional donde se desenvuelven normalmente*' (at pp. 178-179): what I call constitutional guidance is about helping supporting this kind of involvement of society in the institutional decisions about the 'optimisation' of the funding.

Contrast instead the view that the priority would be to 'speed' the implementation of the NG-EU funding through seeing the involvement of local authorities as negatively impacting as 'implementation delays' in R Crescenzi, M Giua, G V Sonzogno, 'Mind the Covid-19 crisis: An evidence-based implementation of Next Generation EU', *Journal of Policy Modeling*, 43(2), 2021: 278–297 at https://www.sciencedirect.com/science/article/pii/S016189382100017X (*'Simplified implementation procedures with clear spatial targeting and limited involvement of regional and local authorities are necessary conditions for the avoidance of implementation delays'*) and quoting C Lagarde, President of the ECB, at the plenary session of the European Parliament to debate on the ECB Annual Report, Brussels, 8 February 2021 (*'It is essential that the Next Generation EU funds are disbursed quickly and used to support structural reforms and growth-enhancing investment projects. This would boost potential growth and contribute to reaching the EU's objectives in the areas of climate change and digitalisation'*).

Council decision to make the NG-EU.[54] In deciding to resort to enacting the NG-EU Recovery Plan, the states have acted out of necessity.[55] Let's recall some key passages of the European Council's Conclusions that started off the NG-EU Recovery Plan, all revolving around the legal concepts of necessity through protecting the citizens, through the exercise of emergency, exceptional, extraordinary powers:[56]

> As Europeans continue to face extraordinary challenges and uncertainty in their daily lives, all our efforts will remain focused on protecting citizens and overcoming the crisis.
>
> The COVID-19 crisis presents Europe with a challenge of historic proportions. The EU and its Member States have had to adopt emergency measures to preserve the health of the citizens and prevent a collapse of the economy. We are slowly exiting the acute health crisis. While utmost vigilance is still required on the sanitary situation, the emphasis is now shifting to mitigating the socio-economic damage. This requires an unprecedented effort and an innovative approach, fostering convergence, resilience and transformation in the European Union. At the request of the Heads of State or Government, the Commission presented at the end of May a very wide-ranging package combining the future Multiannual Financial Framework (MFF) and a specific Recovery effort under Next Generation EU (NG-EU).
>
> It is an ambitious and comprehensive package combining the classical MFF with an extraordinary Recovery effort destined to tackle the effects of an unprecedented crisis in the best interest of the EU.
>
> The exceptional nature of the economic and social situation due to the COVID-19 crisis requires exceptional measures to support the recovery and resilience of the economies of the Member States.

[54] https://www.consilium.europa.eu/en/press/press-releases/2020/07/21/european-council-conclusions-17-21-july-2020/.

[55] Constitutional scholars have noted the exceptionalism of the NG-EU in its setting aside '*the most important constitutional principles*': see eg Nettesheim, 'Legally feasible, constitutionally dubious: Establishing 'Next Generation Europe' on the basis of EU secondary legislation', *Verfassungsblog*, 12 April 2020, available at www.verfassungsblog.de/legally-feasible-constitutionally-dubious/ (on the EU 'pushing aside' 'even the most important constitutional principles when it seems politically opportune to do so). Politically opportune in my view signifies decisions made in the mode of exceptionalism.

For the conscious dealing with exceptionalism see the EU Council Legal Service, 'Opinion on the Proposals on Next Generation EU', 9062/20 (24 June, 2020): '*In order to respond to the exceptional situation, it is thus also required that financial means are available which are commensurate in volume to the challenge that the Union and its Member States face. It is for the Union legislator to decide, under the applicable procedures, what is considered appropriate and commensurate to the specific situation. In making such a decision, the legislator enjoys a wide margin of discretion, provided the safeguards described in paragraphs 67 to 69 below – which in essence aim at safeguarding the integrity of the system of own resources as well as the principles of unity and universality applicable to the Union budget – are respected*'. Emphasis added.

And at para 67: '*The substantial amount of external assigned revenue may, therefore, exceptionally be considered justified insofar as it is strictly circumscribed to cover measures linked to the COVID-19 pandemic and limited, in size and duration, to what is necessary to that end*'.

[56] On 21 July 2020, the European Council adopted conclusions on the recovery plan and multiannual financial framework for 2021–2027: https://www.consilium.europa.eu/en/press/press-releases/2020/07/21/european-council-conclusions-17-21-july-2020/. Emphasis is my own.

Scholarship, both constitutional and political science, has been scrutinising the NG-EU details yet we lack an understanding of the implications of crisis as emergency in comparative constitutional terms. In particular, as the relationship between constitutionalism and politics is being altered by new (crisis) governance through the fact of power interventions towards crisis resolution, as with the NG-EU/RRF, there is urgent need for an assessment of the state of that relationship from the vantage point of normative constitutionalism with its necessary democratic dimension.[57]

This is needed because, first, there is a risk of a justificatory approach[58] that creates an impression whereby the EU institutions may do as they wish without any limits to their operations, once the legality question is resolved positively or, by contrast, that EU institutions may not do anything at all (and that they even should somehow revoke their determinations, with paralysing effects)[59] once that legality question is decided negatively.

Second, the question concerning the democratic legitimation of the NG-EU as the currently prominent EU governance model is open and unresolved and needs to be assessed in its relationship with constitutionalism, that is, as the question concerning democratic legitimation at supranational level.

Third there is a risk of continuous negative reactions from the populist and nationalist fronts unless the democratic legitimation question is really addressed and engaged with.

Here one must note that executive constitutionalism as exceptionalist comes to life not out of a normally legitimated polity but out of a polity, the EU, that is not a real constitutional federation: as executive constitutionalism as exceptionalist is an extreme form of political power that reaches beyond normal politics and is as such constitutionally problematic within the state then *a fortiori* it must be at the EU level as quasi-federative polity: for, whether the EU can become a new kind of legitimised polity, in other ways than the states' and yet no less 'validly', is a question yet open. As things stand, the EU has acted through the NG-EU out of necessity[60] in the sense of an act (the NG-EU) that constitutes the most visible and explicit way to '*exercise sovereign public power in an explicit fashion*'[61], which, in my view, and contrary to what has been argued, constitutes an inversion from within

[57] See eg chapter by MS Kuo in this book: 'It is hard to see how debate, deliberation, persuasion, and judicial articulation required of fundamental constitution-reshaping can result from such a rushed temporality'.

[58] See critically on the legalistic position L Niglia Ch 4 in this book.

[59] See M Nettesheim https://verfassungsblog.de/legally-feasible-constitutionally-dubious/blog.

[60] On state of exception and integration see discussion in L Niglia, 'The New Transformation of Europe. Arcana Imperii' (2020) 68 *American Journal of Comparative Law* 151.

[61] Compare Menendez and Dani in J Komarek: '*Not even at the height of the crisis was the European Union capable of exercising sovereign public power in an explicit fashion. The European Union can act as a vincolo esterno (exerting negative powers), but not as an autonomous political actor (making use of positive powers). It lacks the institutional, the material, and, above all, the legitimacy resources to do so, to a considerable extent because its functional and material constitutions are far from those presupposed by democratic and social constitutionalism*': Dani and Menendez conflate the exercise of public power and explicitness of doing this as sovereign state power and, at pp 72–73, note the cloaking of political power, on the part of the ECB, as technical.

of the patterns of the EU regulatory activities as it has been arguably the case of the European Central Bank's Euro-crisis interventions.[62] And yet even against the grain of that visibility, EU constitutional scholarship has managed to construct a layer of legalism under which to justify the NG-EU intervention.[63]

3.2 Structure of the book

The book explores these issues by adopting three interrelated yet distinct perspectives organised into three parts:

Part I expores the perspective of general constitutionalism and crisis as emergency seen in relation to how general constitutionalism – that is, established theories of constitutionalism at the EU level – perceives and relates to crisis governance as constitutional *problématique*. This is more than the perspective of conventional EU law scholarship that sees the NG-EU as just a matter of concern in terms of legality/illegality as to the relevant Treaty rules. The analysis here is about testing how constitutionalist theories re-understand governance in the light of the history and of the present role of crisis in the context of integration. Crisis may be a constant dimension of integration, as in the conventional EU law scholarship approach to the NG-EU – which assumes that the NG-EU is about crisis interventions as somehow part of a normal cycle of a Europe made through crisis – and yet it is important to reflect on the peculiarity of new governance as crisis resolution as to its constitutional dimensions.

Part II deals with the interrelated perspectives of crisis governance constitutionalism, as seen through the lenses of *theoretical* constitutional material including sociolegal and normative political perspectives.[64] This is a perspective that sees constitutionalists engaging with the two aspects of constitutionalism and of crisis governance as deeply interrelated – as if somehow conflating through the reference point of 'populism' and the reference point of 'emergency' respectively made in the chapters by Priban and by Kuo: where the two 'conflate' not in a reductionist sense, whereby law becomes one and the same thing with politics, but in a normative sense of the constitutional as autonomous, and stressing the danger of

[62] Ibid. 'it is telling that the ECB could only act in a decisive manner by pretending that it was merely discharging its modest role of implementing monetary policy in a fully rule-based manner. Only by means of cloaking its political role as purely technical could the ECB take the decisions it took. Had the ECB fully disclosed the nature of what it was doing, its authority would have been immediately depleted'.

[63] See below at ch 4. Of course, in order to see into this exercising of explicit sovereign political power, we need to not act under the constraints of the legalistic cloak: for this criticism see below at chapter 4 (as to the NG-EU: the EU is seen as acting under the legalistic cloak, through holding that its powers are fully justified under the Treaty, rather than just under 'emergency').

[64] Whether crisis governance constitutionalism as other than 'general' in its three (and the further two at Part 3) declinations is about 'sectoral constitutionalism' (see Tuori, Kaarlo, and Klaus Tuori. *The Eurozone Crisis: A Constitutional Analysis* (Cambridge, Cambridge University Press, 2014) is a question that will be addressed in another volume of this book project.

reductionism of constitutionalism to politics,[65] which in my view means avoiding a reductionism that would make constitutionalism miss its own hermeneutical[66] and epistemic dimensions.[67] Here, constitutionalism is no longer distinct from (as if it ever was) crisis as an 'outside objective' to manage, but is internalised with the effect of changing the constitutionalist discourse from within due to its reacting to crisis.

Part III explores the interrelated writings closer to the EU institutional context of crisis constitutionalism. Here, the book engages with political science and economic voices that closely look at the EU crisis governance schemes of intervention, respectively covering the NG-EU and EU governance by public goods' thinking.[68] In my view, these governance theories raise certain dilemmas that are then discussed and addressed in Chapter 9.

On this basis, the book maps eight declinations of crisis governance constitutionalism including a-constitutional renditions of governance, while also exploring their tensions and the related open questions regarding their coexistence through conflicts in the landscape of the emerging discourse of crisis governance constitutionalism.

[65] Eg Kuo in his chapter in this book: '*That the executive constitutionalism as manifested in the EU's recent emergency response comes closer to an executive exercise of (derived) constituent power in Schmitt's teachings than political constitutionalism resting on a normative view of democratic politics should not be missed.*'

[66] Chapters 4 and 9.

[67] Ibid.

[68] See the 2024 reports by E. Letta https://www.consilium.europa.eu/media/ny3j24sm/much-more-than-a-market-report-by-enrico-letta.pdf and by M. Draghi above.

INTRODUCTION TO PART 1

Four Declinations of Crisis Governance Constitutionalism: Legalistic, Ordoliberal, Democratic/ Social State and Reflexive

LEONE NIGLIA

The influence of ordoliberal thinking on the fabric of the EU constitutional order has been widely acknowledged and studied. Out of these studies, competing readings have emerged that concern the relationship between ordoliberalism and integration. Two of them are re-presented here as standing at the core of the debate on the current crisis governance. In both, the crisis imaginary takes hold of the constitutional mind in a first declination, that is, it draws on previous constitutional materials towards adapting it to the new crisis circumstances. These positions inevitably reflect scholarly discussions of the past regarding Europe's economic constitution and its characterisation, whether liberal or social, as respectively in the pathbreaking works of Böhm and Sinzheimer, among others.[1] Yet Ernst-Ulrich Petersmann[2] warns against these parallelisms, between the 1930s and today, which are instead for others compelling.[3]

Chapter 2 by Petersmann proposes the need for rethinking EU constitutionalism, defended by Petersmann as ordoliberal (EU law as ordo-liberal), in the face of crisis situations, as a project of constitutional ordoliberal adaptation and evolution.

Petersmann sees here a transformation of Europe's economic constitution taking place as part of the *evolution* of ordoliberal thinking. The general constitutionalist narrative of ordoliberalism and of EU law as ordoliberal constitutionalism, is subjected to a renewed scrutiny that aims at governing the EU crisis interventions under the 'old materials' now reread as *evolutionary constitutionalism* as part of a new chapter in that long term story. The EU crisis intervention through the

[1] Respectively F Böhm, (ed), *Wettbewerb und Monopolkampf: Eine Untersuchung zur Frage des wirtschaftlichen Kampfrechts und zur Frage der rechtlichen Struktur der geltenden Wirtschaftsordnung* [1933] (Baden-Baden, Nomos,2010); H. Sinzheimer in *Arbeitsrecht und Rechtssoziologie: gesammelte Aufsätze und Reden* (2 volumes, Otto Kahn-Freund and Thilo Ramm (eds).

[2] Petersmann at Chapter 2 below.

[3] Menendez at Chapter 3 below.

NG-EU is seen as 'stabilising' 'social support for EU governance' under the 'EU mandate for a 'social' market economy protecting human rights and 'cohesion'', against a background of a re-reading of the history of integration as a governance (ordoliberal) continuum rather than having undergone a radical transformation, and as a model for future crisis interventions.

The following statements are representative of the crisis of general constitutionalism and of crisis governance constitutionalism seen as ordoliberalism as applied to the governance of crisis as discussed in chapter 2:

The view of the *'development of EU law and policies responding to economic, environmental, social and security crises in conformity with 'ordoliberal principles''* as *'rejecting business-driven self-regulation neglecting human rights'*

And the view that:

> *The EU mandate for a 'social' market economy protecting human rights and 'cohesion' is increasingly used (eg for post-Covid 19 recovery projects financed through common EU borrowing in capital markets) to stabilise social support for EU governance in Europe's transnational society, economy and demoi-cratic polity.*

and the consideration that:

> *'As EU law protects individual and democratic autonomy and only limited EU competences for protecting transnational PGs, EU crises governance requires interpreting and developing EU law as a citizen-driven 'living constitution' different from national Constitutions based on state sovereignty'.*

and, further, that:

> *'Europe's successful integration law can be explained by its unique merging and extension of republican, democratic and cosmopolitan constitutionalism to multilevel governance of PGs'*

thus placing public goods under ordoliberal constitutionalism (as opposed to the economic theories of governance of public goods as discussed at chapter 8 below), and setting these arguments in a geopolitical perspective where it is held that 'the geopolitical 'permacrises' require adjusting EU law and EU politics by transforming intergovernmental EU emergency governance into democratically and constitutionally better controlled forms of EU internal and external crises governance'.

Petersmann's contribution stands in stark contrast to accounts of 'neo-ordo-liberalism' as unconcerned with social aspects in that he argues that: 'The EU's prioritization of comprehensive human and constitutional rights of citizens limiting public and private powers[4] reflects ordoliberal rather than neoliberal EU governance of PGs' and referring to the document of the EU Commission

[4] Cf EU Commission, 70 Years of EU Law. A Union for Its Citizens (EU, 2023).

'EU Commission, *70 Years of EU Law. A Union for Its Citizens* (EU, 2023)'. The implications of this opening to the social will no doubt need to be discussed and elaborated in the near future. In turn Menendez restates a contrasting argument about what he critically calls 'neo-ordo-liberalism'.[5]

Chapter 3 by Menendez is a restatement and defence of integration seen as democratic and social (democratic/social) economic constitutional project with the associated thesis of a critical analysis of the EU political economy seen as remaining *neo-ordo-liberal* since the Maastricht Treaty despite the current, assumed as only rhetorical, shift to *Keynesian* interventionism. We can note at least a double set of conflicting views:

First, to Menendez, ordo- and neoliberal thought and action overlap and hybridise (under the compound 'neo-ordo-liberalism' thesis) in that they are seen as disciplinary modes of governance, as opposed to Petersmann who defends the view of ordoliberalism as distinct from neoliberalism and as somehow characterised by social elements. In the chapter by Menendez crisis emerges as a context in which the EU would manage to preserve its neo-ordo-liberal (austerity) characterisation.

Second, where Menendez sees neo-ordo-liberalism as the basis for the continuing austerity management of the EU, with a background 'socio-economic vision' of democratic/social dirigisme (drawing on socio-legal analysis) also considered in the terms of a political economic approach, which takes into account a descriptive take on what is happening on the ground, it seems to me that Petersmann prefers emphasising a constitutional-normative orientated perspective which also defends his view of the social as transnational. Context sheds light on constitutionalist theories. In two passages representative of Menendez's approach in assessing and facing the crisis of general constitutionalism, by closely looking at what results out of the chosen socio-legal and political economic framework, it is argued that:

> The role of the European Union in the upholding of the European economic order is no longer mainly identified with *unleashing* the economic power of (big) corporations by means of setting aside national norms restraining the power of property owners, but rather to ensure, through its own expenditure and through the expenditure of Member States, the *profitability* of (big) corporations.

and that:

> EU Next Generation is a complex and, in many ways, yet-to-be-completed arrangement. For all the rhetoric about "infectious solidarity", there is little solidaristic in the provision of financial assistance when the creditor stands to benefit as much, if not more, than the debtor and when the power

[5] Menendez, ch 3 in this book; H Lokdam and MA Wilkinson, 'The European Economic Constitution in Crisis: A Conservative Transformation?', in G Grégoire and X Miny (eds), *The Idea of Economic Constitution in Europe. Genealogy and Overview* (Brill Nijhoff, 2022) 458.

imbalance between creditor and debtor is preserved. It is only in regards to the grants part of the European Recovery Fund, and not to the loans part, that it makes sense to speak of solidarity.

Legalism stands as the background to the analysis of chapters 2 and 3, against which the post-legalistic ordoliberal and the democratic/social views are developed. Chapter 4 re-describes legalism as a peculiar reading of the NG-EU as based on secondary legislation whereby the NG-EU would be consistent with the Treaties. It also holds that, whilst legalism confirms the view of letting EU institutions do unlimitedly what they choose to in conditions of emergency, following on a deferential mode of complacency that has been criticised,[6] constitutionalism is about limiting power politics particularly in the extant conditions of emergency as part of a second level analysis of the implementation of the NG-EU as opposed to the first level analysis of the legality of the NG-EU legislative programme. Chapter 4 takes the view that there is need for recovering aspects of the constitutionalist heritage that constitute the living constitutional law understood as plural constitutional heritage. This involves the need for considering counter-movements.[7] It is argued that the proposal of a 'reflexive governance' perspective goes towards unveiling organisational principles whose purpose is to limit and contain power politics.

* * *

Whilst in Chapters 2 and 3 *crisis governance constitutionalism* is articulated as a project of adaptation of the general, and competing, constitutional narratives that stands at the core of the EU project, with the thesis of reflexive governance adding to this picture, Chapters 5 and 6 take the opportunity and challenge of crisis governance to advance a renovated kind of constitutionalism grounded respectively in the public sphere and in constituent power. Reversing the argument whereby contemporary constitutionalism is irremediably bound to betray demos,[8] the two authors argue for the compatibility of demos (democracy) and governance as transnational in conditions of crisis.

[6] C Joerges, above.

[7] K Polanyi, *The Great Transformation* (New York, Farrar & Rinehart, 1944). See C Joerges and J Falke (eds), *Karl Polanyi, Globalisation and the Potential of Law in Transnational Markets* (Oxford, Hart Publishing, 2011); C Joerges 'A New Type of Conflicts of Law as the Legal Paradigm of the Postnational Constellation' in C Joerges and J Falke (eds), *Karl Polanyi, Globalisation and the Potential of Law in Transnational Markets* (Hart, 2011).

[8] Loughlin, Martin. Against Constitutionalism (Cambridge, Massachusetts, Harvard University Press, 2022).

2

EU Crises Governance and 'Evolutionary Constitutionalism' in a Multipolar World of 'Permacrises'

ERNST-ULRICH PETERSMANN

1. Introduction

The UN, WTO, European and national governance of public goods (PGs) are challenged by geopolitical rivalries leading to systemic 'polycrises' such as abuses of veto powers and military aggression undermining the UN security system, the suppression of human and democratic rights by authoritarian governments, failures of UN health and environmental treaties to prevent global health pandemics, climate change, biodiversity loss, and pollution, and illegal US trade protectionism disrupting the WTO legal and dispute settlement systems. The more the largest emitters of greenhouse gases (China, Russia, India and the USA) disregard the Paris Agreement goal of decarbonising economies by 2050 and other sustainable development goals (SDGs), the more EU regulatory responses to 'permacrises' risk undermining EU 'competitiveness' and 'strategic autonomy' in the new 'geoeconomic security order' prioritising security interests and de-risking of supply chains.

EU constitutionalism differs from constitutional nationalism outside Europe by its acknowledgment that – just as globalisation transforms national into transnational PGs that cannot be protected without international law and institutions – state-centered 'constitutionalism 1.0' needs to be transformed into multilevel constitutionalism that limits abuses of national policy powers undermining multilateral governance of transnational PGs. This contribution explains why the EU's internal and external 'crises governance' cannot be separated. The EU responses to the financial and monetary crises of 2008–2012, Russia's aggression against Ukraine since 2014, continuing environmental and migration crises, and the Covid-19 health pandemic of 2020 revealed the need for 'constitutional politics' that strengthen EU emergency governance through constructive interpretations of EU law without formal amendments of the Lisbon Treaty. The 2024 Draghi Report identifies 'existential challenges' resulting from the productivity and investment gaps between Europe, North America and China, and the 'need for Europe to radically change' to reignite economic growth by promoting innovation through advanced technologies, decarbonisation, greater competitiveness and stronger European defence capacities.[1] Even though Draghi does not propose treaty amendments, the latter remain democratically desirable for reforming the 1992 'Maastricht compromise' limiting the EU's Economic and Monetary Union (EMU) and for promoting a stronger EU budget and EU defence union.

Contrary to Anglo-Saxon neoliberalism perceiving self-regulatory markets and government regulation as opposites, Europe's multilevel democratic, republican and cosmopolitan constitutionalism is committed to limiting market failures (eg by competition, environmental and social law and institutions), governance failures (eg to protect PGs such as Europe's common market, rule-of-law) and constitutional failures (eg by the 1950 European Convention on Human Rights (ECHR) and EU treaties limiting national policy discretion). Non-discriminatory market competition and its information, coordination and welfare-enhancing functions are perceived as legal constructs rather than as gifts of nature and of business-driven (self)regulation. Section 2 explains why – in the geopolitical rivalries with authoritarian countries and business-driven neoliberalism neglecting human and democratic rights – Europe's unique 'ordoliberal constitutionalism' requires 'constitutional politics' that explain to EU citizens the need for 'constitutionalising' EU emergency governance (eg based on Article 122 TFEU and intergovernmental agreements supplementing the EU budget by issuance of common EU debt for financing agreed EU emergency policies). Section 3 recalls why – the more the UN security system, UN human rights law, and other UN and WTO agreements and international adjudication are undermined by hegemonic power politics – the more EU policies defending UN and WTO law assume existential importance for protecting human and democratic rights inside and outside Europe. As the EU cannot change American, Chinese and Russian power politics and the 'tragedy of the commons', the geopolitical 'permacrises' require adjusting EU law and EU politics by transforming intergovernmental EU emergency governance into democratically and constitutionally better controlled forms of EU internal and external crises governance.

2. Next Generation EU Governance in a Multipolar World of Polycrises

All human beings and societies are confronted with the 'constitutional challenge' of reconciling our human passions and desires with what human reason and morality require. Constitutional democracy and republican constitutionalism remain Europe's most important 'political inventions' – initiated some 2,500 years ago in ancient Athens and Rome – for responding to governance crises by strengthening

[1] *The Future of European Competitiveness*, EU Commission September 2024.

democratic input-legitimacy and republican output-legitimacy through stronger involvement of citizens in protecting PGs (like citizen rights to participate in democratic governance, citizen duties of military service, judicial remedies). Over centuries, constitutionalism tolerated 'market failures' (such as slave trades and exploitation of labour) and related 'governance failures' (such as gender discrimination, colonialism and the genocide of indigenous tribes); its social and democratic support by 'the people' remained weak until the emergence of communitarian city republics in Europe with more inclusive, social and constitutional contracts that protected religious tolerance (eg by separating secular from religious governance powers) and constitutional rights of citizens. Outside Europe, many UN Member States remain governed by authoritarian rulers without effective constitutional guarantees of human and democratic rights; most democracies prioritise constitutional nationalism and business-driven, neoliberal policies and reject Europe's multilevel regulation limiting abuses of public and private power.

2.1 EU law requires defending 'ordoliberal' rather than 'neoliberal constitutionalism'

England's 'democratic revolution' in the 17th century led to civil war introducing 'parliamentary sovereignty' and 'representative democracy' (with the Monarch, the Lords and the Commons representing the people); yet the 'Hobbesian social contract' justified monarchical powers, and the parliamentary reforms maintained feudal and colonial governance systems. France's 'democratic revolution' in the 18th century aimed at more ambitious human rights protection and more inclusive democratic reforms; but it remained short-lived due to revolutionary 'political terror' and feudal counterrevolutions. The libertarian 'Lockean foundations' of America's 'democratic revolution' contributed to common market regulations without effective limitations of 'market failures' (such as restraints of competition) and 'governance failures' (such as racial discrimination and neoliberal exploitation). The Swiss constitutional reforms of 1874 complemented a communitarian, federal democracy (inspired by Rousseau's social contract theory) by a common market based on judicial protection of rule-of-law among the cantons. Europe's most important economic and 'constitutional revolution' was initiated only after World War II with the ECHR and the European community treaties transforming constitutional nationalism into multilevel democratic and republican governance of transnational PGs (such as Europe's common market, European institutions protecting human rights and transnational rule-of-law). This merging of democratic and republican constitutionalism with transnational cosmopolitan constitutionalism remains Europe's most important 'political innovation' in the 20th century.[2]

[2] Cf EU Petersmann, *Multilevel Constitutionalism for Multilevel Governance of Public Goods* (Hart, 2017); *idem*, Neoliberalism, Ordoliberalism and the Future of Economic Governance, in: *JIEL* 26 (2023),

Ordoliberalism emerged as an economic, political and social project in Germany in response to the ubiquity of market failures, governance failures and constitutional failures revealed by World War I and by the economic, political and social crises in Germany's Weimar Republic (1919–1933). Following World War II, ordoliberal scholars in the 'Freiburg school of law and economics' (such as the economist W. Eucken and the lawyer F. Böhm) and in the 'Cologne school of social market economy' (notably Müller-Armack) successfully influenced the German government (especially under economy minister and later chancellor L. Ehrhard) to design a 'social market economy' embedded into constitutional protection of equal liberties and democratic rights, legal protection of non-discriminatory conditions of competition, equal opportunities, labour rights and social rights, and a 'private law society' protected by a rule-of-law state with strong judicial remedies and commitments to promote European and worldwide economic integration.[3] German ordoliberals actively influenced the negotiations and institutions of the 1957 Treaty establishing the European Economic Community (EEC). Yet the EEC practices avoided references to the diverse, national varieties of market economies, for instance because many national discussions (eg about ordoliberalism in the 1950s) remained contested. German ordoliberals were influenced by Germany's particular national context (such as constitutional guarantees of a 'social State'); and they disagreed on questions of European and worldwide market integration (like the association of overseas territories of EEC Member States with the common market, the interventionist EU agricultural policies).[4] The EU founding

836–842. For comparative analyses of American, European and Asian common market regulations see EU Petersmann, *Constitutional Functions and Constitutional Problems of International Economic Law. International and Domestic Foreign Trade Law and Policy in the United States, the European Community and Switzerland* (Routledge, 1991; reprinted 2019 and 2020); M Hilf, EU Petersmann (eds), *National Constitutions and International Economic Law* (Kluwer, 1993); E U Petersmann, A Steinbach (eds), *Constitutionalism and Transnational Governance Failures* (Brill, 2024).

[3] The Austrian and German ordoliberals advocated interdisciplinary 'Smithian', rather than merely economic 'Ricardian justifications' of non-discriminatory conditions of competition, rule-of-law and economic, monetary, social and legal, national and international rules and institutions establishing a 'market order' aimed at reconciling private and public interests. Their emphasis on the 'constitutional functions' of international guarantees of equal freedoms, non-discriminatory treatment, rule-of-law and judicial remedies as a 'second line of constitutional entrenchment' (provided citizens can enforce such guarantees in domestic courts as inside the EU) distinguishes EU ordoliberalism from Anglo-Saxon neoliberalism. The 74 annual volumes of the *ORDO Jahrbuch für die Ordnung von Gesellschaft und Wirtschaft* edited (since 1948) by leading members of the 'Freiburg school of law and economics' (like Eucken, Böhm, Hayek) document the historical evolution of this school inside and beyond Germany. On current discussions of ordoliberalism and 'Ordnungspolitik' (in the sense of 'constitutional economics' justifying 'economic governance rules') from the diverse, national economic and legal perspectives in EU Member States see the books edited by G Grégoire and X Miny, The Idea of Economic Constitution in Europe (Brill, 2022); T.Biebricher, W.Bonefeld and P.Nedergaard, *The Oxford Handbook of Ordoliberalism* (OUP, 2022); A.Skordas/G.Halmai/L.Mardikian, Economic Constitutionalism in a Turbulent World (Elgar, 2023).

[4] At the 1938 Walter Lippmann conference in Paris, the economist W.Rüstow coined the term 'neoliberalism' in a broad sense (including ordoliberalism) for exploring the normative foundations of a humane, liberal economic order that would avoid the past governance failures of laissez-faire liberalism; totalitarian central planning in communist and socialist countries; the 'social disembedding' and poverty in Germany during the 1920s; and the global financial and economic crises and

fathers agreed that the success of the European integration project depended on a common market increasing the economic and social welfare of European citizens. The creation of Europe's common market and its successive enlargements from initially six to now 27 member countries promoted high economic growth since the 1950s. Yet, since the 1990s, Europe's increasing social, labour and energy costs and – compared with nation states prioritising neoliberalism or state-capitalism – multilevel (over)regulation (eg in the context of Europe's 'legal harmonization', green and digital transition) began to stifle economic growth and technological innovation, as explained in the 2024 Draghi report.[5] How should Europe respond to its decreasing international competitiveness in the current 'multipolar rivalries' with competitors in third countries benefitting from lower energy and manufacturing costs and less ambitious economic, environmental, internet, social and legal regulation?

2.2 Adjusting European constitutionalism to neoliberal and autocratic competition?

The 1957 EEC Treaty, and notably its common market and competition rules, were progressively interpreted by the EEC institutions as being embedded into common market freedoms and other civil, political, economic and social fundamental rights that must be 'balanced' and reconciled through legislation, administration and adjudication. Just as the German Constitutional Court avoided economic dogmas in protecting the economic policy discretion of German government institutions, the European Court of Justice (CJEU) protected the economic policy discretion of EU institutions (eg in developing a more 'economic approach' in EC competition policies) without referring to economic ideologies (eg about neoliberalism or ordoliberalism, or how 'consumer welfare standards' guiding competition policies should be reconciled with protecting 'total welfare standards' and the competitive process itself). The EU's constitutional, parliamentary and representative, demoicratic governance and 'provisions on democratic principles' (Articles 9–12 TEU) emphasise rights of citizens 'to participate in the democratic life of the Union', where 'decisions shall be taken as openly and as closely as possible to the citizen' (Article 10.3 TEU); participatory and deliberative democracy and 'active EU

mutually harmful protectionism during the 1930s. But 'neoliberalism' is usually defined narrowly (eg by US President Reagan and British Prime Minister Thatcher based on 'Chicago school' beliefs in self-regulatory markets) as prioritisation of liberalisation, deregulation, privatisation, financialisation of economies and business-driven regulation. W Eucken emphasised the categorical differences of his conception of ordoliberalism from neoliberalism and state-capitalism. Recent descriptions of 'Bidenomics' as 'post-neoliberal' neglect the utilitarian 'cost-benefit justifications' of business-driven US economic regulations due to the very incomplete limitations of market and governance failures in the US Constitution.

[5] Cf note 1 (explaining why the EU's extensive and stringent regulatory environment may, as a side effect, restrain innovation and face EU companies with higher restructuring costs compared to their US peers).

citizenship' are promoted through various rights (eg to launch citizen initiatives, to elect – and petition to – the European Parliament, or to the EU Ombudsman) and EU programs (eg for promoting citizen assemblies).

EU law and policies avoid references to the 'ordoliberal DNA' of EU common market regulation. EU citizens and public discourse often confuse EU policies with neoliberalism. For instance, academic claims that the German Constitutional Court's insistence on democratic, parliamentary control of financial assistance to over-indebted EU Member State governments was based on 'neoliberal austerity conditionality'[6], or that Britain's 'Brexit' was justified by the EU's neoliberalism[7], or that EU leadership for compulsory WTO adjudication protecting transnational rule-of-law and non-discriminatory conditions of competition is a 'neoliberal policy'[8], are misleading; they neglect the categorical differences between citizen-driven 'ordoliberal constitutionalism', business-driven 'utilitarian neoliberalism', and constitutionally unbound 'totalitarian state-capitalism'. Discrediting Europe's 'competitive social market economy' (Article 3 TEU) as neoliberal unduly alienates EU citizens and does not contribute to clarifying Europe's policy options.[9]

Democratic responses to geopolitical rivalries and climate change require explaining why neoliberal prioritisation of 'negative freedoms' (in the sense of absence of governmental restrictions) privileges the wealthy and the powerful, especially if competition laws and 'polluter pays' principles are not effectively enforced and if private corporate financing of political elections is protected as 'free speech' thereby enabling plutocracy (as, arguably, in the USA). Ordoliberal prioritisation of equal human and democratic rights in Europe's transnational 'European society' (Article 2 TEU) and 'demoi-cracy' (Arts 9–12 TEU) promotes 'positive freedoms' (such as equal access to education and vaccines), equal competitive opportunities and voluntary cooperation among legal equals beyond national frontiers. Stronger

[6] For example, E Luce Scali, in her book on *Sovereign Debt and Socio-Economic Rights Beyond Crisis* (CUP, 2022), attributes the 'austerity-conditionality' of the EU's financial assistance in response to Greece's sovereign debt crises to an 'anti-humanist Hayekian neo-liberalism'; this appears unjustified in view of the emphasis on 'democratic constitutionalism' (eg requiring parliamentary control of fiscal and debt policies) in the relevant jurisprudence by the German Constitutional Court. The economic justification of fiscal and public debt disciplines (eg as agreed upon in the Lisbon Treaty and in the German Basic Law) for reconciling monetary and financial stability with economic growth, and of the conditionality of EU/IMF financial assistance for indebted EU Member States like Greece, remains contested; it requires democratic legitimation avoiding economic dogmas.

[7] M Loughlin's book *Against Constitutionalism* (OUP, 2022) justifies Brexit by his conception of representative British democracy (as represented by the Monarch, the Lords and the Commons in Parliament) rejecting EU neoliberalism – without acknowledging the ineffective UN/WTO protection of the universally agreed sustainable development goals and offering no strategy for protecting transnational PGs demanded by citizens.

[8] Q Slobodian's book on *Globalists: The End of Empire and the Birth of Neoliberalism* (Harvard UP, 2018) discredits WTO law as neoliberal without acknowledging ordoliberal WTO principles (eg on compulsory WTO adjudication protecting rule-of-law, WTO jurisprudence interpreting WTO rules as protecting non-discriminatory conditions of competition) and the ordoliberal advocacy of 'WTO globalists' for interpreting WTO law consistently with the human rights obligations of WTO members, as required by the customary rules of treaty interpretation endorsed in Article 3 of the WTO Dispute Settlement Understanding.

[9] Cf Petersmann/Steinbach (note 2), chapters 2 and 3.

citizen support for Europe's 'competitive social market economy' promoting 'sustainable development' inside and outside Europe (as required by Arts 3, 21 TEU) requires helping citizens to understand why neither Anglo-Saxon neoliberalism nor authoritarian power monopolies are consistent with the Lisbon Treaty's recognition of the major 'constituent principles' (such as labour and social rights, economic freedoms, property rights, rule-of-law, monetary stability, and fiscal and budgetary disciplines) and 'regulative principles' (such as competition and social policies and independent central bank policies) that ordoliberals and 'constitutional economists' have long advocated . The EU's prioritisation of comprehensive human and constitutional rights of citizens limiting public and private powers[10] reflects ordoliberal EU governance of PGs that excludes emulating inside the EU 'neoliberal under-regulation' (like US withdrawal from the 2015 Paris Agreement on climate change mitigation) and authoritarian disregard for UN law:

(a) The ordoliberal principle of normative and methodological individualism explains why EU law (like Articles 2, 6 TEU, the EU Charter of Fundamental Rights (EUCFR)) derives values from voluntary, informed individual and democratic consent of citizens in open economic, democratic, social and 'legal markets' that protect non-discriminatory conditions of competition and equal opportunities for individual and democratic self-development (eg through economic competition, social contracts, democratic voting and 'regulatory competition' at different levels of governance). Protecting citizen-driven 'consumer welfare' in economic market competition, 'citizen welfare' in democratic governance, human and fundamental rights and 'equal opportunities' in social cooperation (such as the 'European society' as legally defined in Article 2 TEU), and rule-of-law leaves broad economic policy discretion and scope for diverse 'social', 'constitutional', economic and 'democratic contracts' among citizens with often diverse preferences. EU Commission President von der Leyen, in her speech in the European Parliament on 17 July 2024 before the parliamentary approval of her re-appointment, described 'social dialogue' as 'the hallmark of our social market economy'.[11]

(b) EU law implements the ordoliberal insight that constituting, limiting, regulating and justifying multilevel governance of PGs requires limiting market failures, governance failures and constitutional failures across the interdependent social, economic, democratic and legal, national and transnational orders. This is reflected, *inter alia*, in the EU Treaty provisions for a 'competitive social market economy' and 'sustainable development' (eg in Article 3 TEU) as integral parts of a European 'society, in which pluralism, nondiscrimination, tolerance, justice, solidarity and equality between women and men prevail', and which is characterised by 'respect for human dignity, freedom, democracy, equality, the rule of law and respect for human

[10] Cf EU Commission, *70 Years of EU Law. A Union for Its Citizens* (EU, 2023).

[11] Statement at the European Parliament Plenary by President Ursula von der Leyen: https://enlargement.ec.europa.eu/news/statement-european-parliament-plenary-president-ursula-von-der-leyen-candidate-second-mandate-2024-2024-07-18_en#:~:text=Our%20focus%20now%20will%20be,they%20can%20rely%20on%20us.

rights, including the rights of persons belonging to minorities' (Article 2 TEU). The ordoliberal emphasis on the 'interdependence of orders' is reflected also in many other EU requirements, for example, to 'offer its citizens an area of freedom, security and justice without internal frontiers, in which the free movement of persons is ensured' (Article 3.2 TEU), and to base the EU's external relations law on the same constitutional principles as internal EU law (Arts 3.5, 21 TEU). The common EU responses to the financial and monetary crises since 2008, to climate change and other environmental crises, the Covid-19 health pandemic, Russian military aggression and weaponisation of energy supplies limited market failures (like pollution and climate change, insufficient supply of vaccines), governance failures (like illegal immigration) and constitutional failures (like countermeasures against illegal military aggression and suppression of human rights by Russia in Ukraine). This EU focus on the interactions between citizen-driven economic, political, social and constitutional, transnational orders distinguishes EU ordoliberalism from neoliberal constitutional nationalism and authoritarianism.

(c) The EU's multilevel democratic, republican and cosmopolitan constitutionalism protecting democratic input-legitimacy, republican output-legitimacy and cosmopolitan, transnational rule-of-law for the benefit of citizens responds to the ordoliberal call for constitutional limitations of market failures, governance failures and constitutional failures. The EU's unique 'EMU', with only limited EU economic and social policy powers, has raised constitutional controversies (eg about the powers of the European Central Bank, (ECB)); their political and judicial settlement focused on protecting democratic governance principles rather than economic dogmas. The EMU remains a constitutional experiment requiring further legislative clarifications and political compromises (eg regarding the EU 'own resources', fiscal deficits, excessive public debt and the issuing of common EU bonds). The 2024 appointments of new EU Commissioners for new regulatory challenges (such as EU security and the housing crises inside several EU Member States) illustrate this crisis-driven evolution of many EU laws and policies.

(d) The explicit commitment to a 'competitive social market economy' acknowledges that competition among diverse economies and democracies creates winners and losers; to remain socially and democratically supported, the EU must respond to changing social, environmental and political circumstances and crises. The EU mandate for a 'social' market economy protecting human rights and 'cohesion' is increasingly used (eg for post-Covid 19 recovery projects financed through common EU borrowing in capital markets) to stabilise social support for EU governance in Europe's transnational society, economy and demoi-cratic polity. EU law clarifies – eg in the EUCFR and in the 2024 EU Corporate Sustainability Due Diligence Directive – that the EU legal conceptions of 'social market economy' and 'sustainable development' exclude neoliberal, business-driven (self)regulation neglecting human and environmental rights and judicial remedies. Authoritarian conceptions of a 'socialist market economy' (eg in China), with communist 'social surveillance' and censorship, are even more inconsistent with EU law. The EU

Commission proposals for a 'new Clean Industrial Deal', a 'European Savings and Investments Union', and a 'European Affordable Housing Plan', as announced by the President of the EU Commission in July 2024, illustrate this development of EU law and policies responding to economic, environmental, social and security crises in conformity with 'ordoliberal principles' that reject business-driven self-regulation neglecting human rights. Past neoliberal criticism of the term 'social' as a 'weasel-word' (FA Hayek) lacking precise meaning is refuted by the EU law guarantees of civil, political, economic, social and cultural rights that offer justiciable, legal definitions of 'social welfare' and of related legal and political remedies.

2.3 'Strategic autonomy' requires interpreting EU Law as a 'living constitution'

The transformation of economic partners into potential adversaries (like Russia) has prompted the EU Commission to call for 'EU strategic autonomy' de-risking economic dependencies (eg on Russian energy supplies and on the Chinese supply of rare earths and technologies) that risk being 'weaponised'. EU Member States remain characterised by diverse national Constitutions and only limited conferral of EU competences, in conformity with the 'subsidiarity principle' (Article 5 TEU) and Europe's decentralised development throughout centuries. As EU decisions regarding the EU budget and other revenues (eg financed through issuance of common EU debt) require unanimity and approval by all Member States (Article 311 TEU), EU financial decisions (eg on financial assistance for Ukraine) have been repeatedly vetoed for political reasons (eg by Hungary); this uncertain EU capacity to agree on urgent fiscal responses to unforeseen events limits the EU's 'strategic autonomy'. Diverse national responses to European crises – as in the financial and sovereign debt crises since 2008, in the migration crisis of 2015, or in the current security crisis caused by Russian aggression – risk undermining European integration, for instance by national border closures, increasing sovereign bond spreads, national referenda (like 'Brexit') or by political vetoes that reject EU initiatives. As EU law protects individual and democratic autonomy and only limited EU competences for protecting transnational PGs, EU crises governance requires interpreting and developing EU law as a citizen-driven 'living constitution', different from national Constitutions based on state sovereignty. The more the geopolitical rivalries and diverse value priorities of European constitutionalism, Anglo-Saxon neoliberalism, authoritarian state-capitalism and 'third-world development policies' become permanent facts, the more EU law and practices must adjust to the new geopolitical and geoeconomic challenges caused by international legal policy competition and 'lawfare' disrupting the UN and WTO legal systems.[12]

[12] Cf E.U.Petersmann, Transforming UN and WTO Legal Systems through International Legal Policy Competition and 'Lawfare', in: *German Yearbook of International Law 2024*, 67 (2025), 255-290.

3. From Exceptional EU Crisis Governance to Evolutionary Constitutionalism

As explained in section 2, Europe's successful integration law can be explained by its unique merging and extension of republican, democratic and cosmopolitan constitutionalism to multilevel governance of PGs. The EU's multilevel constitutionalism differs from neoliberalism by its 'ordoliberal' acknowledgment that the proper functioning of economic, democratic and social, citizen-driven 'markets' (as decentralised information, coordination and sanctioning mechanisms) depends on multilevel legal limitations of market failures, governance and constitutional failures. The 1992 'Maastricht compromise' for the EU's EMU provided for centralised EU monetary policy conducted by the ECB and decentralised, national economic policies (including fiscal and debt policies) subject to national parliamentary control, national financial responsibility, EU policy coordination, EU fiscal and debt disciplines, prohibitions of monetary financing (Article 123 TFEU), a no-bail-out clause (Article 125 TFEU), and EU emergency and solidarity safeguards (eg in Arts 120ff TFEU). According to Article 311 TFEU, the EU budget 'shall be financed wholly from own resources' without prejudice to other revenue; the 'Union shall provide itself with the means necessary to attain its objectives and carry through its policies'. As the Lisbon Treaty does not confer powers on the EU to issue common bonds for financing the EU budget, the transformation of the initially nationalist responses (such as border controls) to the Covid-19 global health pandemic in 2020 by the common Next Generation EU (NG-EU) recovery program – distributing grants and loans to EU Member States worth up to €750 billion based on Arts 122, 175 TFEU from 2021 to 2026, and financed through common debt issued by the EU in conformity with Article 311 TFEU – required ratification of the EU Council decision by all national parliaments in EU Member States.[13] This 'NGEU governance model' – distributing emergency loans and grants based on Arts 122, 175 TFEU, and financing them on the basis of Article 311 TFEU through a Council Decision approved by national parliaments, thereby effectively doubling the EU's annual budget without changing the EU Treaties – also inspired the EU financial and military assistance for Ukraine in response to Russia's full-scale invasion of the country in 2022.[14] In view of the political difficulties and uncertainties of EU treaty amendments, the 2024 Draghi report on a 'competitiveness strategy for Europe' referred, again, to the NG-EU governance as a model for promoting and financing needed EU reforms responding to the 'emergency context' of geopolitical rivalries.

[13] Cf B de Witte, The European Union's Covid-19 Recovery Plan: The Legal Engineering of an Economic Policy Shift, in *CMLRev* 58 (2021) 635.

[14] Cf F Fabbrini, From the Pandemic to the War: the EU Fiscal Response to Russia's Aggression of Ukraine, the Legacy of NGEU, and the Challenge to 'Promote the General Welfare', in *AJIL Unbound* 118 (2024), 177.

3.1 Exceptional and discretionary nature of NG-EU Crisis Governance

Germany's constitutional court, in its judgment approving the NG-EU recovery and resilience program of December 2020, emphasised the temporary, exceptional nature of EU emergency governance based on Article 122 TFEU and financed through issuance of common EU debt.[15] The Court insisted that constitutional democracy in Germany requires that the overall financial burden imposed on German citizens must be decided by the German Parliament. Also, the type and level of public spending, and German financial liability for decisions of other states or international institutions, cannot be decided only at the supranational level. Without a treaty amendment, it is legally not possible to recognise common borrowing as a permanent source of EU financing; yet the Court accepted the EU Council Decision 2020/2053 of December 2020 on the EU system of own resources as a sufficient legal authorisation to borrow on the capital markets 'other resources' provided the borrowing was limited in time and amounts, and was spent for the specific purposes justified under Article 122 TFEU. Considering the diverse emergencies and recovery projects inside Member States, the Court accepted a wide margin of appreciation of the Council and Commission under Article 122 TFEU without insisting that each national recovery project was linked to the pandemic.

The 'ordoliberal principles' underlying Europe's multilevel constitutionalism confirm this EU policy discretion for responding to the unique European context. For instance, interpreting EU law as protecting equal dignity rights (Title 1 EUCFR), liberty rights (Title 2 EUCFR), equality rights (Title 3 EUCFR), solidarity rights and principles (Title 4 EUCFR), citizen rights (Title 5 EUCFR) and 'justice' (Title 6 EUCFR) may justify diverse 'balancing' of democratic, economic and social policy priorities (eg for promoting 'cohesion' and equal opportunities like gender equality).[16] The NG-EU resilience and recovery project also used the EU cohesion policy rules (Arts 174-178 TFEU) for justifying preferential treatment of (eg southern) EU Member States in the allocation of EU grants and loans. EU promotion of a 'competitive social market economy' differs fundamentally from utilitarian

[15] BVerfG, 2 BvR 547/21 (Interim Decision of 15 April 2021), 2 BvR 798/21 (Judgment of 6 December 2022).

[16] My textbook on *International Economic Law in the 21st Century* (Hart, 2012) discusses dozens of relevant CJEU judgments (eg on balancing economic freedoms with dignity rights, social and labour rights inside the EU's rights-based common market); it explains the philosophical foundations of focusing on non-discriminatory conditions of competition and equal opportunities for the benefit of citizens, rather than only on libertarian freedom and autonomy. Competition among individuals with unequal capacities and scarce resources is seen as a pervasive social fact creating social injustices unless human rights and equal opportunities are protected. Economic efficiency standards must be complemented by agreed social justice principles and judicial remedies against abuses of policy discretion. Governmental 'social engineering' must remain limited and justifiable by agreed constitutional rules and procedures reconciling individual and democratic self-determination. For a similar approach, see P Lamy, *The Geneva Consensus. Making Trade Work for All* (CUP, 2013).

prioritisation of 'libertarian freedom' and mere 'Kaldor-Hicks-efficiency' in the US common market, or of authoritarian market distortions in autocracies.[17]

'Ordoliberal interpretations' of EU law – for instance, for justifying common market regulations that promote EU competitiveness based on the 'commerce clause' in Article 114 TFEU, and EU emergency assistance based on the emergency clause (Article 122 TFEU) in combination with TFEU provisions for cohesion policy outside of regular funds (Article 175) with EU agreements supplementing the EU budget (Article 311) – facilitate justifying EU crises governance. The creation of the NG-EU recovery program, and its approval by national legislatures, showed how dynamic interpretation of EU Treaty provisions – without changing the EU fiscal and budgetary constitution – can enable effective EU crisis responses.

Reconciling individual and democratic autonomy (as protected by human and constitutional rights) with 'state sovereignty' and the quest for EU 'strategic autonomy' inevitably differs from conceptions of national sovereignty outside Europe. The EU Treaties remain embedded into other worldwide (eg UN, GATT, WTO) and regional treaty obligations of EU Member States (like the ECHR) as integral parts of European integration. The geopolitical changes – caused by authoritarian power politics, climate change, the digital revolution and the emergence of a multipolar world with 'permacrises' challenging the EU's multilevel governance - require EU crisis responses taking into account the EU obligations (as prescribed in Arts 3, 21 TEU) to comply with UN and WTO law. So far, EU responses to the changing geopolitics (like adjustments of EU trade and industrial policies, competition and state aid policies, internet governance and data protection laws, common foreign security and defence policies) avoided treaty changes. Whether the limited fiscal and budgetary EU competences - and the dangerously insufficient EU security system – can be adequately complemented through *ad hoc* agreements among EU Member States without changing the Lisbon Treaties remains, however, contested.

3.2 Democratically legitimate, alternative forms of EU crises governance

Do the global 'permacrises' (such as climate change), and the undermining of the UN security and WTO trade systems by geopolitical power politics, justify interpreting EU emergency governance (eg based on Article 122 TFEU) as a permanent NG-EU governance model? Repeated invocations of Article 122 in 'permacrises' are justifiable. However, Article 122 does not prescribe participation

[17] A Applebaum, *Autocracy, Inc: The Dictators Who Want to Run the World* (Doubleday, 2024) describes the common characteristics of modern autocracies (like Belarus, China, Cuba, Iran, North Korea, Russia, Venezuela) as being based on oppressive, (para)military security services; kleptocratic networks; corrupt financial structures; technological experts providing surveillance, propaganda and disinformation; and internal and external power politics suppressing human and democratic rights (eg in Ukrainian territories occupied by Russia as confirmed by European and international courts of justice). For a similar diagnosis, see I Williams, *Vampire State: The Rise and Fall of the Chinese Economy* (Birlinn, 2024).

of the European Parliament in EU emergency governance; this makes other treaty provisions for common EU actions with the consent of the European Parliament (like Arts 175, 352 TFEU) democratically preferable. Amendments of Article 122 TFEU may be pragmatically avoided by agreements among the EU institutions ensuring participation of the European Parliament in EU emergency governance. Treaty amendments conferring EU powers to issue common debts without approval by national parliaments remain contested, however, at least in view of Germany's requirements of national parliamentary budget responsibility subject to a 'debt brake' (Arts 109, 115 German Basic Law). NG-EU emergency governance and cohesion policies (Article 175) offer policy alternatives for circumventing this 'debt brake' if proposals for amending the Basic Law lack sufficient democratic support.

The succession of financial crises (such as bankruptcies threatening financial stability), sovereign debt crises (such as sovereign debts threatening the monetary Euro-system), illegal migration, 'Brexit' and rule-of-law crises, health pandemics, military security, competitiveness and environmental crises since 2009 forced the EU institutions to design crises responses through evolutionary, contextual interpretations of EU treaty provisions[18] that did not specifically foresee such agreed crises responses:

(a) EU Treaty provisions conferring legislative powers (like Article 114 TFEU for approximation of national laws for the functioning of the EU internal market) have been used extensively, for instance in the banking crisis, to establish a banking union with central supervision of banks, and for responding to the 'digital revolution' by regulating services providers through the Digital Services, Digital Markets and the Artificial Intelligence Acts. While Article 114 shall be applied by the European Parliament and the Council in accordance with the ordinary legislative procedure, some other treaty provisions enable only unanimous Council actions 'on a proposal from the Commission and after obtaining the consent of the European Parliament', for instance, if 'the Treaties have not provided the necessary powers' for attaining treaty objectives 'within the framework of the policies defined in the Treaties' (Article 352 TFEU).

(b) Emergency powers (notably under Article 122 TFEU) have been used frequently in the debt, pandemic, energy and security crises since 2009; they do not provide for parliamentary consent and are subject to the constitutional principles of necessity, proportionality and only temporary use. Even though the NG-EU recovery program was adopted as an exceptional emergency measure, its legal and political governance methods have been followed in the financial and military EU assistance for Ukraine which – in addition to national financial and military assistance by EU Member States – was financed by common debt raised

[18] Cf A de Gregorio Merino, The EU Treaties as a Living Constitution of the Union in Times of Crisis, in *AJIL Unbound* 118 (2024) 162.

on the financial markets.[19] It remains to be clarified – by the CJEU or by democratic agreements – to what extent pluricrises can justify regular invocations of the NG-EU governance model for responding to permacrises like climate change and systemic EU competitiveness challenges in a multipolar world where state-capitalist and neoliberal competitors avoid many regulatory costs (such as those of complying with higher environmental, human rights and labour standards) and, thereby, undermine Europe's social and competition models.[20]

(c) EU emergency responses have often been agreed through international agreements among EU Member States, for instance if EU treaty provisions (like the lengthy treaty amendment procedures) and/or EU budgetary resources were deemed insufficient, or the needed consensus was blocked by one or a few states. Examples include the 2012 'Fiscal Compact' on Stability, Convergence and Growth as well as the European Stability Mechanism created in response to the Euro-crisis with the possibility of mobilising up to €500 billion in loan assistance to an overindebted Eurozone member country (like Greece at the time), or for financing EU assistance for migrants in Mediterranean countries, such as Turkey. These treaties often confer additional competences on EU institutions (such as the EU Commission and the CJEU) to ensure their coherence with EU law. Control of these treaties by EU Member States and their national parliaments secure democratic legitimacy. Yet, as the preponderant role of the European Council in crisis governance avoids the normal EU co-legislative procedures involving the Commission, the European Parliament and the Council of Ministers, there are deliberate efforts at involving the EU Commission for initiating and implementing EU crises measures (such as the European Peace Facility for supplying munitions to Ukraine, and for NG-EU borrowing in financial markets and controlling the spending of loans and grants in EU Member States).

(d) Arguably, even if the NG-EU governance model risks circumventing the European Parliament, the consent from Member States (Article 122 TFEU), ratification by national parliaments (Article 311 TFEU), and judicial approval by national constitutional courts maintain democratic legitimacy of its innovative policy tools (such as national recovery projects, performance-based supervision, redistributive 'cohesion policy', common EU borrowing, rapid macroeconomic stabilisation, rule-of-law conditionalities and the diversification of energy supplies through REPowerEU projects). Crisis measures adopted by 'republican EU institutions' (like the ECB), and the protection of the rule-of-law by the CJEU, illustrate how multilevel 'demoi-cracy' bridging the national and European democratic decision-making procedures is complemented and 'stabilised' by republican and cosmopolitan EU constitutionalism limiting democratic discretion by constitutional constraints protecting public reason against volatile, populist emotions.

[19] Cf note 14.

[20] Cf P Lindseth, P Leino-Sandberg, *Democratizing Draghi: Why the "Competitiveness Report" Demands Treaty Reform*, *VerfBlog*, 2024/9/12, https://verfassungsblog.de/draghi-report-investment-eu-competition-treaty-reform/, DOI: 10.59704/36728ff8ed7b538d.

Judicial and regulatory institutions (like the ECB) have democratically agreed mandates for institutionalising public reason. EU constitutionalism recognises judicial clarifications of indeterminate legal rules (such as judgments on environmental policy inaction violating human rights to climate change mitigation) as an indispensable part of constitutional democracy. Withholding NG-EU funds vis-à-vis Member States with illiberal governments undermining rule-of-law (eg in Hungary and Poland) set effective financial incentives for national legal and democratic reforms. Europe's constitutional demoi-cracy rejects claims that democratic discretion should include power to abolish democracy, human rights, or governmental duties to protect PGs. Cosmopolitan constitutionalism protecting human rights and rule-of-law across national frontiers, and republican constitutionalism protecting agreed PGs (including 'rule-of-law conditionalities'), distinguish Europe's multilevel 'ordoliberal constitutionalism' from constitutionally less restrained nationalism outside Europe.

4. Conclusions: 'Systemic Challenges' for Internal and External EU Crises Governance

There is no other multilateral organisation outside Europe with 27 democratic Member States, whose courts protect a regional 'rule-of-law' system with a transnational 'constitutional identity' as defined in Article 2 TEU.[21] Compared with process-based, constitutional nationalism with autocratic or neoliberal policies, the Lisbon Treaties' commitments to protecting human and constitutional rights, democracy and rule-of-law not only inside and among EU Member States, but also in EU external relations, entail 'multilevel constitutional self-restraints' that states outside Europe do not accept. Past EU attempts at complementing Europe's 'foreign policy constitution' by a transatlantic free trade agreement (FTA) and compulsory international economic adjudication were rejected by successive US governments.[22] The financial and monetary EU crises since 2009, like the subsequent migration, environmental, health, energy, security and 'competitiveness crises' inside the EU, were all related to governance crises outside Europe, for instance in the US financial system, emigration from failed states in Africa and Asia, global climate change, biodiversity losses and pollution (eg of the oceans), weaponisation of energy supplies and military aggression by authoritarian

[21] In *Republic of Poland v European Parliament and Council of the EU*, C-157/21, ECLI:EU:C:2022:98 (16 February, 2022), the CJEU defined the values in Article 2 TEU as 'the very identity of the European Union as a common legal order' (para 327). On the extension of these constitutional principles to third European states (eg through the European Economic Area with EFTA states) see: A Petti, *EU Neighborhood Law: Wider Europe and the EU's Extended Legal Space* (Hart, 2024).

[22] Cf EU Petersmann, The EU's Cosmopolitan Foreign Policy Constitution and its Disregard in Transatlantic Free Trade Agreements, in: European Foreign Affairs Review 21 (2016), 449–469; Petersmann/Steinbach (note 2).

dictatorships, and loss of European competitiveness vis-à-vis third competitors benefitting from lower human rights and environmental standards, production and energy costs. Internal and external EU crises governance interact and cannot be separated. The EU's multilevel constitutionalism increasingly prompts the EU to assume leadership for promoting sustainable development reforms beyond the EU (below 4.1). Yet, the limited conferral of EU competences, the subsidiarity principle (Article 5 TEU), and the political, economic and social diversity inside and among EU Member States render democratic EU crises governance increasingly difficult (4.2-3); as ordoliberal constitutionalism excludes emulating 'neoliberal under-regulation' and authoritarian power politics, the EU needs additional, external 'interface safeguards' protecting the EU's international competitiveness and 'strategic autonomy' against neoliberal and authoritarian power politics (4.4).

4.1 EU constitutionalism prescribes sustainable development reforms beyond the EU

As explained in sections 2 and 3, EU law (eg Arts 3, 21 TEU, 208 TFEU) prescribes EU compliance with UN and WTO law and their SDGs. The more authoritarian and neoliberal power politics impede UN and WTO reforms, the more necessary become second-best plurilateral governance reforms which make membership conditional on promoting human rights and rules-based, multilevel private-public partnerships for realising the universally agreed SDGs. The polycrises have induced the EU to resort to new regulations and directives responding to foreign market distortions, environmental pollution, and violations of UN and WTO rules by collective countermeasures. For instance, to protect EU citizens, the EU has introduced new regulations for:

- screening foreign investments inside the EU;
- limiting access of non-EU companies to government procurement inside the EU unless reciprocal access of EU companies is secured;
- EU 'anti-coercion measures' providing for unilateral EU countermeasures against economic sanctions by third countries (such as China);
- EU prohibitions of importing 'conflict minerals' and products made by forced labour, and EU 'sustainability sanctions' in response to foreign violations of labour rights, human rights and sustainable development commitments, including also a 2024 EU corporate sustainability due diligence directive requiring large companies to protect human rights, worker rights and environmental standards in their supply chains;
- EU emergency powers for responding to supply chain problems (as they emerged during the Covid-19 and energy crises);
- stronger EU anti-subsidy and emergency export control regimes;

— unilateral EU carbon border adjustment measures (CBAMs) supplementing the European carbon emission trading system (ETS) by avoiding 'carbon leakage' (ie relocation of production outside EU borders to countries with lower environmental standards), greening the Union's supply chains, and promoting climate change mitigation beyond EU borders;
— an EU deforestation regulation compelling exporters of six commodities (including coffee, palm oil and rubber) to prove they were not produced on land that was recently deforested, and imposing mandatory due diligence obligations on firms trading such products in Europe.[23]

The EU emphasises its commitment to WTO-consistent regulations. Hence, in response to criticism of the EU CBAMs and a 2024 WTO dispute settlement finding of certain legal inconsistencies in the EU 'tropical deforestation regulations', the EU confirmed its determination to bring its measures into conformity with WTO law. At the same time, the EU exercises leadership for promoting sustainable development reforms in third countries, especially in the following four areas:

(a) Since the 2010 EU-Korea FTA, the EU includes provisions on trade and sustainable development (TSD chapters) into all EU FTAs. The TSD-chapters include provisions relating to domestic law (such as labour, environmental and sustainable development policies subject to non-regression obligations), international standards and agreements (eg referring to ILO conventions, ILO core labour standards, multilateral environmental agreements), FTA institutions with civil society participation, and FTA dispute settlement procedures. Past evidence suggests that the TSD chapters and their institutionalised supervision (eg promoting labour law reforms in Vietnam) and enforcement (eg in the context of EU-Korea panel procedures concerning Koreas's non-compliance with ILO core labour rights like freedom of association) have rendered the sustainable development obligations of FTAs more effective in conformity with the UN SDGs.[24]

(b) The rules-based internal and external EU mandates and judicial remedies pushed the EU to become a leading advocate for compulsory adjudication in international trade law, investment law, international criminal law and the Law of the Sea. For example, when the WTO Appellate Body (AB) was rendered dysfunctional in 2019 by illegal US vetoes of the consensus-based nominations of AB judges, the EU introduced voluntary Multi-Party-Interim Arbitration agreements (based on Article 25 DSU [Dispute Settlement Understanding]) providing for compulsory appellate arbitration among WTO Members pending the blockage of the WTO AB, thereby limiting abuses of 'appeals into the void of a dysfunctional AB' that

[23] These various EU Regulations and Directives are published in the EU Official Journal and explained on the EU website on EU trade policies: *Making Trade Policy*, European Commission, https://policy.trade.ec.europa.eu/eu-trade-relationships-country-and-region/making-trade-policy_en.

[24] Cf Velut et al. (2022) Comparative Analysis of Trade and Sustainable Development Provisions in Free Trade Agreements, LSE, 02/2022, p. 39, https://circabc.europa.eu/rest/download/150a55ee-fd11-491d-a9f1-c6347cfe9800?ticket

prevented adoption of WTO panel reports. The bilateral and UN negotiations on transforming investor-state arbitration into more transparent, and more accountable investment adjudication were promoted by the CJEU ruling that investor-state arbitration was inconsistent with EU constitutional law and had to be reformed in both the EU's internal and external relations; the EU continues to actively participate in the ongoing negotiations (eg in the UN Commission on International Trade Law and in the International Center for the Settlement of Investment Disputes) on reforming investor-state arbitration in the EU's external relations.[25] The EU's participatory and deliberative democracy has also pushed EU institutions to withdraw in 2024 from the 1998 Energy Charter Treaty in response to the increasing use of its investor-state arbitration procedures by fossil fuel industries to challenge climate change policies.

(c) EU common market regulations often have global 'Brussels effects' if access of foreign goods, services and investments to the EU market is made conditional on compliance with EU common market regulations (like EU product and production standards, EU regulations of digital services and artificial intelligence).[26] The EU's environmental constitutionalism, climate legislation and related climate litigation illustrate how domestic constitutional reforms inside the EU set incentives for governments and non-governmental organisations also outside the EU to increase their environmental and human rights protection standards, for instance by introducing carbon taxes on products and services exported to the EU.[27] The EU's internal ETS and external CBAMs – aimed at reducing Greenhouse Gas (GHG) emissions, inducing industries to use greener technologies, and to prevent 'carbon leakage' – illustrate the transformative nature of the EU's environmental constitutionalism inside and beyond the EU, for instance by setting incentives for increasing insufficient 'nationally determined contributions' for GHG reductions under the 2015 Paris Agreement on climate change mitigation. The EU remains committed to regulating and implementing its CBAM in conformity with both UN law and WTO law. Even if collecting carbon tariffs at the border as an integral part of the EU ETS could violate GATT Articles II or III, Article XX GATT justifies the EU's ETS/CBAM system to the extent it is non-discriminatory and necessary for protecting the human right to protection of the environment (Article XX, para. a), human, animal and plant life or health (para. b), non-discriminatory internal product and production standards like ETS systems (para. d), or is related to the conservation of exhaustible natural resources 'in conjunction with restrictions on domestic production or consumption' (para g). The EU Commission initiated bilateral negotiations with third countries (such as India, African countries, the USA) on, *inter alia*, defining agreed production standards (eg for carbon-intensive 'dirty

[25] On the EU initiatives for reforming trade and investment adjudication see Petersmann/Steinbach (note 2), 308–361.

[26] Cf A Bradford, The Brussels Effect: How the European Union Rules the World (CUP, 2020).

[27] Cf J Delbeke, How CBAM Can Become a Stepping Stone towards Carbon Pricing Globally, European University Institute STG Policy Paper 2023-6. There are now about 40 third countries cooperating with the EU in designing their own CBAM systems.

steel'), agreed procedures for calculating the carbon content of traded products and services, mutual recognition of diverse climate change mitigation policies in import and export countries (eg environmental taxes and subsidies), and 'common but differentiated responsibilities'. Yet, following the blocking by fossil fuel exporting countries in 2025 of UN negotiations on multilateral treaties on reducing plastic pollution and on imposing 'green shipping levies', the EU-led group of more than 80 countries in the COP 30 climate mitigation negotiations accepted in November 2025 that their demand for a 'road map to transition away from fossil fuels' could not be included into the consensus-based, COP 30 final agreement. As burning oil, coal and gas remains the chief cause of climate change and the final COP 30 agreement acknowledges that the world is now likely to exceed the 1.5C warming target in the 2015 Paris Agreement, EU leadership for 'coalitions of the willing' participating in the EU's CBAM system as of 2026 has become even more important.

(d) EU leadership for democratic and human rights reforms is pursued, *inter alia*, by including references to human rights in all external EU trade and investment agreements and continuing EU accession negotiations aimed at enlarging the EU from now 27 to about 35 Member States by 2030. The inclusion of human and democratic rights guarantees in EU trade and association agreements and related EU enforcement measures go beyond similar treaty provisions and judicial remedies in the external FTAs by non-European democracies (like the USA); they render UN human rights law more effective.[28]

4.2 EU multilevel demoi-cracy constrains discretionary emergency governance

There is no continent outside Europe with 'democratic principles' as in the Lisbon Treaty (eg Arts 9–11 TEU) prescribing multilevel constitutional, parliamentary, participatory and deliberative democratic governance at national and regional levels protected by civil, political, economic, social and cultural rights, multilevel judicial remedies of EU citizens, and principles of limited conferral of EU powers subject to constitutional restraints such as the subsidiarity principle (Article 5 TEU). Similarly, on no continent outside Europe have more than 46 democracies accepted regional treaty systems protecting human rights and multilevel judicial and other republican institutions as comprehensively as in the numerous Council of Europe treaties (like the ECHR). Yet, this dense 'legal integration law' with

[28] A recent example is the judgment by the CJEU of 4 October 2024 annulling the EU Council Decision approving an EU-Morocco trade and fishery agreement on the ground of violating international law by extending the scope of the agreement to the territory of the Western Sahara without respect for the right to self-determination of the indigenous Sahrawi people which had not consented to the agreement, and whose consent could not be assumed: CJEU Joined Cases C-779/21 P, Commission v Front Polisario and C-799/21 P, Council v Front Polisario (not yet reported). Yet, the judgment has not prevented the subsequent recognition by President Macron of Moroccan sovereignty over Western Sahara.

numerous obligations of solidarity (eg in Arts 42.7 TEU, 122, 162, 222 TFEU) has not prevented 'democratic back-sliding' inside the EU (eg in Hungary, Poland and Slovakia) and among members of the Council of Europe (eg leading to the exclusion of Russia). The social, economic, political and legal diversity inside and among EU Member States renders democratic majority governance a constant challenge, especially in crises governance as discussed above. The emergence of ordoliberalism responded to Europe's social, economic and political crises following the First and Second World Wars; it confirmed why – in Europe – democratic and social support for a common market never depended only on protecting market freedoms and economic efficiency (as the prevailing 'neoliberal justifications' of the US common market); it also depended on transnational social order responding to citizen demand for social security, full employment, diversity and solidarity.

Sections 2 and 3 explained why Europe's 'ordoliberal constitutionalism' protects wide democratic discretion at national and European levels of governance, for instance regarding limitations of market failures, governance failures and constitutional failures. The EU's 2020 post-pandemic Recovery and Resilience Program allocated more grants and loans to southern EU Member States based on macroeconomic justifications (such as comparatively lower per capita GDP, larger economic harm during the pandemic in these recipient countries); yet, such democratic value decisions remain *ad hoc* compromises.[29] Reducing public debt and annual budget deficits in EU Member States (as prescribed by the fiscal and debt disciplines in the TFEU to promote monetary, financial and economic stability, economic growth and competitiveness in the EMU) and rebuilding stronger financial safety nets for financing innovative investments require finding a more sustainable balance between public finances, private investment and economic growth.[30] The national 'balancing efforts', and the national responses inside the EU 'welfare states' to the financial, health, environmental and security crises since 2008, remain diverse.[31] National parliamentary responsibility for fiscal and debt policies, and proposals for joint financing of common European PGs, have to be reconciled through consensus-based EU decisions which, according to the 'passerelle clause' in Article 48(7) TEU, may legalise qualified majority decisions. Enhanced cooperation among nine or more EU Member States (Arts 20 TEU, 326ff TFEU), EU social policies pursuant to Arts 151ff TFEU, EU cohesion

[29] Macroeconomic data (like national GDP per capita) say little about domestic 'social welfare'; for example, more than 80% of Italian households live in their own house or apartment and are exempt from property taxes on their first house (apartment); in Germany, less than 50% of households live in their own home, which is subject to property taxes aimed at reducing social inequalities. The comparatively lower public and private investments in European technologies and innovation (than in the USA) are partly due to the fact that the EU cohesion funds distribute about a third of the EU budget to reduce social and economic gaps between richer and poorer parts inside the EU, and agricultural subsidies account for more than a quarter of the EU budget.

[30] On the difficulties of solving Europe's 'budgetary trilemma' and 'investment gap' of more than 1 trillion € per year see the Draghi report (note 1).

[31] For example, seven EU Member States have recently been put forward for an excessive deficit procedure.

policies (Arts 174ff TFEU), the EU treaty commitments (eg in Arts 42.7 TEU, 222 TFEU) to collective responses to natural disasters and foreign aggression offer many EU policy instruments for promoting a 'competitive social market economy', solidarity and social justice in European integration.[32]

4.3 EU republican constitutionalism 'stabilises' European demoi-cracy

Section 2 explained how the EU 'republican commitments' to protecting rule-of-law and other PGs inside and beyond the EU institutionalise public reason based on democratically agreed mandates, depoliticise and stabilise EU decision-making. As explained in section 3, EU law offers multiple legal procedures – like the NG-EU governance method and more 'enhanced cooperation' among 'coalitions of the willing' – for progressively moving towards more qualified-majority decisions and joined financing of new EU initiatives for promoting technological innovations, digitalisation and decarbonisation of economies, social and democratic support of EU common market and capital union reforms. As proposals for common EU social policies remain confronted with democratic opposition against transferring discretionary social welfare powers to EU institutions without agreed standards limiting 'moral hazards' in distributing EU funds among 27 Member States, consensus-requirements in EU decision-making offer incentives for needed compromises. Replacing neoliberal 'shareholder strategies' by inclusive stakeholder and environmental, social and governance (ESG) strategies helps aligning company interests with governmental responses to environmental, health and other social crises and private-public partnerships (eg for collective EU procurement of 'green technologies', vaccines and military supplies for Ukraine).

Practising 'EU solidarity' inside and beyond the EU in conformity with the 17 universally agreed UN SDGs facilitates reconciling the EU's internal and external legal obligations (such as EU commitments to preferential treatment of less-developed countries) and related treaty commitments of the EU (eg to comply with the 2015 Paris Agreement on climate change mitigation). For instance, the EU's financial contributions to the 'Loss and Damage Fund' established in the context of the 2015 Paris Agreement on climate change mitigation for assisting

[32] The need for such 'supranational social incrementalism' - as increasingly practised (eg with the EU's 'Civil Protection Mechanism' since 2001, and the common EU health and defence policy initiatives) – is explained by M.Ferrera, Politics and Social Visions: Ideology, Conflict and Solidarity in the EU (OUP, 2024). It is consistent with ordoliberal advocacy for a 'social market economy' assisting the losers in economic and social competition to maintain decent living standards and adjust to competitive pressures. As climate change has made Europe the world's fastest warming continent with increasing numbers of wildfires and other natural disasters, invocations of the EU's 'Civil Protection Mechanism' continue to increase every year (pooling resources such as planes and firefighters dispatched from other EU Member States when a government or EU candidate countries request assistance in case of a natural disaster, and financing 75 per cent of the operational costs).

less-developed countries in adjusting to the harmful changes caused by global warming (like rising sea levels, sea temperature changes, increase in ocean acidity caused by the absorption of carbon dioxide from the atmosphere) take into account the EU legal commitment (eg in Article 3 TEU) to promoting 'sustainable development', with due recognition of the historical accountability of industrialised countries for about 80 per cent of GHG emissions. EU FTAs promoting economic development and job opportunities in Africa and Latin-America may offer effective strategies also for EU policies reducing illegal immigration. The complex interactions between internal and external EU policies must be explained by EU institutions also in the current 'neoliberal challenge' that demand by EU citizens for high EU social standards undermines EU competitiveness vis-à-vis authoritarian and neoliberal competitors.

Third countries increasingly challenge (eg in WTO dispute settlement proceedings) what they perceive as 'green imperialism' and 'social protectionism' of the EU. For instance, EU CBAMs aimed at requiring third exporting countries to comply with the higher carbon emission reduction standards inside the EU's common market will be effectively enforced only progressively as of 2026. At the request of third countries, the entry into force of the 2023 Deforestation Regulation was delayed by one year; it aims at greening the Union's supply chains and mitigating climate change beyond its borders by prohibiting imports of major agricultural commodities into the EU market if they have been produced on recently deforested land. Respect for the principle of 'common but differentiated responsibilities and respective capabilities' in EU climate change policies needs to be further specified.[33] Imposing mandatory due diligence obligations on firms in third countries exporting to Europe, and EU invocations of 'security exceptions' on grounds of economic and democratic rather than only military security,[34] must be legally justified.

4.4 Geopolitical permacrises as existential threat to Europe's integration model

Constitutionalism emerged in response to the bounded rationality of human beings so as to limit domination of politics by power struggles, human passions and rational egoism. Constitutional democracy requires 'active citizenship'. Section 2 described how the emergence of ordoliberalism after World War I, and Europe's multilevel constitutionalism since the 1950s, prioritise values different from

[33] See G.Marin Duran/J.Scott, *Global EU climate action and the principle of common but differentiated responsibilities and respective capabilities*, in: EUI Law Working Papers 2024/2. In the WTO, the EU emphasises its commitment to design its trade and environmental policies in compliance with WTO law.

[34] Cf *Robust. Resilient. Sustainable. Integrated Security for Germany: National Security Strategy* (Bonn, 2023), which defines 'integrated security' in three dimensions: 'protection from war and violence'; 'the freedom to be able to shape our lives, our democracy the way we want'; and 'focusing on people's individual security needs', using the rights of women and vulnerable groups as a social barometer.

autocracies and democracies outside Europe. As emphasised already by Kant in his definition of 'enlightenment' as 'courage to know' ('*aude sapere*'),[35] 'enlightened citizens' insistance on 'public justification' of the exercise of all public and private power remains a precondition for 'democratisation' and 'constitutionalisation' of legitimate governance. The history of constitutionalism demonstrates how such citizen-driven 'struggles for justice' aimed at institutionalising reasonable rules and institutions are resisted by communities and rulers prioritising human passions (like religious beliefs, gender and racial discrimination) and self-interests in abusing power (eg through slavery, feudalism, colonialism, dictatorship and neoliberalism). Most citizens prioritise individual survival and self-development through professional specialisation and collaboration in families and local communities; they tend to remain 'rationally ignorant' about European and global politics, for instance due to their limited knowledge about governance failures in distant UN and WTO institutions.[36] Authoritarian and populist denial of 'constitutional failures' ignores the historical lessons from Europe's 2,500 years of 'constitutional experimentation' with democratic and republican constitutionalism, like the frequent destruction of democracies (eg in ancient Athens) and of city republics (eg in Rome, Florence and Venice) by intergovernmental power politics. Inducing EU citizens to support Europe's multilevel constitutionalism requires linking 'constitutional politics' and 'constitutional economics' to EU social policies and daily concerns of EU citizens.

Globalisation has rendered 'national constitutionalism 1.0' an outdated, incomplete model for governing transnational public goods. UN and WTO models of 'international constitutionalism 2.0' have failed to protect human rights and the SDGs effectively. Europe's 'multilevel constitutionalism 3.0' has proven to be the most effective form of governing PGs like 'democratic peace' and social welfare for the benefit of EU citizens. Neither business-driven, neoliberal constitutional nationalism nor authoritarian 'fake constitutions' without effective limitation of power monopolies – and without constitutional protection of human rights (as in authoritarian states like China, Iran and Russia) – offer legitimate alternatives for empowering individual and democratic self-government protecting the SDGs. Overcoming the 'constitutional failures' to limit the ubiquity of abuses of public and private powers in multilevel governance requires protecting citizens in their 'struggles for justice' by insisting on citizen-driven, democratic and republican accountability and constitutional protection of 'open societies'. Europe's

[35] Kant defined 'enlightenment' as 'man's emergence from his self-imposed immaturity. Immaturity is the inability to use one's understanding without guidance from another. This immaturity is self-imposed when its cause lies not in lack of understanding, but in lack of resolve and courage to use it without guidance from another'; cf I.Kant, *An Answer to the Question: What is Enlightenment?* (1784).

[36] Most EU citizens participating in EU elections do not know why their democratic support for Europe's 'competitive social market economy' implies support for 'ordoliberalism' rather than for Anglo-Saxon neoliberalism. Without knowledge of the diverse kinds of 'market failures' (like restraints of competition, harmful externalities, social injustices, information asymmetries, public goods) and of related 'governance failures' (like failures to protect human and constitutional rights, limit market failures and protect public goods), citizens cannot evaluate neoliberal faith in self-regulatory market competition ('markets know best').

ordoliberal constitutionalism for protecting a 'competitive social market economy' has institutionalised more 'public reason' and has empowered citizens across national frontiers more than other treaty systems, albeit limited to European integration and in need for further protection against the 'polycrises'. Outside Europe, the number of democracies declines because citizen struggles for extending 'constitutional politics' (ie transforming agreed social contracts and constitutional principles into democratic legislation, administration and adjudication protecting rule-of-law and human rights) to multilevel governance of PGs remain resisted by vested interests.[37] Similarly, 'constitutional economics' (eg protecting non-discriminatory conditions of competition, equal opportunities, monetary stability and social justice through rules of a higher legal rank, as in EU law and WTO law)[38] is resisted by authoritarian and neoliberal interest group politics. Authoritarian and populist disinformation keep many citizens ignorant vis-à-vis the requirements of multilevel governance of transnational PGs in a globalised world.

'Democratic progress' remains a slow, collective learning process. EU politics must continue emphasising: *Aude sapere*, dare to assume political responsibility for multilevel governance of transnational PGs demanded by citizens! The EU must resist both autocratic and neoliberal abuses of power, like US practices of refusing international judicial control of 'security exceptions' (eg in WTO dispute settlement procedures) and making everything a matter of 'national security' (such as climate change, critical minerals, artificial intelligence). Even if US President Trump is expected to repeat his earlier policies of withdrawing from UN agreements and disregarding many SDGs (such as climate change mitigation and protection of the environment), EU law requires the EU to comply with UN law (notably its *jus cogens* and *erga omnes* obligations such as respect for democratic self-determination of people and the prohibition of recognising the acquisition of foreign territory by force).[39] EU protection of civil, political, economic, social and cultural human rights and the universally agreed SDGs require 'social market economies' that are supported by citizens with due respect for the diversity of national social contracts. As European law is founded on the principles underlying the UN and WTO legal systems, the geopolitical rivalries undermining the UN and WTO legal systems and also the EU's 'competitive social market economy' (Article 3 TEU) risk becoming the biggest regulatory challenge of EU crises governance in the foreseeable future. Instead of outsourcing Europe's critical data, defence and satellite infrastructures to American tech companies attacking democratic institutions and supporting far-right parties in Europe, Europe must transform itself into an independent technological and military power capable of

[37] On constitutional politics see Petersmann/Steinbach (n 2).

[38] On constitutional economics see Petersmann/Steinbach (n 2), chapter 3 and E.U.Petersmann, *Transforming World Trade and Investment Law for Sustainable Development* (OUP, 2022), chapters 4 and 5.

[39] On *jus cogen* rules see the Advisory Opinion by the International Court of Justice of 19 July 2024 on the Legal Consequences arising from the Policies and Practices of Israel in the Occupied Palestinian Territory, including East Jerusalem.

protecting European citizens against neoliberal and authoritarian power politics. Yet, Europe's loss of international competitiveness is not only caused abroad by neoliberal 'under-regulation' (eg of environmental protection in the USA) and authoritarian disregard for UN and WTO law. Europe's insufficient economic growth and innovation, 'regulatory overkill' and often excessive 'integration through law' (eg harmonising 27 different national laws rather than enforcing mutual recognition principles promoting 'regulatory competition') also require reviewing European 'governance failures' of neglecting the regulatory costs of European integration and of unnecessary EU 'mission creep'.[40] Avoiding de-industrialisation (eg by imports of subsidised Chinese over-production) and abuses of market power (eg by US tech oligopolies) require stronger EU enforcement of trade remedy and competition laws.

[40] For criticism of Europe's 'regulatory overkill' and high 'regulatory costs' impeding innovation, and proposals for internal EU reforms prioritising economic growth and innovation without EU treaty amendments, see L.Garicano, B.Holmström, N.Petit, *The Constitution of Innovation: A New European Renaissance* (Nov 10, 2025). The EU commitment to a 'competitive social market economy' requires reconciling economic growth with social integration protecting a 'European society' as defined in Article 2 TEU.

3

Neo-ordo-liberalism by Other Means: The Economic Constitution of the European Union Revisited

AGUSTÍN JOSÉ MENÉNDEZ

'[N]ever was a hope more forlorn'.[1]

The European Union implies the concept of the 'minimum state', the abandonment of the mixed economy, the abandonment of economic planning, the redefinition of the way in which expenditure is made up, a redistribution of responsibilities that reduces the power of parliamentary assemblies and increases that of governments, fiscal autonomy for local authorities, the rejection of the principle of widespread free provision (with the consequent reform of the health and welfare systems), the abolition of the automatic indexing of wages to past inflation (with the rejection of the principle of automatic recovery from past inflation and the linking of wage trends to programmed inflation), the drastic reduction of privileged areas, the mobility of the productive factors, the reduction of the State's presence in the credit and industrial system, the abandonment of inflationary proclivities not only by workers but also by producers of services, the abolition of the regulations establishing administered prices and tariffs. In a word, a new pact between the State and the citizen, in favour of the latter. Well, a legal change of this magnitude, with these consequences, has passed almost unnoticed, without hitting the headlines.[2]

[1] E Wiskemann, 'Whither Germany?', *The Nineteenth Century*, July 1932, p. 28, cited in Geoffrey Field, *Elizabeth Wiskemann: Scholar, Journalist, Secret Agent*, (Oxford, Oxford University Press, 2023, p. 51).

[2] G Carli, *Cinquant'anni di vita italiana*, a cura di P Peluffo, Bari and Roma: Laterza, 1993, 436. My translation. The original goes: 'L'Unione Europea implica la concezione dello "Stato minimo", l'abbandono dell'economia mista, l'abandono della programmazione economica, la ridefinizione delle modalità di composizione della spessa, una redistribuzione della responsabilità che restringa il potere delle assemblee parlamentari ed aumenti quelle dei governi, l'autonomia impositiva per gli enti locali, il ripudio del principio della gratuità diffusa (con la conseguente riforma della sanità e del sistema previdenziale), l'abolizione della scala mobile (con la sconfessione del principio del recupero automatico dell'inflazione passata e l'aggancio della dinamica retributiva all'inflazione programmata), la drastica riduzione delle aree di privilegio, la mobilità dei fattori produttivi, la riduzione della presenza dello Stato nel sistema di credito e dell'industria, l'abbandono dei compartimenti inflazionistici non soltanto da parte dei lavoratori, ma anche da parte dei produttori dei servizi, l'abolizione delle normative che stabiliscono prezzi amministrati e tariffe. In una parola: un nuovo patto tra Stato e cittadini, a favore di

1. Introduction

A growing number of voices in European Union (EU) studies are claiming that the EU has entered a process of radical transformation. The policy responses deployed to face the COVID-19 syndemics,[3] climate change[4] and, last but not least, the changing geostrategic circumstances (in particular, the reemergence of Russia as a world power[5] and the 'disengagement' of the United States from European defence)[6] would have resulted in fundamental changes of political vision, from which it would be following a rapid and radical transformation of the EU. That transformation would concern very especially its 'economic constitution'. The play-book of 'hyper-globalisation', dominant from the 1980s to the 2010s, would have been abandoned in a relatively short period of time.[7] Instead, the Union and its Member States would have rediscovered the virtues of the 'activist' and 'the interventionist' state. To put it differently and more concisely, while the EU emerged as a neoliberal Union from the Eurozone fiscal crisis, it would be now in the process of mutating into a neo-Keynesian union. One intervention after the other, a new Europe would be in the making.

This chapter strikes a discordant note. I do not contest the fact that the never-ending cycle of crises that have hit the EU in the last decade and a half has resulted in many changes. What I challenge is the conclusion that this has brought about a radical transformation of the European economic constitution. In a nutshell, my main thesis is that what we are witnessing is something much more modest, namely a reconsideration of the means through which the old neo-ordoliberal vision is realised and sustained. In concrete, the role of the state in the capitalist order, which has always been decisive, is shifting. The European state, either through the EU, through the Member States or through a combination of the two, is now expected to provide legal guarantees of the appropriation of wealth and to unleash private power (through deregulation),[8] but also, and

questi ultimi. Ebbene, un cambiamento giuridico di questa portata, con queste conseguenze, è passato pressoché sotto silenzio, senza conquistare le prime pagine dei giornali'.

[3] C Fasone, N Lupo, 'Learning from the euro crisis: A new method of government for the European Union's economic policy coordination after the pandemic', *International Journal of Constitutional Law*, Volume 22, Issue 3, July 2024, Pages 882–904, https://doi.org/10.1093/icon/moae064

[4] D Bevilacqua and E Chiti, *Green Deal: Come Costruire una Nuova Europa* (Bologna: Il Mulino, 2024).

[5] N Hajiyeva, 'La guerra en Ucrania y la política de globalización económica de la UE: nuevos retos y cuestiones de seguridad', 137 (2024) *Revista CIDOB d'Afers Internacionals*, 141-165; Davide Genini, 'How the war in Ukraine has transformed the EU's Common Foreign and Security Policy', (2025) *Yearbook of European Law*, 1–43, available at https://doi.org/10.1093/yel/yeaf003

[6] E Chiti, 'Il rafforzamento della difesa europea', 2 (2025) *Giornale di Diritto Amministrativo*, 145–151.

[7] Something epitomised by the rewriting of the German Fundamental Law to recalibrate the 'balanced budget' provisions. See AJ Menéndez, 'Editorial: Rewriting the German Fundamental Law in a Blitz?' 3:4 (2024) *European Law Open* 687–704, available at https://doi.org/10.1017/elo.2025.18.

[8] At the same time, of course, the state may keep on unleashing private power from pre-existing regulations introduced to sustain the public interest (a central plank in the programme of the Von

crucially, to 'derisk' corporate investments.[9] Or what is the same, in (partial) discontinuity with what was the case during the 90s to the 00s, public Treasuries are assuming a good deal of the costs of private investments, while reserving most profits to corporate actors. That marks a discontinuity with some of the key components of the 'neo-ordo-liberal' constitutional settlement of the 1990s, such as 'free competition' and 'sound money', but not with the underlying socio-economic vision, which places private accumulation through private property at the heart of the socio-economic arrangements.

The chapter is structured in three parts.

First, I set the European economic constitution in its context. This allows me to do three things. First, to lay out the foundational ambivalence of the process of European integration that is somehow suspended between democratic interventionism and ordoliberalism. Second, to draw the attention of the reader to the relative flexibility with which the socio-economic visions are implemented in practice, the result not only of the transformation of how democratic interventionism, and above all, neo-ordo-liberalism has been understood over time, but also of the extent to which different legal institutions can be placed at the service of different socio-economic visions. Third, to emphasise the extent to which changing socio-economic circumstances account for the different colouring of the European economic constitution over time. If the democratic interventionists managed to leave a visible imprint in the European economic constitution in the 60s and early 70s and made of the European Communities an external enabler of national Democratic and Social States, the first 'polycrisis' of the 1970s paved the way for the ascendancy of neoliberal ideas, which in Europe were hybridised with ordoliberal ones (thus the term neo-ordo-liberalism). This turned the European Communities first, and later the European Union, into an external constraint on national Democratic and Social states.

Second, I consider how the second 'polycrisis' of the 2010s resulted in the consolidation of the neo-ordo-liberal settlement, which came to be concretised via the 'holy constitutional trinity' of economic freedoms, sound money and free competition.

Third, I analyse the three set of EU 'crises' responses that would have triggered the ongoing 'interventionist' turn of European Union politics, leading to the creation of the rudiments of a European Treasury (Next Generation EU) in response to the Covid syndemics), a new relationship between economic

der Leyen II Commission, in many cases undoing the very regulations and directives approved by the Von der Leyen I Commission) and providing legal guarantees so that private actors may appropriate new fundamental assets (as is happening in a very explicit manner on what concerns the development of Artificial Intelligence, developed through the commercial exploitation of what are public commons.

[9] D Gabor, 'The (European) derisking state', in (2023:1) *Stato e mercato, Rivista quadrimestrale,* 53–84, doi: 10.1425/107674.

and non-economic goals (the European Green Deal in response to the climate change) and the mainstreaming of interventionism, at the heart of the new European industrial policy (in response to geopolitical changes, not least the refusal of the US to keep on playing as the buyer of last resort of goods in the international trade order). I find that not only all these transformations are still far from being fully concretised (including Next Generation EU), but also that they essentially point to the generalisation of the role of the EU and of the Member States as guarantors of the level of private profits through a new policy mix, in which the transfer of public resources plays a fundamental role. The geo-strategic turbulence which has marked the second presidential term of Donald Trump seems to be consolidating such a trend.

The last section holds the conclusions.

2. The Socio-Economic Ambivalence of European Integration: From the Founding to Neo-Ordo-Liberal Europe

In this section, I highlight the ambivalence of the foundational Treaties of the European Communities, open to be reconstructed as a compromise between democratic interventionist and ordoliberal ideas (section 1). In the sixties and the seventies, the democratic interventionists managed to win the day to a far from negligible extent, and made the European Communities into an enabler of national Democratic and Social States (section 2). The first 'polycrisis' of the 1970s radically altered the circumstances, and paved the way to the neoliberalisation of national and supranational politics. Quite decisively, such ideas hybridised (and transformed) ordoliberal views (giving rise to what is referred as neo-ordo-liberalism in this chapter) (section 3). Through the Single European Act, and above all, the Maastricht Treaty, the core tents of neo-ordo-liberalism were codified into the legal marble of the European Treaties (section 4).

2.1 The Foundational Ambivalence of European Integration: A Social and Economic Vision torn between the Democratic and Social State and the Neo-ordo-liberal project

In this section, I start by considering the two socio-economic visions (ordoliberalism and democratic interventionism) that competed to define the basic social and economic choices at the heart of the process of European integration (section A); I then try to determine to what extent those visions managed to leave their imprint in the founding Treaties of the European Communities. I approach the texts not only as formal legal documents, but also as embryos of future institutional renderings of social and economic blueprints (section B).

A) Two visions of Europe, two conceptions of the European economic constitution

The project of European integration has been, since its early days, ambivalent.[10] In particular, two social and economic visions competed at the inception of the Communities to shape the project. Such visions can be referred as democratic interventionism and as ordoliberalism. [11]

a) The social and economic vision of democratic interventionism

The advocates of democratic interventionism regarded the European Communities as an institutional and normative structure capable of complementing and supplementing the national Democratic and Social constitutions.

Paradigmatic examples of the latter were the 'resistant' and 'anti-fascist' 1946 French and 1948 Italian constitutions.[12] These legal documents laid the grounds of a social contract that did not only promise higher levels of welfare, but also a radical transformation of the socio-economic structure. And that on three accounts. First, the state, as ultimate institutional embodiment of the public interest, was to assume direct or indirect responsibility for the provision of a number of essential services, including education, housing, health and insurance against basic social risks. Second, economic and social policy was to be modelled in such a way as to not only sustain the economic growth needed to reconstruct and modernise the European economies, but also as to allow shaping the direction and forms of growth, so as to realise *material equality*. That required not only *politicising* monetary policy,[13] but also a sizeable public and social sector.[14] Third, democratic labour law (which compromised the right to collective bargaining and the collective right to strike) was regarded as a fundamental part of the social contract. Its point and

[10] M Dani and AJ Menéndez, 'È ancora possibile riconciliare costituzionalismo democratico-sociale e integrazione europea?', 42:1 (2020) *DPCE online*, 289–326, available at https://www.dpceonline.it/index.php/dpceonline/article/view/899.

[11] Ordoliberalism, as we will see, was later "hybridised" with neoliberalism. This resulted in neo-ordo-liberalism. Cf. AJ Menéndez, 'En el 50° aniversario de la CES7ETUC: las dos constituciones económicas de la Unión Europea (por qué la unión económica y monetaria convirtió el trabajo en variable de ajuste por excelencia y por qué es necesario modificar los tratados para hacer posible la Europa social)', (2024) 105 *Revista de derecho social*, 213–243.

[12] On France, see the fundamental anthology by H Michel and B Mirkine-Guetzévitch, *Les idées politiques et sociales de la Résistance*, Paris: PUF, 1954; for Italy, see C Franceschini, S Guerrieri and G Monina (eds.), *Le Idee Costituzionali della Resistenza* (Roma, Presidenza del Consiglio di Ministri, 1995).

[13] As presciently argued by Jeremy Leaman. See his *The Bundesbank Myth: Towards a Critique of Central Bank Independence*. Basingstoke: Palgrave, 2001. On the independence of central banks, see now M Dani, *La banca centrale nel diritto pubblico europeo* (Milano, Franco Angeli, 2024).

[14] F Briatico, *Ascesa e Declino del capitale pubblico in Italia: Vicende e protagonisti*, Bologna: Il Mulino, 2004.

purpose was not only the maximisation of workers' welfare, but also to ensure that the constitution entered the workplace and turned workers from exploited subjects into active producers, and at the end of the day, that they were citizens also when working (democratic labour law was to play an essential role in that regard). Not only equal members of the polity when coming to the voting box every four or five years, but also every day in the factories and the fields. The ultimate horizon in that regard was that of economic democracy.[15]

From that perspective, common European institutions, policies and norms should be conceived as levers to facilitate the required societal changes to transform European societies through public action. In particular, European integration would allow reconciling the opening of the Western European economies (a move regarded as necessary to increase productivity levels and thus improve material living conditions) with the consolidation of Democratic and Social states at home.

Integration represented a chance to counter the dynamics of competition among states that had had devastating consequences in the 1920s and in the 1930s. But it was also an occasion to create the political space necessary to render harmonious the co-existence of different national socio-economic models and policies and, gradually, to project them onto the supranational level. In other words, the point was to increase the political capacity to govern economic relationships that 'cut' across borders within Western Europe.[16]

In sum, European institutions were imagined as *external enablers of the Democratic and Social Constitutional States.* To this was added the horizon of the projection of solidarity to the continental level. This required first redefining national communities of insurance in an inclusionary fashion (or what is the same, decoupling access to social security and work benefits from the condition of national, and instead basing them on residence).[17] And then creating means to

[15] The most influential articulation of the idea of economic democracy through constitutional and labour law is to be found in Weimar's Germany. Cf. G Grégoire, 'The Economic Constitution under Weimar: Doctrinal Controversies and Ideological Struggles' in G Grégoire and X Miny (eds.), *The Idea of Economic Constitution in Europe* (Leiden, Brill/Nijhoff, 2022) doi: https://doi.org/10.1163/9789004519350_004. On the French tradition, with deep links to Proudhon's mutualisme, see B Borrits, *Vers la démocratie économique*, Paris: L'Harmattan, 2005; B Borrits, *Au-delà de la propriété : pour une économie des communs*, Paris: La Découverte, 2018. On democratic labour law, see R Dukes, *The Labour Constitution: The Enduring Idea of Labour law* (Oxford, Oxford University Press, 2014).

[16] Such ideas aligned with the assumptions originally underpinning both the Bretton Woods monetary arrangements and the failed International Trade Organisation. Helleiner stresses the extent to which the model underpinning Bretton Woods was open to participation by countries that favoured state-led development and even central planning. Cf. E Helleiner, *States and the Reemergence of Global Finance*, Ithaca: Cornell University Press, 1994. To viz, national policy autonomy had to be secured by means of providing collective coordination of policies. JG Ruggie 'International Regimes, Transactions, and Change: Embedded Liberalism in the Postwar Economic Order' (1982) 36 *International Organization.* 379–415; E Helleiner, 'The life and times of embedded liberalism: legacies and innovations since Bretton Woods' (2019) 26 *Review of International Political Economy*, 1112–1135.

[17] See AJ Menéndez and EDH Olsen, *Challenging European Citizenship* (Basingtoke: Palgrave, 2019).

coordinate economic and monetary policies at the European level, which would eventually lead to mechanisms of supranational solidarity.[18]

This was a view that, with many nuances, influenced the action of the (admittedly weak) French governments of the IVth Republic, and would become very influential on Italian governments, most evidently with 'centre left' cabinets of the 1960s. The result was a specific breed of interventionism. In economic terms, the politics of productivity was central, with all its ambivalences. But not withstanding them, capitalist markets were to be constituted and regulated in such a way as to render them compliant with openly non-market objectives. This was so because the social vision of the Democratic and Social State was not founded on property (on the liberty of the property owner), but on labour (on the freedom of the worker who is a full citizen).[19] This was not only a rhetorical proclamation, it rather, had tangible implications, partially reflected in the sustained improvement of the socio-economic conditions of European populations during the *treinte glorieuses.*

b) The ordoliberal social and economic vision

Other actors, however, believed that the point and purpose of supranational integration could and should be a different one, namely, the recreation of a 'liberal' European economic order. An order that, for all purposes, had collapsed with the breaking of the hostilities leading to the First World War. And which had never been fully re-established in the interwar period, not least because of the inability to rethink the foundations of economic liberalism, and to offer alternative institutional and policy visions to recreate that order in very changed circumstances.

The 'liberal' economic order was sometimes advocated on the assumption that it was possible, even necessary, to combine democratic interventionism at home with liberalism at the European and international levels. This was a view largely shared by British governments from the mid-1940s to the 1960s, independently of their political orientation.[20] This goes a long way (but not a complete way) to account for the preference, on the side of British governments, for free trade arrangements (the failed European Free Trade Area first, and the EFTA afterwards). Given that the UK was not a founding Member of the Communities, we will not pay much attention now to that view.

Alternatively, 'liberalism' could be favoured as constituting the necessary supranational discipline, needed to first tame and then, eventually, undo some of the institutional, policy and normative choices fostered by democratic interventionists. Choices which, it was argued, threatened the integrity of the socio-economic

[18] On the embryonic components of solidarity in the Treaty establishing the European Coal and Steel Community, see S Giubboni, *Diritti sociali e mercato* (Bologna: Il Mulino, 2003).

[19] A Pepe, 'Le parole della costituzione', in F Farina (ed), *Le Parole di Giuseppe Di Vittorio. La persona, il lavoro, il sindacato, la costituzione*, Roma: Ediesse, 2016, 41–61, 55.

[20] The kind of approach that would be basically followed by the United Kingdom, resulting in their non-participation in the Communities and the favouring of looser European free trade agreements.

order necessary to sustain a thriving market economy.[21] As is well-known, this was the view held by German ordoliberals. Who had a moderate success in shaping the postwar constitutional order in the mould of their beliefs, although they encountered opposition, and not only from the 'left'.[22] It is quite obvious that ordoliberals grounded their claims on a specific reading of the history of the Weimar Republic, in particular, of its collapse due to the instability of its socio-economic arrangements, brought about by a democratic interventionism propelled by mass proletarianisation.[23] In addition to fearing a replay of Weimar, ordoliberals were apprehensive of French hegemony, which could lead to the 'Europeanisation' of democratic interventionism (in public parlance characterised as a form of dirigisme). The most outstanding European ordoliberal was, by all accounts, the German Chancellor of the Exchequer, Ludwig Erhard. He chose many of his collaborators in the ordoliberal circles.[24]

When it came to European integration, the ordoliberal aspiration was to make of the European Communities a lever which would allow the European economy to be released from the 'straitjackets' built in the interwar period (and quite obviously, during the Second World War) through a bold definition of transnational economic freedoms. While the forms of interventionism at the heart of *dirigisme* were openly rejected, it was explicitly affirmed that the recreation of a (Western) European economy would not happen spontaneously but required a fundamental decision establishing the European economic *ordo*. That would make it possible to create the basic infrastructure of a market economy. Which comprised not only the institutions and institutional guarantees literally *constituting* markets (from private property to fundamental contractual norms), but also the necessary legal structures to avoid the transformation of politics into an *agonistic* contest. This rendered necessary some form of agricultural policy and a specific discipline of labour relations through labour law. The key criterion to distinguish what could be done from what was anathema was whether interventions where market conform (*marktkonform*), to use the terms cherished by ordoliberals.

The result was expected to be a form of interventionism pitched against 'really existing' interventionism, or, to continue with the paradoxical formulas, a specific political choice which presents itself as the guarantee of a peculiar form of

[21] Additionally, some saw in the process of European integration a unique chance to rectify in a liberal direction the constitutional commitments reflected in the constitutions drafted in the immediate postwar. See Carli (n 2).

[22] On the complex trajectory of German constitutional law, see M Hailbronner, *Traditions and Transformations: The Rise of German Constitutionalism* (Oxford, Oxford University Press, 2015). A fresh look at the influence that ordoliberalism played on German competition law, and how that reverberated on EU law can be found in A Klüsters, *The Making and Unmaking of Ordoliberal Language. A Digital Conceptual History of European Competition Law* (Frankfurt am Main, Vittorio Klostermann, 2023).

[23] W Röpke, *The Social Crisis of Our Time,* (Chicago, Chicago University Press, 1946). W Bonefeld, 'Crisis, Free Economy and Strong State: On Ordoliberalism' 2:3 (2015) *European Review of International Studies*, 5–14.

[24] A J Nicholls, *Freedom with Responsibility. The Social Market Economy in Germany 1918-1963* (Oxford, Clarendon Press, 1994).

depoliticisation of socio-economic policy.[25] If you wish, *technical* interventionism, not *democratic interventionism*. In such a view, all institutional structures, including fundamental social rights, were not seen as 'irreversible conquests', but were contingent on the 'soundness' of the economic structure, and also, of economic performance. It is for this reason that ordoliberals did not rule out in fact that 'welfare' provisions could be used as *adjustment variables* if the need arose. How that balance worked out depended, at the end of the day, on the actual macro-economic performance.

B) The ambivalence of the founding Treaties

The 1957 Treaty establishing the European Economic Community (TEEC) can be regarded as a compromise between the visions of democratic interventionism and ordoliberalism.[26]

This can be shown by means of rereading the text of the Treaties, to determine what specific provisions (and what parts of their drafting) were favoured by democratic interventionists or by ordoliberals. This assumes that the bargaining

[25] Quite obviously, by means of 'blocking' further political discussion a very asymmetric form of depoliticisation ensues, one that guarantees an implicit and silent political choice in favour of ordoliberal ideas.

[26] L Warlouzelet, 'The EEC/EU as an Evolving Compromise between French Dirigism and German Ordoliberalism (1957–1995)', 57 (2019) *Journal of Common Market Studies* 77-93. More in extenso in his *Europe contre Europe: Entre Liberté, Solidarité et Puissance*, Paris: CNRS Editions, 2022. See also B Shaev, 'Left Internationalisms, Past and Present' 27 (2019) *Renewal*, 31–40. Two caveats must be made. First, it could be argued that the ambivalent relationship of the 'progressive' parties to the process of European integration may cast some doubt about the interpretation that underpins this section. Social-democrats, and even more clearly, communist parties have expressed major reserves towards European integration. Thus, the Social Democratic Party of Germany opposed the creation of the Coal and Steel Community and most communist parties were vocally opposed to European institutions (from which, it must be added, they were basically excluded, including the European Parliament). However, it should be added that the SPD shifted its course in the mid 1950s, leading to its support of the Treaties establishing the European Economic Community and Euroatom in 1957. (See M Dreyfus, *L'Europe des Socialistes*, Brussels, Editions Complexe, 1991, 216–231; W E Paterson, *The SPD and European Integration*, Westmead and Lexington, Saxon House and Lexington Books, 1974, especially chapters 2 and 3; K Featherstone, *Socialist Parties and European Integration*, Manchester, Manchester University Press, 1988, 141–2). Communist parties shifted course in the late 1960s. Especially significant in that regard was the case of the Italian Communist Party, which was instrumental in the emergence of what was later called Euro-communism. From the Single European Act, opposition to successive Treaty amendments is amenable to be interpreted as opposition to the mutation of the European Communities, later European Union, into a vehicle of the ordoliberal constitution (see M di Donato, 'Europe et gauche européenne: les multiples défis des communistes italiens au moment du lancement de l'eurocommunisme (1969–1977)', 46 (2022) *Histoire Politique* 1–14, available at https://doi.org/10.4000/histoirepolitique.2510. Second, some actors endorsing an ordoliberal vision were rather reluctant to embrace the project of the European Economic Community, and indeed were hoping its more 'dirigiste' traits (in close affinity to the labour constitution) would be diluted through a free trade area encompassing both the 'little Europe' of the Economic Communities and other Western European countries, including the United Kingdom. This hope will be frustrated by De Gaulle's double move in 1958, endorsing the Communities and rejecting the free trade area. On ordoliberal scepticism vis-á-vis the European Communities, see S Quirico, 'The Constructive Side of Fear: Wilhelm Röpke's Discourse on Europe between Crisis and Integration', 1 (2018) *De Europa*, 63–73. On the free trade area, see Europeus (Pierre Uri), *La crise de la zone de libre-échange* (Paris, Plon, 1959).

game played during the drafting was one in which both parties favoured reaching a compromise but tried to be as successful as possible in planting seeds of their visions, so that they could be made to flourish later, pushing European integration in the direction of their preference. As we will see, what mattered was not so much the isolated drafting of each provision, but the overall 'system' to which they pointed. This reflects the close relationship between specific socio-economic visions and concrete legal renderings, but also the extent to which the former can be realized through different legal settlements.

The German negotiation team was led by ordoliberals. They managed to insert into the TEEC many provisions that could be regarded as the legal translation of their socio-economic vision. In particular, the very idea of a fusion of national markets into an internal European market[27] was accepted and spelled out in the four economic freedoms: free movement of goods,[28] freedom of movement of workers and freedom of establishment and free movement of capital, as well as free provision of services.[29] Further confirmation of the Treaty being a potential force for the 'ordoliberalisation' of the European Communities was found in Article 110 TEEC, which defined the abolition of restrictions and the lowering of customs barriers in world trade as key aims of the common commercial policy. By the same token, the German negotiators succeeded in inserting strong provisions on competition, open to be constructed as supranational constraints on national *dirigiste* policies, to the extent that, in a context of economic growth marked by the diffusion of democratic interventionist ideas, they could be used to curb the power of the state to encroach on private initiative. In a typical ordoliberal move, those provisions were also applicable to privately held power, to be more precise, when private actors could distort markets in ways similar to public actors. Thus, states were in principle barred from granting public aid to private or public enterprises (Article 92 TEEC), as they were prevented from establishing either special or exclusive rights to public undertakings (Article 90 TEEC). The prohibition of private cartels and the abuse of dominant position were understood as exceptional, but relevant cases in which private enterprises accumulated so much power as to become as dangerous to the competitive order as state-owned or state-funded enterprises (Articles 85 and 86 TEEC).

On its turn, several seeds were planted by the advocates of a European Community embracing democratic interventionism. A number of provisions were drafted in such a way that it would be possible to reconcile the opening of national economies (notably, trade in goods and movement of workers) with politically defined activist policies.[30] Accordingly, the Treaties were designed so that economic freedoms could remain embedded, states were given time to readjust

[27] In the Spaak report, reference is made to the 'fussion progressive des marches', see 'Rapport des chefs de delegation aux Ministres des Affaires Etrangeres', 21 April 1956, http://aei.pitt.edu/996/, 10. See also Article 3 TEEC.

[28] Part I, Title I of the TEEC.

[29] Part I, Title III of the TEEC.

[30] See above chapter 2, section 3.3.

their socio-economic policies to the new conditions resulting from trade liberalisation, and, quite decisively, integration was not only about negative integration, but also about the coordination of national policies and the creation of governing capacities at the supranational level through the development of common positive policies. This general notion resonated first of all in the distinct regulatory frameworks devised for each factor of production.[31] Moreover, the choice of framing economic freedoms not as self-standing principles applying across the board, but as more specific norms instrumental to the attainment of a wider set of goals enshrined in the Treaty[32] was reinforced by the notion that nothing that was said in the Treaty affected national property regimes.[33] This pre-empted a reading of the Treaties inimical to the nationalisation of specific industries or whole economic sectors of activity. Finally, states were given plenty of time to adjust their socio-economic regulations to the new conditions resulting from trade liberalisation. The internal market was to be built in four stages, with ample transitional periods.[34] Moreover, numerous safeguards allowed Member States to slow down or even temporarily reverse liberalisation in order to reconcile it with other socio-economic goals.[35] Finally, market principles were flanked by clauses allowing their derogation in a range of specific and less specific circumstances.[36]

[31] On free movement of goods, see Articles 9, 13, 16, 18, 30, 34 TEEC; on freedom of movement of workers, see Articles 48.1 and 48.2 TEEC. Freedom of establishment and free provision of services were set as goals, but subject to the condition of the drawing up of programmes of positive legislation; see, respectively, Articles 54 and 63 TEEC. On what concerned free movement of capital, liberalisation is conditioned to the issue of directives (Article 69 TEEC). Article 71 reflects the extent to which the liberalisation of capital required by the Treaty was mainly and foremostly the freedom of payments (as reflected in Article 67.2 TEEC).

[32] Indeed, the immediate objective was not so much free movement of goods (article 3, title I of part I) as the more specific and concrete removal of customs duties (articles 9; 13; 95) and the elimination of quantitative restrictions (articles 30 and 34). By the same token, the Treaties did not so much set as a short-term objective the full affirmation of the freedom of nationals to move to seek work in another Member States (article 3, title III of part I), but the faculty of accepting work offers and establishing oneself in the territory of another Member State for that purpose (48.1 in view of 48.3 (a))

[33] Article 222 TEEC and 68 TECSC.

[34] The transitory period was expected to last twelve years and could be extended to fifteen. As mentioned, the transition to each new stage of the transitory period was not left to a discretionary decision of the Member States. The French government failed to persuade others to accept that solution. That, however, did not result in full automaticity, but rather (Article 8.3 TEC) into a Council decision which would declare the occurrence of the set of objective circumstances referred in the Treaties. Crucially, were the Council failed to take that decision unanimously, or later, by qualified majority, the decision would be left in the hands of an arbitration board nominated by the European Court of Justice.

[35] Article 108 TEEC (balance of payments crisis); Article 115 TEEC (development of common commercial policy); Article 226 TEEC (serious difficulties liable to persist in any sector of the economy or serious deterioration in the economic situation of a given area).

[36] While competition rules (Articles 90 and 91 TEEC) could limit both the use of state aid to shape socio-economic activity and the activities of public undertakings, the number of exceptions limited the extent to which such norms constraint the steering capacities of states. On what concerned state aid, such exceptions included the promotion of economic development in areas suffering abnormally low standards of living or serious levels of unemployment (Article 92.3a TEEC); remedying serious disturbances in the economy of a Member State (Article 92.3b TEEC); developing economic activities in areas where aid does not adversely affect trading (Article 92.3c TEEC); and, above all, allowing further exceptions as decided by the Council acting unanimously (Article 93.2 third paragraph TEEC); on what regards public undertakings, the application of competition rules to those entrusted with

Compromise was facilitated by the importance assigned by many political actors to the objective of fostering economic growth through external trade, which could be regarded as contributing to the realisation of both the democratic and social and the ordoliberal visions.[37] Indeed, the high and sustained growth experienced by the Member States of the European Communities in the late forties, the 1950s and 1960s rendered possible a marked improvement in the standards of living, whether their governments followed interventionist (as was paradigmatically the case in the Fourth French Republic and, to a considerable extent, also in the Fifth) or ordoliberal policies (as was from 1948 to 1966 the case in Germany).

In addition, it should be stressed that, in the specific socio-economic and geopolitical circumstances of the late 1950s, ordoliberals integrated that the acceptance of a 'capitalist' political order, and the avoidance of radical political conflict, required that economic freedoms were flanked by many of the policies which were part of the regulatory ideal of the Democratic and Social State. What they aimed at was not at 'unleashing' private power per se, as at 'embedding' capitalism so as to render it possible to thrive. Intervention, to reiterate the point, was not ruled out, but had to be made *marktkonform*.[38]

2.2 The dominance of democratic interventionism in the early years of the European Communities

The 'founding' ambivalence of the Communities was temporarily solved in the 1960s and early 1970s in favour of democratic interventionism.

In particular, economic freedoms were interpreted as operationalisations of the principle of non-discrimination on the basis of nationality, not as harbingers of a socially unencumbered right to private property. In the spirit of postwar embedded liberalism,[39] the common market fostered trade in goods while respecting national autonomy to choose a fiscal and monetary policy attuned to the specific needs of each Member State, and rendered possible by the legal and economic technology of capital movements. Concerning the latter, economic freedom was not about the radically free disposal of one's capital but rather meant the liberty to trade and to pay for goods and services across borders. At the same time, high and sustained economic growth favoured the recognition of the rights of foreign workers to be treated equally.[40]

services of general economic interest or having the character of a revenue-producing monopoly could not obstruct, neither in law nor in fact, the performance of the particular tasks assigned to them (90.2).

[37] A Milward, *The European Rescue of the Nation-State* (London, Routledge, 1992).

[38] Things will change in the mid and late 1970s, and with it, ordoliberalism as a policy platform. The influence of neoliberal thought will not only lead to the de facto abandonment of democratic interventionism on the left, but also to a transformation of ordoliberalism itself. This is why it seems to me it makes sense to speak of neo-ordo-liberalism.

[39] Ruggie (n 16).

[40] It could even be argued that the different socio-economic models interacted in largely complementary fashion, with a slow process of mutual learning resulting in some degree of experimentation in Western Germany with 'Keynesian' policies, albeit in an 'ordoliberal' framework. See J Leaman, *The Political Economy of West Germany, 1945–1985: An Introduction* (Basingstoke: MacMillan, 1988, 176–181).

To summarise: The common market allowed economic integration to be reconciled with national policy autonomy through an interpretation of economic freedoms as operationalisations of the principle of non-discrimination. The European currency, as planned in the early 1970s, aimed at recreating at the European scale the conditions under which monetary policy could be embedded in the wider economic and social policy, as had been the case under the European Payments Union and later under the Bretton Woods arrangements.

In the conceptual framework that organises this chapter, the European Communities of the period created the conditions under which democratic interventionism could thrive at the national level. The European economic order was defined as a common market, or to be more precise, a space where borders persisted but were to a large extent rendered predictably porous. A European political order slowly but steadily emerged, characterised by a degree of convergence around the values of the Democratic and Social State, but in which states retained a considerable degree of political autonomy. Within the overall geopolitical framework, marked by the 'imperial-by-invitation' role of the United States, the Member States of the European Union acquired, through concerted action, the means to design and implement policies which were to a considerable extent in line with the preferences of their citizens.

2.3 The slow-motion neo-ordo-liberal turn: From economics of turbulence of the 1970s to the 'Maastricht' economic constitution

This section considers the shift in the direction of movement of the European economic constitution in the 1970s, and the confirmation of its direction in the 1980s.

This was the result of the combined monetary and economic shocks of the early 1970s. First, a monetary crisis (the Nixon moment, which dismantled the short-lived Bretton Woods arrangements), which was rapidly followed by an economic crisis (section A). I then consider how ordoliberal ideas were hybridised with neoliberal ideas, and how the compound 'neo-ordo-liberalism' came to shape the fundamental supranational norms governing the vision underpinning supranational policy (section B). The Treaty of Maastricht and some of the legal documents through which it was rounded off (notably, the 'Maastricht' ruling of the German Constitutional Court and the Stability and Growth Pact of 1997) wrote into the marble of European primary law the socio-economic vision characteristic of neo-ordo-liberalism (section C).

A) The economics of turbulence of the early 1970s challenges the Democratic and Social State

The economic shocks of the 1970s rapidly altered the European social and economic landscape. The monetary (1971) and economic crises (1973, 1979) served as the pivotal moments of a European transformation. Repeated crises plunged the West (and also the East)[41] into an 'economics of turbulence'.[42]

European integration had proceeded far enough as to render a collective response to the crises needed, but not far enough as to render such response probable, or perhaps even feasible. Western European economies were simultaneously hit by stagnation and inflation (stagflation).

This resulted in a fundamental transformation of the way in which monetary and fiscal policy were conducted.[43]

At first, there were attempts at coordinated reflation[44] and also at the recreation of a partial monetary order within the EEC, modelled on the Bretton Woods arrangements (the so-called 'snake').[45] Beyond the attempts at fixing the different structures, the consensus around the Democratic and Social State started to weaken.

Clear signals were found not only on the election of conservative cabinets to government, but perhaps even more significantly in the shifts of left-wing politicians to 'austerity' policies. This was the case when Schmidt replaced Brandt as chancellor of West Germany in 1974, or when Callaghan replaced Wilson as prime minister of the United Kingdom in 1976. It would be even more obvious when French Socialists led by Mitterrand undertook their austerity turn in 1983.[46]

B) Neo-ordo-liberalism is born and comes to Brussels

Change at the national level ended up being reflected at the supranational level. Retelling that story in full is beyond the scope of this chapter. What is of special interest now is that the European Union experienced a process which may be proper to characterise as one of 'constitutional mutation'.[47]

Long regarded as marginal, neoliberal ideas gained renewed attention once the crises and stagflation proved sticky. Neoliberals interpreted these developments

[41] F Bartel, *The Triumph of Broken Promises: The End of the Cold War and the Rise of Neoliberalism* (Cambridge, Harvard University Press, 2022).

[42] I am obviously paraphrasing the title of R Brenner's famous book: *The Economics of Global Turbulence: The Advanced Capitalist Economies from Long Boom to Long Downturn, 1945–2005* (London, Verso, 2006).

[43] See P Armstrong, A Glynn and J Harrison, *Capitalism since 1945* (Oxford, Basic Blackwell, 1991, chapters 11 and 12).

[44] 'Council Directive 74/121/EEC of 18 February 1974 on stability, growth and full employment in the Community', OJ L 63, of 5.3.1974, 19–20; 'Council Decision 74/120/EEC: of 18 February 1974 on the attainment of a high degree of convergence of the economic policies of the Member States of the European Economic Community', OJ L 63, of 05/03/1974, 16–18.

[45] B Eichengreen, *The European Economy since 1945: Coordinated Capitalism and Beyond* (Princeton, Princeton University Press, 2007, 246–251).

[46] Rightly or wrongly, it was widely perceived that the French Socialists had felt they had to choose between their political programme and European integration (as embodied in the discipline of the European Monetary System). See AD Andry, *Social Europe: The Road not Taken: The Left and European Integration in the Long 1970s* (Oxford, Oxford University Press, 2022, 258).

[47] AJ Menéndez, 'A European Union in Constitutional Mutation', 20 (2014) *European Law Journal*, 127–141.

as evidence that the pretence of 'governing' the economy was futile. Instead of democratic interventionism, what was needed was a 'neutral' and 'apolitical' *governance* of the economy. This would render state action foreseeable for private actors. In other words, discretionality would be encased and, in the process, room would be created for private planning,[48] rendered possible by the 'neutralisation' of politics. In such a context, the full enjoyment of private property, entrepreneurial freedom and sound money would be guaranteed, and the conditions would be created for the flourishing of free competition. Governance by numbers[49] becomes the technique through which discretionary steering can be replaced by automatic steering, rendering it possible to reconcile the fragmentation of public power with stability.

The state should retreat, private power should be 'unleashed'. The 'animal spirits' of capitalists will give a necessary boost to economic activity, restarting the virtuous cycle of growth.

This narrative represented a challenge not only to democratic interventionism but also to ordoliberalism. However, the advocates of the latter were in a position to reinterpret their views in line with the neoliberal platform. And indeed, what we can observe, as already anticipated, is a hybridisation of neoliberalism and ordoliberalism. This new vision combines a recovery of the centrality of legal rules with the coopting of economic knowledge, redeployed at the service of constraining and fragmenting public power. The vision is epitomised by the emergence of the very idea of 'constitutional economics',[50] which decouples constitutional commitments from democratic legitimacy, in the process generating 'new' forms of 'constitutionalism'.[51]

These developments exerted a considerable influence on Community law. The 'constitutional' reading of Community law, which had timidly emerged in the 1960s with exclusive regard to the structural principles governing the relationship between EEC law and national constitutional law (the so-called doctrines of direct effect and primacy, which claimed to govern the relationship between EU and national laws), was now projected into to the substantive principles of Community law. Economic freedoms (first free movement of goods; from the early 1990s, all economic freedoms, and outstandingly free movement of capital) and 'free' competition were reinterpreted as operationalisations of the right to private property, and once and at the same time, transformed into the 'canon' of validity by reference to which the European Court of Justice (ECJ) reviewed all national norms, eventually

[48] M Friedman, 'A Monetary and Fiscal Framework for Economic Stability', 38 (1948) *American Economic Review*, 245–64; F Kydland and EC Prescott, 'Rules Rather than Discretion: The Inconsistency of Optimal Plans', 85 (1977) *The Journal of Political Economy* 473–492.

[49] A Desrosiéres, *Gouverner par les nombres. L'Argument Statistique II* (Paris, Presses des Mines, 2008); A Supiot, *La Gouvernance par les nombres* (Paris, Fayard, 2015).

[50] J Buchanan, 'The Constitution of Economic Policy', 77 (1987) *The American Economic Review*, 243–250.

[51] S Gill, 'New Constitutionalism, Democratisation and Global Political Economy', 10 (1998) *Pacifica Review*, 23–38.

setting aside those it reputed in breach of Community law.[52] At the same time, the principle of 'sound money' came to be imposed on the conduct of the monetary policy of all Member States, initially not so much through the force of legal norms, but through the 'economic force' and implications of the economic arrangements enshrined in the European Monetary System agreed in late 1978.[53]

This legal shift implied a massive and fundamental normative change. However, this new vision was not at first translated into a formal amendment to the Treaties, but entered into the law and politics of European integration through other means. The new vision of economic freedoms and of free competition was part of new lines of jurisprudence decided by the ECJ, while the European Monetary System (EMS) was at first presented as a mere exchange arrangement, with a thin legal infrastructure, approved through the Conclusions of the Presidency of a European Council. The significance of the changes was openly constitutional, in the double sense that the fundamental supranational norms were transformed, and so were the national constitutions. The transformations, at first sight technical, had massive political implications, largely pre-determining the fundamental norms according to which political and economic activity will unfold. In particular, the objectives of establishing a common market and a common currency were replaced by those of creating a single market and a single currency. Monetary stability, economic freedoms and 'free' competition were no longer to be understood as means but became goals in themselves.[54]

2.4 Writing neo-ordo-liberalism in the marble of the Treaties: the Maastricht Treaty

From the perspective that has just been fleshed out, the Maastricht Treaty not only accelerated the path of change, but largely codified the previous constitutional mutation. In other words, the neo-ordo-liberal shift was entrenched into the primary law of what became now the European Union.

In this regard, four sets of changes were fundamental.

Firstly, and most obviously, European Monetary Union (EMU) implied the removal of the lever of the exchange rates. From 1999, the parities between national currencies were irreversibly fixed.[55] From 28 February 2002, national currencies

[52] See for example W Sauter, 'Proportionality in the EU: A Balancing Act' 15 (2013) *Cambridge Yearbook of European Legal Studies*, 439–466. See also AJ Menéndez, 'The Guardianship of European Constitutionality: a Structural Critique of European Constitutional Review', in M Andenas, T Bekkedal and L Pantaleo (eds.), *The Reach of Free Movement* (The Hague, TMC Asser Press, 2017, 173–203).

[53] On SME, see F Masini, *Smemorie della lira: Gli economisti italiani e l'adesione al sistema monetario europeo* (Milano, Franco Angeli, 2004).

[54] AJ Menéndez, 'The Crisis of Law and the European Crises: From the Social and Democratic *Rechtsstaat* to the Consolidating State of (Pseudo-)technocratic Governance' 44 (2017) *Journal of Law and Society*, 56–78.

[55] Joint communiqué on the determination of the irrevocable conversion rates for the euro, 2 May 1998, available at https://www.ecb.europa.eu/press/pr/date/1998/html/pr980502.en.html.

were replaced by a new and single currency, the euro.[56] This implied eliminating the exchange rate as an instrument that allowed the different national economic and social policies to be reconciled, and consequently, the very possibility of *significantly different* economic and social policies in different Member States, in response to different preferences of the electorate. With no room for exchange rate adjustments, there were new structural limits to the extent to which policies could be divergent without resulting in a dangerous loss of economic ground in comparative terms (what is usually referred as a loss in competitiveness).[57] This would ultimately force the hand of national governments and legislatures.

Secondly, the commitment to 'sound money', initially pursued through the essentially economic arrangements of the EMS as pointed, became a legal one, identified as a fundamental principle of economic government. This was reflected not only in the independence of the European System of Central Banks, which included both the ECB and national central banks (Article 130 TFUE), but also in the mandate extended to the ECB to make use of its exclusive competence to define and shape the monetary policy of the Eurozone with a view to ensure monetary stability (Article 127.1 TFUE, first sentence). Other objectives were to be secondary and to be considered only as long as monetary stability was fully guaranteed (Article 127.1 TFUE, second sentence). Such commitment was further supported by the strict prohibition of the monetisation of public debt (Article 123.1 TFUE), which implied a complete divorce between the European Central Bank (ECB) and the supranational and the national Treasuries. That implied a radical transformation of public debt, as it was could seriously undermine its condition as a privileged form of debt, and consequently, as the ultimate safe asset. This would have the effect of radically limiting the capacity to pursue any policy that could result in deficits, as they would not be funded by the ECB and would be enormously costly if the 'financial markets' 'voted' with their money against such policies.

Thirdly, the necessary coherence between one single monetary policy, determined by the ECB, and a plurality of national fiscal policies was guaranteed by means of subordinating fiscal policy to monetary policy. Two fiscal rules set upper ceilings to both annual deficits (3 per cent of the GDP) and the stock of debt (60 per cent of the GDP) (Article 126.2 TFUE by reference to Article 1 of the Protocol on the excessive deficit procedure—originally numbered as Protocol 12). The constraints that stemmed from this were amplified by the principle of strict separation of national Treasuries, reflected in the no bail out principle (Article 125.1 TFUE), and by the intentional exclusion of financial aid being provided between Eurozone states (according to Article 122 TFUE interpreted *a contrario* and the non-projection of the balance of payments aid to the Eurozone). Finally, the extension of free movement of capital beyond the European Union, to third states (Article 63.1 TFUE), was intended to create a further disciplinary device, by

[56] 'Commission Communication to the European Council: Review of the introduction of euro notes and coins', COM (2002) 124 final.

[57] A Bagnai, *Il Tramonto dell'euro* (Reggio-Emilia, Imprimatur, 2014).

means of facilitating financial markets 'sanctioning' or 'rewarding' Member States on account of their national fiscal policies.

Fourthly, EMU literally created a monetary union that was not supported by a common Treasury, even less by a Treasury capable of engaging into significant expenditure. A Treasury capable, if needed, of stabilising or restabilising the Eurozone. The increase in supranational structural funds, even if regarded as significant by some Member States, was not only decoupled in operative terms from the macroeconomic conjuncture, but was extremely small when compared to what several institutional reports, most significantly the McDougall report,[58] had estimated would be necessary to ensure a federal power to stabilise the Union. If the latter estimated that the common budget should be established, at the very least, at 5 per cent of the area GDP, the EU budget was only slightly over 1 per cent of GDP at the time, and has since then, with the sole exception of the effect of Next Generation EU (NG-EU), declined.

The combination of these four changes created the conditions under which democratic interventionism was basically pre-empted, so that the fundamental objectives and the fundamental rights at the heart of the regulatory ideal of the Democratic and Social State became dependent on productivity growth. Were such growth to become negative, or significantly lower than average, in one or in some of the states making up the Eurozone, social rights and social policy were bound to become the variables through which states expected to regain 'competitiveness' and rebalance the economy. With no external devaluation possible anymore, and with no relevant budget for centralised macro-economic stabilisation, the only avenue left open to a Eurozone state experiencing economic difficulties was to reduce the costs that capital was to bear. The day of the reckoning could be postponed through a more or less sophisticated form of financial engineering, as was the case from 1999 to 2010, when massive financial flows from the core of the Eurozone to its periphery created the illusion of convergence. But such a strategy was bound to end up in one form or another of austerity, meaning a redistribution in favour of capital and to the detriment of labour, as it did from 2009 onwards.

3. The radicalisation of the neo-ordo-liberal constitution: Austerity Europe

In this section, I show how the policycrisis of the 2010s radicalised the neo-ordo-liberal turn that had proceeded since the late 1970s. The punctual decisions and the structural reforms undertaken to govern the Eurozone crisis accelerated the constitutional mutation that had started in the 1970s. The fundamental

[58] See the 1977 Report of the study group on the role of public finance in European integration (the 'McDougall Report'), available at https://op.europa.eu/en/publication-detail/-/publication/907775d1-93ce-4824-b0b0-cedc2389731b.

norms of economic freedoms, sound money and free competition that organised public power in Europe became amplified. That seemed to provide the ending point of the neo-ordo-liberal settlement, in which a socio-economic vision (wealth through capitalism) came hand in hand with specific 'constitutional' principles (economic freedoms, sound money and free competition). I start by considering how a web of cross-border loans contributed to create the mirage of a convergence between the Eurozone core and its periphery (section 1). Then I analyse how the financial crisis mutated into the Eurozone fiscal crisis (section 2) and how the latter was governed in such a way as to protect the interests of the financial institutions of the Eurozone core (section 3). This leads me to consider the extent to which austerity was not only a policy choice but above all a structural consequence of the design of the Eurozone and how it revealed the true configuration of the European economic constitution (section 4). Finally, I consider how the European economic 'settlement' had come, by the mid 2010s, to be based on the holy quartet of economic freedoms, sound money, free competition and neo-mercantilism (section 5).

3.1 False convergence during the first decade of EMU, facilitated by a web of cross-border loans

The first decade of EMU seemed to lead to economic convergence between the core states and the periphery states of the Eurozone, thanks to higher rates of growth in the latter. It was thought that the new neo-ordo-liberal settlement had produced a stable economic and political order.

Behind the apparently encouraging figures, it was possible to observe three less reassuring developments: (1) a progressive loss of 'competitiveness' of the periphery, as a result not only of higher inflation rates, but also of the repression of wages in the core, especially in Germany, which resulted in massive current account imbalances (growing surpluses in the core; growing deficits in the periphery); (2) massive flows of credit flowing from core to periphery, which rendered the growing current account deficits of the periphery sustainable for a time; and (3) the rapid growth of private debt, especially in the periphery (but not only: also in some core Eurozone states, such as the Netherlands).

These developments resulted in a massive debt web woven with cross-border loans. It was such a web that disproved the most pessimistic predictions regarding the prospects of the EU. However – as would be rendered evident since 2008, but should have been evident all the time – these dynamics were unsustainable in the long run. The loans were keeping the Eurozone stable only at the price of preparing a later explosion in which the risks implicit in the loans would become losses. But because EMU had not come hand in hand with a banking union, the cross-border character of the losses rendered unclear who was to bear the costs at the end of the day when the financial crisis started to unfold.

3.2 The financial crisis and its mutation into the Eurozone fiscal crisis

Western states, including the EU Member States, tackled the financial crisis of 2008 by means of bailing out financial institutions. Or what is the same, they transferred to the public treasury the problematic financial assets that threatened the viability of (mostly private) financial institutions. Doing this certainly protected the interests of shareholders, and in general, of the holders of financial assets. It was argued, however, that this was secondary to the main objective, which was to 'save main street', and thus, also the jobs of millions of workers. Keeping financial assets whole, no matter the immediate distributive implications, was necessary to keep afloat all boats, and especially the smaller ones. The absorption of economic losses by the Treasuries preserved capital profits, but was presented as the most progressive course of action that was possible, given the alternatives.

What was less noticed at the time was not only that these actions composed wealth inequalities (or what is the same, they disproportionately benefitted the wealthy), but, in the specific case of the European Union, the way in which the transfer to the public of financial losses was undertaken resulted in a very specific pattern of nationalisation. This was so because the risks were assumed by the different Member States, and not by the Union through a common fund, despite monetary (and financial) integration in the Eurozone. This also affected, obviously, cross-border loans. By means of extending wide guarantees of the 'national' financial institutions through different instruments and techniques, debtor states assumed, without really reflecting about the consequences, the liability in case the potential risks turned into actual financial losses. In such a way, the Treasuries of the debtor states were to find themselves on a slippery slope in that they would not be able to escape from becoming responsible for the eventual losses resulting from cross-border loans.

As is well-known, doubts about the solvency of the Greek State – which had resulted from a rather peculiar turn of events in Greece in the aftermath of the 2009 elections, together with the repeated refusal of European institutions and the other European Member States to support the Greek republic during the fall of 2009 and the winter of 2010 – led to the triggering of the Eurozone fiscal crisis. When belated and insufficient decisions aimed at containing the Greek crisis came in the spring of 2010, it was not only too late, but the response was based on the wrong diagnosis, leading to an extremely problematic prognosis.

3.3 The Eurozone Fiscal Crisis

The rhetoric of the 'rescue' of the Greek state (and the fetishisation of the Greek public debt) cloaked in plain sight that it was basically a private financial crisis (including the collapse of the mountain of cross-border loans) that the Eurozone was dealing with. 'Financial assistance' provided by the Eurozone (and the

International Monetary Fund (IMF)) to Greece, as agreed in April 2010 and later in March 2012, was subject to the condition that Greece used most of the money to contain and overcome the crisis of its financial institutions. In fact, as was later established beyond doubt, the financial assistance provided to the Greek state only circulated through the Hellenic Exchequer, as it was immediately transferred to the creditor banks in France and Germany on account of the credits they had vis-á-vis the Greek state or the Greek financial institutions. In other words, the Hellenic state was, to a far from small extent, the *vehicle* through which the Eurozone as a whole provided financial assistance to Eurozone core financial institutions.[59] This entailed, de facto, 'bailing out' the creditors of Greek institutions, and particularly, the Eurozone banks that had lent to Greek financial institutions. What was supposed to be highly problematic in the Maastricht Constitution, ie state intervention, was resorted to, only this time to prop up profits, by means of transferring losses and or risks to the Greek Treasury. In concrete, the Hellenic Exchequer was required to *nationalise* the economic risks involved in the web of debt, or what is the same, to *transfer* to the Treasury the losses stemming from cross-border *private* debts. Given the parallel fiscal crisis in which the Greek state was submerged, that could only work if, at the very same time, all the other states of the Eurozone provided financial assistance to the Greek state. In such a way, the reckless management of Greek public accounts served to hide the recklessness of the Eurozone core creditors, with all the costs being absorbed by the Hellenic Exchequer, or subsidiarily by the taxpayers of the other Eurozone states, while private creditors (in the Greek case, mainly French and German banks) escaped unscathed. Austerity policies were the rather brutal methods by which the payments of these debts by the Greek Treasury were to be guaranteed. A similar story, with specific variants, could be told in the case of the programs of financial assistance to Ireland and Portugal. The Spanish and the Cypriot cases were not completely different, but there were specific factors rendering them slightly idiosyncratic. For reasons of space, such cases cannot be considered in detail here.[60]

The unfolding of events was, as pointed out, decisive in the diagnosis of the root causes of the crises put forward by European institutions. Instead of focusing on the structural shortcomings of an asymmetric European Union, institutions stuck to a less complex, more simplistic analysis. In particular, it was argued that the crises had been caused by the breach of the *fiscal rules* at the core of the European constitution of money. Had the periphery governments respected the deficit and debt ceilings, there would have been no crises to speak about. That was an appealing diagnosis in view of the discrepancy between predictions and realities, but

[59] ATTAC Austria has shown in detail that at least 77% of the funds of the first bailout ended up being paid to financial institutions. Cf. 'Greek Bail-Out: 77% went into the Financial Sector', 17 June 2013, available at https://www.attac.at/news/details/greek-bail-out-77-went-into-the-financial-sector.

[60] In the short run, the Eurozone core benefitted considerably, precisely because Germany and France avoided having to rescue their own banks. The impact upon the economies and the social structures of the periphery states was devastating.

it was one that fundamentally misunderstood the nature of the Eurozone fiscal crisis. Moreover, the overfocus on Greek infringements resulted in insufficient attention being paid to the fact that the decisions taken to contain the fiscal crisis were themselves in breach of the fiscal rules of the Eurozone.[61] When forced to produce reasons, European institutions would resort to a *principled* interpretation of their actions, arguing that the prohibition of financial assistance was at the end of the day the operationalisation of national fiscal autonomy, but even more deeply the subjection of national fiscal policy to *market discipline*,[62] or that the conditions for market discipline to kick in, to an equivalent of it, in the form of *conditionality* were absent. Consequently, financial assistance subject to strict conditionality was regarded as being in accordance with the ultimate telos of the Treaty, to the extent that conditionality ensures that the state remains subject to a logical *equivalent* to that exerted by financial markets when seeking financing.[63]

3.4 The true nature of austerity: Not a policy choice, but the ultimate implication of the neo-ordo-liberal social vision

Scholars, pundits and institutions failed to realise the extent to which austerity was not a mere policy choice, but was basically the only policy response left to a Member State experiencing a fiscal crisis within EMU as designed in Maastricht. They also failed to recognise the unsustainable character of the balance that was reached in the Eurozone during its first decade. It was only the exponential growth of cross-border loans that had rendered skyrocketing current account deficits possible, which in their turn created the mirage of economic convergence. This left the periphery states in a highly vulnerable position, and was bound to result in a major financial, economic and fiscal crisis, as it did. Moreover, the decisions through which Member States extended guarantees to *their* financial institutions in the immediate aftermath of the collapse of Lehman Brothers, and the parallel non-decision that no common fund would be created for that purpose had massive consequences, not least in pushing the Eurozone down a path that would result in periphery states serving as the vehicle through which core financial institutions would be bailed out at the cost of the periphery taxpayer.

[61] In particular, the principle of full national fiscal autonomy and responsibility, from which stemmed the rule forbidding the provision of financial assistance among EMU states (as already referred to above, the so-called no bailout clause, Art. 125 TFUE). It is perfectly possible to claim, at the very same time, that such a norm was being breached, and that such a norm, to paraphrase a former President of the European Commission, was deeply silly, or to be more precise, actually bound to be broken if the Eurozone was to survive over time.

[62] C-370/12, *Pringle*, ECLI:EU:C:2012:756; C-62/14, Gauweileir, ECLI:EU:C:2015:400.

[63] Ibidem.

3.5 The neo-ordo-liberal constitution of Europe: Sound money, economic freedoms, free competion (and neomercantilism)

The result of the long process of constitutional mutation of the European Union, unleashed by the crisis of the 1970s, partially codified by the Treaty of Maastricht, and radicalised and accelerated by the Eurozone crises, is the emergence of a 'functional' neo-ordo-liberal supranational economic constitution. This can be reconstructed around three basic principles: sound money (section 1), economic freedoms (section 2) and free competition (section 3). To this, the government of the fiscal crises added a fourth principle, fundamental in terms of defining the economic relationships between the EU and the rest of the world: which we can refer to as 'neo-mercantilism' (section 4).

A) 'Sound' money

The 'soundness' of money refers to its capacity to keep its power to command goods or services. 'Sound' money is money that can serve as the store of value, thereby creating the conditions for capital accumulation and the preservation of the value of the capital already accumulated.[64]

The 'soundness' of European money is guaranteed by means of a specific discipline of monetary and economic policy. This is three-fold. First, monetary stability is the paramount goal of monetary policy. Article 119.2 TFEU clearly defines monetary stability as the primary objective to be pursued by the independent ECB, and subjects the 'support' of the 'general economic policies in the Union' to the previous satisfaction of this objective. Second, fiscal policy cannot but also be oriented towards the realisation of the objective of monetary stability in line with the ideal of 'sound' money. In particular, the coherence between a single and centralised monetary policy (run by the ECB) and a plurality of national fiscal and economic policies (decided by national parliaments and national governments) is guaranteed by a number of limits to the latter, not the former. This accounts for the most conspicuous components of the 'sound budgetary' canon, the fiscal rules setting ceilings to the stocks of public debt (60 per cent GDP) and to public deficits (3 per cent GDP).[65] In the wake of the 2010 fiscal crisis, new fiscal rules have been added to the set constraining national fiscal policy, from tighter limits to the 'structural' deficit of Member States,[66] to those fixing trajectories of deficit and debt reduction,[67] closely associated to a peculiar form of automatic stabilisers in

[64] This is, in itself, preeminently in the interest of those who already have cumulated capital, and not so much of those who live off their wages.

[65] Article 1 of Protocol 12 to the TFEU.

[66] Article 2A and Article 9.1, first paragraph of the consolidated text of Regulation 1466/97.

[67] Article 5.1, second paragraph and Article 9.1, second paragraph of the consolidated text of Regulation 1466/97 (deficit reduction), Article 5.1 of the consolidated text of Regulation 1466/97 and Article 1.1 of the consolidated text of Regulation 1467/97 (debt reduction).

reverse, the automatic expenditure cuts.[68] The room for discretionary fiscal policy is further constrained by the panoply of indicators of macroeconomic imbalances, which reach into all corners of economic policy.[69] These rules substantiate the ideal of 'sound' budgetary policy, and are rendered effective through a complex set of procedures (now referred as the European Semester) that are formally aimed at the coordination of fiscal policy in the European Union, but which have acquired an increasingly hierarchical and disciplinary character. Third, supranational and national public institutions are expected to play a major role in preserving the stability of the financial system as a whole, something that may well require state intervention to underpin the value of financial assets when there is a serious risk (now labelled a 'systemic risk') that the market will undermine itself, threatening the stability of the economy as a whole.

B) *Economic freedom(s)*

The literal tenor and the structure of the provisions of the Treaty establishing the European Economic Community defining the 'four' economic freedoms (Article 30 TEC – elimination of quantitative restrictions; Article 48 TEC – free movement of workers; Article 52 TEC – right of establishment; Article 59 TEC – freedom to provide services; and Article 67 TFEU – elimination of (some) limits to the movement of capital) were ambivalent. This reflected the lack of a consensus among the drafters on the point and purpose of European integration. Was the European Economic Community to be an *external enabler* of national Democratic and Social states, rendering their consolidation possible through the expansion of external trade, but without constraining the power of states to steer socio-economic activity? Or rather, was the EEC to serve as an external constraint that set limits to national socio-economic powers in view of realising the liberal ideal of economic freedom? This ambivalence has marked the evolution of European institutions, oscillating between the paradigm of the 'common' market proper of the external enabler vision, to that of the 'single' market, in which the EU comes closer to an external constraint.

As I already hinted at, from the late 1950s to the early 1970s, the constellation of political forces at the national and supranational levels favoured the building of an internal market that gravitated towards the freedom to trade goods and the right to cross borders to pursue gainful employment, at the very same time that all economic freedoms were to a considerable extent socially, politically and culturally 'embedded' through national (and supranational) regulation.[70]

[68] Fiscal Compact, Article 3.1. e.

[69] Article 2 of Regulation 1176/2011.

[70] The extremely difficult act of squaring liberalisation with the consolidation and development of social states was to a large extent rendered possible by an exceptional political and economic climate, which was not deprived of its dark elements, from the resilience of patriarchy to the realpolitik of the Cold War.

From the mid and late 1970s onwards, the political and economic constellations radically changed, giving way to a balance of forces in which economic freedoms came to be understood as actionable subjective rights, largely emancipated from national law and politics into a 'single market'. The odd combination of economic stagnation and high inflation eroded the intellectual and political consensus around the Democratic and Social State, resulting in the decline of political parties and trade unions as constitutional forces, and the parallel rise of courts and central banks, promoted as actors that could solve the 'governability' crisis. Non-financial corporations and financial institutions, largely subdued during the 'treinte glorieuses' regained, slowly but steadily, the political and legal means to translate their economic power into political might. The Commission and the ECJ were key actors in these transformations, and saw their decisions partially codified with the deep reforms to the literal tenor of the Treaties, with economic freedoms strengthened and articulated as general subjective rights.[71]

This radical transformation has deeply marked the prevalent construction of economic freedoms.[72] Not only are they characterised as subjective rights, but each of them is regarded as a manifestation of a wider and encompassing 'economic freedom', that, as we will see in section V, is closely related to a specific conception of private property. And at the heart of such wider economic freedom, we find the right to fully command one's own capital. At one time understood as the (relatively modest) freedom to make payments corresponding to non-financial transactions (Articles 67.2 and 67.1 TEEC), free movement of capital was first turned into a fully-fledged subjective right by Directive 88/361[73] and then into the most fundamental of the economic freedoms. This primacy of free movement of capital is reflected in its legal force. Not only is it the only freedom that applies 'erga omnes', beyond the territory of the European Union (Article 63 TFEU), but it may eventually defeat conflicting Treaty provisions, including Article 345 TFEU. In particular, the ECJ has concluded that the full realisation of free movement of capital may require a narrow construction of the national power to define property regimes.[74] That reveals, as we will see in Section V, that beyond the economic freedom(s) (and indeed of the whole trio of principles at the heart of the fundamental European norms) lurks a radically strong conception of private property.

[71] Cf. the referred provisions with articles 28, 45, 49, 56, 63 TFEU.

[72] This transformation was led by the ECJ, which first "decoupled" free movement of goods from non-discrimination on the basis of nationality (case 120/78, *Cassis de Dijon*, ECLI:EU:C:1979:42) and then sidestepped the very structure of the Treaties to regard all four economic freedoms as making up a single normative block, on the basis of which projected the new understanding of free movement of goods to the other economic freedoms. Cf. rulings in C-76/90, *Säger*, ECLI:EU:C:1991:331; C-55/94 *Gebhard*, ECLI:EU:C:1995:411; C-415/93 *Bosman*, ECLI:EU:C:1995:463 and C-163/94, *Sanz de Lera*, ECLI:EU:C:1995:451.

[73] Council Directive 88/361/EEC of 24 June 1988 for the implementation of Article 67 of the Treaty, OJ L 178, 8.7.1988, p. 5–18.

[74] C-367/98, *Golden Shares*, ECLI:EU:C:2002:326.

C) 'Free' competition

The principle of 'free' competition prescribes that the allocation of goods and services must take place through 'competitive' markets, so that the welfare of the consumer is maximised.[75]

While the principle was originally interpreted as empowering the Commission to monitor and eventually to constrain private activity that could undermine the effectiveness of economic freedoms,[76] the centre of gravity of the principle shifted in the 1980s, leading to its transformation into a yardstick that determines the validity of public regulation of economic activity and, above all, the direct public engagement in the provision of goods and services (for example, through public ownership of corporations).[77] At the same time, the rise of 'consumer welfare maximisation' (and not sheer economic size and power) as the criterion by reference to which the legality or illegality of corporate structures and practices is determined has favoured the concentration of economic power, fuelling the further oligopolisation of the European economy. The de facto suspension of competition law in the aftermath of the financial crisis in 2008 and of the coronavirus crisis in 2020 proves the malleability of the principle of 'free' competition when constructed in the image and semblance of consumer welfare maximisation. In both cases, national Treasuries have been deployed to inject massive amounts of capital in 'ailing' companies (financial institutions in 2008–2009, all kinds of corporations in 2020). Actual practice seems thus to diverge radically from the theoretical ideal models that inspired the drafting of Article 119.1 TFEU ('open market economy with free competition'), and to basically point to a discipline of state intervention, which should not meddle with private control over the investment of capital. Quite tellingly, even nationalisations ceased to be a taboo during the coronavirus crisis, provided, however, they were temporary, and private ownership and control remained the rule and the goal.

D) 'Neo-mercantilism'

The Eurozone fiscal crisis played a major role in consolidating the neo-ordo-liberal turn of the European Union in the terms that I have considered in the three subsections of this part of the chapter. In addition, the government of the crisis also resulted in a new development that can be summarised as a process of

[75] H Hovenkamp, *The Antitrust Enterprise: Principle and Execution*, (Cambridge, Harvard University Press, 2006).

[76] For example, through the abuse of market power that rendered difficult access to different national markets European Court of Justice. Cf. rulings in cases 56 and 58/64, *Consten Grundig*, ECLI:EU:C:1966:41; 6/72 *Continental Can*, ECLI:EU:C:1973:22; 85/76, *Hoffmann*, ECLI:EU:C:1979:36; 322/81, *Michelin*, ECLI:EU:C:1983:313; *Ford vs. Commission*, ECLI:EU:C:1985:340.

[77] Cf. rulings in cases 18/88, *Régie des télégraphes et des téléphones*, ECLI:EU:C:1991:474; C-41/90, *Höfner*, ECLI:EU:C:1991:161; C-218/00, *Inail*, ECLI:EU:C:2002:36; C-399 and 401/10, *Bouygues*, ECLI:EU:C:2013:175; and T-296/97, *Alitalia*, ECLI:EU:T:2000:289.

Germanisation of the Eurozone, in the sense of all states, and especially those on the periphery of the Eurozone, were pressed into shifting to a growth model based on exports. Several legal and economic instruments were instrumental in this transformation, but perhaps none played such an important role as the debt brake.

The so-called debt brake was made part of the German constitution in 2009. The reform was ultimately (but not exclusively) triggered by the 2008 financial crisis; in particular, by the huge cost to the German taxpayer of bailing out the big German banks in the aftermath of the Lehmann Brothers' debacle.[78] The *Schuldenbremse* was regarded by a CDU/SPD supermajority as the cure to German ills.[79]

When the Eurozone fiscal troubles became a full-blown crisis in the spring of 2010, the German chancellor came to regard the debt brake as its ultimate constitutional export.[80] As was already pointed regarding Greece, most financial assistance to states experiencing major fiscal problems merely transited through their Treasuries, and ended up in the hands of financial institutions of the Eurozone core, not least Germany.[81] Such 'assistance' came hand in hand with the request of implementing 'structural reforms', which aimed at nothing less than the restructuring of periphery economies.[82] Having lost the adjustment variable of the exchange rate, external competitiveness was to be regained through internal devaluations, in which wages (that is labour, that is workers) were actually devalued.[83] In the mid run, it was expected, the structure of those economies would and should come to resemble that of Germany, with its neo-mercantilist reliance on constant surpluses as the engine of growth.

Such a vision was translated into legal norms, which have already been covered in this chapter. It is worth repeating that the jewel of the crown was the Fiscal Compact.[84] Not by chance, Article 3 of said peculiar 'quasi-Treaty' required all

[78] See Feld and Reuter (n 25).

[79] The Bundestag approved the amendment on 29 May 2009, the Bundesrat on 12 June 2009. The law amending the Fundamental Law came into force on 1 August 2009. However, the provision did not enter fully into force until 2016 (on what regarded the Federal Government) and 2020 (regarding the federal states). As is known, it was "suspended" in that same years due to the massive effects of the corona syndemics. It was reactivated in 2023.

[80] W Schäuble, 'Why austerity is only cure for the eurozone', *Financial Times*, 5 September 2011, available at https://www.ft.com/content/97b826e2-d7ab-11e0-a06b-00144feabdc0.

[81] Cf. J Rocholl and A Stahmner, 'Where did the Greek Bailout Money Go?', Working Paper 16-02 of the European School of Management and Technology, 2016, available at https://www.astrid-online.it/static/upload/esmt/esmt_wp-16-02.pdf.

[82] F Scharpf, 'Forced structural convergence in the eurozone: Or a differentiated European monetary community', MPIfG Discussion Paper, No. 16/15, Max Planck Institute for the Study of Societies, 2016, https://www.econstor.eu/bitstream/10419/150047/1/879422955.pdf.

[83] A devastating critique in C Lavapitsas, *The Left Case Against the EU*, London: Polity, 2019, especially pp. 67–82, on the Eurozone crisis. See also K Armingeon and L Baccaro, 'Political Economy of the sovereign debt crisis: The limits of internal devaluation', 41 (2012) *Industrial Law Journal* 254–275.

[84] 'Treaty on Stability, Coordination and Governance in the Economic and Monetary Union', available at https://eur-lex.europa.eu/legal-content/EN/TXT/?uri=celex%3A42012A0302%2801%29.

Member States to write into their fundamental norms, preferably in their constitutions,[85] the European equivalent of the German debt brake. The famous letters addressed by Trichet and Draghi to Zapatero and Berlusconi[86] resulted in the Spanish and the Italian Constitutions being amended in line with the requirements of the Fiscal Compact (through the amendments to Articles 135 of the Spanish Constitution and 81 of the Italian Constitution). Slovenia followed somehow later (cf. Article 148 of the Slovenian constitution).

In such a way, the 'mutated' national economic constitutions pre-determined that states had to commit to become 'export-led' economies, practising new forms of mercantilism through the constant repression of wages. The Eurozone had been transformed into a neo-mercantilist pact.

4. 'Hamiltonian' Moments, 'Green' Europe and the 'Geopolitical' Rearmament Turn: A New Economic Constitution?

In this section, I turn to the analysis of the three main 'crises' that are said to have prompted a new set of punctual decisions and structural reforms that allegedly have deeply transformed the EU: the corona syndemics; the 'climate change' emergency; and the geostrategic shifts rendered evident by the recrudescence of the war in Ukraine and the gyrations in US foreign policy brought about by the second Trump administration, and which will trigger the launch of a new European industrial policy (as of late in the form of a common defence policy). I highlight the extent to which these transformations are more inconclusive than they seem. The character of the response of the EU to Covid-19 is yet to be settled, because no final decision has been taken on how to pay for NG-EU. The fight against climate change defines the problem in rather narrow terms, ignoring the extent to which climate change is part of a wider problem, the trespassing of planetary limits; in addition, there are clear indications that the commitments reflected in the 'Green Deal' are being scaled down when not silently repudiated. Finally, the new 'industrial policy' is not only yet to be defined, but is tied to the rather imprecise concept, to say the least, of strategic autonomy, apparently fuelled by the sudden realisation of the need to acquire an autonomous capacity to defend Europe. Above all, what all these changes signal is not a return to democratic interventionism, but the instrumental use of the repertoire of policy tools

[85] Article 3.2 of the Fiscal Compact reads: 'through provisions of binding force and permanent character, preferably constitutional, or otherwise guaranteed to be fully respected and adhered to throughout the national budgetary processes'.

[86] The texts were pretty similar. The letter to Berlusconi can be read at https://www.ecb.europa.eu/ecb/access_to_documents/document/pa_document/shared/data/ecb.dr.par2021_0001lettertoItalianPrimeMinister.en.pdf. The letter Zapatero was published by the latter in his memoir on the crisis years. See JL Rodríguez Zapatero, *El Dilema: 600 días de vértigo*, (Barcelona, Planeta, 2013), 169. Zapatero dwells in detail on the context of the letter, and of the reply given to it.

of the latter at the service of the neo-ordo-liberal socio-economic vision. What is being proposed are massive transfers of public resources to 'derisk' corporate investments. The costs of innovation are socialised, the eventual benefits kept in private hands. That is by no means neo-Keynesianism, but neo-ordo-liberalism by other means.

4.1 Greening Europe

In a context marked not only by the legacies of 'austerity policies' but also by the outcome of the Brexit referendum and the socio-economic policies implemented by the first Trump administration, a new European Commission came to office in December 2019.

Quite immediately, the Commission launched a new policy initiative, the so-called 'European Green Deal'.[87] Its declared aims were two. First, reducing greenhouse gas emissions by at least 50 per cent by 2030 (compared with 1990 levels). Second, making Europe the first climate neutral continent by 2050. The level of ambition was perhaps only comparable to that which was the hallmark of the Lisbon Strategy of 2000.[88] Indeed, the Commission claimed that the Green Deal would transform 'the EU into a modern, resource-efficient economy while addressing environmental and social challenges'.

Such goals have been said to be bound to radically transform the economic constitution of the European Union.[89] The main reason why this would be so is that the Green Deal aims at redefining the 'European' model of economic growth. In particular, growth should be 'decoupled' from the consumption of non-renewable material resources, very especially fossil fuels.[90] That was supposed to have major requirements. First, it was said to require the development of 'clean' and renewable sources of energy, at the same time as doubling up efforts on energy efficiency (ie reducing the consumption of energy through different saving measures).[91] Doing so would render it possible to both 'de-carbonise' economic activity

[87] 'Communication from the Commission to the European Parliament, the European Council, the Council, the European Economic and Social Committee and the Committee of the Regions, The European Green Deal, COM/2019/640 final, 11 December 2019, available at https://eur-lex.europa.eu/legal-content/EN/TXT/?uri=celex:52019DC0640.

[88] Lisbon European Council, 23 and 24 May 2000, available at https://www.europarl.europa.eu/summits/lis1_en.htm: 'the most competitive and dynamic knowledge-based economy in the world capable of sustainable economic growth with more and better jobs and greater social cohesion'.

[89] In the terms of Annette Bongardt and Francisco Torres, (The European Green Deal: More than an Exit Strategy to the Pandemic Crisis, a Building Block of a Sustainable European Economic Model, 60:1 (2022) Journal of Common Market Studies, 170-85), echoed by Bevilacqua and Chiti (n 4) , the Green Deal not only constitutes a new pillar of the European economic constitution (alongside the single market and the single currency), but has a transformative character of the whole European economic constitution. Bevilacqua and Chiti stress that to render the Green Deal possible, the *economic constitution* of the EY had to be changed.

[90] Green Deal (n 87) 2: 'It is a new growth strategy (. . .) where economic growth is decoupled from resource use'.

[91] Ibid 6.

(very especially industry,[92] agriculture,[93] building[94] and transport[95]) and sustain the present levels of economic growth (with the latter 'liberated' from the shackles of the dependency of non-renewable sources of energy). Second, 'extractivism' should be progressively replaced by the reuse and repurposing of natural goods (the 'circular economy').[96] Such transformation was to come hand in hand with the drawing of a new relationship with nature. If, until then, 'sustainable growth' was to be achieved *within the single market*, now the Union would aim at 'ecosystem sustainability', which would set the parameters of economic activity *in the single market*.[97] Nature should not only be protected but eventually restored,[98] even if that resulted in restraining or constraining economic development. In other words, the *inner normative logic* of the Green Deal pointed towards the transformation of the preservation of the integrity of ecosystems into the overriding public interest of the Union, capable of defeating, when in conflict, the goals of economic growth and economic (admittedly short term) welfare[99] Third, such ambitions required a new array of policies and instruments to be put in place. Massive amounts of private and public investment were to be mobilised.[100] New

[92] Key in that regard is the reference to a 'zero-carbon steel making process', to be achieved by 2030, Cf. Ibid, 8,

[93] That largely corresponds to the so-called 'fork to farm' strategy. Ibid, 11–14. See also 'Communication from the Commission to the European Parliament, the Council, the European Economic and Social Committee and the Committee of the Regions, A Farm to Fork Strategy for a fair, healthy and environmentally-friendly food system', COM/2020/381 final, 20 May 2020, https://eur-lex.europa.eu/legal-content/EN/TXT/HTML/?uri=CELEX:52020DC0381.

[94] Green Deal (n 87) 9.

[95] Ibid, 10–11

[96] Ibid, 7 and 8. The circular economy should also include 'measures to encourage business to offer, and to allow consumers to choose, reusable, durable and repairable products'. The Commission was considering fleshing out, among other things, a right to repair.

[97] Bevilacqua and Chit (n 4) 88. The authors admit that implementing that shift would not be a straightforward process. The tension between the old 'sustainable development' goal and the new of integrity of ecosystems was unresolved, and is bound to remain unresolved.

[98] Cf. Bio-diversity Strategy 2030, available at https://environment.ec.europa.eu/strategy/biodiversity-strategy-2030_en; Forest Strategy 2030, https://environment.ec.europa.eu/strategy/forest-strategy_en; Soil Strategy 2030, https://environment.ec.europa.eu/publications/eu-soil-strategy-2030_en. Even more decisive is Regulation (EU) 2024/1991 of the European Parliament and of the Council of 24 June 2024 on nature restoration and amending Regulation (EU) 2022/869, *OJ L, 2024/1991, 29.7.2024, ELI: http://data.europa.eu/eli/reg/2024/1991/oj*, available at https://eur-lex.europa.eu/legal-content/EN/TXT/HTML/?uri=OJ:L_202401991.

[99] Bevilacqua and Chit (n 4) 114: 'Ma ci interessa qui per la sua carica innovatrice: l'integrità ecologica presuppone inevitabilmente che, nel caso di conflitto tra integrità degli ecosistemi ed esigenze sociali ed economiche, la prima prevalga sulle seconde, perché risponde a parametri che solo la scienza può individuare e ai quali non si può rinunziare senza compromettere la stessa integrità degli ecosistemi". Cf. also ibid, 66-7 on the primacy of the preservation of nature: 'ridefinisce la sostenibilità come il dovere di proteggere e ripristinare l'integrità dei sistemi ecologici e presuppone che la salute degli ecosistemi prevalga sulle esigenze sociali ed economiche (. . .) un piano i cui effetti vanno oltre i risultati perseguiti dall'istituzione che del Green Deal è il principale motore politico'. This leads to a rebalancing of ultimate goals. Ibid, 115: 'Implica che la tutela della salute degli ecosistemi prevalga sulle esigenze sociali ed economiche eventualmente confliggenti'.

[100] Green Deal (n 87) 2: 'It will require massive public investment and increased efforts to direct capital towards climate and environmental action'.

forms of interventionism might be required.[101] The social impacts might be many, as in-depth changes are disruptive.[102] By the same token, a panoply of measures would be needed that aimed at avoiding disproportionately burdening the least well-off in society with the costs.[103] The Union, and not only the states, should play an active role in the governing of the transition, leading to the need to introduce genuinely European taxes (not least, the plastic tax and the carbon adjustment tax).[104] Fourth, greening Europe was regarded as essential, but also as insufficient. The EU could and should lead by example, in the process deploying the means to persuade other polities to follow its cue. This had two major implications. The EU should protect itself against the *unfair* economic advantage of other regions of the world that were not internalising the ecological constraints (not least, through the carbon border adjustment mechanism)[105] while preventing the climate objectives being undermined through the externalisation of production (what is referred as 'carbon leakage').[106] By the same token, the EU should use its economic power to persuade trading partners to undertake their own plans to fight climate change.[107]

The Green Deal[108] has given rise to a flurry of legislative and policy initiatives. Most voluminously, we find the 'Fit for 55' legislative package. Although the label

[101] This was represented as requiring not so much the development of a strong public sector, not even heavy handed regulation, but rather as public institutions 'sending' the 'right' signals to the private sector, so that the incentives are there for private investment. See Green Deal (n 87) especially p. 16 and 17: 'The private sector will be key to financing the green transition. Long-term signals are needed to direct financial and capital flows to green investment and to avoid stranded assets'. A similar approach is applied to the 'greening' of finance, with the EP and the Council adopting 'the taxonomy for classifying environmentally sustainable activities'. Such an approach can be categorised as corresponding to the 'derisking state', and is at odds with what the type of intervention in the form of planning favoured in the ecologist literature. See for example C Durand and R Keucheyan, *Comment Bifurquer. Les Principes de la Planification Écologique* (Paris, Zones, 2024).

[102] Chiti and Bevilacqua (n 4) 56.

[103] Green Deal, (n 87) 16: 'The need for a socially just transition must also be reflected in policies at EU and national level'. That concern has resulted in the creation of the Just Transition Mechanism, supposed to mobilise 55bn euro during the period 2021–2027. Such monies are supposed to be spent in the 'most affected regions', so as to alleviate the socio-economic costs of transitioning. At its heart we find the Just Transition Fund, part of the NG-EU Programme. See Regulation (EU) 2021/1056 of the European Parliament and of the Council of 24 June 2021 establishing the Just Transition Fund, *OJ L 231, 30.6.2021, p. 1–20*, https://eur-lex.europa.eu/legal-content/EN/TXT/HTML/?uri=CELEX:32021R1056.

[104] Green Deal, n 84, 15–7.

[105] Ibid 5.

[106] Ibidem.

[107] Ibid, 21: 'On climate change more specifically, the EU's most recent agreements all include a binding commitment of the Parties to ratify and effectively implement the Paris Agreement. The Commission will propose to make the respect of the Paris agreement an essential element for all future comprehensive trade agreements'.

[108] Although I am presenting the post-2018 period in three steps, and in the process distinguishing between the Green Deal and the NG-EU programme, the two are deeply intertwined. Not only the 'greening' of the EU has been made into a fundamental objective of NG-EU, but the actual funding of the Green Deal was articulated through NG-EU. Cf. C Papa and J Sachs, 'Implementing the European Green Deal through Transformative Change: A Review of EU Climate Action through the lens of the "Six Transformations"', Enel Foundation, 2001, available at https://openinnovability.enel.com/content/dam/enel-foundation/news/2021/11/sdsn/211019-EGD-report.pdf. On the 'reverse' links, that is, on how the Green Deal may end up producing the sources of revenue to pay for NG-EU, see M Bryk-Zwolska, 'The EU ETS and the European Green Deal – the Struggle for Compromise', in A Sikora and I Kawka (eds.)

refers to the 2030 objective of cutting emissions by 55 per cent, most of the norms have relevance and implications extending beyond that date. That is clearly the case of the 'European Climate Law' of 2021,[109] and of the Regulation establishing the Carbon Adjustment Mechanism.[110] Or, for that matter, of the Regulation establishing the Social Climate Fund.[111] Alongside the package, we should also consider the Nature Restoration Regulation[112] and the Regulation establishing the Just Transition Fund.[113]

It should be noticed that the ambitions of the plan were progressively curtailed. The aggravation of the war in Ukraine, following the Russian invasion of February 2022, led to an energy crisis that facilitated the dilution of the Green Deal's goals.[114] Moreover, the elections to the European Parliament in 2024 resulted in a configuration of the assembly, and consequently, of the European Commission in which the majority was much less enthusiastic about climate neutrality.[115] Even a report of the research services of the European Commission was not especially upbeat.[116] The actual proposals put forward by the Commission (the so-called 'Omnibus Act') point in the direction of a radical scaling down of ambitions.[117]

The European Green Deal and the Impact of Climate Change on the EU Regulatory Framework, (Bruxelles, Presses universitaires Saint-Louis, 2024), available at https://doi.org/10.4000/12kex. An assessment of the extent to which NG-EU has managed to contribute to fulfil the goals set by the European Green Deal, and considerations on how to change course, in J Pisany-Ferry and S Tagliapietra, *An Investment Strategy to Keep the European Green Deal on Track*, Policy Brief, (Bruegel, 2024), available at https://www.bruegel.org/policy-brief/investment-strategy-keep-european-green-deal-track.

[109] 'Regulation (EU) 2021/1119 of the European Parliament and of the Council of 30 June 2021 establishing the framework for achieving climate neutrality and amending Regulations' (EC) No 401/2009 and (EU) 2018/1999 ('European Climate Law'), OJ L 243, 9.7.2021, p. 1–17.

[110] 'Regulation (EU) 2023/956 of the European Parliament and of the Council of 10 May 2023 establishing a carbon border adjustment mechanism', OJ L 130, 16.5.2023, p. 52–104.

[111] 'Regulation (EU) 2023/955 of the European Parliament and of the Council of 10 May 2023 establishing a Social Climate Fund and amending Regulation' (EU) 2021/1060, OJ L 130, 16.5.2023, p. 1–51, ELI: http://data.europa.eu/eli/reg/2023/955/oj.

[112] 'Regulation (EU) 2024/1991 of the European Parliament and of the Council of 24 June 2024 on nature restoration and amending Regulation' (EU) 2022/869, OJ L, 2024/1991, ELI: http://data.europa.eu/eli/reg/2024/1991/oj,https://eur-lex.europa.eu/legal-content/EN/TXT/HTML/?uri=OJ:L_202401991.

[113] 'Regulation (EU) 2021/1056 of the European Parliament and of the Council of 24 June 2021 establishing the Just Transition Fund', *OJ L 231, 30.6.2021, p. 1–20*, ELI: http://data.europa.eu/eli/reg/2021/1056/oj.

[114] M Doğan, *The Ukraine-Russia War and its Relationship with Climate Change* (Istanbul: Istanbul University Press, 2024), available at https://cdn.istanbul.edu.tr/file/JTA6CLJ8T5/B56AA66B4B554595BD12A33840E67BE6.

[115] 'EU struggles to balance its green and growth goals', *Financial Times*, 28 February 2025, https://www.ft.com/content/6f74926a-6ab3-46ee-a434-573c588b7ff4. But see the upbeat S Mundy, 'Why the EU's competitiveness push could be good news for the green agenda', *Financial Times*, 7 February 2025, https://www.ft.com/content/7be67276-3755-4cdd-b72e-ffa1e5daf531

[116] European Commission, 'Delivering the EU Green Deal – Progress towards targets', available at https://publications.jrc.ec.europa.eu/repository/handle/JRC140372.

[117] N de Sadaleer, 'The European Green Deal: greenwashing compounded by deregulation (Omnibus law) or a genuine paradigm shift?', *European Journal of Risk Regulation*, early view, at https://www.cambridge.org/core/journals/european-journal-of-risk-regulation/article/european-green-deal-greenwashing-compounded-by-deregulation-omnibus-law-or-a-genuine-paradigm-shift/EAD181DF582BB92ACF6EAFD5D709CC22: 'we shall see that traditional economic interests have largely prevailed over the fight against pollution and the ecosystemic approach, whereas nature conservation and the social pillar of sustainable development risk being the big losers of the green transition'.

Even more decisive is the fact that the implementation of the European Green Deal was bound to fall short of the ambitions of the Commission due to the very design of the project. The diagnosis that underlies the Green Deal is hard to contest. The world is certainly facing an increase in the levels of CO2 in the atmosphere, leading to a rise in temperatures that may disastrously alter environmental conditions. Still, the objective of making Europe, and by its example, the world climate neutral by 2050 may be a tall order in social and political terms, but if anything is insufficiently ambitious when we consider the factual situation. In particular, it would have been preferrable to approach the issue from the perspective provided by 'planetary limits', that stress the extent to which we have overexploited the Earth, pushing the planet beyond the capacity to sustain human lives in several dimensions.[118] But there is more. The incomplete diagnosis results in a misleading prognosis. The key goal set by the European Commission is to decouple growth from the consumption of fossil fuels. This allows Eurocrats to assume that solving the environmental crisis does not require a fundamental change in the way we live, and consequently, on the European economic constitution, but rather a technical fix, which calls for important but at the end of the day marginal adjustments.[119] In the view of the vision that underpins the Green Deal, the changes that are needed are fundamentally related to the effort required to discover and render ready to use the new technologies that will allow us to 'transition' from finite and polluting fossil fuels to renewable and clean new sources of energy.

If we consider this assumption carefully, however, we notice two things. The first is that it assumes that economic history has been marked by the transition from one source of energy to the next (human power, wood, coal, oil and now 'clean sources of energy'). That is, however, wrong. Economic history has been marked by the successive addition of new sources of energy. When oil becomes the dominant source of energy, coal does not disappear; actually, coal is deeply involved in the overall energy mix that we have at present. The second is that the prognosis implies a rather blind faith on the existence of clean technologies that will allow us to fully replace the present sources of energy, so that we can 'decouple' from 'fossil' fuels. If only we invest the right amounts of resources in researching them and do it in the right way, the sources of energy will be discovered. Such assumptions get history wrong and, by means of doing so, present the problem as being much easier to solve than it is. What we need is not only a new energy technology, but an energy technology that allows us to do what no energy technology has so far rendered possible, which is to stop using previous sources of energy. And there is more than 'unlimited optimism' involved in the assumption that the new source of energy is bound to be readily available.

This reveals the extent to which the European Green Deal is deeply attached to the status quo, and indeed to the economic constitution as has emerged from the

[118] A Turiel, *El Futuro de Europa* (Barcelona, Destino, 2025).

[119] Adjustments that can be duly calculated and integrated into a blueprint, such as the European Green Deal.

process of normative mutation described in the previous pages. This is so because while scholars claim that the European Green Deal *radically changes* the European economic constitution, the blind faith of a technological fix being around the corner pre-empts a discussion of the role that the present economic constitution has played in causing the environmental crisis we are confronting. An in-depth transformation of our economic constitution, not only as a capitalist constitution based on the triad of sound money, economic freedoms and free competition, but also based on an unlimited supply of energy, is as a result ruled out from the very beginning. Even if some thought is applied to measures that increase energy efficiency, the emphasis is placed on renewable sources of energy capable of replacing fossil fuels. A different future, in which energy austerity is unavoidable, is simply beyond the bounds of the thinkable for the European Commission. This is proven by the fact that no consideration is given to measures rendering a drastic reduction in actual energy consumption possible . Measures that will be unavoidable if the 'scientific breakthrough' does not take place. This is particularly intriguing, given that the European Commission was once led, even if briefly, by one of the few institutional figures in world politics who openly advocated for what is usually labelled as 'degrowth', Sicco Mansholt.

For those reasons, the changes that are being proposed do not amount to a radical reconfiguration of the economic constitution of the European Union, but rather consist in variations aimed at rendering it possible to uphold the said economic constitution *by other means*. In that regard, what the Green Deal clearly signals is a shift in the terms of the relationship between public institutions and corporations, especially between the EU and corporations. The role of the EU in the upholding of the European economic order is no longer mainly identified with *unleashing* the economic power of (big) corporations by means of setting aside national norms restraining the power of property owners, but rather to ensure, through its own expenditure and through the expenditure of Member States, the *profitability* of (big) corporations. This is why the Green Deal marks a radical shift, already in the wings since the 2010s, regarding so-called industrial policy. The European Green Deal requires, among other things, a new industrial policy.[120] The amounts of capital needed were bound to be daunting (especially in the form of initial costs);[121] by the same token, the risks involved were not only too numerous but were also very difficult to calculate. Both the Commission and the academic commentators did not even consider that such investments would be undertaken through a revival of public enterprises, combined with state-led forms of planification. What was needed was something different: a derisking state. The Union and the Member States have a major role to play in both sending the right signals over investment (something that assumes that 'market' signals are wrong, and should be replaced by signals *produced* by public institutions, regarding for example the long-term sustainability of investments), and fostering investment that would not

[120] Bevilacqua and Chiti (n 4) 30, 41, 114
[121] Ibid 41.

take place unless *incentivated* by public institutions. They are capable of shaping the commercial and industrial operators' choices through balancing public objectives backed by the use of public resources to 'derisk' investment (what used to be regarded as forms of illegal state aid, in breach of the principle of fair competition). Such form of industrial policy requires Member States to spend big, basically to *derisk* investment. Or what is the same, the investment costs are socialised, while profits remain fully allocated to the shareholders of corporations. This accounts for the visionary tones in which the European institutions express themselves, when they characterise the climate crisis as a major challenge if not an epochal crisis, which, however can be turned into an opportunity, and decisively, into an *economic* opportunity. That is true, in a literal sense, but only applies to some: the corporate beneficiaries of public subsidies.

4.2 Hamiltonian Moments? Shifting Course to Stay Put

The spread of Covid-19 in the early weeks of 2020 resulted in a rapid increase of excessive mortality in the EU (and in most of the rest of the world). This posed major challenges from the standpoint of human health. In most EU states (with basically the sole exception of Sweden) it was decided that massive lockdowns were needed to slow down the spread of the virus and avoid a collapse of the capacity to take care of the seriously ill. That had immediate and massive implications, not least socio-economic.

The protection of public health seemed to require imposing a massive demand shock. The consequences of such decision could only be mitigated by countervailing public intervention. Such intervention could not be undertaken through the European common budget, because the EU lacked the means. The EU budget stood at 1 per cent EU GDP and to increase spending would require following a very convoluted and long procedure. Theoretically speaking, Member States could coordinate their use of fiscal tools with such a goal in view. However, two obstacles stood in the way. First, Eurozone states lacked the most obvious means to procure the massive amounts of resources needed, as they had renounced monetary power, and with it, the monetisation of public debt. Second, European fiscal rules, 'hardened' after the cycle of reforms triggered by the fiscal crisis, forbade states to incur the kind of deficits that would be needed to meet the present needs. This accounts for the reluctance with which the Commission and the ECB acted in the first days of February 2020. In particular, Christine Lagarde, as president of the ECB, rejected any form of extraordinary intervention to reduce the borrowing costs of Italy, which was the first country seriously affected by Covid-19. By the midle of that month, however, the Council took the extraordinary decision to suspend the Stability and Growth Pact, making use of the 'collective' escape clause placed at its heart. At the same time, the ECB launched its Pandemic Quantitative Easing (QE), which in a nutshell provided unlimited and unconditional funding to Member States. This created the conditions under which Member States could engage into massive support programmes, which allowed the EU economies to 'freeze' and mitigate the socio-economic consequences of a phenomenal simultaneous decline in economic activity and employment levels.

De facto, a financial state of emergency was declared again (the first time was in the period 2010–2015), and extraordinary measures were adopted. There were considerable differences, however, between the European government of the fiscal crisis and that of the Covid-19 syndemic. While in the former, the cost of the crisis was imposed on the shoulders of citizens as workers and as recipients of public services and transfers, in the latter, state power was also used to mitigate the social consequences of the crisis. It is proper to speak of the Union contributing to 'shielding' social protection systems in 2020, while in 2010–2015 such mechanisms were undermined by the EU. However, it is important to notice three additional things. First, that the crisis opened by Covid-19 affected all Member States and it was much harder to redistribute the costs through legal and political forms of 'inverted solidarity' as was done during the fiscal crisis. Second, that in both cases, state intervention aimed at preserving the capitalistic infrastructure of the system; capital was rescued in 2008, in 2010 and in 2020. Only, in 2020, such a rescue was part of an overall attempt at freezing the whole economy. Third, that the Stability and Growth Pact was only suspended, not eliminated; so even if states faced no immediate limit to their capacity to indebt themselves, they were in very different positions when they considered the mid run, when the suspension of the Pact would come to an end.

The asymmetric capacity of states to absorb new debt affected the readiness of states to intervene. Germany made use of the temporary framework to grant a massive amount of aid to German companies, while other states were much more parsimonious. The Commission and several national governments soon noticed that this was bound to have a major effect, placing German companies in a privileged position within the single market. In addition, the impact of the syndemic had been different in different Member States, something that was related not only to epidemiological factors, but also to social factors (thus the pertinence of using the more encompassing term of syndemic). This created momentum in favour of a collective, European intervention, which the Commission calculated would have to be in the vicinity of €1.2 billion. The negotiation process seems to have been affected and accelerated by the famous ruling of the German Constitutional Court on 5 May 2020, which declared prima facie unconstitutional the QE programme, although through a complicated legal formula left open the possibility that the ECB would provide a detailed justification of the proportionality, and thus constitutionality, of the programme.

At the end of May, Macron and Merkel agreed on the basic outlines of a European programme, in the vicinity of €750 billion, to support the efforts of reconstruction but also to provide funding to meet the long-term objectives of the EU, including climate neutrality and digitalisation. After a tense negotiation, an agreement was found between all Member States. The total amount of the programme was kept intact, but a sizeable part of them (more than half) was to consist of loans, not grants. All states were to benefit from the funds (something which eased the approval, in both political and legal terms, but diluted any redistributive potential), but those states that had been more deeply affected by Covid-19 would receive a higher share.[122]

The NG-EU is a complex and, in many ways, yet-to-be-completed arrangement. For all the rhetoric about 'infectious solidarity', there is little that is solidaristic in the provision of financial assistance when the creditor stands to benefit as much, if not more, than the debtor and when the power imbalance between creditor and debtor is preserved. It is only in regards to the grants part of the European Recovery Fund, and not to the loans part, that it makes sense to speak of solidarity. There is no doubt that the approval of the NG-EU entails that the EU, acting as a collective, issues common debt at unprecedented levels and then makes use of the funds thus collected to distribute grants and loans to each and every Member State in proportion to the degree to which their economies were affected by the syndemic. Thus, a common solidum is created, and we find legal norms allocating the resources raised on the basis of principles that claim to correspond to the requirements of mutuality and reciprocity.

And still, five caveats are due:

First, it is important to keep in mind that the actual macroeconomic size of the programme is smaller than its advocates suggest, not least when comparing the programme with the series of decisions that led to the forging of a common federal treasury in the US. Consider the following three sets of considerations:

a) The real size of the NG-EU is smaller than the one advertised by European institutions. I will not consider the tendency of the European Commission to quote a constantly bigger figure without explaining that the new amount results from adjusting the original figure to inflation. More relevant is the fact that the original figure of €750 billion is only indicative of the maximum amount of the programme, which would only be reached if all Member States would borrow the maximum quota of loans allocated to them. Suffice it to say that in the case of the countries that financial markets perceive as representing a lesser risk, such as Germany or the Netherlands, it is cheaper to issue debt than to borrow money from the common fund. France does not have much of an incentive to borrow, if only because the meagre eventual financial benefits would not compensate for the loss of goodwill and face (leading to eventual higher interest rates in the future). So, in 2021 prices, we are talking approximately about €325.9 billion of grants and €166 billion of loans, that is, slightly under €500 billion.
b) European institutions fail to emphasise that the amount of funds will be spent not in one single year but basically over a five-year period. This entails that the actual macroeconomic impact is much smaller than it may seem at first sight, or what is the same, a trifle more than 4 per cent of the EU GDP, spread over

[122] 'European Council Conclusions, 17-21 July 2020', available at https://www.consilium.europa.eu/media/45109/210720-euco-final-conclusions-en.pdf.

five years, or what is the same, and an average of 0.8 per cent GDP per year, if (a big if) all grants and requested loans would lead to actual expenditure and investment. This is far below the level of expenditure that the European Commission itself calculated was necessary to serve the most modest objective of the programme, namely, to compensate for the impact of the massive but unequal state aid granted by states from March 2020.

c) Additionally, it should be noted that the increase in real expenditure of €390 billion comes hand in hand with reducing the 'ordinary budget' of the EU, of the order of €100 billion for the seven-year fiscal cycle. The result is that the new financial perspectives will have an expansionary effect in the first three years (2021–2023) but will have a deflationary impact from year four (in particular, the cuts to the EU budget will have a major impact on the expenditure associated to the common agricultural policy and research and development).

Second, raising funds through loans contributes, and not insignificantly, to the financialisation of the European economy. It could be argued that under the conditions prevailing in 2020 and 2021, there was not much of an alternative to funding most of the common expenditure except through the issuance of new public debt. Still, part of the costs could have been met through taxes collected on excessive profits, as famously John Maynard Keynes proposed when considering ways of paying for the Second World War.[123] As this was not done (despite Article 310.1, third paragraph), it is hard to avoid the conclusion that the programme contributes even further to the growth of financial assets, and, consequently, to the process of financialisation of the economy, even if at a smaller scale than the 'standard' and the 'pandemic' programmes of QE.

Third, the limits to the capacity of the EU to steer expenditure and of the Member States to channel the funds into public investment, both a consequence of the way in which European integration curtails public power, rendered it very probable from the very beginning that most of the money would be applied to the subsidisation of private investment projects. As was pointed out in the previous subsection, all money is transferred from the Union to national exchequers, with no money being spent from the centre. States are subject to a layer of conditionality requirements that are more oriented to reinforce the capacity of the Commission to influence the overall design of national fiscal and social policies than to determine the way in which the funds are spent. Additionally, the radical downsizing of the public sector since the 1970s, compounded by the reduction of administrative capacities and accelerated by austerity policies, rendered it extremely difficult for Member States and their regions to actually make direct and effective use of the funds within the tight deadlines imposed upon them. As a result, a high percentage of the money is unlikely to end up being channelled to the creation and improvement of existing collective goods through public investment

[123] JM Keynes, *How to Pay for the War* (MacMillan & Co, 1940).

but rather would fund the public subsidisation of private investment. Or rather, the programme will likely turn out to be a means to socialise risks while privatising benefits, an old practice which, as already pointed, is now aptly labelled as 'derisking' and which has become dominant in the profile of contemporary states.[124] That can hardly be described as a way to realise solidarity. Rather, it seems to be another form of 'inverted' solidarity.

Fourth, it remains unsettled how the cost of the programme will be funded, or rather, how the debt incurred to pay the grants will be repaid when it will become due. This is essential to determine the actual economic and normative effect of NG-EU, and more particularly, the extent to which it can be described as a solidaristic programme. While it was generally agreed that the EU would recognise the power to collect new taxes or participate in the collection of existing ones at a level which would cover the costs of returning the principal of the debt issued to fund the NG-EU programme,[125] so far only the tax on the consumption of non-recycled plastic[126] and the carbon border adjustment mechanism[127] have been approved. The former raised €7 billion euro in 2023, less than 4 per cent of total EU revenue.[128] Being a sin tax, if successful it would raise even less money in the future. The latter only entered into force in January 2026, but only after a major modification which dented its revenue gathering capacity.[129] There were also plans to generate revenue through emissions trading and through one corporate income tax part of the proposed new framework of corporate taxation of the OCDE/G20 agreement. In addition, by June 2023 the Commission proposed a fourth tax, a specific form of tax on corporate profits (expected to generate €16 billion per year from 2024).[130] But, as such plans have not materialised, we still do not know to what extent this leads to a shift from the logic of apportioning common expenses to Member States, as is now the rule. In other words, the decision to issue debt has been taken and acted upon while leaving open the question

[124] Gabor (n 9).

[125] European Commission, 'The Commission proposes the next generation of EU own resources' (European Commission, 22 December 2021) https://ec.europa.eu/commission/presscorner/detail/en/ip_21_7025 accessed 17 March 2024.

[126] 'Council Regulation (EU, Euratom) 2021/770 of 30 April 2021 on the calculation of the own resource based on plastic packaging waste that is not recycled, on the methods and procedure for making available that own resource, on the measures to meet cash requirements, and on certain aspects of the own resource based on gross national income', OJ L 165, 11.5.2021, p. 15–24, ELI: http://data.europa.eu/eli/reg/2021/770/oj.

[127] 'Regulation (EU) 2023/956 of the European Parliament and of the Council of 10 May 2023 establishing a carbon border adjustment mechanism', OJ L 130, 16.5.2023, p. 52–104, ELI: http://data.europa.eu/eli/reg/2023/956/oj.

[128] https://renewable-carbon.eu/news/challenging-start-for-the-eus-revenue-based-on-non-recycled -plastic-packaging-waste/.

[129] 'Regulation (EU) 2025/2083 of the European Parliament and of the Council of 8 October 2025 amending Regulation (EU) 2023/956 as regards simplifying and strengthening the carbon border adjustment mechanism', OJ L, 2025/2083, 17.10.2025, ELI: http://data.europa.eu/eli/reg/2025/2083/oj.

[130] European Commission, 'EU budget: Commission puts forward an adjusted package for the next generation of own resources', 20 June 2023 https://ec.europa.eu/commission/presscorner/detail/en/ip_23_3328.

of what taxes would be levied to pay such debt. If no decision is taken, the NG-EU programme would be paid through the EU budget, or what is the same, most of the grants would be paid by the very Member States receiving them. The redistributive impact, in that case, would be very small between states, and an uncertain among individuals qua nationals. If new taxes are collected, whether the NG-EU reinforces solidarity would depend on the distribution of the tax burden, on the very characteristic of those taxes.

Fifth, the NG-EU, much as with the Green Deal it contributes to fund, results not only in expenditure occurring at the EU level, as the EU level is being used to facilitate national expenditure that is intended to shape and mould the socio-economic structure in view of a number of objectives, crucial among them the speeding up of both digitalisation and climate neutrality. This sees the public sector not only shaping investment decisions, but also providing the finance to undertake them. The dismantling of state capacities to undertake such investments through publicly owned companies and structures renders it extremely probable that most of these expenditure will be channelled through private companies. This is being rendered possible by a 'flexible' interpretation of competition law, in particular, of the norms governing state aid. This implies a discontinuity with the 'Maastricht' constitution. But as already pointed when dealing with the Green Deal, the modus operandi is that of the derisking state. Public investment reduces private risk, while leaving untouched the prerogative of private actors to collect benefits.

4.3 A European industrial policy?

Industrial policy was not part and parcel of the competences assigned to the European Communities in the founding Treaties. A transfer of power in favour of supranational institutions on that matter was not considered as being needed to build the foundations of a European economic and political order. At least *not at the time*. Also, a determinant of such a decision was the disagreement around socio-economic visions, which also entailed major differences on how to shape industrial policy. The question was not so much whether or not to have an industrial policy (reconstruction and modernisation would have been inconceivable without them) but *how* to articulate it. The deep differences that divided the *democratic interventionists* and the *ordoliberals* at the national level were also projected to the supranational level. Keeping the competence at the national level would therefore help to avoid the disagreement becoming a major obstacle to the establishment and consolidation of the European Communities. The only provision that could be regarded as touching, even if indirectly, on industrial policy was Article 82 TEEC, which introduced a 'German exception' to competition rules: 'The provisions of this Title shall not form an obstacle to the application of measures taken in the Federal Republic of Germany to the extent that such measures are required in order to compensate for the economic disadvantages caused by the division of Germany to the economy of certain areas of the Federal Republic affected by that division'.[131]

In the 1960s and early 1970s, the development of community law, and in particular, of competition law, left its mark on the autonomy that Member States enjoyed to design their industrial policies. Having said that, the states' leeway was not seriously narrowed until the passing of the Single European Act. This was not least because the Treaty provisions on state aid were left largely unimplemented until the early 1980s and the development of national competition law was rather variable (Italy and France, the countries that were most keen to intervene, only introduced national statutes framing competition in the late 1980s and early 1990s). Proof of that can be found in the fact that the economic crisis of the 1970s resulted in massive national interventions to prevent deindustrialisation and layouts (with state still representing around 2 per cent of the EEC GDP in the 1980s). Indeed, it is at that time that we find the first attempts on the side of the Commission to lay the ground for forms of a supranational industrial policy,[132] not least in the steel sector.[133]

From the mid 1980s, however, the progressive triumph of neo-ordo-liberal ideas led to a point at which national industrial policies were scaled down, while the embryonic supranational industrial policy was essentially dismantled. Developments were very marked from the Treaty of Maastricht onwards. Some of the decisions taken were, at least at first sight, paradoxical. Industrial policy became part of the set of policies of the now European Union. At the same time, the meaning of industrial policy, in particular its substantive content, was redefined. This was at work in the three main changes that resulted from the entry into force of the Maastricht Treaty. First, we have the 'general provision' on industrial policy. The role of the Union as 'supportive' of national industrial policies was enshrined in Article 130 of the TEEC as amended by the Treaty of European Union (now Article 173 TFEU). The key sentence was contained in the first paragraph: 'The Community and the Member States shall ensure that the conditions necessary for the competitiveness of the Community's industry exist'. The meaning of that provision was further clarified when the actions to be developed were required to be in accordance with a 'a system of open and competitive markets'. Industrial policy was thus redefined in *marktkonform* (market-driven) terms, with the market increasingly understood as capable of self-adjusting. The last paragraph of Article 130 TEEC as then drafted left no doubts in that regard: 'This Title shall not provide a basis for the introduction by the Community of any measure which could lead to a

[131] See the referred Article 82 of the original Treaty on European Economic Community. The provision seems, however, not to have been much used, perhaps as a result of the strength of the German economy.

[132] SM Ramírez Pérez and S van de Scheur, 'The Evolution of the Law on Art 81 and Art 82: Ordoliberalism and its Keynesian Challenge', in KK Patel and H Schweitzer (eds.), *The Historical Foundations of EU Competition Law* (Oxford, Oxford University Press, 2013, 19–53).

[133] Y Mény, V Wright, M Rhodes, *The Politics of Steel: Western Europe and the Steel Industry in the Crisis Years (1974–1984)* (Berlin, Walter de Gruyter, 1987).

distortion of competition'. Second, regional policy was expanded via the introduction and development of cohesion and structural funds. In the framework defined by the just analysed Article 130 TEEC, the far from small amount of supranational funds were destined to be transformed into a 'competitiveness' oriented industrial policy with a territorial (essentially regional) basis.[134] Third, the 'East German' exception got rephrased. Article 82 TEEC, later 'renumbered' to 78, was kept, but given a new sense and meaning. During reconstruction, it could have provided an explicit basis for a 'competitiveness' oriented industrial policy at a rather vast scale. Instead, now it was largely used as a means to legalise the transfer of public funds to private enterprises at the same time that the Eastern German corporate structure was subordinated to the West.[135]

It can thus be said that the normative ethos of the Maastricht Treaty largely codified the socio-economic vision of neo-ordo-liberalism, according to which it was highly inefficient to have public actors second guessing market forces. Muscular state aid rules started to be applied in earnest by the Commission, under the assumption that the best possible industrial policy was to have no industrial policy at all.[136] States had perhaps a role to play in smoothing the social fallout of markets picking winners and losers (through *social* policy), but the Commission preferred that states refrained from determining the volume and direction of private investment (through *industrial* policy). In the actual world, a modicum of industrial policy would unavoidably exist. That should be developed *with a view to render the policy tendentially self-effacing*, once the temporary obstacles to a competitive private order were surmounted. As a matter of fact, levels of state aid declined through the 1990s and the 2000s, with the ECJ vigorously supporting the actions started by the Commission against the granting of state aid on the side of Member States.

Until the 'polycrisis' of the late 2000s, industrial policy remained rather constrained. The Lehmann Brothers' moment started to change things. The near collapse of international financial markets in September 2008 revived the spectre of the 1930s major economic and social crisis. Under such circumstances, national Treasuries intervened as means of last resort to 'rescue' financial and non-financial enterprises. On the one hand, such interventions followed the neo-ordo-liberal script. State actions were justified as 'last resort' and 'temporary' measures aimed

[134] MC Barbieri Góes and G Viesti. 'The Revival of Industrial Policies in the EU?' 37:2 (2024) *Review of Political Economy*, 344–68, available at doi:10.1080/09538259.2024.2368210.Barbieri/Viesti 348.

[135] Christina Wolf, 'The making and unmaking of uneven development: the role of anchor firms in creating and overcoming industrial decline in East Germany'(2025), *Journal of Economic Geography*, early view, available at https://doi.org/10.1093/jeg/lbaf055.

[136] Neglect was based on the intellectual obliteration of the history of industrial policy, which was for almost thirty years the policy that 'should not be named'. R Cherif and F Hasanov, 'The Return of the Policy That Shall Not Be Named: Principles of Industrial Policy', IMF Working Paper 2019/074, 26 March 2019, https://www.imf.org/en/Publications/WP/Issues/2019/03/26/The-Return-of-the-Policy-That-Shall-Not-Be-Named-Principles-of-Industrial-Policy-46710. The authors vindicate the past achievements of interventionist states, at the same time that contribute to the reframing of industrial policy in the mould of the 'derisking state'.

at protecting the market order from an (admittedly massive) market failure. States would do whatever it took, save from making use of the circumstances to radically change the social and economic system. In fact, when nationalising banks or companies the view remained that of an economic order based on private property. This was why, from the very first moment in which the state took control, the perspective was reprivatisation. Something that excluded a radical transformation of the way in which the companies were run and operated. On the other hand, the scale of the intervention was phenomenal. If the disbursement of state aid represented in 2007 a mere 0.5 per cent of the EU GDP, in 2008 it reached 2.2 per cent, and in 2009, 3.5 per cent. Or to say the same thing in a different way, a seven-fold increase in two years.

Even if the European Commission insisted on a rapid return to the pre-crisis framework, something had changed. It can be said that the second 'polycrisis' paved the way for the role of the state as the direct guarantor of the levels of private profitability through direct or indirect transfers to become a permanent feature of the EU policy order. The ambivalence toward the ongoing transformation was reflected in the first systematic blueprint of a European industrial policy, put forward by the European Commission in 2010. 'An Integrated Industrial Policy for the Globalisation Era: Putting Competitiveness and Sustainability at Centre Stage'.[137] While the text was clearly shaped by the growing concerns about 'de-industrialisation', which had been basically disregarded in the previous two decades out of a distorted understanding of the benefits of international trade, the two main tools that were considered to develop a European industrial policy were 'smart regulation' (ie, ensuring that all regulation fosters instead of hampers the competitiveness of European industry) and the improvement of access to private finance for business.[138] The rhetorics were thus formally in line with the neo-ordo-liberal approach. Industrial policy was imagined as a fully *marktkonform* policy. And yet, it is undeniable that it was not insignificant that *industrial policy* was back, and was linked to the themes of sustainability, which were not easy to contain within the neo-ordo-liberal framework.[139]

An additional factor added to the equation was the feeling, which became widespread during the 2010s, that the EU was falling behind in the technological revolution associated with that vague concept of 'digitalisation'. It became abundantly clear that the European Union had failed to fulfil the core objective it had set to itself in the Lisbon Agenda to make the EU 'the most competitive and dynamic knowledge-based economy in the world, capable of sustainable economic growth with more and better jobs and greater social cohesion'.[140] This contributed to add

[137] COM/2010/0614 final, 28 October 2010, available at https://eur-lex.europa.eu/legal-content/EN/TXT/HTML/?uri=CELEX:52010DC0614.

[138] Ibid, 5 and 7.

[139] See also the follow up, 'A Stronger European Industry for Growth and Economic Recovery Industrial Policy Communication Update', COM/2012/0582 final, available at https://eur-lex.europa.eu/legal-content/EN/TXT/HTML/?uri=CELEX:52012DC0582.

[140] 'Lisbon European Council 23 and 24 May 2000, Presidency Conclusions, available at https://www.europarl.europa.eu/summits/lis1_en.htm.

a second theme to the numerous calls for both opening the space for national industrial policies and developing a supranational one. Europe had to catch up, and this catching up was not going to happen spontaneously. Such development was later intertwined with the narrative about the 'strategic autonomy', occasionally declined as 'strategic sovereignty' of the European Union.[141] This admittedly vague talk was projected in 2019 into the EU's industrial policy. In that year, the Commission started to refer to the risk of the Union losing its 'digital sovereignty'.[142] This opinion was then repeated in several other documents.[143]

This is the perspective from which we need to consider both the Green Deal and the NG-EU Programme; and from early 2025, the so-called 'Readiness 2030'.[144] The key policy tool through which such initiatives ended up being implemented were the use of public money to 'steer' private investment. The collective goals of fighting climate change, achieving a successful digitalisation of European societies and since late 2024 becoming capable of defending Europe without relying on the United States,[145] justified interventionism, insofar as such interventionism also contributed to recreate the future economic order based on private property. While in principle there was no in-built preference for the favouring of private over public investment, three decades of dismantlement of state capacity, aggravated in the case of the countries that were eligible for a higher proportion of the grants and loans of EU-Next Generation by a targeted scaling down of the capacity of states to intervene, have resulted in the European funds being used as forms of state aid in which the costs of investment are socialised while the benefits are enjoyed by private corporations.

A similar conclusion can be reached regarding the different plans, yet to be implemented, which have been produced at the request of European institutions. The most famous of these, by a long stretch, is the so-called 'Draghi report'.[146] Its rapporteur, the former central banker, national technocrat and circumstantial prime minister Mario Draghi, left no doubts regarding the extent to which the document proposes a radical departure from neo-mercantilism and consequently from external growth as the key dynamising factor of European economies. In Draghi's view, Europe should now rely on internal growth. That factor in itself would require

[141] The turn of phrase was popularised by Emmanuel Macron. See 'Discours d'Emmanuel Macron pour une Europe souveraine, unie, démocratique', 26 September 2017, https://www.elysee.fr/front/pdf/elysee-module-795-fr.pdf.

[142] 'A Europe Fit for the Digital Age', https://commission.europa.eu/strategy-and-policy/priorities-2019-2024/europe-fit-digital-age_en.

[143] 'Technological trends and policies: Advanced Technologies for Industry', https://monitor-industrial-ecosystems.ec.europa.eu/sites/default/files/2021-01/EU%20Report%20-%20Technological%20trends%20and%20policies.pdf, p. 16.

[144] 'White Paper for European Defence—Readiness 2030', 6 March 2025, available at https://commission.europa.eu/document/download/e6d5db69-e0ab-4bec-9dc0-3867b4373019_en.

[145] See M Dani and A J Menéndez, 'The (not so) European talk on defence', 4:3 (2025) *European Law Open* 425–440.

[146] 'The Draghi Report on EU Competitiveness', https://commission.europa.eu/topics/eu-competitiveness/draghi-report_en. The report is actually made of two parts, the first delineating a 'competitiveness' strategy for Europe, and the second made of the 'in-depth analysis and recommendations'.

re-emphasising the need of massive new investments. Complementing Draghi's report, two rationales have been part of the case for (*marktkonform*) industrial policy in European debates since the 2010s. These are the danger of falling behind against competitors (China and the USA) and environmental sustainability (always understood in the narrow sense of fight against climate change). Add to this a third rationale: the *imperative* of becoming more self-reliant, which updates the topos of 'strategic autonomy' from the specific angle of a sort of geopolitical reading of the security threats Europe faces in the aftermath of the recrudescence of the war in Ukraine.[147] While the Draghi report is mostly written in the lexicon that has dominated European policy documents since the 1980s, it is clear that this last component exacerbates major tensions.

The report has one clear virtue, which is to offer a realistic quantification of the amount of resources that would be needed to try to achieve the goals it sets. Namely, an annual investment of €800 billion, or to put it a different way, 5 per cent of the EU GDP. There is a very solid reason why such investment should be undertaken mostly by the EU, and through European 'own resources', because investment at such scale, fragmented along national lines, would result in very different levels of investment in different states, with asymmetric implications for the competitiveness of companies. To keep on pretending that after a number of years we will keep on having something coming close to a levelled playing field would require a leap of the imagination beyond human capacity.

Despite that being the case, the actual plans being considered and debated at the European level point to a rather modest role of supranational institutions. This is clearly the case of the already mentioned Readiness 2030, or what is the same, the plans to embark the EU in a rearm programme. While at first sight this may seem to concern rather different matters, rearmament not only always has major industrial implications (the arms have to be produced) but in this case, institutional actors have confirmed the extent to which the *dual nature* of Readiness 2030 makes rearmament into the closest thing to a new European industrial policy. It is true that the European Commission has proposed, and got approved, a SAFE Regulation that will result, when implemented, in a sizeable common expenditure (€150 billion) at the European level. That is dwarfed, however, by the amounts to be spent by Member States. The expenditure has been facilitated by the convoluted process of a coordinated activation of the national escape clauses of the Stability and Growth Pact. The Commission envisages additional security and defence expenditure at the value of 1.5 per cent GDP of the Eurozone *annually*. The U-turn resulting from the (admittedly asymmetric) reform of the German Fundamental Law is closely related to that change. The fact that German authorities intend to spend much more than what is being envisaged under the coordinated activation

[147] The intertwinement between industrial policy and war economy was already visible in the first major intervention by Draghi in his post Prime Minister period. Cf. Draghi, 'On the path to fiscal union in the Eurozone', *The Economist*, 6 September 2023, available at https://www.economist.com/by-invitation/2023/09/06/mario-draghi-on-the-path-to-fiscal-union-in-the-euro-zone.

of national escape clauses is, to say the least, indicative of the weakness of centralised supranational control over the process.[148]

5. Conclusions

Recent scholarship has highlighted the extent to which the transformations that EU law has undergone in the last five years have resulted in major changes in the economic constitution of the EU. There is no doubt, as we saw in section III of this chapter, that the attempts at containing and overcoming the effects of the Covid-19 syndemic, what is too narrowly defined as the 'climate change' crisis, and the geopolitical shifts which are reconfiguring the world order, not least in its economic dimension, have brought important changes to the policy and the law of the European Union.

What I have contested in this chapter is that this change implies the abandonment of the neo-ordo-liberal vision that has dominated the European level of government since the late 1970s. At least for the time being, what is going on is something far more modest, namely a change of the means through which the far from new neo-ordoliberal vision is realised and sustained. The European state, either through the EU, through the Member States or through a combination of the two, is now expected not only to provide legal guarantees of the appropriation of wealth (through 'sound money' and economic freedoms) and to unleash private power (through deregulation), but crucially to 'derisk' corporate investments. Or to say the same thing a different way, Public Treasuries now assume a good deal of the costs of investments, while reserving most profits to private actors. Unsurprisingly, some of the 'tools' of postwar interventionism are being redeployed, following years in which even their invocation was regarded as anathema. This is clearly the case with 'industrial policy'. However, the purposes to which industrial policy is put are very different from those characteristic of democratic interventionism. This is evident by what is *not* being even debated in European discussions, be them in parliaments or in the public sphere. Namely, political intervention with a view to radically change the power balance in society, be it through public/social ownership of the means of production or through extensive interventions to reinforce the collective power of workers through democratic labour law. Conspicuously absent in the European debate is any ambition to transform socio-economic practices, arrangements and institutions in line with the regulatory ideal of the Democratic and Social state, contrary to what was the case in 1945. Interventions aimed at a deep transformation of the socio-economic order, even less so at laying the ground of transcending capitalism, are completely off bounds, again contrary to the postwar democratic constitutions. As has been argued in detail, especially in the last section of this chapter, what is being proposed is essentially the same old neo-ordo-liberal order, only *by other means*.

[148] Cf. Menéndez (n 7).

4

The Structure of Crisis Governance Through Constitutionalism: The New Legitimation Crisis and the Promise of a 'Constitutionally Reflexive Governance' in Conditions of 'Debt Constitutionalisation'

LEONE NIGLIA

1. Constitutionally Reflexive Governance Crisis as Legitimation Crisis and the Promise of 'Principled (Autonomy and Equality) Reflexive Constitutionalism'

The structure of crisis governance constitutionalism stands in an uncertain relationship between acting towards resolving the relevant steering problems on the one hand, and the interrogation of normative structures towards that purpose on the other. Let me explain:

Recalling *J. Habermas*' thoughts on crisis:

> By 'principles of organisation' I understand highly abstract regulations arising as emergent properties in improbable evolutionary steps and characterising, at each stage, a new level of development. Organisational principles limit the capacity of a society to learn without losing its identity. According to this definition, steering problems can have crisis effects – if (and only if) they cannot be resolved within the range of possibility that is circumscribed by the organisational principle of the society.[1]

[1] J Habermas, *Legitimation Crisis* (Cambridge, Polity Press, 1998, (Polity Press, 1988, reprinted 1992, translated by Thomas McCarthy), translation of J Habermas *Legitimationsprobleme im Spätkapitalismus* (Frankfurt, Suhrkamp Verlag, 1973).

My own identification of constitutional principles in this chapter and in chapter 9 attempts to explore a dimension entailed in the current crisis as to the exceptional/emergency[2] crisis governance remedies being taken, primarily the NextGenerationEU (NG-EU). The current chapter considers the constitutional crisis resolution capabilities that consist of a range of available, yet still not deployed, organisational principles in the face of the crisis-ridden steering problems as these threaten the existence of Europe (the EU) and of the State.[3]

We are experiencing crisis-produced structural alterations (asymmetries of power) as *system integration* steering problems that threaten the continued existence of the project of integration and of the States themselves, considering that the solidarity bonds at the core of the States are negatively affected, through the calling into question of *social integration* in terms of an 'impairment' of the relevant 'consensual foundations of the normative structures'. This is explained below in section 3. Recall that:

> . . . only when members of a society experience structural alterations as critical for continued existence and feel their social identity threatened can we speak of crises. Disturbances of system integration endanger continued existence only to the extent that social integration is at stake, that is, when the consensual foundations of normative structures are so much impaired that the society becomes anomie. Crisis states assume the form of a disintegration of social institutions'[4]

The extant asymmetries of power that undergird crisis[5] call for transformative constitutional-normative interventions that tackle and hopefully reverse them rather than keeping perspectives that aim at their stabilisation (as crisis irresolution).[6] I gather that the current political science and economic governance theories (Chapters 7–9), alongside with legalism,[7] only go towards legitimating stabilisation (power reproduction processes)[8] whenever they lack a deployment of the available constitutional materials understood as countering and limiting power through long standing constitutional principles (a condition I label 'a-constitutionality').

I aim at identifying these in-depth constitutional/institutional capabilities towards complementing and integrating the tenets of general constitutionalism

[2] On exceptionalism/emergency see above at Introduction and below and at Ch 5, 9.

[3] Including the UK as former Member State as increasingly once again engaging with continental European countries and the EU in the crisis context.

[4] Habermas, *Legitimation Crisis*, above, at p. 3. On disintegration and regional integration see L. Niglia, 'Regional Integration' in *Max Plank Encyclopedia of Comparative Constitutional Law 2025*, https://oxcon.ouplaw.com/display/10.1093/law-mpeccol/law-mpeccol-e449.

[5] See e.g. ch 3 by Menendez and Niglia, *AJCL*, 2020.

[6] Petersmann is more optimistic on the stabilisation effects of the EU crisis interventions (as to the 'social' see ch 2) whilst Menendez (ch 3) sees a real danger in the preservation of old austerity policies.

[7] On the relationship between legalism and governance theories see Part 3 and Chapter 9.

[8] In other words, they tend to be deferential positions.

adapted to crisis (chapters 2 and 3) and the theoretical tenets, which are somehow external to, and yet close to, institutionalised constitutional materials (chapters 5 and 6), without neglecting the lessons that come with governance theories, in the belief that intercepting the actual constitutional-governance capabilities requires an inquiry into the depths of constitutional organisation (understood as 'social integration' and not just as 'systemic integration').

Part 3 of this volume presents positions that lean more towards 'system integration' than 'social integration' given their readings through economics (economic variables) and political science (power variables) to which one must contrast the normative-constitutional capabilities deriving from Parts 1 and 2 towards complementing the economic and political science readings of the EU crisis intervention measures.[9]

This is what the perspective of discursive validity claims [*Geltungsansprüche*] can do: to reflexively identify constitutional principles (in chapter 9 I consider two of them: autonomy and equality)[10] that enable us to better tackle the steering problems from within the integration system (constitutional) with the effect of countering the dangers of disintegration.[11]

Note that in conditions of crisis '*organisational principles limit the capacity of a society to learn without losing its identity*' and that '*steering problems can have crisis effects – if (and only if) they cannot be resolved within the range of possibility that is circumscribed by the organisational principle of the society*', and, also, that the issues underlying crisis (the macro and micro asymmetries of power) can be tackled through consented-to organisational principles, that is constitutional equality and autonomy --- given these premises, by becoming aware and by adopting the constitutional tools of autonomy and equality we will move closer to a re-acquisition of the capacity to learn and act as European polity (a 'weak identity' of 'acting together'). To say it in another way: the visible organisational principles, as they connote the debate on crisis and governance, do not enable the resolution of the steering problems (crisis); yet, the constitutional heritage regarding emergency/exceptional situations contains other ways for coping with crisis, that is, equality and autonomy, through their potential for addressing the steering problems and for framing a new solidarity ('altruistic' as opposed to the legalistic interpretation as 'egoistic').[12]

[9] On the aspect of methodology (comparative) for doing the job of actively engaging with the heritage of constitutional principles see the next volumes in the series (post-legalistic deployment of comparative knowledge, and see L. Niglia, 'Regional Integration' in *Max Plank Encyclopedia of Comparative Constitutional Law 2025,* at https://oxcon.ouplaw.com/display/10.1093/law-mpeccol/law-mpeccol-e449).

[10] See below at ch 9, as complementary principles.

[11] L Niglia, *Regional Integration* 2025 https://oxcon.ouplaw.com/display/10.1093/law-mpeccol/law-mpeccol-e449 (on disintegration). On the grounding of validity claims in constitutional ordering see L Niglia, *The Structural Transformation of European Private Law. A Critique of Juridical Hermeneutics* (Hart Publishing, 2023). Compare the chapter by Priban.

[12] See eg P Hilpold, *Understanding Solidarity within EU law: An Analysis of the 'Islands of Solidarity' with particular regard to the Monetary Union.* 34 Yearbook of European Law (34) 2015, 257 (on 'altruistic' vs 'egoistic' solidarity).

This is what I label '*constitutionally reflexive governance*' as compound of autonomy, equality, solidarity.

Here, I refer the reader to chapter 9 where I say more about the content of principled reflexive constitutional governance. In that chapter, I juxtapose the systematic modalities through which the system of crisis governance operates in tackling the steering problems (by eliciting the ways in which the insiders describe these operations – as system integration) with the potential for social integration resources (principled constitutionalism) to tackle those steering problems: at that point it should become evident how crisis governance constitutionalism can 'govern' the extant asymmetries of power by carefully balancing the relevant factors.

I argue that, in dealing with the NG-EU elements of *ownership* and of the *conditionalities*, we need to introduce forms of balancing towards taking into account the interests of the State (under the normative constitutional categories of autonomy and equality) as part of moderating the condition of debt constitutionalisation (or the EU constitutionalisation of debt) initiated by the NG-EU as exceptional intervention. To the one-sided balancing contained in the Recovery and Resilience Facility (RRF) (the structure of the conditionalities and the power of the European Commission in overviewing and deciding over the 'correct' implementation of the national plans) we need to contrast the possibility of a plural kind of balancing that redeems and is informed by autonomy and equality.[13] Namely:

In mobilising the NG-EU financial resources, the States have been unable to do this on their own –– thanks to the notorious financial constraints descending both from the EU and from the financial markets' overseeing State behaviour regarding budgetary and financial stability, as well as from the contingency of their own actions explained as an inability to act in the face of contemporary crisis situations such as the pandemic without imposing burdens on the other Member States –[14] and, States have also given up their power to decide autonomously about that mobilisation,[15] with national parliaments voting in favour of the NG-EU under necessity

[13] On balancing, for a genealogy in the context of integration, see L Niglia et al. *The Foundations of European Private Law* (2011) and Niglia, *The Structural Transformation.*

[14] See on this latter point C Joerges Economic Constitutionalism and 'the political' of the 'economic' in in G Grégoire and X Miny (eds) *The Idea of Economic Constitution in Europe.*

[15] States have had to notify their acceptance of the Own Resources Decision: see Art 311(3) TFEU 'enter into force [once] it is approved by the Member States in accordance with their respective constitutional requirements'. Notably the Federal Constitutional Court rejected a preliminary injunction against the ratification of NG-EU which then entered into force in June 2021 once notification by all member states took place: see BVerfGE 157, 332 (see www.bundesverfassungsgericht.de/SharedDocs/Entscheidungen/EN/2021/04/rs20210415_2bvr054721en.html).

Notably the Second Senate of the Federal Constitutional Court rejected two constitutional complaints directed against the Act Ratifying the EU Own Resources Decision (Eigenmittelbeschluss-Ratifizierungsgesetz – ERatG): Judgment of 6 December 2022 - 2 BvR 547/21, 2 BvR 798/21and see in English language at https://www.bundesverfassungsgericht.de/SharedDocs/Pressemitteilungen/EN/2022/bvg22-103.html (The Act Ratifying the EU Own Resources Decision does not violate the complainants' right to democratic self-determination derived from Art. 38(1) first sentence of the Basic Law (Grundgesetz – GG) in conjunction with Art. 20(1) and (2) and Art. 79(3) GG. The 2020 EU Own Resources Decision does not manifestly exceed the current European integration agenda (Integrationsprogramm) and does not impair the overall budgetary responsibility of the Bundestag) also (the *Own Resources Decision* as ratified),[16] with the overall radical effect of *constitutionalising fiscal power through common debt from State to EU* (which I label EU 'debt constitutionalisation').

Whilst not creating an autonomous capacity to tax nor formally constituting and conferring on the EU full EU fiscal policy powers,[17] the NG-EU funding creates a new condition of administering common debt funds under the constraints of undertaking major structural reforms (with the formula of conditional lending, demand-driven funding)[18] which, I am arguing, calls for the need for constitutional rationality to balance and contain the newly autonomous (EU) power decisions, with a view to confer upon them a degree of legitimation which must involve, rather than exclude, the nation State interests.[19] Autonomy and equality

---

holding that '*a request for a preliminary ruling from the Court of Justice of the European Union (CJEU) is not necessary*.'

The extent of this giving up entails 'becoming a debtor' (as to the loans, but note that where loans and grants have been given together the States receiving them are accountable for both) and as such being obliged to return the loaned funding. Whilst many politicians and scholars have claimed that taking the loans is just 'good', on reflection it is about taking loans in conditions under which it may not be administratively possible to actually use part of them (no real administrative capacity) and may also produce new debt related to the fact that once a sum is spent on a project, the costs of keeping that project going on entail new costs (eg the case of kindergartens as part of the national plans' projects), let alone that taking a loan means to 'choose' to live on debt rather than to reduce debt (on the significance of debt as to State sovereignty in terms of prejudicing state autonomy, see J L Villacañas Berlanga Europa: de Habermas a Kant pasando por el populismo in L Niglia, *Europe and "Crisis"*, *European Papers*, Vol 3, 2018, 2, 601 with reference to I. Kant and note on fiscal power as liberty as to organisation C Joerges 'Economic Constitutionalism and 'the political' of the 'economic'' in in G Grégoire and X Miny (eds) *The Idea of Economic Constitution in Europe* at p 793, on the *'liberty to organise national life at will' as a democratic essential. Has this command been overruled by Europeanisation and globalisation? I suggest that we should care about its survival and that a survival is conceivable under a re-conceptualisation of European and international economic law as 'conflicts law'*.

[16] Reference is here made to the Own Resources Decision (ORD) (EU, Euratom) 2020/2053 (Next Generation EU), as unanimously adopted by the Council on 14 December 2020, as requiring ratification by all 27 of the EU Member States according to their own national constitutional rules (ratified by all Member States by 31 May 2021, and entered into force on 1 June 2021.

[17] This seems to be what stops scholarship from acknowledging what I call 'debt constitutionalisation'– an imperfect institutional arrangement such as debt brought at the EU level without establishing EU taxes nor full EU fiscal power formally constituted cannot make us blind to the complex reality of 'debt constitutionalisation'. Fiscal power alienated from the State level lives off in the negative state of being exceptional fiscal power transferred at the EU level as common debt through the NG-EU.

[18] See eg A Heritiers Quo Vadis, Europa? Five Paths, their Plausibility and Impact, RSC Working Papers 2021, at https://cadmus.eui.eu/server/api/core/bitstreams/6a08b00b-5a75-5a40-932a-2e1686c7cc89/content: 'Only more recently the pandemic Covid 19 crisis with its symmetric impact on all Member States and the ensuing economic crisis which are not considered to be self-inflicted, at the difference of the Eurozone crisis, brought a change of preferences of important decision-makers and resulted in the adoption of the Recovery and Resilience Facility of 2020 or Recovery Fund EU Next Generation on pooling debts and sell European bonds funded with EU own resources and market capitalisation (Wolff and Ladi 2020). In other words, we can observe a crisis-induced preference change in important member states regarding path one of deeper formal integration'. But here *the 'crisis-induced preference change'* is excessive in that the state have found themselves in a situation of 'emergency' when signing up to the NG/EU.

[19] Eg according to Heritiers *Quo Vadis, Europa? Five Paths, their Plausibility and Impact 'Kielmannsegg argues that the nation state has legitimation resources and solidarity resources that the EU does not command'* commenting on P von Kielmannsegg Graf, 2020, Europa Neu Denken. Podcast. *Frankfurter Allgemeine Zeitung*, 29.4.2020.

constitutional criteria go towards this necessary constitutional job to legitimise the necessity driven EU crisis determinations. Constitutionally reflexive governance, as I here introduce it as workable notion, is both a necessity and a choice for anyone wishing to keep a minimum of legitimation with regard to the major NG-EU spending decisions and related structural reforms.

* * *

Scholars believe that not creating an EU autonomous capacity to tax nor formally constituting full EU fiscal powers (political and economic)[20] would make us operate under a gap situation, which would in turn call for reforms, notably, it has been suggested, by Treaty changes as allegedly being the only tools capable of legitimating the reforms towards at least formally constituting full EU fiscal powers. Yet we do live under the conditions of a radical change of the economic constitution of the EU and of the Member States, which must be contained by way of constitutional rationality. One must therefore search for constitutionally organised principles that enable that job to be done.

In Chapter 9, I identify two such constitutional principles: applying constitutional autonomy and constitutional equality to the administration of the spending and of the related reforms meant as anti-emergency measures towards restoring the required and ineliminable legitimation balance of powers between the state and the EU.

As within States, constitutionalism has been producing anti-emergency measures towards restoring the legitimate conditions under which the state must operate, now it is necessary to Europeanise such measures by a re-constitutionalisation of 'debt constitutionalisation' if we are not to live under an economic constitutional regime only built on the legalistic premises of enabling power politics to do as it pleases unlimitedly through the exercise of exceptional powers by the relevant technocratic (Commission and experts including national experts), juristocratic (the CJEU, see the judgments Pringle and Gauweiler)[21] and executive (State) actors (as to the NG-EU national plans).

New policies – Keynesian[22] as opposed to neo-ordo-liberal[23] – are allegedly being advanced in a situation in which they lack a constitutional legitimation basis comparable to that of a standard constitutional federation. This is not a theoretical question but a question concerning the constitutional basis of the crisis interventions, which in turn calls for the job of reconstituting them on a credible constitutional basis. This can be done under the proposed autonomy (preserving a minimum of respect for national constitutional laws) and equality (ensuring

[20] Yet, notably, the distinction between monetary and political economic powers is blurred.

[21] See CJEU case 370/12 Pringle (holding the validity of the ESM); Gauweiler case 62/14 (holding the validity of the ECB operations for saving the euro).

[22] See ch 3.

[23] H Lokdam and MA Wilkinson, 'The European Economic Constitution in Crisis: A Conservative Transformation?', in G Grégoire and X Miny (eds), The Idea of Economic Constitution in Europe. Genealogy and Overview (Brill Nijhoff 2022) 458; also see chapter 3.

equal distribution) principles applicable to the administrative organisation of the NG-EU and to the relevant judicial control mechanisms.

Not to trust this legitimation potential of crisis governance constitutionalism would mean falling into the trap of a problematic situation that can be labelled 'constitutionalisation (debt) without constitutionalism' which is similar in form to what happened for long time in Europe regarding the so-called phenomenon of 'constitutionalisation without constitutionalism'.

Instead of the argument whereby emergency gives rise to forms of rigid and reified centralisation – presented in the Schmittian argument, declined in various directions, or in the neo-ordo-liberal criticism by Lockdam and Wilkinsson, or in the Hegelian state conception according to von Bongandy –[24] I am exploring the contrary constitutionalist experience of the 'living constitution' producing democracy-defence mechanisms that preserve the constitution in times of crisis as opposed to leaving the crisis measures intact and self-standing. These mechanisms I call the principles of autonomy and equality.

Moreover, autonomy and equality are correlated in that equality implies, according to Fredman, redistribution (adapting here: the actual financial conditions and, adapting, the actual financial conditions of the Member States) and recognition (adapting here: State constitutional law as self-government and the need to counter violence), and participation and transformation as structural change and accommodation.[25] I consider constitutional autonomy to be a constitutive dimension of constitutional integration without which, at least as things stand today, we cannot do, given that the State is the democratic unit of legitimation par excellence and the ineliminable parameter of democratic practices beyond the State – until and unless new forms of transnational legitimation emerge. Constitutional autonomy is related to equality in our context in the sense that it preserves the self-governmental element.[26] I foresee the possible application of equality and autonomy to the NG-EU as design and as implementation through measures at both the macro and the micro levels of asymmetries of power, an application I consider to be needed towards reversing the relevant and extant asymmetries of power. To deal with the NG-EU only in the vocabulary of 'governance' and of 'law' (primacy, effectiveness, sovereignty) – as if they were neutral and at best linked to an opaque, not really developed, and ultimately mystifying and justificatory notion of 'solidarity',[27] rather than necessarily open to the demands of equality and autonomy – would be to

[24] Respectively H Lokdam and MA ', above, 'The European Economic Constitution in Crisis; Menendez in Chapter 3 of this book; von Bongandy Society 2024.

[25] S Fredman *Discrimination Law* (Oxford, Oxford University Press, 2022 and ICON 2016). See now the application of the equality perspective to the case of veiling bans by S C Ibold *The added value of equality* (Baden-Baden, Nomos, 2025).

[26] See discussion below at Chapter 9 as to 'ownership' (to be differentiated from autonomy understood as self-government) and as to 'equality' (as to the asymmetries of power among the Member States towards the needed forms of 'reasonable accommodation' in settling the relations between Member States and the EU).

[27] See below at section on solidarity, for discussion of this point. On solidarity see also Menendez in this volume.

condemn us to subject ourselves to a constitutionalism by emergency that would be bound to destroy the conquests of constitutionalism made since post-war times. In my view, it is through these organisational principles that we can envisage an effective and normatively orientated way for dealing with and hopefully resolving the problem of governance under conditions of debt constitutionalisation. In other words, we need to rethink solidarity in terms of equality along the lines noted above. And I see the judgment of the CJEU on energy[28] as paradigmatically embodying that kind of framework of analysis in that it embraces balancing as key to resolving the conflicts between EU governance and state law (under 'solidarity balancing' as I discuss this in chapter 9).

* * *

Principled constitutionalism around autonomy and equality as discussed in this chapter is intelligible both in relation to the ordoliberal and to the social democratic readings of crisis governance. Namely:

If ordoliberal thinking is about protecting the social (as Petersmann argues in chapter 2)[29] then the question of whether the NG-EU manages, at the implementation stage, to achieve that objective, constitutionally, becomes central and the principled constitutionalist thesis that I am proposing is a way to look effectively into that pathway.

If democratic/social state thinking is the background to the thesis that at stake in EU crisis governance is an ordo-neo-liberal hybrid complex that preserves austerity (as Menendez argues in chapter 3) then this position must also subscribe to the Polanyian reading whereby counter-movements are and must be part of any crisis situation.[30] From this vantage point, the principled constitutionalist thesis as reflexive governance helps to unveil what the social means in practice as part of the engagement of constitutional actors towards reversing the relevant power asymmetries.

Moreover, the politics/law continuum, so central to various chapters in this book, cannot explain it all: one must also consider the relevance of hermeneutical material towards developing a 'reflexive governance' mode of tackling crisis situations in terms of social integration. In a sense, both the ordoliberal and the democratic/social traditions of thoughts are traceable to liberal and social thinking (Habermas)[31] with their irresolutions as to the delivery of the social as statist welfarist agenda in contemporary conditions of crisis, which now applies to their

[28] CJEU C-848/19 P Germany v Poland *ECLI:EU:C:2021:598:* see L Niglia, *The Dual Character* (manuscript 2026, on file with author).

[29] But there is no consensus in this: see H Lokdam and MA Wilkinson, 'The European Economic Constitution in Crisis: A Conservative Transformation?', in G Grégoire and X Miny (eds), The Idea of Economic Constitution in Europe. Genealogy and Overview (Brill Nijhoff, 2022) 458 and Chapter 3 in this book.

[30] K Polanyi, *The Great Transformation* (New York, Farrar & Rinehart, 1944).

[31] Habermas, *Legitimation Crisis*, above.

managing crisis conditions (and innovation), and is in need of reflexivity towards identifying ways for governing the relevant steering problems arising from such crises.

As to the contributions in Parts 2 and 3 of this book, principled constitutionalism focuses on the living law as applied in time of crisis and emergency, towards filling a gap from within constitutional thinking on crisis by bridging theories and the practice of constitutionalism through principles (autonomy, equality).

* * *

As to the thematising of the relevant principles for coping with crisis conditions so as to redeem or dismiss and call for modifying – on the basis of judicial review and public discussion through participatory fora – the work of the relevant administrative bodies, here one must apply the distinction between reflexive and non-reflexive learning positions, considering that the crisis predicament makes 'learning' more complex:[32]

> Non-reflexive learning takes place in action contexts in which implicitly raised theoretical and practical validity claims are naively taken for granted and accepted or rejected without discursive consideration. Reflexive learning takes place through discourses in which we thematise practical validity claims that have become problematic or have been rendered problematic through institutionalised doubt, and redeem or dismiss them on the basis of arguments. The level of learning which a social formation makes possible could depend upon whether the organisational principle of the society permits (a) differentiation between theoretical and practical questions and (b) transition from non-reflexive (prescientific) to reflexive learning.[33]

Once the relevant organisational principles have been identified, we will be able to proceed with the 'differentiation between theoretical and practical questions' and with the 'transition from non-reflexive (prescientific) to reflexive learning'.

* * *

Referring to a contribution by Hernández Andreu,[34] the thesis of constitutionally reflexive governance finds support in the notion of 'optimisation' understood as the critical need to optimise the use of the relevant resources. [35] Here, I uphold what can be labelled the constitutional optimisation thesis, which requires a deeper understanding of solidarity as engaging with the actual changing relationships; the

[32] See eg the chapter by Kuo in this book and see DA Innerarity, *A Theory of Complex Democracy* (London, Bloomsbury Academic, 2025).

[33] J Habermas, *Legitimation Crisis*, above.

[34] See J H Andreu *¿Que Hemos Aprendido De Las Crisis Economicas? Una Perpectiva Historica* (Delta, 2021).

[35] See such 'optimisation' as participatory, as discussed above at Niglia, Chapter 1.

above identified constitutional principles aim at enabling such 'optimisation' of constitutional materials towards the resolution of the steering problems – today's steering problems including climate change, digitisation, authoritarian constitutionalism within Europe and populism.[36]

2. A Contest of Approaches in a Contested Field: On Ordoliberal, Democratic/Social State and Reflexive Crisis Governance Constitutionalism vs. Legalist Crisis Governance Constitutionalism

2.1 A Contest of Approaches

Crisis 'governance constitutionalism' is not a monolith but a compound of conflicting narratives that mark a new paradigm of rethinking of (and of fragmentation of) the heritage of general constitutionalism as developed in the context of Europeanisation (both as ordoliberal and as democratic/social state).[37] By 'conflicting' I refer to the deep tensions between the rising crisis governance constitutionalism positions on the one hand, and constitutional legalism on the other.[38]

What I label constitutional legalism is the prevailing mode of reading and tackling crises through governance, against which the constitutional reawakening that this book aims at pursuing must be read. The ordoliberal and the democratic/social state positions, and the (autonomy and equality) principled/reflexive governance position, have in common their post-legalistic methodological approach. As against the neutralisation effects of legalism,[39] given its a priori justification of the NG-EU as part of the project of avoiding the relevant conflicts, here is the need instead to address the relevant redistributive issues ('redistributive Europe') through a post-legalistic approach, considering that legalism does not allow nor is interested in exercising a control over redistribution through funding. The minimal understanding of solidarity as principle is a constitutional concern for EU law scholarship only in relation to

[36] See Petersmann at ch 2 listing them including authoritarian constitutionalism within Europe and see Priban at ch 6 on populism. By adopting the perspective of crisis as steering problem we can include, comparatively speaking, under crisis governance also the cases of authoritarian constitutionalism and of constitutional populism. On the comparative method and constitutionalism, see L Niglia 'Regional Integration' in R Grote, F Lachenmann, R Wolfrum (eds) *Max Plank Encyclopedia of Comparative Constitutional Law* (Oxford, Oxford University Press, 2025) and L Niglia 'Private Law Public Law Divide' in R Grote, F Lachenmann, R Wolfrum (eds) *Max Plank Encyclopedia of Comparative Constitutional Law* (Oxford, Oxford University Press, 2025).

[37] See chapters 2 and 3 in this book.

[38] Here, I leave aside the obvious tensions between the three positions of ordoliberalism, social democratic and reflexive constitutionalism themselves (above all the characterisation of the former two for staying within the liberal and the social as opposed to principled constitutionalism as transcending both in their reflexive framing: see the thoughts of J Habermas on reflexivity vs. the liberal and the social) in that I focus on their common post-legalistic characterisation as 'crisis governance constitutionalism'.

[39] See at n 2 on 'constitutional legalism'.

the macro-issue of the act of borrowing and lending, arguing that the NG-EU is about implementing solidarity insofar as the mutual debt has been agreed upon, without considering the underlying asymmetric relations involved in that act nor the micro-issues of power asymmetries involved in how the funding is actually allocated and spent.[40]

Whilst Part 3 adds further material to this picture, including two more post-legalistic crisis governance constitutionalist positions, and two non-legal (political science and economic) positions that appear to end up reinforcing the legalistic view, in this chapter, I would like to expand more on constitutional legalism and on the possibility of overcoming it with a view to re-describing it towards clarifying the said tensions.

2.2 Constitutional legalism

Constitutional legalism in our context consists basically of interpreting the relevant Treaty articles (including Art 122, 125, 173 TFUE) with a view to justify the activities of the EU legislative institutions through their having enacted the NG-EU legislative measures. Against a block of Treaty articles normally interpreted – before the coming into force of the NG-EU – in the sense of barring any attempt at market correcting interventions, one now observes an emerging yet massive literature that reinterprets those very articles as enabling such interventions under the Treaty.[41] All is seen in this literature in terms of the legality/

[40] On the macro-issues see ch 3 Menendez in this book and L Niglia, 'The New Transformation of Europe. Arcana Imperii' (2020) 68 *American Journal of Comparative Law* 151. The macro- ('inverted solidarity', 'unequal relations', including the aspect of the eventuality for some states to not possess a real capacity to spend, see chapter 3 by Menendez) and micro- (distribution of the funds by who and to whom and how and with what effects) aspects are no doubt related (the social effects of the spending of the funding may go towards contributing to the objective of balancing macro-imbalances of power; I am referring here to the policy choices made regarding redistributing towards those who most need the funds (micro power asymmetries) and also in terms of the deadline for using the funds, eg extending it for the debtor states, and in terms of enabling on the part of the states a re-prioritisation of the objectives of ecology and of digitisation vis-à-vis those concerning the social (macro power asymmetries). Note eg the European Court of Auditors, review 02/2025: 'Performance-orientation, accountability and transparency – lessons to be learned from the weaknesses of the RRF', Publications Office of the European Union, 2025 at n 30 on risks of 'unequal treatment' across countries, which clearly calls for administrative and/or judicial corrective interventions and see also at nn 24–29 to which the framework of autonomy and equality should apply towards remedying these proportionally related questions of 'underperformance'.

[41] See for the legality of the NG-EU triad of legislative instruments as inaugurating a solidaristic and redistributive Union eg K Laenertz and S. Adam La solidarité, valeur commune aux États membres et principe fédératif de l'Union européenne, in *Cahiers de droit europeen* 57 2021 2, at p. 307 (on Articles 122, 123 and 125 TFUE, and with reference to the NG-EU at pp. 405–406, and viewing the NG-EU as justified insofar as being a concretisation of the principle of solidarity ex Art 3 (3) TUE); and see, for further views converging on the point of the legality of the NG-EU, B De Witte, 'Integration Through Funding: The Union's Finances as Policy Instrument'. In R Weber (Ed.) *The Financial Constitution of European Integration: Follow the Money?* (Oxford, Hart Publishing, 2023) pp. 221–236 (on Articles 8 to 13 TFUE as 'help remove any doubt'; then discussing the legal basis of the NG-EU, on the NG-EU as serving as a tool for fostering 'integration through funding'); The EU Council Legal Service, 'Opinion on the Proposals on Next Generation EU', 9062/20 (24 June 2020); G Merino, 'The Recovery Plan: Solidarity and the living constitution', EU law live, 6 March 2021,Weekend Edition N° 50 (2021), at 1:

illegality paradigm in relation to the relevant Treaty articles (Articles 122, 125, 173 TFUE) and therefore as a form of 'constitutionalist crisis governance' that neglects the above noted reflexive conditions as well as the tenets of democratic based normative constitutionalism.[42]

The neutralisation effects of legalism consist of a configuration whereby it does not really matter what happens at the implementation stage as far as solidarity is concerned when instead it is the implementation stage that make solidarity intelligible in the making.

2.3 Beyond constitutional legalism

We can describe crisis governance constitutionalism as a path towards taking distance from legalism and tackling the crisis demands as a concrete challenge to be faced on the ground. As a result, crisis governance constitutionalism unfolds as a manifestation of a post-legalistic mode of analysis and action that aims at gaining knowledge about the actual impact of the NG-EU funding and the actual redistribution under the aspects of *to whom, by whom and how* in the context of the range of missions as identified in the national plans.

Moreover, solidarity should be seen, in post-legalistic mode, not as an abstraction that validates it all as a priori justification, as with the legalistic position, but as in need of concrete steps towards assessing the ways it is articulated on the ground (ie, the implementation of the NG-EU) in that, as solidarity embodies many meanings, one must assess how actors are implementing it – as egoistic or as altruistic: to mention one key aspect of the debate about solidarity.[43] The latter

---

'The EU's response to the COVID-19 crisis can be qualified as historic and commensurate to the gravity of the circumstances. . . . it consists of a very innovative legal architecture. Yet, ***however historic and unprecedented it may be, the so-called recovery plan, also known as the Next Generation EU (NGEU) is solidly founded in the Treaties****'*. [Emphasis added].

On a similar understanding regarding Art 175 TFUE as the legal basis of the RRF see B De Witte *Integration Through Funding*, above. See also von Bongandy at p 156: '*The EU's measures in response to the COVID-19 pandemic could propel this transformation by significantly advancing European solidarity*', and '*Such transformations require doctrinal reconstructions that imbue the Union's economic and monetary constitution with the principles of Article 2 TEU, Article 3(3) TEU, Article 119 TFEU, and the provisions concretising them should be interpreted in the light of Articles 2 and 3(1) TEU*'.

Note the Opinion of AG Campos Sánchez-Bordona in the judgment C-848/19 P Germany v Poland ECLI:EU:C:2021:598 *('The adoption at the European Council of 10 and 11 December 2020 of the Multiannual Financial Framework 2021-2027 and the European Union Recovery Facility (Next Generation EU) is arguably the biggest step forward in terms of solidarity which the European Union has taken in its history')* and, in another context, the CJEU on solidarity seen as one of the fundamental principles of EU law in the judgment C-848/19 P Germany Poland ECLI:EU:C:2021:598, para 39.

In political science studies, see Fabbrini, Sergio; Buti, Marco. (2023). Next generation EU and the future of economic governance: towards a paradigm change or just a big one-off?. Journal of European Public Policy, (ISSN: 1350-1763), 30:4, 676–695 (on the 'exogenous' nature of the crisis, induced by the pandemic, as having helped promote a narrative based on collective solidarity, rather than on individual national interest).

[42] See eg chapters 4 and 5 and 6.

[43] See eg P Hilpold, 'Understanding Solidarity within EU Law: An Analysis of the 'Islands of Solidarity' with Particular Regard to Monetary Union', 34.1 (2015): yev02 *Yearbook of European law*.

(altruistic solidarity) is the position I am defending and it seems to me that the other declinations of crisis governance constitutionalism take a similar position on this point: the ordoliberal view of Petersmann regarding its support for the social; the democratic/social view with its attention to the need for reversing the relevant asymmetric power configurations; and the public sphere positions held by Kuo and by Priban who point our attention to the central relevance of the collective.[44]

The determinations of the EU Commission as to the national plans, their renegotiations and eventual amendments, and their assessment of the achievement of the relevant targets and milestones, should be justiciable in the specific constitutional sense of being subject to the principles of constitutional autonomy and equality through balancing these principles with the requirements of *relevance, effectiveness, efficiency and coherence of the recovery and resilience plan* as stated in the RRF.[45] The disciplinary character of the conditionalities should be turned around into an assessment by balancing. I have labelled this mode of judicial review 'solidarity balancing'[46] as meaning an understanding of solidarity as technique that enables the constitutional respect for autonomy and for equality. Chapter 9 further illustrates this argument by looking at the details of the RRF.

3. Conclusion

The remainder of this book aims at mapping further declinations of crisis governance constitutionalism.

The thesis that I am here proposing of a 'Constitutionally Reflexive Governance' stands in between recovering and adapting constitutional material (institutional, as discussed in chapters 2 and 3, and normative, as in chapters 4 and 5) and capturing the principled normativity that enables fully deploying the resources for crisis resolution from within the plural tradition of constitutionalism (and not just EU). This thesis is then contrasted in Part 3 with the governance theories that lean towards system integration materials that are rehearsed in a way not yet fully aware of the constitutional organisational heritage regarding crisis situations. Two chapters (7 and 8) expose this position whilst chapter 9 draws on crisis governance constitutionalism towards re-reading these positions as to their *a-constitutional* characterisation and potential for constitutionalisation.

[44] Whether experimentalism, as discussed at chapter 9, is characterised by and can give rise to forms of altruistic solidarity, is an open question: for my view on experimentalism as democratically (reflexively) justifiable however under what I call constitutional guidance: see below at ch 9.

[45] Art 19 c 3 of the RRF: 'The Commission shall assess the relevance, effectiveness, efficiency and coherence of the recovery and resilience plan and, for that purpose, shall take into account the following criteria which it shall apply in accordance with Annex V'.

[46] L Niglia, *The Dual Character of Solidarity* (manuscript 2026).

INTRODUCTION TO PART 2

Crisis Governance Constitutionalism: The Public Sphere and the Normative Political Dimensions

LEONE NIGLIA

As constitutionalism is mutating into crisis governance constitutionalism, to its ordoliberal, democratic/social, (autonomy and equality) principled reflexive, and legalistic declinations are to be added two more theoretical views whose focus is on the public sphere and on the normative political.

Again, these two further analyses must be contrasted to the legalistic position and can be labelled as post-legalistic in the same way as the ordoliberal, the democratic/social and the (autonomy and equality) principled reflexive. To the arguments of an epochal decline of the public sphere the two chapters in this part 'respond' with a renewed faith placed in the role of the public sphere and in the normative political as part of the rising crisis governance constitutionalism understood as constructive reaction to the doings of crisis governance. Where crisis is associated with the disappearance of the public sphere here the two authors reinstate trust in the central place of the public sphere in times of crisis governance. And, where crisis is associated with the argument about democracy as not able to cope with it[1] here normative constitutionalism is relied on to try the opposite argument.

Critical scholars have noted the need for a *transnational* democracy,[2] which the chapters in this book touch upon, with chapters 4 and 5 clarifying the aspects of the role of public sphere and of normative constitutionalism, and of the mediation of constitutional categories, thus going towards attempting at filling a gap: there is need to contextualise the arguments about a transnational democracy as basis for governing crisis transnationally in relation to the current crisis situations.

In his *Post-Constitutional Crisis, Democratic Governance and the European public spheres: on the concept of EU constitutional demoicracy* Priban puts forwards arguments about the public sphere understood as *European demoicracy* that go

[1] See eg DA Innerarity, *A Theory of Complex Democracy* (London, Bloomsbury Academic, 2025).

[2] C Joerges Economic Constitutionalism and 'the political' of the 'economic' in in G Grégoire and X Miny (eds) *The Idea of Economic Constitution in Europe.*

towards reinforcing the potential for a constitutionalism that takes seriously a range of principles (such as representation, *quod omnes tangit* principle, 'epistemic subsidiarity') so as to tackle the crisis steering problems by making us aware once more about the available constitutional resources for limiting the doings of power politics. In my view[3] Priban contributes to thinking about the needed space of a possible EU constitutional demoicracy by rethinking any self-referential conception of reflexivity, for his arguments for the need to 'translate … specific expert knowledge to the generally shared rules and normative regimes' that should connote the 'legitimate demoi' share a common ground with what I propose in this book as the autonomy/equality constitutionally reflexive framework, and by opening up to a new way of seeing populism ('*need to move beyond its normative depictions as either the ultimate danger of constitutional democracy, or the most effective remedy of its current crisis*') as opposed to only focusing on its 'negative' aspects (e.g. impact on the rule of law). Here conflicts are seen positively as enhancing democracy, not dissimilarity to and thus falling in the tradition of the works of C Joerges and of G Teubner with their respective references to the opus of J Habermas and of N Luhmann. In my view this is about focusing on the space dimension of crisis governance through constitutionalism, though, with regard to Priban's chapter, one should consider that what I label reflexive governance reflects a 'dual constituent' legitimation rather than the demoicratic view of the one only legitimation from the bottom.[4]

The following statement illustrates the articulation of what I label crisis governance constitutionalism in the version discussed in Priban's chapter:

The EU's transnational constitutionalism subsequently offers responses to the rising constitutional populism, most notably through the emergence of the plurality of European public spheres and demoicracy. Without the constitution of an anti-explosive and anti-populist transnational and democratically legitimised community, further enhancement of power of EU institutions and their forms of democratically limiting and limited governance will always lead to the populist backlash at national and local levels of its Member States. Transnational European constitutionalism thus can integrate elements of constitutional populism while preserving the European integration's initial critique of the imaginary of nations living authentically and exclusively in their states.

Arguments about emergency, in the chapter by Kuo, go towards reinforcing the potential for constitutionalism to tackle the steering problems by stressing the problem of the need for governance to be based on any available (in terms of the timing needed) knowledge rather than on limited-in-time gathered information. From the vantage point of my view about reflexive governance, this take contributes towards thinking about the latter's time dimension.

[3] See ch 1, 4, 9.

[4] See J Habermas, *The Crisis of the European Union* (Polity, 2012); K Nicolaidis 'The Idea of European 'Demoicracy'; in Julie Dickson and Pavlos Eleftheriadis (eds.) *Philosophical Foundations of European Union Law*. (Oxford, Oxford University Press, 2012).

The following statements are representative of what I label crisis governance constitutionalism in the version discussed in Kuo's chapter, in a declination of it as executive constitutionalism:

> ... a two-part argument. The first part concerns the tension between constitutionalism and crisis governance in general; the second focuses on the emergence of executive constitutionalism in the EU from its responses to the euro crisis to the Covid pandemic emergency and beyond. Taking on the question of time in constitutional governance, I argue that how to manage the intertemporal conflict between the state of exception/emergency and that of normalcy lies at the core of the constitutional domestication of emergency powers and holds the key to the prognosis of executive aggrandisement in increasingly crisis-minded governance; yet, driven by successive crises, the recent changes to the EU's constitutional configuration results from an 'always present' executive-led race against time, heralding the culmination of executive constitutionalism that is set in a temporality structured by the fast-changing financial market and the highly contagious SARS-CoV-2 – which is distinct from the steady-paced temporal order of democratic dynamics that incubate normative political constitutionalism.

And:

> Recognising the 'political' character of the EU's crisis-induced reform, I questioned the characterisation of such constitution-reshaping in terms of political constitutionalism. Instead, I suggested that the EU's crisis-driven constitution-reshaping reflects executive constitutionalism, whose speedy, rapid-fire character renders its attendant constitutional reform dubious.

Here then crisis governance constitutionalism amounts to control and disciplining devoid of the characterisation of 'normal' constitutionalism. Under this view it appears that the state of experimentalism-as-implementation through the NGEU – seen by Zeitlin et al. in a positive light, that is, as reinforcing national ownership[5] – paves in comparison as it becomes only an instance of executive constitutionalism whenever based on information not acquired in the due time or, otherwise said, in knowledge not adequate for constitutional deliberation. The recent reflection coming out of the EU Court of Auditors illustrates

[5] For my view on experimentalism as democratically (reflexively) orientated however under what I call constitutional guidance, see below at ch 9. For my understanding of experimentalism through the NG-EU as in the chapter by Zeitlin et al see below at introduction to part 3.

the cogency of this criticism as an implicit call for any experimentalism-as-implementation through the NGEU to be informative as part of the however deeper argument from constitutional guidance that I make in chapters 4 and 9.[6]

[6] See at https://www.eca.europa.eu/en/news/NEWS-RV-2025-02 the EU court of auditors criticising the RRF/recovery fund for a lack of transparency as to ITS results and as to the related actual costs, in their review of 8 April 2025: Ivana Maletić, named at the above link as 'one of the two ECA Members behind the review' holds that '*EU policymakers must draw lessons from the RRF, and not allow any future similar instrument without having information on actual costs, final recipients and a clear answer to the question of what the citizens actually get for their money,*' and, in the opinion of Jorg Kristijan Petrovič, the review's co-author '*For future performance-based budgets, funding must be better linked to results and clearly defined rules, otherwise such a system should not be used*'.

5

Post-Constitutional Crisis, Democratic Governance and the European Public Spheres: On the Concept of EU Constitutional Demoicracy*

JIŘÍ PŘIBÁŇ

1. Introduction

The post-1945 history and general process of European integration and its legal and political forms offer a unique opportunity to study constitutionalism beyond structural and semantic limitations of the modern nation state. Recent crises of transnational European society and even its limited disintegration caused by the United Kingdom's withdrawal from the EU further illustrate polyvalence and polysemy of constitutionalism beyond modern statehood.

Like the modern nation states, the history of transnational European integration has been informed by two general political goals, namely economic prosperity and social stability. These goals are formulated through imaginaries,[1] which are also typical of the nation states, that is market as free exchange of mutual advantages and benefits, rights equally shared by their subjects and power democratically accountable and operating and conditioned by the public sphere. However, these typically modern liberal imaginaries cannot be simply translated from the nation state to the transnational supra-state constitutional structures of the EU, which are expected to be socially and morally pluralistic, efficiently and rationally governed, economically prosperous and sufficiently democratised to challenge populist and illiberal responses to the European integration.

*This chapter integrates revised versions of the first and final chapters of the monograph *Constitutional Imaginaries: A Theory of European Societal Constitutionalism* (London, Routledge 2022).

[1] For the concept of social imaginaries, see C Taylor, *Modern Social Imaginaries* (Durham NC, Duke University Press, 2004); for the emerging concept of constitutional imaginaries, see particularly J Přibáň, *Constitutional Imaginaries: A Theory of European Societal Constitutionalism* (London, Routledge, 2022); J Komárek (ed), *European Constitutional Imaginaries* (Oxford, Oxford University Press, 2023); M Belov (ed), *Legal Imaginaries of Crisis and Fear* (London, Routledge, 2025).

The rise of populism is a consequence of recent transnational economic and political crises and growing public distrust of technocracy and expert knowledge. Populist politics draws on public anger vis-a-vis growing economic insecurity and the general failure of anti-majoritarian institutions to address issues of social justice and equality. However, populists mainly exploit the framework of constitutional democracy without dissolving and replacing it with a different political regime. Their politics thus remain the subject of political contestations and opposition challenges in free elections. Nevertheless, some populists seized the opportunity to challenge this constitutional order and transformed into full-scale autocrats by reconstituting their power, such as the Hungarian Prime Minister Viktor Orbán whose rule transformed Hungary into the illiberal clientelist state in the last two decades.

The problem of constitutional populism and transnational democratic governance, therefore, needs to be addressed as both self-identification of democratic polity and style of power that increases the risk of constitutional regime changes. Theoretical inquiries into populism need to move beyond its normative depictions as either the ultimate danger of constitutional democracy, or the most effective remedy of its current crisis.

Populism evolving in individual Member States of the EU is both power formation and polity's self-identification and self-constitution.[2] Different forms and ideologies of populism and their constitutional risks and excesses, rather than being considered as external destabilising threats, can be treated as an intrinsic part of constitutional democracy. In explorations of post-constitutional crises, democratic governance and European politics, the typically democratic imaginary of the public sphere is distinguished from the imaginary of the authentic polity in which constituent power of the people is protected against the corrupting effect of representative institutions and their forms of governance.

The promise of authenticity is behind the recent political crisis and the resurgence of populism in the EU and its Member States and the constitution of what Zygmunt Bauman described as 'explosive communities'.[3] The EU's transnational constitutionalism subsequently offers responses to the rising constitutional populism, most notably through the emergence of the plurality of European public spheres and demoicracy. Without the constitution of an anti-explosive and anti-populist transnational and democratically legitimised community, further enhancement of power of EU institutions and their forms of democratically limiting and limited governance will always lead to populist backlash at national and local levels of its Member States. Transnational European constitutionalism thus can integrate elements of constitutional populism while preserving the European integration's initial critique of the imaginary of nations living authentically and exclusively in their States.

[2] T Donnelly, 'Making Popular Constitutionalism Work' (2012) *Wisconsin Law Review* 159–94, 161–162.

[3] Z Bauman, *Liquid Modernity* (Cambridge, Polity Press, 2000), 193–199.

2. Democratic governance, constitutional statehood and the public sphere

In the context of democratic constitutional politics, the general possibility of a legitimate political order depends on the imaginary of collective self-rule. The constitution of modern society as a community of democratic values and self-governing people has coevolved with the imaginary of the public sphere.

The public sphere imagines moral bonds and mutual obligations of members of political society through the constitution of a pluralistic space open to contestable opinions and reasonable arguments of all members of society.[4] It draws on the idea of moral order constituted by the belief that individuals participating in this sphere are equal and enjoy freedoms and rights limiting government.[5] Political power thus needs to be consented to by those subject to it and to be legitimised by its societal benefits constituted through the public sphere.

This differentiation between political order constituted by power and societal order constituted by mutual benefits and expectations of individuals communicated through the public sphere is typical of modern democratic societies. Using the image of modernity as social differentiation, Taylor considers the public sphere a dimension of civil society differentiated from the polity with its governmental power. Like the market economy, the public sphere constitutes a common space evolving independently of political power and communicating through other media and forms of disciplinisation of individuals.

Furthermore, the public sphere imaginary introduces the idea of a common space in which people can share opinions, beliefs and actions and reach a common mind constituting the social and moral order. As Taylor, following Habermas, states: 'So what the public sphere does is enable the society to come to a common mind, without the mediation of the political sphere, in a discourse of reason outside power, which nevertheless is normative for power'.[6]

In short, it is the imaginary of commonality that constitutes collective identity through social communication and independently of the political system and its institutions. At the same time, its function is to limit and legitimise political power by something outside the political system.

The public sphere is to facilitate free discussion and the identification of social problems as political ones. Structures of the public sphere are expected to transform diverse and conflictual views into rational judgements and political consensus. As Jürgen Habermas observed, public opinion was imagined as constitutive force of reason limiting political power by the authority of reason and thus

[4] J Habermas, *The Structural Transformation of the Public Sphere* (Cambridge, Polity, 1989) 239.

[5] P M Garry, *Limited Government and the Bill of Rights* (Columbia MO, University of Missouri Press, 2012).

[6] Taylor, supra n. 1, 91.

transforming the Hobbesian *auctoritas non veritas facit legem* into the Kantian *veritas non auctoritas facit legem*.[7]

The force of reason gets communicated through the public sphere and opinion and subsequently legislated for and constituted as the democratic rule of law. It legitimises operations of politics including the state organisation and its legal constitution signifies a profound shift in constitutional politics, especially the problem of political representation. It becomes a matter of public knowledge representing the sovereign reason. Instead of expressing the sovereign subject's will as constituent power, representative bodies of the political constitution are expected to represent knowledge constituted by the primarily non-political public sphere and validated by reason.

Democratic constitutional power represents its people through knowledge of their political interests, preferences and views constituted by public debates and opinion. The public sphere thus becomes an imaginary of societal limitation and non-political control of political power constituted by the modern state. The public sphere represents civil society as a subsystem of particular social and economic needs and interests and transforms it into the plurality of public opinion which, however, operates as the source of legitimacy of the constitutional state in its unity. It is imagined as the representation of society and its democratic ethics of non-domination, participation, civility and tolerance that externally constitute and internally control hierarchical structures of the state and other political institutions, such as political parties and public media.

Public opinion is the medium of societal power that constantly communicates social problems to the constitutional representative bodies and demands their political solutions. Direct expressions of the popular will can thus only be formulated as indirect societal representations constituted as general opinion by the public sphere. This check and balance between opinionated civil society and open-minded constitutional politics makes democratic regimes more flexible and reflective of their social environment.

For Habermas, Taylor and others, the public sphere functions as an external societal guarantor of limitation (and therefore legitimation) of political power by public opinion. Legitimacy is not a matter of internal procedures. It is secured through external normative criteria constituted and protected by the public sphere. Its space of public discussion and critical scrutiny is constituted outside political power, yet this power is expected to listen to the public sphere's voices and opinion. While non-political in the sense of being constituted outside the system of political institutions, the public sphere, nevertheless, exercises societal power over politics and directly leads to another typically modern social imaginary, the imaginary of the self-governing and self-constituting people.

The public sphere is considered a 'metatopical space' that, according to Taylor, 'constituted a metatopical agency, but one that was understood to exist

[7] J Habermas, *The Structural Transformation of the Public Sphere* (Cambridge, Polity, 1989) 53, 82.

independent of the political constitution of society'.[8] This constituent power of the public sphere as a common agency and societal force legitimising the political constitution depends on its capacity to simultaneously communicate different themes related to individual and collective interests and opinions. However, this appeal of heterogeneity also paradoxically presumes the possibility of value homogeneity and moral commonality, which dominate many classic and recent theories of modern constitutionalism.

The public sphere imaginary thus constitutes non-political moral and societal forces that push the modern individual to accept and conform to this social order and to obey its rules. Modern individualism turns out to be the very essence of collective social pressure and the power of morally justified social norms precedes political power operating through legal norms and the rule of law. The public sphere limits political power and gradually transforms it into democratic government of the people, by the people and for the people. The imaginary of the public sphere thus becomes inseparable from the imaginary of the sovereign self-governing people.

3. Truth and falsity: On the imaginary of authenticity in constitutional politics

The imaginary of one people living under one rule of law assumes normative limitations of political power as much as its constitution through democratic mobilisation. It is exactly in this sense that modern populism in all its varieties and forms, from ethno-nationalist to inter-nationalist, is an intrinsic part of democratic societies.

The public sphere is a theatre of permanent conflicts between different values shared in different regimes of the soft *doxa* of public opinion that never have a clear-cut rational solution, but for all that, claim permanent validity. The technocratic sphere, on the other hand, is an expanse of clear, but always temporary, solutions of the *episteme* – expert knowledge.

The distinction between expert knowledge and public opinion is an intrinsic part of modern democratic constitutionalism that draws on the imaginary of the public sphere. However, the populist critique of expert knowledge is also informed by another constitutional imaginary, namely *the imaginary of authenticity* of polity's existence and the claim of political living in truth.

Like every imaginary, the imaginary of authentic polity finds its counterpoint in the negative process of alienation.[9] Any polity striving to constitute its authentic being is allegedly under the permanent risk of alienation separating the political constitution from its true self-expression. Categories of truth and falsity thus

[8] Ibid, 99.
[9] R Jaeggi, *Alienation* (New York, Columbia University Press, 2014).

permeate the systems of politics and law and redraw the imaginary of constitutional polity as an authentic community of shared values.[10]

The original tension of constitutional politics between the populist and expert reason thus gets the secondary coding of the distinction between authenticity and alienation. Authenticity is another name for truth and honesty while alienation is marked by falsity and corruption. The process of legitimation by democratic mobilisation is subsequently conditioned by the possibility of self-identification of members with the true nature of their imagined polity.

The truth/falsity distinction also affects imaginaries of different social systems and, for example, in Marxism amounts to the distinction between alienating forces of the market rationality which allegedly have to be confronted by a common political will and revolutionary action.[11] However, the contrast between the market forces and a socially authentic and ethically meaningful life commonly permeates a great variety of critical theories, including Habermas's theory of communicative action and discourse ethics.[12]

The imaginary of authenticity, introduced to the public life by the Romantics in the 19th century, radicalised the democratic identity question by asking who we *really* are as one polity. The principle of representation of nations through states thus became a matter of irresolution because state institutions, socially constructed and politically encoded through power, became considered to be both expressing and distorting the authentic will of the people and the true spirit of the nation.

Modern political constitution-making thus became inseparable from societal expectations of authentic self-expression, self-determination and self-elevation of the popular will through constitutional politics. However, this historically new imaginary of authenticity of collective identity, expressed through representative political institutions, is constituted by the paradox of permanent coeval normative expectations and factual deficits of representative bodies, such as parliaments, to correctly represent what people think, want and struggle for in their collective existence.

Appeals to 'the real will of the people' or 'the silent majority' are as old as democracy itself and populists can hardly claim their invention.[13] The imaginary of authenticity has been an intrinsic part of democratic political mobilisation as much as criticisms of the power holders and their institutions as failing to speak the people's voice. The argument from the real and authentic will of the people then often bears a hallmark of 'the True Scotsman Fallacy'.[14]

[10] D Schecter, *Sovereign States Or Political Communities?: Civil Society and Contemporary Politics* (Manchester, Manchester University Press, 2000) 112.

[11] C Castoriadis, *The Imaginary Institution of Society* (Cambridge MA, The MIT Press, 1987) 101–112.

[12] J Habermas, *The Theory of Communicative Action, Volume 2: The Critique of Functionalist Reason* (Cambridge, Polity, 1987) 332–373.

[13] A von der Goltz and B Waldschmidt-Nelson, *Inventing the Silent Majority in Western Europe and the United States: Conservatism in the 1960s and 1970s* (Cambridge, Cambridge University Press, 2017).

[14] The fallacy, which is a popular version of the argumentative attempt to protect a universal generalisation from counterexamples by changing the definition in an ad hoc fashion to exclude the counterexample, unfolds in these steps: 'No Scotsman eats sugar with his porridge'; 'My uncle Angus is a Scotsman, and he eats sugar with his porridge'; 'Ah, but no *true* Scotsman eats sugar with his porridge'.

However, the imaginary of authenticity involves one particular risk, namely turning the problem of political representation into the question of corruption of common values and the popular will. Populists of all kinds more or less successfully exploit this moralistic appeal of authenticity and use it to delegitimise the establishment or political opposition as morally corrupt and obstructing the will and welfare of the people.[15] Any political conflict thus can be personalised and turned into a matter of moral corruption of politics which, according to the authenticity imaginary, always has to express the 'real' interests and 'true' values of polity of 'shared destiny'.

Furthermore, this existential concept of constitutional politics and identity draws on the images of threats and enemies. Who the real people are and who is identified as their enemy have always been strategic questions behind political operations of both the powerful governments and the powerless opposition or dissent. The imaginary of authenticity is used as a reference to the mystical body of constituent power betrayed by procedures and outcomes of 'the system'. Opposition can question, for instance, election results as manipulated or achieved through the misrepresenting electoral system. The normativity of constitution can be presented as just a machinery that safeguards the interests of the power elite. On the other hand, those in power can claim to speak on behalf of the people and protect their real interests against the opposition, which is the enemy of the people financed by those threatening its homeland, national identity, revolution, etc.

The imaginary of authenticity contradicts the imaginary of the public sphere. It portrays polity as a collective person that stands in contrast to the impersonal rules of public life. Authentic community promises personal bonds and feeling of collective togetherness, which is all but ignored by societal structures of standardised and ritualised public action. It is in this context that Richard Sennett reformulated the classic sociological distinction between heart-warming personal community and rationally cold impersonal society by stating that, in modern politics and culture of authenticity 'community becomes a weapon against society'.[16]

According to Sennett, the imaginary of authenticity leads to the tribalisation of modern democratic politics and the destruction of the public sphere by mutually hostile and combative tribes. Politics is trivialised by the conviction that the true and authentic individual and collective selves have to combat the alienating impersonal and complicated structures of public life. Emotional relations have wounding effects on polity members and the image of an authentic collective personality becomes the ultimate purpose of their political engagement.

Sennett warns against the political violence and exclusion present in the imaginary of authenticity by stating that 'the logic of the collective personality is the purge'.[17] These originally ethno-fantasies of the mystical collective body of a

[15] See P Blokker, 'Populist constitutionalism' in C De la Torre (ed), *Routledge Handbook of Global Populism* (Oxford, Routledge, 2018) 113–127, 125.

[16] R Sennett, *The Fall of Public Man: On the Social Psychology of Capitalism* (New York, Vintage Books, 1978) 339.

[17] Ibid, 223.

nation have been politically and militarily both offensive and defensive, yet always socially draw on the basic exclusionary distinction between 'us' and 'them'. The imaginary of authenticity, therefore, requires a sociological inquiry into the relationship between states and nations.

4. Democracy, authenticity and identity politics

Democratic politics is identity politics. It always has been and continues to be, even in the global information age.[18] Modern nations became effective containers of the authenticity calls and were even reimagined as political units of the ancient collective existence. For Romantic nationalists, they merely had to be 'reawakened' and brought back into their modern existence.[19] This semantic paradox of an already existing nation brought into its existence by reawakening through interpretive constructions of its members, however, means that the nation's true and authentic voice has to be represented by those speaking on behalf of that nation.

The imaginary of authenticity is an intrinsic part of political existentialism that draws on the imaginary of the people as a secular continuation of the medieval notion of the sovereign's two bodies – one real and the other mystical.[20] Modern nations require a minimum cultural and moral homogeneity that can form a basis of mystical collective identity behind popular sovereignty.[21]

Democratic politics is societally constituted as the imaginary of collective self, beyond its political existence. However, the question of political identity and constitutional self-identification does not have a simple answer in symbols of constitutional settlement. It, therefore, gets temporalised and reformulated as Renan's famous 'daily plebiscite'[22] and delegated to the more technical question of political constitution and representation of the nation. The nation-*ethnos* as imagined community and symbolic unity of shared culture thus meets the nation-*demos* as a daily plebiscite or polity represented by parliament and other constitutional institutions.

The *demos/ethnos* distinction is irreducible to the normative ethical difference between 'good' inclusive democratic patriotism and 'bad' exclusive ethnic nationalism. Rather, it signifies the political distinction between the nation and the state

[18] See, for instance, M Castells, *The Information Age: Economy, Society and Culture: The Power of Identity* (Oxford, Blackwell, 1997); A Mellucci, *Challenging Codes: Collective Action in the Information Age* (Cambridge, Cambridge University Press, 1996).

[19] E Gellner, *Nations and Nationalisms* (Oxford, Blackwell, 1983) 47–48.

[20] E H Kantorowicz, *The King's Two Bodies: A Study in Medieval Political Theology* (Princeton, Princeton University Press, 1957); for a liberal critique of populism as a doctrine allegedly drawing on the mystical body of a people, see M Kumm, 'The Best of Times and the Worst of Times' in M Loughlin and P Dobner (eds), *Twilight of Constitutionalism?* (Oxford, Oxford University Press, 2009) 201.

[21] L Corrias, 'Populism in a Constitutional Key: Constituent Power, Popular Sovereignty and Constitutional Identity' (2016) 12(1) *European Constitutional Law Review* 6–26, 16–18.

[22] E Renan, 'What Is a Nation?' in A E Zimmern (ed), *Modern Political Doctrines* (Oxford, Oxford University Press, 1955 [the French original 1882]) 186–205.

as part of the constitutional semantics of modern democratic politics. Social structures of modern state-building coincide with the semantics of national identity politics. The problem of identity thus becomes a matter of circularity of nations and peoples finding their exclusive representation in state institutions while states achieve their legitimacy as far as they can be imagined as representing the authentic will of these nations.

The principle of national unity as the supreme communal bond preceding all other societal loyalties and identifications politically materialised in modern statehood. The nation state was the only organisation successfully combining societal expectations of 'cold' rationality and efficiency and communal expectations of 'hot' feelings of belonging and collective self-determination constituted by the national identity. Its legitimacy thus drew on the successful organisation and operationalisation of the distinction between society and community.[23]

The nation state had to be constituted by suppressing local communities with their traditions, dialects and culture and politically enforcing the official unifying language and compulsory education, including history, which could facilitate the symbolic constitution of collective memory.[24] In this historical process, modern nations were constituted by their states and legal constitutions granting civil rights under the condition and official promise of national unity. Liberal patriots and illiberal nationalists thus share the illusion of political unity coinciding with the practical goal of eliminating diversity, which is perceived as a threat to both the identity of the nation and functionality of its state.

The modern state has the unique ability of operating as both the societal institution of rational steering and the communal organisation of pre-political bonds.[25] It represents rational societal organisation as much as it represents irrational communal bonds. In modern statehood, community and society coevally operate and the imaginary of particular folkways and histories is thus as strongly present as the imaginary of universal modernisation by reason. So far, no supranational and transnational political or legal organisation has managed to achieve this capacity of coeval political self-organisation and cultural self-identification.

In the context of constitutional sovereignty, the self-authenticating authority of the nation's supreme will is reconstituted as the sovereignty of constitution legitimised by public reason and representative institutions. The principle of representation, allegedly alienating the people, takes over the authenticating principle of direct democracy as the people's uncorrupted voice.

Nevertheless, this capacity of modern state organisation also means that its structures will always be affected by the tension between the authentic popular will and its potentially alienating and corrupted representation by the state organisation and any other political institutions and agents. The sociological distinction between community and society is politically reformulated as the value choice

[23] Ferdinand Tönnies, *Community and* Society (Mineola NY, Dover Publications, 2002) 230.
[24] Jiří Přibáň, *Legal Symbolism: On Law, Time and European Identity* (Aldershot, Ashgate, 2007).
[25] Gellner, supra n. 18.

between security and freedom, authority and choice, etc. It, therefore, is even more important to examine the imaginary of authentic polity as the commonly shared meaningful and valuable life in its political and legal contexts and the semantics of both locally evolving national and globally evolving transnational constitutionalism.

5. The constitution of 'explosive communities': On the globalised structures of populist tribalism

As Eric Hobsbawm noted in the mid-1990s, politics of identity and authenticity invoke the promise of a safe haven for those who feel threatened by and alienated from the forces of the endless and seamless processes of modernisation currently taking the form of globalisation with its contradictory and conflictual constitution of world society. Hobsbawm observed that terms like 'collective identity', 'identity politics', 'identity groups' and even 'ethnicity' had been largely missing from the vocabulary of social and political sciences and discourse fifty years ago and the Oxford English Dictionary of the early 1970s listed the 'ethnicity' entry as a rare word mainly indicating social 'superstition' of the past.[26]

Historically, the development of the concept of community coincided with the weakening of communal bonds in real life.[27] However, the initially Romantic distinction between community and society continues to affect ideological debates and value conflicts between liberalism, communitarianism, multiculturalism, nativism and all other imaginaries at local as well as global levels. Tensions associated with constitutional imaginaries and identity politics of modern nation states, therefore, affect supranational and transnational constitutional politics.

According to the persisting imaginary of authenticity, corrupting money and a globalised economy represent an existential threat to the honestly working and living people in their local polities. The sociological distinction between society and community thus gets its political expression based on the contrast between politically destructive effects of economy, industry and technology and political heroism of leaders speaking the authentic 'true' voice and representing 'real' interests of people.

Populist arguments typically draw on the distinction between the alienating power of the political system and authentic power of the people. Populists promise to be 'honest' and 'true' representatives of the people's will, which is constantly being betrayed by the ruling economic and political elites. The figure of a banker is contrasted to that of a political leader. Business-people and engineers, with their industrial machineries, are considered to be enemies of the people in particular and politics in general because they can only follow the diktat of profit and

[26] E Hobsbawm, 'Identity Politics and the Left' (1996) 217 *New Left Review*, 38–47.
[27] E Hobsbawm, *The Age of Extremes* (London, Michael Joseph, 1994) 428.

administrative efficiency, which trumps any form of political decision-making. Populists, therefore, mobilise the public by the promise of tackling this depoliticising power and replacing it with authentically popular politics. Saint-Simon's utopia of self-administering industrialist society is confronted by the Napoleonic heroism committed to the new political and societal order.[28]

The accelerating process of globalisation and postmodernisation of culture[29] transforms this tension between nationally entrenched mobilising populism and globally floating depoliticising powers of economy and politics. Globalisation in general and Europeanisation in particular radically change the concepts of nationhood and citizenship. Imaginaries of the nation beyond the state are stretching beyond the traditional notion of diaspora and ethnic or national minority rights and transnational legal and political structures lead to the new meaning of political identity and participation.

Dual nationalities and citizenship can be ethnically exploited by countries of both origin and residence, and emigrant/immigrant dynamics have profound effects on economic and political rights of people living in transnational economic and legal settings.[30] Driven by the call of authenticity, they are often divisive as regards politics of democratic engagement, inclusion and participation. Ethnic imaginaries are not simply eliminated by global societal structures and cultural experiences. Nationalist rhetoric thrives in transnational politics while citizenship laws invite both inclusive and exclusive political mobilisation in both minority diasporas and majority societies.

Sociologists, such as Zygmunt Bauman, then speak of ethnic identity politics and populism as a communitarian response to the global nomadism that reinvents specific globalised forms of societal tribalism and leads to the constitution of 'explosive communities' filling the void of meaning created by globalisation.[31] These communities react violently to the social insecurity, instability and fears of global developments and the world they perceive as out of control and beyond comprehension. These are defensive mechanisms that constitute the shared 'we' identity that promises to collectively protect the community's members against the outside chaos and decline. They promise to establish security borders against 'terrors of the global' and effects of 'negative globalisation'[32] breaking social boundaries and former rules in economy, politics, culture, technology, science or the media. They draw on the imagination of predictability and regularity of the world in times of increased unpredictability and non-calculability of global risks and dangers.

[28] O Spengler, *The Decline of the West: An Abridged Version* (Oxford, Oxford University Press, 1991) 398–414.

[29] D Harvey, *The Condition of Postmodernity: An Enquiry into the Origins of Cultural Change* (Oxford, Blackwell, 1989).

[30] R Rubio-Marin, 'Transnational Politics and the Democratic State: Challenges and Prudential Considerations' (2006) 81 *New York University Law Review*, 117–147, 145.

[31] Z Bauman (n 3) 197.

[32] Z Bauman, *Liquid Fear* (Cambridge, Polity, 2006) 96.

The absence of positive counterpoints of global justice and lasting peace contributes to the negative state of global lawlessness and armed violence and this 'globalization of harm and damage rebounds in the globalization of resentment and vengeance'.[33] This trend is further complicated by the weakening of the nation state with its monopoly of political violence. The weakening power of the state does not necessarily mean the reduction of political violence. Violence only becomes deregulated, like so many other forms of global society, and devolved from state to local communal levels.[34]

This deregulation of violence from the state to explosive communities is part of the process described by social and political theorists as 'new tribalism'[35] or the 'retribalisation'[36] of global politics. The end of the Cold War fundamentally changed the geopolitical system, and globalisation both weakened the nation state and strengthened aspirations and struggles for local autonomy and separatism. Local identity politics thus became considered a counterpoint to the globally free movement of capital, goods, services, people and cultures.[37]

6. The constitution of Europe, its epistemic communities, and the political spectre of identitarian authenticity

The post-1989 rise of identity politics is part of the reflexive modernisation and globalisation of society.[38] It also informs the process of European integration and its constitutional imaginaries of authentic political identity and alienating depoliticisation of both the people and beyond it.

The imaginary of authenticity in populism, which leads to the description of the EU as a politically deficient and even morally corrupt empire of money and profit,[39] needs to be comprehended in the historical context of European integration and its profound impact on typically modern imaginaries, such as nation, democracy, technocracy, rights or the very concepts of market and legality.

European constitutionalism incorporates the general goals of economic prosperity and social stability, which are applicable to all politics. Imaginaries of the

[33] Ibid, 97.

[34] Bauman (n 3) 193–194.

[35] M W Hughey (ed), *New Tribalisms: The Resurgence of Race and Ethnicity* (New York, New York University Press, 1998); M Maffesoli, *The Time of the Tribes: The Decline of Individualism in Mass Society* (Thousand Oaks CA, Sage, 1996).

[36] R J. Antonio, 'After Postmodernism: Reactionary Tribalism' (2000) 106(1) *American Journal of Sociology*, 40–87, 55.

[37] See, for instance, H-G Betz and S Immerfall (eds) *The New Politics of the Right: Neo-Populist Parties and Movements in Established Democracies* (New York, St. Martin's Press, 1998).

[38] U Beck, A Giddens and S Lash, *Reflexive Modernization: Politics, Tradition and Aesthetics in the Modern Social Order* (Stanford CA, Stanford University Press, 1994).

[39] For an analysis of Eurosceptic attitudes from critics of the EU's current regime to the critics of EU policies and supports of exits from the EU, see C E De Vries, *Euroscepticism and the Future of European Integration* (Oxford, Oxford University Press, 2017) 8.

economic market, legal rights and democratic power, typical of the modern nation state as its background legitimation power,[40] played an important role in the societal constitution of a transnational European polity. Nevertheless, the historical process of European integration was also affected by political excesses and failures of the nation state. The constitution of transnational Europe, therefore, has been confronted by the most general political and sociological questions regarding the state and nation and their forms of organisation and functions in modern society.

The utopian imaginary of 'the withering-away state' significantly contributed to the theoretical knowledge and normative expectations of post-national Europe. It was strengthened by the horrors of War World Two and the role of nation states in mobilising political violence and destruction through nationalist and racist imaginaries and ideologies. 'Authentic' ethnocentrism of the nation state always operated as the negative legitimation of European integration 'beyond the people'.[41]

However, the European 'withering-away' nation state was also constituted against another utopia – the utopia of communism which, under political and imperial ambitions of the Soviet Union, promised its own version of the post-state and post-national communist constellation and the perpetual peace that would be established after the world revolution that overthrew the capitalist system with its market economy, labour exploitation and corrupt political systems that defended bourgeois constitutional rights and freedoms.

In short, the process of European integration originally had to confront authenticity imaginaries promised by both state nationalism and communist internationalism, and constitute viable political, economic and societal alternatives to them. The history of European integration is a critique of the imaginary of authenticity materialising in either the nation state, or the communist internationalism. It favours alienating institutions of the common market, administration and legal justice as alternative forms of commonality shaped by epistemic communities of experts: economists, bureaucrats and lawyers.

Functionalist theories of EU governance also argued that these institutions would eventually constitute the EU's transnational democratic political system, including the public sphere.[42] Paradoxically, these theories of further integration through epistemic communities of experts without democratic consolidation have made the EU exposed to the Marxist fallacy described by Ernest Gellner in his *Nations and Nationalism* as an expectation that the boundaries between nation states will be weakened and eventually disappear when members of those nations realise that their nationalist sentiments are only ideological masks that hide the real causes of their conflicts and existential hardship.[43]

[40] Compare Taylor (n 1) 21–22.

[41] E O Eriksen and J E Fossum (eds) *Democracy in the European Union: Integration Through Deliberation?* (London, Routledge, 2000).

[42] J Přibáň, 'The Self-Referential Semantics of Sovereignty: A Systems Theoretical Response to (Post) Sovereignty Studies' (2013) 20(3) *Constellations*, 406–421.

[43] Gellner, (n 19) 12.

Similarly, theorists of European integration used to believe that transnational structures would be gradually strengthened as citizens of the EU experience benefits of expert knowledge and realise the humanist potential of European integration. Nationalist prejudices were expected to disappear, together with further weakening of the nation state and its replacement by transnational networks and regimes of multiple rationalities of expert *episteme*, which would successfully substitute for nationally practiced and constrained procedures of democratic legitimation.

In the second decade of the twenty-first century, the EU, however, has been experiencing an unprecedented series of crises – from the Eurozone and migrant crises to the Brexit and coronavirus ones – resulting in illiberal, yet democratically enacted politics in many of its Member States. These institutional failures lead to both the segmented structural tensions between Member States and EU institutions, and the functional systemic tensions between European economy, politics, law, and administration.

The historically justified imperative of limitation of state sovereignty and national politics of totalitarian and war extremities became destructive itself by ignoring the other historical fact that the nation state also represents the most legitimate organisation of constitutional democratic politics. Despite a number of well-intended efforts, the EU has never managed to match or substitute for democratically elected and publicly accountable and representative bodies operating at a level of its Member States.

European integration used to be imagined as a political and democratically appealing alternative to the modern history of ethno-nationalism and politics dominated by nation states. However, the EU with its democratic deficit and expertise-driven 'elitist' decisions by epistemic communities of economists, administrators, lawyers and other professionals cannot avoid increasing conflicts and collisions with 'populist' responses emerging within and beyond democratic institutions of its Member States.

7. *Quod Omnes Tangit*: Legitimacy by *episteme* and *demoi* in European societal constitutionalism

One way of tackling the problem of the power of epistemic communities and their expert knowledge is offered by Gunther Teubner, who links the question of constitutional subjects to the self-constitution of the system's *episteme* as the source of the system's constitutional authority, including the intrinsic political tension between democracy and technocracy, respectively the public and expert reason. If constitutional modernity means the differentiation of the economic, political and legal rationalities, part of which was the process of inventing the people as the subject of sovereign power,[44] constitutional postmodernity of soci-

[44] E S Morgan, *Inventing the People: The Rise of Popular Sovereignty in England and America* (New York, Norton 1988)

etal constitutionalism, according to Teubner, involves abandoning this ultimate subject of politics and constituting non-human and non-political subjects imaginable as fragmentation and the plurality of knowledge regimes and networks within the system of global law.

Teubner, nevertheless, admits that democratic legitimacy and its deficits are 'the Achilles' heel' of transnational regimes, including those evolving in the EU and societal constitutionalism.[45] Addressing the 'universal core of democracy',[46] he even argues that the conditions of global transnationalisation of law require a re-thinking and re-contextualisation of democracy, including its relational aspect and self-identification of the authors of rules and decisions and those affected by them, even if these new 'constituencies' and 'demoi' of transnational regimes are fluctuating and involve the affected outsiders as much as the corporate members in possession of expert knowledge that are 'the sources of regime authority.'[47]

Teubner's reflections on democratic politics effectively mean that the general principle *quod omnes tangit* become the basic political norm of transnational law. Instead of consensus-building, it constitutes itself by internal proceduralisation of dissent and institutionalised self-contestations of rules and decisions, which vary due to the epistemic diversity of different transnational legal regimes. The *quod omnes tangit* principle, therefore, needs to be supplemented by the principle of 'epistemic subsidiarity',[48] which reflects on the variety of legitimising knowledge circulating in global law and supports the development of self-contestation procedures in different regimes.[49]

These two principles legitimise transnational regimes both internally, as the democratic inclusion of all affected parties, and externally, as the societal exclusion of totalising knowledge and arguments that come from other social systems, such as economy, science or religion. Furthermore, the principles reformulate the concept of *demos* by removing the supremacy of consensus and unity from its political self-identification. Teubner's critique of the existentialist concept of *demos* as the constitution's sovereign power and subject is thus further qualified by his proceduralist understanding of *demoi* as agencies constituted by the system's internal self-contestations and dissent capacities.

Teubner's comment on democratic legitimacy as the 'Achilles' heel' of transnational constitutionalism indicates a more general problem of the EU in particular and global society in general, which is the surplus of power and the shortage of authority. The absence of a global constitutional polity and its fragmentation into different subjects of the varied societal constitutions cannot obscure the fact that

[45] G Teubner, 'Quod Omnes Tangit: Transnational Constitutions Without Democracy?' (2018) 45(S1) *Journal of Law and Society*, 5–29, 7

[46] Ibid, 11

[47] Ibid, 21

[48] S Jasanoff, 'Epistemic Subsidiarity: Coexistence, Cosmopolitanism, Constitutionalism' (2013) 2 *European Journal of Risk Regulation* 133–141

[49] G Teubner (n 45) 27

these constitutions are power organisations impossible to be exclusively legitimised by their social efficacy and steering capacity.

The general distinction between legitimation by the governing capacity and authorised power finds its specific formula in Teubner's poetic expression of the transnational regimes' 'tunnel vision'. It is caused by the regimes' highly specialised policy fields and expert knowledge which, therefore, require the adoption of international public law principles, especially the 'constitutional toleration' and 'constitutional compromise'.[50]

These normative strategies and procedures of authorisation in global legal pluralism and its European context cannot be easily dismissed, for instance, by the labelling of pluralism as 'the laziest of all compromises'[51] because Teubner's notion of pluralism and the call for transnational constitutional compromises and toleration are primarily informed by the systemic and epistemic plurality of European and global law and cannot be simply re-interpreted as normative expectations of political pluralism. Using Unger's concept of 'institutional imagination',[52] Teubner invites his reader to engage in the construction of new imaginaries of legal legitimation and authorisation that are suitable for transnational European and global law to operate independently of the differences between international and transnational, public and private, or substantive and procedural law. However, Teubner's approach also shows that the theory of societal constitutions cannot ignore constitutional imaginaries of modern national and international politics and law or their potential to address legitimation deficits in European and global societal constitutionalism.

The power of expert knowledge is the source of authority in societal constitutions due to its ability to produce social norms and to establish the conditions and criteria of efficient governance. The tension between democracy and technocracy in societal constitutions may be managed by internal constitutions of *demoi* with the power of dissent and its execution through the procedures of self-contestation. The theory of societal constitutions, therefore, has to analyse not only power without legitimacy but also powerful knowledge regimes – economic, administrative, clinical, educational, scientific, digital, etc.

However, societal constitutionalism cannot disconnect from the idea of sovereignty and territorial control only to reconnect with some reflexive ideas of the collective self-rule of the multitude and the plurality of political subjects constituted at global level. The reflexive and differentiated images of *demoi* pushing back the expansive power of expert knowledge and conditioning it by the varied procedures of democratic legitimation are not enough for the legitimation of transnational societal constitutions. It is important to analyse, rather, how these constitutions manage to turn the affected populations into legitimate *demoi* and

[50] G Teubner, (n 45) 25.
[51] N Luhmann, *Observations on Modernity* (Stanford CA, Stanford University Press, 1998) 27
[52] G Teubner (n 45) 13.

how they translate their specific expert knowledge to the generally shared rules and normative regimes.

8. Constitutional recurrence of the European pluralistic and democratic *doxa*

Hegel's note that once none had the state, then some had it, and finally all have it in modern times has been pushed by the process of European integration into its post-national constellation. The imaginary of polity as an authentic community of shared destiny and values[53] compensating for legitimation gaps in the alienating systems of positive law and politics keeps its persuasive force in supranational and transnational conditions. It operates within modern nationhood and Statehood as much as beyond their structural and semantic limitations.[54]

It was no coincidence that increasing politicisation of European integration and subsequent attempts at democratisation of European institutions particularly in the post-Maastricht European Union led to the coeval processes of constitution-making and identity-building of European supranational polity of peoples. The constitution-making failure and subsequent searches of post-constituent constitutionalism without a constitution and its people only highlight the inseparability of constitutionalisation and democratisation and the coevolution of political representation and identity beyond the semantics and structures of the modern nation state.

8.1 European public spheres

The EU's democratic deficit is closely related to the weak parliamentarianism and party politics as much as it is to the absence of the European public sphere and strong collective identity. Different political interests, combined with the diversity of political cultures and historical experiences, make transnational normatively binding debates generated through civil society structures hardly achievable.[55] The quixotic search of the European identity 'we-feeling' that matches the ambitious goal of constitution-making at the turn of the twenty-first century did not lead to the constitution of authentic post-national polity.[56] Attempts at identity-building through European

[53] See, for instance, N Bolleyer and C Reh, 'EU legitimacy revisited: the normative foundations of a multilevel polity' (2012) 19(4) *Journal of European Public Policy*, 472–490.

[54] H Brunkhorst, 'Globalising Democracy without a State: Weak Public, Strong Public, Global Constitutionalism' (2002) 31(3) *Millenium*, 675–690.

[55] C Closa, 'Requirements of a European Public Sphere: Civil Society, Self, and the Institutionalization of Citizenship' in K Eder and B Giesen (eds) *European Citizenship between National Legacies and Postnational Projects* (Oxford, Oxford University Press, 2001) 181–201.

[56] Ol De Schutter, 'Civil Society in the Constitution for Europe' in E O Eriksen, J E Fossum and A J Menéndez (eds), *The Chartering of Europe. The European Charter of Fundamental Rights and its Constitutional Implications* (Baden Baden, Nomos, 2003) 133–160.

constitutional patriotism backfired in public revolts against the EU in the French and Dutch national referenda on the Constitutional Treaty in 2005.

The question as to whether a transnational polity can be constituted without pre-political authentic self-identification is accompanied by specific questions regarding the constitutive power of transnational citizenship, social and economic solidarity and plural identities.[57] Does the process of the self-constitution of polity through a collective self-understanding generated by public reason still need to be pre-politically guaranteed by social and cultural we-feeling? Can the public sphere be conceived of as a non-identitarian communicative network and power structure that limits and balances the growing power of the EU's systems of positive law and politics?[58]

A transnational European public sphere cannot be symbolically shaped by a democratic sovereign as constituent power. Deontology of liberty, equality, social solidarity and the democratic self-rule is impossible to achieve by constitutional symbolism and collective identity. However, the European public sphere can be constituted as a communication network that channels this deontology as part of the European public *doxa* operating through the public media network[59] and critically observes and pluralistically limits the expansion of power formed through EU political institutions.

Instead of one public sphere that expresses the authentic spirit of the European people, EU democratised politics is being constituted as a specific pluralistic structure of public spheres[60] of communication between governing institutions and the governed citizens and peoples of the EU.[61] The constitutional imaginary of pluralistic European public spheres thus integrates democratic conflictual politics and constitutes a symbolic counterpoint to the imaginary of authenticity of political identity.

8.2 European demoicracy

The other response to the imaginaries of authenticity and increasing conflict between elitist and populist legitimations permeating EU structures and critical operations, consists of the constitutional imaginary of European 'demoicracy'.[62]

Like many other core concepts of modern social and political sciences, the concept of demoicracy was originally used in a negative sense only to become a key

[57] F S Pérez, *Political Communication in Europe: The cultural and structural limits of the European public sphere* (London, Palgrave Macmillan, 2013).

[58] E O Eriksen, 'An Emerging European Public Sphere' (2005) 8(3) *European Journal of Social Theory*, 341–63, 344–346.

[59] R Koopmans and P Statham (eds), *The Making of a European Public Sphere: Media Discourse and Political Contention* (Cambridge, Cambridge University Press, 2010).

[60] T Risse (ed), *European Public Spheres: Politics is Back* (Cambridge, Cambridge University Press, 2014).

[61] H-J Trenz and K Eder, 'Democratizing Dynamics of a European Public Sphere' (2004) 7(1) *European Journal of Social Theory*, 5–25.

[62] For the latest summary, see P Eleftheriadis, *A Union of Peoples* (Oxford, Oxford University Press 2020) 115–119.

descriptive tool due to its exceptional capacity of formulating the most persistent social and political problems of contemporary European society. While originally used to describe the impasse of EU politics in the 1990s and the need to move to the constitution of a European demos,[63] Kalypso Nicolaïdis reformulated the concept as the basically Aristotelian mean way between the Eurofederalist hopes of constituting a sovereign European demos and the inter-governmentalist notion of the EU as an association of States governed by their sovereign demoi.[64]

The concept of demoicracy addresses the EU's democratic deficit by claiming that the absence of the European demos does not mean the impossibility of effective democratic control of EU political institutions. The EU as a Union of demoi governing together but not as one abandons the search for one people and federalist identity-building through constitution-making. It gives up the moralist job of one Europe of shared values that further strengthen European bonds and collective identity. Instead, it draws on ideas of deliberative democracy and applies them to the pluralistic political and societal condition of the EU.[65]

The Union's irreducible value and political pluralism requires specific political communication that draws on a mutual recognition of both national differences and increasingly Europeanised and globalised governance structures. Instead of cosmopolitan and anarchist 'no borders' fantasies and sweeping criticisms of Statehood and nationhood, demoicracy aims at political communication evolving horizontally between and vertically beyond borders.[66] Its legitimation formula consists of recognising the interdependence of globalised polities and including all parties and individuals affected by political decisions. It is close to the societal constitutions' legitimation formula *quod omnes tangit* formulated by Teubner and discussed above in this chapter.[67]

The concept of demoicracy highlights the unique political structure of the EU as a polity of mutually fertilised liberal democratic states.[68] It represents a critique of nationalist populism because of its emphasis on the diversity and heterogeneity of political communication and legitimation of the EU.[69] At the same time, it embraces the strategy of public mobilisation and criticisms of 'elitist' politics pursued by EU institutions that allegedly need to be challenged by public involvement of citizens on issues of European governance. Finally, it relies on democratic

[63] P van Parijs 'Should the European union become more democratic?' in A Follesdal and P Koslowski (eds), *Democracy and the European Union* (Berlin, Springer, 1998) 287–301.

[64] K Nicolaïdis, 'European Demoicracy and Its Crisis' (2013) 51(2) *Journal of Common Market Studies*, 351–369.

[65] J Bohman, 'From *Demos* to *Demoi*: Democracy across Borders' (2005) 18(3) *Ratio Juris*, 293–314.

[66] Ibid, 300.

[67] Teubner (n 45).

[68] F Cheneval and F Schimmelfenning, 'The Case for Demoicracy in the European Union' (2013) 51(2) *Journal of Common Market Studies*, 334–350.

[69] J-W Mueller 'The Promise of Demoi-cracy: Diversity and Domination in the European Public Order' in J Neyer and A Wiener (eds), *The Political Theory of the European Union* (Oxford, Oxford University Press, 2010) 187–204.

networks and regimes beyond the nation state and is communicated directly instead of being mediated through the national public media.

In other words, demoicracy is a communication network of the transnational democratic *doxa* constituted by heterogenic and horizontal networks of citizens and organisations in matters of political governance. In line with the original constitution of European integration, it challenges national constitutional imaginaries by recognising the diversely self-constituted demoi, yet both limits their sovereignty claims and uses their legitimacy potential as background power of transnational European governance.

9. Concluding remarks: On the European societal constitution of *communitas*

The constitutional imaginary of European demoi pushing back the expansive power of expert knowledge and conditioning it by the varied procedures of democratic legitimation can hardly close the legitimation gap of the current EU. Similarly, the imaginary of European public spheres as structures of democratic opposition to the EU's political institutions cannot eliminate the growing power of constitutional populism responding to the failures of both European and national politics. Nevertheless, both imaginaries show that transnational structures of EU politics and law cannot operate without addressing the constitutional semantics of authenticity. Rather, they illuminate the self-description of European integration as a historical process that both furthers and challenges constitutional imaginaries of the modern nation state.

Replicating the imaginaries of the public sphere and demoi at transnational European level addresses the problem of collective self-identification beyond structures of the legal constitution. However, this self-identification cannot proceed as self-authentication because both imaginaries are constituted as societal communication networks without a claim to be a 'real' voice of the people speaking 'truth' to power. While drawing on the potential of popular mobilisation and public opinion – the *doxa* challenging the power of expert knowledge – the *episteme*, transnational European democratic constitutionalism keeps its initial critical attitude towards the imaginary of authenticity as a legitimation force of EU law and politics.

Apart from examining the process of turning populations affected by the EU's societal constitutions into legitimate demoi of their self-constituted European polity, the sociology of European constitutional imaginaries, therefore, analyses the process of transformation of specific expert knowledge into democratically accepted rules and generally shared normative power regimes. The function of European constitutional imaginaries is to steer exactly this process of constitutionalisation of systemic facts of societal power as legitimising values of the EU and the transformation of societal immanence into transcendental ideals of the integrated European *communitas*, both inspired by and critical of the imaginary of authenticity originally associated with modern nations and their states.

6

Born out of Crisis? 'Emergency Europe' and the Question of Intertemporal Conflict Management in Constitutional Governance

MING-SUNG KUO

1. Introduction

Political orders are no stranger to crisis.[1] How to govern in crisis, or rather, how to govern crisis, had occupied political thinkers for centuries even before the dawning of modern constitutionalism in the seventeenth century.[2] Despite its design defects,[3] the Constitution of the United States (US Constitution) revealed modern constitutional thinking about crisis governance when it was written in 1787. Normal constitutional norms – the long-held common law privilege of the writ of habeas corpus in this case – can be suspended by the legislature in extraordinary times of invasion and rebellion; with such suspension, the government – to be more precise, the executive branch of the federal government – is thus less constrained and its power increases in such times.[4] The framers of the US

[1] A crisis is a factual condition. It may result from a long-term, structural defect. In such a case, the decisive moment at which the long-term, structural defect turns into a difficult or dangerous situation that needs serious attention seems to be an expression of its preexisting structural condition. On this view, a crisis is different from an emergency. Yet a crisis may be prompted by some unanticipated problem, which suddenly threatens the continuing function of a seemingly healthy system. In this latter sense, a crisis indicates the exceptional circumstances that may trigger emergency powers. Notably, for a crisis that speaks to a long-term structural systematic defect, its decisive moment tends to be magnified and thus eclipse the structural nature of such a crisis. Thus, for present purposes, I focus on the decisive moment in a crisis situation, regardless of whether it results from a system's long-term, structural defect or some unanticipated problem, and draw no distinction between crisis and emergency. cf B De Witte, 'Guest Editorial: EU Emergency Law and Its Impact on the EU Legal Order' (2022) 59 *Common Market Law Review* 3, 4. I thank Jonathan Zeitlin for pushing me to rethink the relationship between crisis and emergency.

[2] See C Schmitt, *Dictatorship: From the Origin of the Modern Concept of Sovereignty to Proletarian Class Struggle* (M Hoelzel and G Ward trs, Polity, 2014) ch 2; see also F Del Lucchese, 'Crisis and Power: Economics, Politics and Conflict in Machiavelli's Political Thought' (2009) 30 *History of Political Thought* 75.

[3] See B Ackerman, *Before the Next Attack: Preserving Civil Liberties in an Age of Terrorism* (Yale University Press, 2006) 122–41.

[4] US Constitution article I, section 2, clause 2 provides, 'The Privilege of the Writ of Habeas Corpus shall not be suspended [by Congress], unless when in Cases of Rebellion or Invasion the public Safety may require it.'

Constitution conceived a compartmentalised constitutional order, under which the state of normalcy and the state of exception or emergency – ie, crisis[5] – are governed by two distinct normative regimes:[6] the normal rule of law and the 'emergency constitution',[7] respectively. This pattern of compartmentalisation has since dominated more sophisticated constitutional designs on governance of, and in, crisis. It is noteworthy that while the *factual* state of exception (or emergency) is to be governed in accordance with the special norms set out in the emergency constitution vis-à-vis the normal rule of law, it does not mean that exception or emergency exists in a norm-free state of lawlessness.[8] On this view, the separation of emergency from normalcy in constitutional governance is central to the constitutional domestication of emergency powers.[9] A good emergency constitution comes down to under what substantive constraints – such as the list of rights that can be suspended or limited and the factual circumstances that can trigger a declaration of a state of emergency[10] – and procedural requirements a constitution allows for the exercise of emergency powers.[11]

Yet, as crisis becomes a constant phenomenon in constitutional orders and no longer exists as exception, emergency powers aimed at crisis governance have gradually turned normal, if you will. The normalisation of the state of exception calls into question the wisdom of compartmentalisation in the constitutional domestication of emergency powers.[12] Confronted with this constitutional development, some commentators warn of the erosion of constitutional governance amid the continuing normalisation;[13] others track

[5] See n 1.

[6] For further discussion of the 'normative duality' in the governance of emergency powers, see M-S Kuo, 'From Institutional Sovereignty to Constitutional Mindset: Rethinking the Domestication of the State of Exception in the Age of Normalization' in R Albert and Y Roznai (eds), *Constitutionalism Under Extreme Conditions: Law, Emergency, Exception* (Springer, 2020) 21, 23–26; see also O Gross and F Ní Aoláin, *Law in Times of Crisis: Emergency Powers in Theory and Practice* (Cambridge University Press, 2006).

[7] Bruce Ackerman, 'The Emergency Constitution' (2004) 113 *Yale Law Journal* 1029.

[8] Kuo (n 6).

[9] ibid; see also J Ferejohn and P Pasquino, 'The Law of the Exception: A Typology of Emergency Powers' (2004) 2 *I-CON* 210, 211.

[10] In this chapter, the 'state of exception', as opposed to the 'state of normalcy', refers to the *factual* situation in which the ordinary rule of law is considered unable to function properly. I refer to those extraordinary powers the government adopts in the *factual* state of exception (or emergency) as 'emergency powers' or alternatively the juridical 'state of emergency'. Thus, in contrast to the ordinary rule of law that governs the state of normalcy, the state of emergency (or emergency regime) in constitutional orders is the alternative juridical regime in response to the state of exception. Notably, as will be discussed, the juridical state of emergency in a constitutional jurisdiction may be differently named or further differentiated.

[11] Ackerman (n 3) 77–100.

[12] Kuo (n 6) 29-32; G Frankenberg, *Political Technology and the Erosion of the Rule of Law: Normalizing the State of Exception* (Edward Elgar, 2014) 145–46, 189–95.

[13] Eg, Ackerman (n 3) 47-49; Frankenberg (n 12); D Dyzenhaus, 'The Permanence of the Temporary: Can Emergency Powers be Normalized?' in R Daniels, P Macklem and K Roach (eds), *The Security of Freedom: Essays on Canada's Anti-Terrorism Bill* (University of Toronto Press, 2001) 21; S Molloy, 'Approach with Caution: Sunset Clauses as Safeguards of Democracy?' (2021) 23 *European Journal of Law Reform* 147; see also JM Balkin and S Levinson, 'The Processes of Constitutional Change: From Partisan Entrenchment to the National Surveillance State' (2006) 75 *Fordham Law Review* 489; RH Fallon, Jr, 'Interpreting Presidential Powers' (2013) 63 *Duke Law Journal* 347.

the trajectory of normalisation in light of the continuous rise of the executive power in constitutional governance.[14] From the first perspective, how to adapt the design of the emergency constitution, with better compartmentalisation, to the long state of exception various constitutional orders find themselves in holds the key to upholding the project of constitutional governance.[15] To the second group, the normalisation of the state of emergency is in essence a function of the development of the administrative state and the expansion of the executive vis-à-vis other constitutional powers. Thus, the normalisation itself is not a concern but needs to be seen as part of the problematics of the expanding administrative state.[16] To both, how to maintain constitutional governance in the 'age of permacrisis'[17] is a question of institutional design – either through smarter compartmentalisation or with tightening of administrative discretion.

Both are laudable efforts to rein in the executive power that has become self-aggrandising in the name of emergency. Yet neither offers an effective remedy on its own for the expansion of the executive power driven by constant crisis. In this chapter, I aim to complement such efforts by taking up the less-noticed question of time in constitutional governance[18] through an examination of the European Union's (EU) emergency-driven constitutional change, starting from the Eurozone crisis. I wish to advance a two-part argument. The first part concerns the tension between constitutionalism and crisis governance in general; the second focuses on the emergence of executive constitutionalism in the EU from its responses to the euro crisis to the Covid pandemic emergency and beyond. Taking on the question of time in constitutional governance, I argue that how to manage the intertemporal conflict between the state of exception/emergency and that of normalcy lies at the core of the constitutional domestication of emergency powers and holds the key to the prognosis of executive aggrandisement in increasingly crisis-minded governance; yet, driven by successive crises, the recent changes to the EU's constitutional configuration results from an 'always present' executive-led race against

[14] Compare A Vermeule, 'Our Schmittian Administrative Law' (2009) 122 *Harvard Law Review* 1095, with M Tushnet, 'Emergency Law as Administrative Law' in FF Davis and F de Londras (eds), *Critical Debates on Counter-Terrorism Judicial Review* (Cambridge University Press, 2014) 121; see also JE Fisch, 'Overseeing the Administrative State' (2024) 47 *Seattle University Law Review* 899, 904.

[15] See generally Ackerman (n 3).

[16] Vermeule (n 14); Tushnet (n 14); Fisch (n 14).

[17] F Zuleeg, JA Emmanouilidis and R Borges de Castro, 'Europe in the Age of Permacrisis', *European Policy Centre Commentary*, 11 March 2021, https://www.epc.eu/publication/Europe-in-the-age-of-permacrisis-3c8a0c/.

[18] Legal philosopher Gerald Postema noted in 2018, 'Until recently, contemporary legal philosophy has often ignored the historical or diachronic and dynamic dimension of law.' GJ Postema, 'Time in Law's Domain' (2018) 31 *Ratio Juris* 150, 161. Noticeably, the question of time has received increasing attention from constitutional scholars. Examples include RS Kay, 'Constitutional Chrononomy' (2000) 13 *Ratio Juris* 31–48; J Rubenfeld, *Freedom and Time: A Theory of Constitutional Self-Government* (Yale University Press, 2001); PW Kahn, 'Political Time: Sovereignty and the Transtemporal Community' (2006) 28 *Cardozo Law Review* 259; L Barschack, 'Time and the Constitution' (2009) 7 *I-CON* 553; M Fichera, *The EU and Constitutional Time: The Significance of Time in Constitutional Change* (Edward Elgar, 2023); P Linden-Retek, *Postnational Constitutionalism: Europe and the Time of Law* (Oxford University Press, 2023).

time, heralding the culmination of executive constitutionalism that is set in a temporality structured by the fast-changing financial market and the highly contagious SARS-CoV-2 – which is distinct from the steady-paced temporal order of democratic dynamics that incubate normative political constitutionalism.

To advance my argument, I start by setting out my analytical framework around an investigation into the distinction of the state of exception from that of normalcy at the centre of the constitutional domestication of emergency powers. Following this introductory section, a deep look at the conventional wisdom of governing crisis by means of compartmentalisation reveals two distinct temporalities in constitutional governance. While the normal rule of law operates on a steady-paced temporal order in which political ideas are turned into real-word policies in an articulated multistage process of decision making, governing in crisis requires urgent government responses that are likely to curtail the normal decision-making process, engendering an accelerated temporal order. As each temporal order cultivates a distinct mindset of governance in the exercise of power, the tension between the normal rule of law and the emergency constitution speaks to an intertemporal conflict. Through this lens, the technique of compartmentalisation at the heart of the traditional governance of crisis turns out to be centred on the management of intertemporal conflict. It follows that what matters in compartmentalisation is not so much about separating two constitutional regimes as it is about aligning distinct governance mindsets framed in different temporal orders with changing circumstances in the workings of constitutional governance. Seen in this light, the challenge posed by the 'always present' executive in blurring the normalcy-exception distinction is not only concerned with how to control administrative discretion. It further casts doubt on the effectiveness of managing intertemporal conflict by compartmentalisation as the 'always present' executive extends the governance mindset moulded in the crisis-induced accelerated temporal order further to constitutional governance in general.

Applying the foregoing analytical framework, I then take on the EU's recent emergency-driven constitutional change from the euro crisis to the Covid pandemic emergency and beyond in the next two sections. Upon closer inspection, these crises have become the EU's constituent moments as the EU takes up more and more functions associated with constitutional orders through institutional re-engineering amid successive crises. Mirroring the EU's race against time, the temporality in these constitution-reshaping moments is a function of the market and of the pandemic. Born out of crisis, the EU's emergency-induced constitutional order reminisces a not so bright executive constitutionalism instead of a normative political constitutionalism. Seen in this light, the intertemporal conflict in the EU's recent constitution reshaping centres on how to align the temporal order required for constitution reshaping to the executive reaction to emergencies in various rescue missions. In the concluding section, I provide further reflections on the management of intertemporal conflict as crisis governance is becoming a constitutional fixture.

2. Taming the Prince in Time: Intertemporal Conflict Management and Governance of Crisis

To shed light on the framing effect of temporality on the mindset of the executive power and its implications to the compartmentalisation strategy in the governance of crisis and emergency powers, I conduct a two-step analysis in the following. I first dig deeply into the perceived dictatorial character of emergency powers and then discuss why variations on the temporal pace in the exercise of executive discretion have implications for the government's application of power to everyday administration and the state of emergency.

2.1 Excavating the Dictatorial Ghost

'Condottiere', 'commissar', and 'prince' may sound like legacy terms to the ear of students of constitutional democracy.[19] As these equestrian, majestic, and formidable images evoke, concentration of power is characteristic of such powerful figures. They are antithetical to the separation of powers and thus repugnant to constitutional ordering.[20] Departing from the precedents of all-powerful magistrates appointed for siege-like situations in history, designers of modern constitutions do not conceive of a present-day prince or condottiere in providing for powers to be deployed in a state of emergency. Instead, under the constitutional project of governance, the deployment of emergency powers in crisis is a multistage process through which power is brought to bear on the factual but exceptional situation, starting with the initiation and comprising further stages of approval, implementation, adjudication, termination, and correction or indemnification.[21] Through this process, a variety of constitutional power holders are involved. This modern image of emergency power speaks to a world set apart from that made in a princely, commissarial, or horse-riding condottiere image.

Yet whether 'the prince' can be tamed still stands at the centre of continuing debates surrounding emergency powers.[22] Moreover, 'dictatorship' and its lexical relative 'dictator' – a no less formidable figure than those signified in the legacy terms mentioned above – still pervade the current literature.[23] It is not just a legacy

[19] Schmitt (n 2) 37–65.

[20] 'Any society in which no provision is made for guaranteeing rights or for the separation of powers, has no Constitution.' The Declaration of the Rights of Man and of the Citizen article 16, available at https://www.elysee.fr/en/french-presidency/the-declaration-of-the-rights-of-man-and-of-the-citizen.

[21] Ackerman (n 3) 77-121; T Ginsburg and M Versteeg, 'The Bound Executive: Emergency Powers during the Pandemic' (2021) 19 *I-CON* 1498.

[22] Compare HC Mansfield, *Taming the Prince: The Ambivalence of Modern Executive Power* (Free Press 1989), with AS Katz, 'Taming the Prince: Bringing Presidential Emergency Powers under Law in Colombia' (2020) 18 *I-CON* 1201.

[23] Schmitt (n 2); Ferejohn and Pasquino (n 9); CL Rossiter, *Constitutional Dictatorship: Crisis Government in the Modern Democracies* (Princeton University Press, 1948); S Levinson and JM Balkin, 'Constitutional Dictatorship: Its Dangers and Its Design' (2010) 94 *Minnesota Law Review* 1789; A Keil, 'A Very British Dictatorship: The Defence of the Realm Act in Britain, 1914–1920' (2023) 14 *First World War Studies* 51.

of Carl Schmitt's corpus of anti-liberalism and his fascination with strong executive leadership.[24] Rather, 'constitutional dictatorship' now seems to stand for the reality: living in the shadow of unforeseen existential struggles, liberal democracies must strive to reconcile their political soul with the needs of survival in times of crisis through constitutional framing.[25] Yet, if the exercise of emergency powers is a multistage process involving various institutional holders of constitutional power, why is the contemporary constitutional construction of emergency power as part of the design of separation of powers still associated with the idea of dictatorship? Is it just a metaphor in rhetorical exercise? What on earth makes the institution of emergency power in modern constitutions still dictatorial?

To answer the above questions, we need to take a deep look at the multistage decision-making process in the exercise of emergency powers. For present purposes, let us focus on the 'ideal situation' of emergency power and leave aside the question of the normalisation of states of emergency by stealth for the time being. Start with the first stages of initiation and approval. In some countries such as France[26] and Taiwan,[27] when some exceptional circumstance – simply call it a crisis – arises, a state of emergency can be constitutionally declared by the executive power without prior consent from the legislature. Once entering a state of emergency, the executive power may immediately take extraordinary measures in responding to the crisis beyond those authorised under the normal legal framework, provided that such measures do not exceed the limits set out in the constitution. It should be emphasised that in such cases, the executive power is still required to obtain approval from the legislature for the already declared state

[24] S Baume, 'Carl Schmitt's Multifaceted Rejection of Political Compromises' (2024) 86 *Review of Politics* 197.

[25] See Levinson and Balkin (n 23).

[26] The French Constitution provides for two types of the state of emergency in articles 16 and 36, respectively. According to article 16, the president may unilaterally exercise emergency powers under specified special circumstances, although the president is required to consult the prime minister, the presidents of both houses of the parliament and the Constitutional Council before invoking such powers. Although the Constitutional Council may intervene to decide whether the factual circumstance that initially triggered the invocation of emergency powers under this provision still exists following a referral (after thirty days of presidential invocation) and on its own (after sixty days of presidential invocation), the legal effect of a negative decision by the Constitutional Council is unclear. In addition, article 36 provides for a 'state of siege', which can be 'decreed by the Council of Ministers', which is chaired by the president, but will lapse in twelve days if the parliament does not give further authorisation during the 12-day period. See The French Constitution, available at https://www.conseil-constitutionnel.fr/en/constitution-of-4-october-1958.

[27] According to the Additional Articles of the Constitution of the Republic of China – amendments to Taiwan's working constitution officially titled the Constitution of the Republic of China – '[t]he president may, by resolution of the Executive Yuan Council [ie, the council of ministers headed by the president-appointed premier], issue emergency decrees and take all necessary measures' under specified special circumstances (article 2 paragraph 3). However, such emergency powers shall lapse if they are not ratified by the Legislative Yuan within ten days. See Additional Articles of the Constitution of the Republic of China available at https://law.moj.gov.tw/ENG/LawClass/LawAll.aspx?pcode=A0000002. Notably, the Constitution of the Republic of China of 1947 proper also provides for the institution of martial-law rule in article 39, which has been left untouched in subsequent amendments. See Constitution of the Republic of China, available at https://law.moj.gov.tw/ENG/LawClass/LawAll.aspx?pcode=A0000001.

of emergency within a specified, and mostly short, period of time.[28] If the required legislative approval fails to materialise, the state of emergency declared by the executive will end and those extraordinary measures taken by government authorities automatically lapse. It follows that the normal rule of law will be restored as the governing framework for government response to the perceived crisis that has prompted the executive declaration of a state of emergency in the first place. Still, in such cases, the executive power plays a forceful initiative role in decision making on emergency powers. Notably, the unilateral declaration of a state of emergency by the executive is far from the global standard in constitutional design. Rather, to close the window of the executive abuse of emergency powers before the legislature can intervene, the Basic Law of Germany, for example, entrusts the power to determine states of emergency to the federal legislature,[29] restricting the executive's initiative role in this multistage decision-making process to requesting the legislature to decide on the existence of a *factual* state of emergency. In this case, acting in good faith, the executive power, in view of the evidence, may conclude that the factual situation is dire and demands government response backed by emergency powers, but its conclusion does not dictate the legislature.

In the above snapshot of the emergency constitution, the executive's role in the initiation of emergency powers seems to be the focus of institutional designers mindful of the separation of powers. Narrow as it may seem, the constitutional window of a unilateral declaration of a state of emergency vested in the executive in cases like France and Taiwan can still be virtually widened by the forceful executive to inflict irreversible damages on the constitutional order. From this window, those who are concerned about the domestication of emergency powers see a constitutional landscape of would-be dictators. Closing this window in the constitution should then be a natural choice. With that window shut, the constitutional institution of emergency power is seen to rid itself of the long-associated dictatorial character. The wiser design as epitomised by the German emergency constitution should be able to steer clear of association with the idea of constitutional dictatorship. Yet, as the prevalence of constitutional dictatorship in the literature suggests, it does not seem to be the case.[30]

From the above comparison, it follows that the emergency measure only taken after the legislature has determined the existence of a factual state of emergency or

[28] In France, this only applies to the state of siege under article 36. For details, see n 26 above.

[29] Apart from the provisions governing responses to grave accidents or natural disasters (articles 35 and 104b), the Basic Law further distinguishes between the state of tension (article 80a) and the state of defence (articles 115a–115l). While the elected lower house (*Bundestag*) is the sole authority to determine a state of tension (article 80a), the power to determine a state of defence – ie, a state of emergency resulting from the attack or the imminent threat of attack on the federal territory by armed force – is vested in the bicameral legislature (article 115a (1)). Under special circumstances, the latter can be exercised by a Joint Committee comprising members of both the lower and the upper (*Bundesrat*) houses of the legislature (article 115a (2)). It is worth noting that the German Basic Law does not rule out the possibility of a state of defence being entered without prior legislative intervention (article 115a (3)). See The German Basic Law, available at https://www.gesetze-im-internet.de/englisch_gg/index.html#gl_p0112.

[30] Levinson and Balkin (n 23); CC Schweitzer, 'Emergency Powers in the Federal Republic of Germany' (1969) 22 *Western Political Quarterly* 112, 112.

crisis is no less dictatorial than emergency powers employed on the executive's own initiative. So, the dictator's spirit still haunting the modern emergency constitution is not manifested so much in the constitutional institution of state of emergency itself as in the instantiation of emergency powers. This explains why compartmentalisation has been central to the constitutional strategy to domesticate emergency powers and to tame the prince. Given that the instantiation of emergency powers – which are vested in the executive – is indelibly tainted with a dictatorial character, it needs to be confined and separated from the executive's exercise of power that is governed by the normal rule of law. With emergency powers confined to a special juridical state of the constitution – to which the state of emergency gives expression – a constitutional order seems able to keep its soul and survive the existential challenge in the shadow of emergency challenges. Seen in this light, keeping the spirit of the rule of law from contamination by emergency powers becomes the key concern in designs of the emergency constitution.

This standard account of the constitutional domestication of emergency powers by compartmentalisation sounds convincing. Yet one unasked question still needs to be answered: If the institution of emergency power is rendered dictatorial in its very instantiation by the executive, is it the *executive* instantiation or the *emergency* power – or something else – that is to blame for the dictatorial character attributed to this constitutional institution? It is to this question that I now turn.

2.2 Having the Right Mindset for the Right Time?

It bears emphasis that under the modern design of emergency constitution, the executive is not vested with uncontrolled powers. First, the executive is indeed headed by a chief officer, but it requires a whole body to function and to make its power effective.[31] Thus, even if in cases such as France and Taiwan, the president as head of state may declare a state of emergency without prior consent from the legislature, he or she cannot make such decisions alone. The president needs to gain support from his or her ministers. Yet the president cannot be sure of how his or her ministerial appointees would respond to the request for support if the factual circumstance is not manifestly clear to justify the invocation of emergency powers in the public eye. Truly, the president eventually may well be able to push through the decision to declare a state of emergency, given the dominant presidential position – including the ultimate power to remove and replace – vis-à-vis the appointed ministers. Nevertheless, the president would be politically exposed and damaged if he or she only gained the support for invoking emergency powers from within the executive branch by replacing ministerial dissenters with obedient

[31] See generally T Daintith and A Page, *The Executive in the Constitution: Structure, Autonomy, and Internal Control* (Oxford University Press, 1999).

loyalists.[32] A state of emergency that is declared against the backdrop of intramural executive dissensus will likely be questioned for its legitimacy, with the authority of derived emergency measures thrown into doubt. Seen in this big picture of its whole body instead of the head-only close-up, the executive is not as dictatorial as it seems.

Moreover, the emergency power in the hands of the executive remains confined to constitutional limits, although it is subject to an governing framework different to the normal rule of law. Granted, the alternative normative control of emergency powers is more of a function of politics – or rather political ethics – than an application of legal precepts.[33] And there is no denying that political ethics is no legal prescription and lacking in enforcement. It is also true that emergency power is liable to abuse, if not full-scale arbitrariness, and cannot rid itself of discretionary character. Yet all of this needs to be appreciated in light of the fact that executive discretion has long been part and parcel of the modern administrative state and has routinely penetrated everyday life in contemporary society under the normal rule of law.[34] Embedded in this constitutional reality, emergency powers do not make a dictatorship just with augmented discretion.

If neither the executive body itself nor the strong discretionary character of emergency powers is dictatorial in nature, can it be the increased discretion granted to the executive in a state of emergency that makes the image of dictatorial emergency powers? Needless to say, compared with the interventionist reality of the modern state, steered by its 'most knowledgeable branch',[35] the strong discretionary character distinctive of emergency powers makes state intervention not only more annoying but also alarming. Still, the increased discretion granted to the executive in a state of emergency does not have to elide into dictatorship. Here enters the sixty-four-thousand-dollar question: What predisposes executive discretion that takes the form of emergency power to dictatorship?

What is distinctive of the executive discretion exercised in the form of emergency measure – ie, emergency discretion – is the factual condition that emergency discretion is brought to bear on. In a genuine crisis – note, we are still in the ideal situation – the situation demanding an emergency power-underpinned response is fickle. It is characteristic of uncertainty and fraught with unknowns.[36] Emergency discretion is expected to be exercised in a way that the response measures coming out of it are able to address such a situation. For this reason, officials and bureaucrats in the executive branch that are making decisions and taking actions under the auspices of emergency discretion are put in a unique mindset. On the one

[32] This is part of the political control of emergency powers, which will be further discussed later in this section.

[33] Ackerman (n 3) 77–121; Kuo (n 6) 32–34; Gross and Ní Aoláin (n 6) 110–70.

[34] C Coglianese and CS Yoo, 'The Bounds of Executive Discretion in the Regulatory State' (2016) 164 *University of Pennsylvania Law Review* 1587; C DeMuth, 'Can the Administrative State be Tamed?' (2016) 8 *Journal of Legal Analysis* 121.

[35] CR Sunstein, 'The Most Knowledgeable Branch' (2016) 164 *University of Pennsylvania Law Review* 1607.

[36] Ginsburg and Versteeg (n 21).

hand, they are expected to stabilise and 'control' the fast-changing situation in a crisis. On the other hand, hampered by unknowns and uncertainties, they hardly ever have much success in getting ahead of the next new situation in an ongoing crisis.[37] The best to be expected of the executive in a factual state of emergency is that those in charge of 'controlling' can catch up quickly. Thus, emergency discretion is exercised as if to stop a rapid fire,[38] either to get ahead of it or simply to catch it up. Under such circumstances, the timescale of an instance of emergency discretion tends to be short, while the temporal pace for decision-making in a crisis is accelerated. The executive is put in a race-against-time mindset in a state of emergency.

In contrast, discretion is made at a less hectic temporal pace in normal times. Although the speed of societal tempo has steadily picked up in the continuing process of social acceleration,[39] administrative discretion under the legal framework in times of normalcy is still embedded in the multistage decision-making structure under the separation of powers. Discretionary measures are part of the appropriate actions the administration is expected to take in the implementation of the law that gives shape to policy proposals and political ideas originating in society.[40] Administrative discretion cannot be exercised without taking into account the relevant statutory provisions, administrative precedents, departmental guidelines, and court judgments. Within this web of legal norms, the executive mindset in everyday administration is different. Officials and bureaucrats can fall back on the rule of law to pace their response to societal needs in everyday life even when facing an unexpected incident.[41] In tandem with this steady-paced time, discretionary measures are likely to be more informed, fact-based, soundly reasoned, and prudential.

Yet, unmoored from the web of legal norms in times of crisis, emergency discretion is exercised in a rushed way to win the race against time. With the timeframe compressed, the fact, reasoning, information, and public participation on which good emergency response relies all fade into the background. Prudence becomes a rare thing in emergency discretion. 'Reassurance', not proportionality, occupies the minds of those under pressure to control the situation.[42] Differently paced in time, the same exercise of discretion by the same executive tends to lead to contrasting results: one is prudential; another lacks balance and smacks of dictatorship.

[37] See M-S Kuo, 'Governing with Limited Learning Capacity? The Question of Institutional Learning and Global Governance's New Legitimacy Challenge' (2023) 55 *Georgetown Journal of International Law* 81, 99–101, 111–12.

[38] cf WE Scheuerman, 'Motorized Legislation? Statutes in an Age of Speed' (2002) 88 *Archiv für Rechts- und Sozialphilosophie* 379, 396.

[39] ibid; WE Scheuerman, *Liberal Democracy and the Social Acceleration of Time* (Johns Hopkins University Press, 2004).

[40] J Waldron, *Political Political Theory: Essays on Institution* (Harvard University Press, 2016) 62–70; M-S Kuo, 'Against Instantaneous Democracy' (2019) 17 *I-CON* 554, 563-64.

[41] See PM Shane, 'The Rule of Law and the Inevitability of Discretion' (2013) 36 *Harvard Journal of Law & Public Policy* 21, 23–25; see also J Heath, *The Machinery of Government: Public Administration and the Liberal State* (Oxford University Press, 2020) 254–99.

[42] Ackerman (n 7) 1037.

The difference in the pace of the temporal order moulds the respective executive mindsets for everyday administration and emergency discretion, shining a light on the dictatorial character of the executive instantiation of emergency powers. Through this lens, the classical strategy in the constitutional domestication of emergency powers by compartmentalisation amounts to a design for managing two conflicted temporalities in the project of constitutional governance. As the mindset of the executive is moulded in the temporal order, the time for emergency discretion and that for normal administrative action must be constructed in a way to cultivate the right and balanced executive mindset for constitutional governance in times of normalcy and crisis at once. Governance of crisis in the emergency constitution means management of intertemporal conflict.

The above discussion reveals that in the ideal situation, the constitutional domestication of emergency powers is centred on managing the intertemporal conflict between the normal state of the rule of law and the juridical state of emergency. Managing conflicted temporalities between normalcy and emergency is meant to cultivate a balanced executive mindset for purposes of governance in constitutional ordering. This ideal picture of the emergency constitution looks orderly and pretty until we shift focus to the real-word governance.

As has been well trodden in the literature, the reach of the administrative state today is pervasive, and its presence is always expected.[43] With the increase of state responsibilities, the executive emerges as an 'always present' power so that the government can live up to the public's high expectations of the welfare state when various societal needs materialise. Notwithstanding being 'always present', the executive should not expect to change its mindset for the sundry routines in everyday governance. Yet, under the pressure of social acceleration, the 'always present' executive is expected to pick up its pace amid the fast-moving societal tempo. As a result, not only is legislation 'motorised' by means of administrative rulemaking[44] but the executive sees its own motorisation in a race against time, only to play catch-up with the fast-changing society.[45] With the executive adapted to coping with the governance challenges posed by an accelerated and complex society, the temporal order in which its mindset in governance is cultivated also changes. The steady-paced temporal order that moulds the executive mindset for the normal state of the rule of law unnoticeably gives way. In its place we see an accelerated temporality approximating that in which the executive mindset for emergency discretion is cultivated. Furthermore, as crisis is seen constantly occurring everywhere, governance evolves as crisis governance.

[43] See GS Lawson, 'The Rise and Rise of the Administrative State' (1994) 107 *Harvard Law Review* 1231; G Scheffler and DE Walters, 'The Submerged Administrative State' [2024] *Wisconsin Law Review* 789, 791–92; see also EL Rubin, *Soul, Self, and Society: The New Morality and the Modern State* (Oxford University Press, 2015); JCN Raadschelders, *The Three Ages of Government: From the Person, to the Group, to the World* (University of Michigan Press, 2020) 27–38.

[44] Scheuerman (n 38).

[45] Scheuerman (n 39) xiv; cf John O McGinnis, 'Laws for Learning in an Age of Acceleration' (2011) 53 *William & Mary Law Review* 305, 335.

With the process of social acceleration pressing on and crisis becoming a governance fixture, the normalcy-exception distinction in constitutional ordering is blurred, resulting in a normalisation of emergency powers by stealth. Here we see a unitary crisis-moulded mindset of the 'always present' executive. In this unitary executive mindset is undercut the constitutional strategy to domesticate emergency powers by way of intertemporal conflict management. How this unitary executive mindset manifests itself in the EU's crisis response is the theme I address next.

3. Constituting Europe in Crisis: Intertemporal Conflict in the Race against Time

To appraise the effect temporality and its attendant mindset exert on the EU's crisis response and its further implications, I first provide a summary account of how the EU's responses to successive emergencies starting from the euro crisis have reshaped its constitutional operation. The EU's emergency-prompted constitution-reshaping exercise is then critically examined in terms of constitutional temporality and mindset.

3.1 Emergency Reordering

The constitutional story of the European Communities of the 1950s evolving into the European Union as we know it today tells us that crisis is an inseparable part of the project of Europe.[46] The EU's constitutional predecessors were founded soon after Europe witnessed a murderous catastrophe, while crises were looming on the eastern horizon in the deepening Cold War.[47] As Jean Monnet's oft-quoted remarks suggested decades ago,[48] the project of Europe as embodied in the EU has been constituted in crises indeed. Yet, to see how the current EU constitutional order has been shaped by crises, we need not go all the way back to the 1950s. Echoing the alignment of the process of state building and the constitutionalisation of political ordering in history,[49] the EU's constitutional configuration has altered in parallel with the recent crises that have effectively revolutionised the

[46] J Zeitlin and F Nicoli (eds), *The European Union Beyond the Polycrisis? Integration and Politicization in an Age of Shifting Cleavages* (Routledge, 2020); FM Ferrara and H Kriesi, 'Crisis Pressures and European Integration' (2022) 29 *Journal of European Public Policy* 1351.

[47] See N Ludlow, 'European Integration and the Cold War' in MP Leffler and OA Westad (eds), *The Cambridge History of the Cold War, Volume II: Crises and Détente* (Cambridge University Press, 2010) 179.

[48] 'Europe will be forged in crises, and will be the sum of the solutions adopted for these crises', quoted in S Fabbrini, 'Brussels in Hard Times: The EU's Executive Deficit' in A Bongardt and F Torres (eds), *The Political Economy of Europe's Future and Identity: Integration in Crisis Mode* (European University Institute, 2023) 43, 43.

[49] See M Loughlin, *Foundations of Public Law* (Oxford University Press, 2010) 238–72.

EU's 'budgetary capacity' or 'fiscal capacity' – a characteristic feature in state building[50] – and governance role in other areas.[51] Let us start where the recent crisis storybook began.

As has been well documented, the EU responded to the euro crisis with a set of emergency policies. The first set of policies can be called economic emergency measures proper. These measures include coordinated bilateral loans to 'bail out' Greece in the early stage of the eurozone debt crisis,[52] the EU law-based emergency assistance programmes such as the temporary European Financial Stabilizsation Mechanism (EFSM) and European Financial Stability Facility (EFSF),[53] and the permanent European Stability Mechanism (ESM) separately established under public international law.[54] Alongside these new mechanisms and the attendant legal instruments, the first set of emergency policies paved the way for the expanded role of the European Central Bank (ECB) in providing financial assistance to the EU Member States through innovative means, including the much discussed Outright Monetary Transactions (OMT) measures.[55] The second set of the EU's responses focused on budgetary and economic surveillance. To address the issues arising under the Stability and Growth Pact (SGP) – which was adopted to ensure that its Member States would not incur excessive government debts through irresponsible budgetary policies – the EU took new measures in the form of regulation and directive in 2011 ('Six Packs') and 2013 ('Two Packs') aimed at establishing budgetary discipline among the Member States.[56] Apart from these measures under the EU law, an international treaty, known as the 'Fiscal Compact',[57] was

[50] C Tilly (ed), *The Formation of National States in Western Europe* (Princeton University Press, 1975); see also J Brewer, *The Sinews of Power: War, Money and the English State, 1688–1783* (Harvard University Press, 1989).

[51] F Fabbrini, *EU Fiscal Capacity: Legal Integration After Covid-19 and the War in Ukraine* (Oxford University Press, 2022); see also F Fabbrini, 'Funding the War in Ukraine: The European Peace Facility, the Macro-Financial Assistance Instrument, and the Slow Rise of an EU Fiscal Capacity' (2023) 11 (4) *Politics and Governance* 52, 53.

[52] For the legal maneuvers to get around the ban on bail-out in the EU law in this regard, see H Schepel, 'The Bank, the Bond, and the Bail-out: On the Legal Construction of Market Discipline in the Eurozone' (2017) 44 *Journal of Law and Society* 79.

[53] Notably, the basis of the EFSF in the EU law is flimsy at best. Formally, it is a limited liability company incorporated under Luxembourg private law, although it originated in an international agreement among the representatives of the Eurozone states meeting within the institutional framework of the Economic and Financial Affairs Council (ECOFIN) under the EU. See C Kilpatrick, 'On the Rule of Law and Economic Emergency: The Degradation of Basic Legal Values in Europe's Bailouts' (2015) 35 *OJLS* 325, 334; see also M-S Kuo, 'Control by Aggregation? Critical Reflections on Global Constitutionalism in the Shadow of Looming Transnational Emergency Powers' (2019) 26 *Constellations* 241, 247.

[54] N De Boer, *Judging European Democracy: The Role and Legitimacy of National Constitutional Courts in the EU* (OUP 2023) 169; see also Kuo (n 53) 247.

[55] De Boer (n 54) 170.

[56] ibid 170–71; Fabbrini (2022) (n 51) 13-14.

[57] Treaty on Stability, Coordination and Governance in the Economic and Monetary Union (2012). Part III of the Fiscal Compact is now incorporated into the EU legal order with the adoption of the Regulation (EU) 2024/1263 of the European Parliament and of the Council of 29 April 2024 on the effective coordination of economic policies and on multilateral budgetary surveillance and repealing Council Regulation (EC) No 1466/97.

concluded between the EU Member States,[58] requiring contracting parties to, inter alia, provide for the requirement for balanced budget in domestic law.[59] As regards the third set, it is centred on measures regarding financial regulation. Under the so-called 'banking union', measures were adopted for the supervision of credit institutions[60] and the wind-down of failing banks[61] of the EU Member States using the euro as their currency.[62]

Apparently, among the three sets of emergency policies the EU adopted amid the euro crisis, only some of the policies in the first set are temporary and emergency measures in nature. Although the EFSM was intended as a temporary measure to mitigate the euro crisis, the ESM was instituted as a permanent mechanism from the outset and has outlived the euro crisis. Moreover, the second and third sets of policies are not obvious for their character as emergency response measures. Rather, they are more of a long-awaited institutional reform to resolve the asymmetry of competence of the EU constitutional architecture of economic governance – with monetary powers centralised at the EU level, and economic powers mostly held by the Member States – than responses to a state of economic emergency as seen in the euro crisis.[63] Outlasting the state of emergency, these measures have significantly increased the EU's role in overall economic governance, although they are still not sufficient to 'complete' the project of the Economic and Monetary Union (EMU).[64] In a word, the EU saw an altered constitutional configuration along with its increased governance capacity when it came out of the euro crisis.[65]

Before the ink of commentaries on the EU's response to the euro crisis and its constitutional implications dried, the EU soon entered another state of emergency in 2020, only this time together with the rest of the world: the Covid-19 Public Health Emergency of International Concern. Despite the Covid pandemic's tremendous toll on citizens of the EU, the crisis prompted by the pandemic that called for responses at the EU level evoked a state of economic emergency.[66] From strict lockdowns imposed by individual Member States – the primary response to the spread of the highly contagious SARS-CoV-2[67] – resulted an abrupt and

[58] At the time of the Fiscal Compact's conclusion in 2012, two Member States refused to join: the United Kingdom (UK) and Czechia (then the Czech Republic).

[59] Fabbrini (2022) (n 51) 14; De Boer (n 54) 171.

[60] The Single Supervisory Mechanism (SSM).

[61] The Single Resolution Mechanism (SRM).

[62] For further details of how these mechanisms work, see De Boer (n 54) 171–72.

[63] See Fabbrini (2022) (n 51) 9–16.

[64] ibid 16–18 (quoting Mario Draghi's Speech at the session of the plenary of the EuropeanParliament in Strasbourg on 15 January 2019, 'EMU remain[ed] incomplete').

[65] G Martinico, 'EU Crisis and Constitutional Mutations: A Review Article' (2014) 165 *Revista de Estudios Políticos* (nueva época) 247; see also A-M Porras-Gómez, 'The EU Recovery Instrument and the Constitutional Implications of its Expenditure' (2023) 19 *EuConst* 1, 6.

[66] J White, 'Emergency Europe after Covid-19' in Gerard Delanty (ed), *Pandemics, Politics, and Society Critical Perspectives on the Covid-19 Crisis* (de Gruyter 2021) 75; V Delhomme and T Hervey, 'The European Union's Response to the Covid-19 Crisis and (the Legitimacy of) the Union's Legal Order' (2022) 41 *Yearbook of European Law* 48, 50; see also P Dermine, 'The EU's Response to the COVID-19 Crisis and the Trajectory of Fiscal Integration in Europe: Between Continuity and Rupture' (2020) 47 *Legal Issues of Economic Integration* 337.

[67] SARS-CoV-2 is the strand of the coronavirus causing the Covid-19 pandemic.

unprecedented economic contraction across the EU.[68] Also, the Member States saw their public spending and budget deficits skyrocketing following their domestic large-scale bailouts. As the sovereign debts of some of the Member States within the eurozone spiked sharply, the stability of the euro became a concern again, raising the prospect of a new euro crisis.[69] With another state of economic emergency looming, the EU began to introduce a set of policies under the umbrella programme of the Next Generation EU (NG-EU) in May 2020 – following earlier responses from the ECB and other existing mechanisms – which only cleared all the political and legal hurdles in 2021.[70] Notably, as its various funds and mechanisms suggest, the NG-EU's reach extends beyond the pandemic's immediate aftermath. At its core is a new EU Recovery Instrument (EURI). Conceived as a one-off programme, the EURI stays outside the EU's Multiannual Financial Framework (MFF). Among the various funds created under the EURI is the Recovery and Resilience Facility (RRF) with 672.5 billion euros at its disposal, which can be disbursed to individual Member States for redistributive purposes.[71] The EURI is noted not only for its plenty funds but also for the way it was sourced. Its total 750 billion euros (including the RRF) came from the common debt the European Commission (the Commission) issued on behalf of the EU on financial markets, backed up by the general EU budget. To make this happen, the legal hurdle set up in the Own Resources Decision (ORD) had been cleared to allow the EU to borrow on financial markets.[72]

As noted above, the asymmetry of the EMU was considered the structural cause of the euro crisis. With the EU's competence confined to monetary policy, the EU's role in coordinating economic policies among the Member States was limited. Lacking a fiscal capacity, the EU's overall influence on the EU-wide governance was constrained, too. Although the line between economic and monetary policies was effectively redrawn by the EU's emergency responses to the euro crisis and the EU's role in economic governance has since been on the rise, the lack of a fiscal capacity was still not adequately addressed.[73] Nevertheless, the emergency mechanisms and measures introduced amid the euro crisis enabled the ECB to intervene in the early stage of the economic crisis prompted by the Covid pandemic.[74] Thus, the EU's crisis response amid the pandemic emergency has built on the institutional groundwork laid during the euro crisis and taken it to the next stage – the EU's fiscal capacity was no longer a political taboo, even if the EURI was still set up as a one-off programme.[75]

[68] See Dirk Ehnts and Michael Paetz, 'COVID-19 and Its Economic Consequences for the Euro Area' (2021) 11 *Eurasian Economic Review* 227; see also Grégory Claeys et al, 'The Great COVID-19 Divergence: Managing a Sustainable and Equitable Recovery in the EU' (2021) 56 *Intereconomics* 211, 212–14.

[69] De Boer (n 54) 243.

[70] Fabbrini (2022) (n 51) 41–47; De Boer (n 54) 243–46.

[71] Porras-Gómez (n 65) 7.

[72] Fabbrini (2023) (n 51) 55; De Boer (n 54) 246.

[73] Fabbrini (2022) (n 51) 156–57.

[74] Fabbrini (2022) (n 51) 44; De Boer (n 54) 243–44.

[75] Porras-Gómez (n 65) 3, 23–24; cf De Boer (n 54) 264 (referring to the establishment of the EURI as the EU's 'Hamiltonian Moment').

The EU's quest for a fiscal capacity did not stop at the wind-down of the pandemic emergency. With another crisis, the Ukraine War, breaking out on its doorstep in 2022, the question of the EU's fiscal capacity was thrown into sharp relief again. To muster the financial resources needed to support Ukraine, the EU first tapped into its European Peace Facility (EPF) – which had already been created in 2021 as part of the 2021–27 MFF – and then established a Macro-Financial Assistance Instrument (MFA+) for Ukraine.[76] Of particular pertinence to the present discussion is that the use of common borrowing and spending initiated in the one-off EURI is replicated in the EU's funding of Ukraine's war effort, despite their technical differences.[77] In sum, building on the innovative measures adopted in the previous rounds of crisis, the EU's overall emergency response has also changed its constitutional configuration.[78]

So far, the summary account of the EU's crisis responses has shown that it has seen structural changes amid crises. Through one crisis after another, it has developed as an entity that is invested with the institutional instruments and financial resources to stabilise the fiscal situation and stimulate economic growth within the EU and even to support its external stance in a geopolitical conflict.[79] As the EU's overall governance competence expands, its policy influence on the Members States increases, and more importantly, its own fiscal capacity is allowed to creep in, the EU has effectively undergone a process of constitution-remaking in an extended three-part state of emergency for just over a decade, reminiscing the history of European state formation.[80]

3.2 Minding Time

The observation made above does not tell us whether the EU's emergency responses are dictatorial in substance or whether they have deviated from the core values of the EU, including the rule of law and democracy.[81] Nor does whether the EU's emergency measures are dictatorial in nature or proportionate to the various crises concern me for present purposes.[82] What interests me here is the transform-

[76] Fabbrini (2022) (n 51) 129–30; Fabbrini (2023) (n 51) 52–55.

[77] Fabbrini (2023) (n 51) 55–56.

[78] See P L Lindseth and P Leino-Sandberg, 'Crisis, Reinterpretation, and the Rule of Law: Repurposing "Cohesion" as a General EU Spending Power' (2024) 16 *Hague Journal on the Rule of Law* 587.

[79] Fabbrini (2022) (n 51).

[80] Fabbrini (2023) (n 51).

[81] Kilpatrick (n 53); C Kreuder-Sonnen, 'Does Europe Need an Emergency Constitution?' (2023) 71 *Political Studies* 125.

[82] On these issues, see Kreuder-Sonnen (n 81); VA Schmidt, *Europe's Crisis of Legitimacy: Governing by Rules and Ruling by Numbers in the Eurozone* (Oxford University Press, 2020) 117–49; J White, 'Constitutionalizing the EU in an Age of Emergencies' (2023) 61 *Journal of Common Market Studies* 781; FB Bastos and A De Ruijter, 'Break or Bend in Case of Emergency?: Rule of Law and State of Emergency in European Public Health Administration' (2019) 10 *European Journal of Risk Regulation* 610; S Grund, 'The Legality of the European Central Bank's Pandemic Emergency Purchase Programme' *Delors Institute Policy Brief* (March 25, 2020).

ative effect of the emergency responses from the EU and its Member States on the EU's constitutional order. As commentaries on the euro crisis have suggested, the EU's emergency responses provide a model case of how a classical situation of exception on an existential scale prompts a (transnational) governance authority into taking responsive actions that were simply unthinkable before the crisis.[83] Seen in this light, the extended three-part state of emergency with which the EU has contended in the past fifteen years or so seems to be the EU's 'constitutional moment'.[84] The crisis-driven reform on the EU's constitutional configuration then should be celebrated.[85] Yet a closer look at the EU's constitution-reshaping amid crises suggests otherwise.

As Bruce Ackerman perceptively observes, the political action of constitution-(re)making is a race against time.[86] To secure and sustain the gains achieved in the collective effort of popular sovereignty by 'We the People' – revolution – they need to be translated into a constitutional order *in time*. Failing constitutionalisation, such collective gains can be swept aside easily once the revolutionary fever cools down, with 'We the People' feeling betrayed.[87] The crisis-prompted change on the EU's constitutional configuration as discussed above seems to be an instance of running a race against time in a constitution-remaking exercise as portrayed in Ackerman's comparative case studies.[88] The problem is that the temporal order the EU's constitution-remaking exercise finds itself in is different from that of a constitutional moment in Ackerman's portrayal of 'We the People' having spoken. According to Ackerman, a constitutional moment manifests itself and lasts for an extended period of time when private individuals rise up as public citizens to address a fundamental issue or a simmering crisis with their collective remaking of the constitutional order through democratic processes.[89] It is a race against time indeed but the race in a constitutional moment is far from a spring. It is an enduring generational movement instead.[90] Through this extended period of political time, debate, deliberation, persuasion, and jurisprudence take shape to place the resolution of a fundamental issue or a simmering crisis on a firm constitutional ground that can stand the test of time.[91] Thus, despite its reminiscences of a fleeting instant, a constitutional *moment* assumes a steady-paced, extended

[83] J White, 'Emergency Europe' (2015) 63 *Political Studies* 300; J White, *Politics of Last Resort: Governing by Emergency in the European Union* (Oxford University Press, 2019); see also Kuo (n 53); White (n 66); but cf J Zeitlin, 'EU Experimentalist Governance in Times of Crisis' (2016) 39 *West European Politics* 1073; F Nicoli and J Zeitlin, 'Introduction: Escaping the Politics Trap? EU Integration Pathways beyond the Polycrisis' (2024) 31 *Journal of European Public Policy* 3011.

[84] Kreuder-Sonnen (n 81) 140; see also White (n 82).

[85] See E Chachko and K Linos, 'Emergency Powers for Good' (2024) 66 *William & Mary Law Review* 1, 41–64; cf Zeitlin (n 83); Nicoli and Zeitlin (n 83).

[86] B Ackerman, *Revolutionary Constitutions: Charismatic Leadership and the Rule of Law* (Harvard University Press, 2019) 3–4, 281.

[87] ibid 281.

[88] ibid.

[89] B Ackerman, *We the People: Foundations, Volume 1* (Harvard University Press, 1991) 266–90.

[90] B Ackerman, 'A Generation of Betrayal?' (1997) 65 *Fordham Law Review* 1519.

[91] Ackerman (n 89).

temporal order that enables the democratic conduct of engagement-requiring, time-consuming higher lawmaking.[92]

In contrast, the EU's crisis-driven constitution-reshaping exercise has taken place in an accelerated temporal order of emergency.[93] Either led by the jittery financial market or conditioned by the exponential tempo of virus spread, such states of emergency are not the right time for debate, deliberation, persuasion, or even to the development of jurisprudence that is central to successful constitution-(re)making in a constitutional moment. Judicial interventions in this situation – as has been vividly exhibited by the 'dialogue' between the Court of Justice of the EU and the German Federal Constitutional Court as well as other apex courts of the Member States – have little to do with the consolidation and articulation of the results of Ackermanian higher lawmaking.[94] Rather, they become a convenient shortcut for the two opposing sides to the EU's emergency measures.[95] In sum, since the pace of such a race against time is determined by the speed of market transaction or epidemic contagion, decisions – including those intended to change the constitutional status quo or just with implications to it – need taking rapidly, leaving no room for the conduct of time-consuming higher lawmaking.

I hasten to add that nothing said above suggests that the measures taken by the EU in response to the extended three-part state of emergency in the past fifteen years or so should not have been adopted or that they are flawed in terms of policy substance. Neither is my present concern. Rather, my point is that such measures have effectively altered the EU's constitutional architecture, and to be persuasive, constitutional changes on this scale need to be debated, deliberated, and articulated through the engagement-requiring and time-consuming process of higher lawmaking.[96] To enable such processes to run in a meaningful way requires a temporality that is distinctive of genuine constitutional moments. This is not the kind of rushed temporality experienced by officials and bureaucrats repeatedly being thrown into a race against time by successive states of emergency.[97] Beneath the surface of doubts cast about the legitimacy of the EU's crisis-prompted change on its constitutional order lies the question of intertemporal conflict between the moment of constitution-(re)making and the state of emergency.[98]

It may be countered that the Ackermanian constitutional moment is based on the revolutionary tradition of constitution-making and it has no place in the

[92] ibid.

[93] See also White (2019) (n 83) 67–69; cf Lindseth and Leino-Sandberg (n 78).

[94] Ackerman (n 89).

[95] De Boer (n 54) 165–218.

[96] cf Lindseth and Leino-Sandberg (n 78).

[97] White (n 82).

[98] cf K Dyson, *States, Debt, and Power: 'Saints' and 'Sinners' in European History and Integration* (Oxford University Press, 2014) 621.

EU's evolutionary mode of constitutional development.[99] On this view, in the EU's crisis-prompted constitutional exercise, there may be no mass mobilisation as Ackerman has championed in instances of revolutionary constitution-making around the globe.[100] Yet it does not make the reformed constitutional configuration less legitimate. Rather, it only reflects the EU's evolutionary tradition. The absence of mass mobilisation does not mean that the EU's recent crisis-prompted change on the constitutional configuration lacks broad *political* support.[101]

It is true that the EU's recent constitution-reshaping exercise is another instantiation of evolutionary change as manifested in its constitutional tradition.[102] Yet not all evolutions take place on the same timescale. While a normal evolution takes an extended period of time to materialise, a mutation in the evolutionary process can happen within a compressed time frame.[103] In the temporally extended process of normal constitutional evolution, debate, deliberation, persuasion, and judicial articulation are not absent but just take place in a scattered manner without much fanfare as seen in mass mobilizisation. Yet, when an 'evolutionary' constitutional change takes the form of mutation, its temporal progression is accelerated. It is hard to see how debate, deliberation, persuasion, and judicial articulation required of fundamental constitution-reshaping can result from such a rushed temporality. Moreover, to paraphrase Jean Monnet, not only has Europe been forged in crises but officials and bureaucrats running the project of the EU have forged their mindsets in crises on end. With their mindsets forged in crises, officials and bureaucrats in charge of controlling crises are unitarily occupied with emergency responses. Under such circumstances, they would be hard-pressed to be mindful of the broad effect of their emergency responses on the EU's overall constitutional configuration and its legitimacy, not to mention whether a constitutional evolution or mutation is being induced. Bypassing cumbersome treaty revision procedures and turning to creative legal reinterpretation in the EU's strategy to rest its emergency response on constitutional grounds[104] speaks to the EU's crisis-driven change as a constitutional mutation. Thus, the 'mutation' that is considered to be the characteristic of

[99] For the centrality of revolution in Ackerman's constitutional theory, see M-S Kuo, 'Authenticity: The Ultimate Challenge in the Quest for Lasting Constitutional Legitimacy' (2021) 41 *OJLS* 261, 281–83; for European constitutionalism's evolutionary character, see Porras-Gómez (n 65); D Piana, 'An Evolutionary Approach to the Constitutionalism of an Enlarged EU: Why will Cognitive and Cultural Boundaries Matter?' in W Sadurski, A Czarnota, and M Krygier (eds), *Spreading Democracy and the Rule of Law? The Impact of EU Enlargement for the Rule of Law, Democracy and Constitutionalism in Post-Communist Legal Orders* (Springer 2006) 219; E-U Petersmann, 'EU Crises Governance and "Evolutionary Constitutionalism" in a Multipolar World of "Permacrises"' *EUI Law Working Paper* (2024/19), https://cadmus.eui.eu/bitstream/handle/1814/77476/LAW_2024_19.pdf?sequence=1&isAllowed=y.

[100] Ackerman (n 86).

[101] De Boer (n 54) 180–98.

[102] Porras-Gómez (n 65); Petersmann (n 99); see also Martinico (n 65).

[103] See K Harris and J K Pritchard, 'Rapid Evolution of the Human Mutation Spectrum' *eLife* (April 25 2017), https://elifesciences.org/articles/24284.

[104] Lindseth and Leino-Sandberg (n 78).

the EU's crisis-prompted constitutional change[105] must find its *political* support from sources other than the processes of debate, deliberation, persuasion, and judicial articulation. What should we make of this 'political' turn in the EU's experience with constitution-remaking? I take up this question next.

4. Whither 'Emergency Europe'? Executive Constitutionalism vs Political Constitutionalism

One criticism about the EU's constitutional development is that it has been pushed chiefly through judicial lawmaking.[106] Engineered by the Cout of Justice of the European Union (CJEU), the EU legal order has taken on constitutional character through what Dieter Grimm calls 'overconstitutionalisation' and become ossified.[107] Against this backdrop, the recent emergency-prompted change on the EU's constitutional configuration has been presented as the evidence that the EU's road towards constitutionalism has taken a political turn as the CJEU no longer occupies the driver's seat.[108] Instead, it is the political branch of the EU that has steered this crisis-driven constitution-remaking exercise, suggesting the emergence of political constitutionalism in the EU's constitutional landscape.[109] At such a political turn in the EU's constitutional development, can political constitutionalism help to refute the long-held view of the project of European integration having been unduly depoliticised?

It should be noted that politics is far from a monolithic phenomenon. It can take myriad forms and may find expression through various channels. Risking the accusation of hyperbole, it can be said that politics is amorphous but we may sense and encounter it everywhere with no specialism in political science needed.[110] Thus, to say that the recent emergency-prompted change on the EU's constitutional configuration marks a political turn in the EU's evolutionary constitutional development only means that this latest round of constitutional reordering by emergency takes an alternative form of politics to that manifested in the CJEU-directed overconstitutionalisation of the EU legal order. To put it bluntly, the EU's much-criticised

[105] Martinico (n 65).

[106] JHH Weiler, 'The Political and Legal Culture of European Integration: An Exploratory Essay' (2011) 9 *I-CON* 678; T Horsley, 'Reflections on the Role of the Court of Justice as the "Motor" of European Integration: Legal limits to Judicial Lawmaking' (2013) 50 *Common Market Law Review* 913; see also KJ Alter and LR Helfer, 'Nature or Nurture? Judicial Lawmaking in the European Court of Justice and the Andean Tribunal of Justice' (2010) 64 *International Organization* 563

[107] D Grimm, *The Constitution of European Democracy* (Justin Collings tr, Oxford University Press, 2017) 27–28.

[108] See C Lequesne, 'The Eurozone Crisis and European Integration: "New Intergovernmentalism" as a Valid Theory' in S Saurugger and F Terpan (eds), *Crisis and Institutional Change in Regional Integration* (Routledge, 2016) 41, 53–55.

[109] See also De Boer (n 54) 17–20, 239–75.

[110] See PW Kahn, *Political Theology: Four New Chapters on the Concept of Sovereignty* (Columbia University Press, 2011) 52, 129, 145.

depoliticised process of constitutionalisation through judicial lawmaking is just another form of politics.[111] It is no less political than the recent emergency-prompted change. Thus, it is one thing to say that the political branch – the Commission, the Council of European Union (the Council), and the European Council in this regard – takes the place of the CJEU in the latest round of the EU's constitutional reform; it is another to imply that this ostensible political turn brings the EU constitutional order closer to political constitutionalism than the CJEU-directed process of constitutionalisation. Then, what is political constitutionalism? Does the EU's crisis-prompted constitutional change live up to political constitutionalism?

Political constitutionalism is not a unitary concept.[112] It can simply mean that politics itself is the constitution. This variety of political constitutionalism rests on political realism: constitutionalism is stripped down to reality of dynamic interactions among politicians and other political actors, and is emptied of normative significance.[113] Notably, political constitutionalists see constitutionalism through the lens of politics, but not all of them hold the foregoing realist view. Departing from political realism, political constitutionalism can be as normative as its conceptual converse – legal constitutionalism.[114] For this normative variety, political constitutionalism looks to politics or political channels – instead of courts – as they are considered the source of constitutional normativity and the mechanism to correct normative breaches in constitutional reality.[115] To allow politics to function as the source of constitutional norms and the correction mechanism for their breach, the normative variety also assumes a normative concept of politics or, to be more precise, a normative view of democratic politics.[116] Such a politics cannot exist independently of democratic processes. Although decisions and choices made by politicians are crucial to a constitutional order, they do not decide the normative content of a constitutional order. Rather, their decisions and policy choices are subject to normative scrutiny through various channels in a dynamic democratic process, including trials in the court of political opinion and duels in periodic elections.[117] Policy choices made by politicians or officials to change established constitutional norms only attain constitutional status after they survive normative scrutiny conducted in democratic politics.[118] Failing this normative test, such policies are nothing but constitutional transgression. Normative political constitutionalism is embedded in politics of 'reflexive democracy'.[119] Is this what

[111] See A Somek and E Paar, 'Europe's Political Constitution' (2023) 2 *European Law Open* 484, 494.

[112] G Gee and GCN Webber, 'What Is a Political Constitution?' (2010) 30 *OJLS* 273.

[113] JAG Griffith, 'The Political Constitution' (1979) 42 *MLR* 1.

[114] See Gee and Webber (n 112) 275.

[115] See A Tomkins, *Our Republican Constitution* (Hart 2005); R Bellamy, *Political Constitutionalism: A Republican Defence of the Constitutionality of Democracy* (CUP 2007).

[116] M-S Kuo, 'Politics and Constitutional Jurisgenesis: A Cautionary Note on Political Constitutionalism' (2018) 7 *GlobCon* 75, 95–96.

[117] Bellamy (n 115) 191–203.

[118] See also D Feldman, 'Political Practice and Constitutional Change' in X Contiades and A Fotiadou (eds), *Routledge Handbook of Comparative Constitutional Change* (Routledge, 2020) 201.

[119] P Rosanvallon, *Democratic Legitimacy: Impartiality, Reflexivity, Proximity* (A Goldhammer tr, Princeton University Press, 2011) 128–36.

underpins the political turn as seen in the latest round of the EU's constitutional reform?

As noted above, political constitutionalism is recently embraced by some scholars to normatively justify the EU's recent emergency-induced constitutional change. Thus, the realist variety of political constitutionalism will not do the trick. What defenders of the EU's emergency responses-turned constitutional change have in mind must be the normative variety of political constitutionalism. Yet the political process in which the EU's emergency-induced constitution-reshaping exercise takes place is a world apart from the reflexive democracy discussed above. Upon closer examination, executive officials of different pedigrees – the EU officials in the Commission, national ministers in the Council, and heads of state or government in the European Council – have dominated the political process leading to the emergency-induced constitutional reform.[120] What came out of this decision-making process – ie, the crisis response policies and the attendant changes on the EU's constitutional configuration – is political indeed, but it did not result from a politics of 'reflexive democracy'. Thus, the variety of political constitutionalism invoked to justify the perceived political turn in the EU's latest emergency-induced constitutional reform turns out to be an 'executive constitutionalism' instead of a normative political constitutionalism.

Whether the nature of executive constitutionalism, which underpins the EU's crisis-driven constitutional change, is lawless or not cannot be fully discussed within this space.[121] Yet one feature characteristic of the EU's constitution-reshaping exercise resting on executive constitutionalism cannot escape attention: it is induced in an extended state of emergency by national and transnational executives. The rise of executive constitutionalism in the EU's recent emergency-prompted constitutional development is the epitome of the 'always present' executive's encroachment on constitutional issues that cannot be properly addressed by rapid-fire responses to persistent crises. This brings home the challenge of intertemporal conflict in constitutional governance. Here arises an issue concerning the constitutional ethos of the project of European integration.

A factual state of exception or emergency is where the *political* component of a constitutional order is most manifest. This is because, as the positive constitutional norms reach their limit, they are forced open to the law of necessity to satisfy the survival needs of the body politic. This perceptive observation of the constitutional phenomenon was made by none other than Carl Schmitt, the foremost champion of executive dictatorship.[122] The extended state of emergency in

[120] See N Scicluna, 'Politicization without Democratization: How the Eurozone Crisis Is Transforming EU Law and Politics' (2014) 12 *I-CON* 545.

[121] Compare E Fisher, *Risk Regulation and Administrative Constitutionalism* (Hart, 2007), with B Ackerman, *The Decline and Fall of the American Republic* (Belknap 2010) 87-116; cf C Casey and D Kenny, 'The Gatekeepers: Executive Lawyers and the Executive Power in Comparative Constitutional Law' (2022) 20 *I-CON* 664.

[122] Schmitt (n 2); see also R Wolin, 'Carl Schmitt, Political Existentialism, and the Total State' (1990) 19 *Theory and Society* 389, 397.

which the EU's latest round of constitutional change took place was no exception. In the extended state of emergency, the EU was forced to gaze at its limit and the political component of the underlying constitutional order. Yet to characterise the constitutional change induced by the EU's emergency measures in response to crises as the political turn in its constitutional development and to justify this emergency-driven constitutional reform in terms of political constitutionalism commits an error of elision. It fails to distinguish between 'the political' distinctive of emergency decisions and the politics required for making fundamental constitutional choices.[123] Blurring these two distinct political phenomena inadvertently gives the Schmittian notion of 'sovereign dictatorship'[124] an unexpected redemption and dampens the EU's normative constitutional ethos.[125] That the executive constitutionalism as manifested in the EU's recent emergency response comes closer to an executive exercise of (derived) constituent power in Schmitt's teachings[126] than political constitutionalism resting on a normative view of democratic politics should not be missed.

5. Conclusion

Time conditions not only individual lives but also human society. Through law, the constitutional project included, and other human works, life can have meaning beyond the time-limited, labouring biological body.[127] Yet law cannot freeze time or stop in time. Rather, it must evolve with time. Failing progress, law only renders itself irrelevant in humankind's continuing grappling with the question of time. The constitutional project is one of humans running a race against time in their political life.[128] Constitutional governance in and of crisis cuts to the heart of how time at varying speeds – or simply temporalities – conditions the constitutional project.

In this chapter, I took up this question in light of the EU's recent crisis-driven constitution-reshaping exercise. Through a close examination of the tension between constitutionalism and crisis governance, I tried to show that at the core of the constitutional domestication of emergency powers is management of the intertemporal conflict between the state of exception/emergency and that of normalcy.

[123] See A Arato, 'Forms of Constitution Making and Theories of Democracy' (1995) 17 *Cardozo Law Review* 191, 205–11.

[124] Schmitt (n 2) 119–29.

[125] Compare Scicluna (n 120) 553–69, with S Tarlea et al, 'Executive Power in European Union Politics' (2024) 37 *Governance* 161. For the normative character of the EU's ethos, see generally A Williams, *The Ethos of Europe: Values, Law and Justice in the EU* (Cambridge University Press, 2012).

[126] Schmitt (n 2). For the distinction between original and derived constituent power, see Y Roznai, *Unconstitutional Constitutional Amendments: The Limits of Amendment Powers* (Oxford University Press, 2017) 105-34.

[127] See also H Arendt, *The Human Condition* (2nd ed, University of Chicago Press, 1998) [1958] 188–98, 220-31 (alluding to the substitution of 'work' for 'action' in the making of laws).

[128] Ackerman (n 86) 3–4.

The distinction between normalcy and exception allows constitutional orders to respond to governance needs that require rapid-fire, reassuring responses without eroding the rule of law. With the intertemporal conflict at the core of constitutional governance in and of crisis brought to the fore, I looked into the EU's crisis responses and argued that they have amounted to a constitution-reshaping exercise of constituent significance. Recognising the 'political' character of the EU's crisis-induced reform, I questioned the characterisation of such constitution-reshaping in terms of political constitutionalism. Instead, I suggested that the EU's crisis-driven constitution-reshaping reflects executive constitutionalism, whose speedy, rapid-fire character renders its attendant constitutional reform dubious.

The EU's implicit embrace of executive constitutionalism as has emitted from its crisis responses is by no means an example of European exceptionalism or the EU as a constitutional polity *sui generis*. Rather, it offers a microcosm of how consecutive crises can impact the constitutional project, shaking to its core the management of intertemporal conflict at the centre of constitutional domestication of emergency powers. With crisis governance becoming a constitutional fixture around the globe, it is past time to take the challenge of time to constitutional governance seriously.

INTRODUCTION TO PART 3

Crisis Governance Constitutionalism and the Perspectives of Experimentalist and of Public Goods' Governance Theories (Political Science and Economics)

LEONE NIGLIA

Part 3 maps the rise of crisis governance constitutionalism in relation to political science and economic studies of governance. This part engages with the often unintended yet strong connection between the legal and non-legal treatments of the NG-EU and the need to explore such connection.

In this Part, further declinations of crisis governance constitutionalism are considered. They are declinations that emerge in more descriptive than normative terms as political science studies measure the dynamics of power politics and as economists measure under their chosen cost benefit analyses.

As constitutionalism keeps mutating into crisis governance constitutionalism, the five versions of this mutation as above mapped – democratic/social, ordoliberal, reflexive, public sphere, normative political – and as critically considered in contrast to the legalistic position, need to be reconsidered in the light of the tensions between their tenet and that of two major strands of political science and of economic scholarship respectively focusing on the implementation of the NG-EU through the national plans and on the theories of 'public goods' applied to governance.

Representative statements of the political science position here under consideration, in addition to their seeing the RRF as reinforcing national ownership,[1] are, to quote from Chapter 7 in this book:

'Building on the Commission's own recent guidance, such a redesigned performance-based financing system would need to give Member States greater flexibility on the means for achieving the milestones and targets, while remaining firm on the underlying objectives and purpose of the reforms and investments they represent. Such a system would also require more flexible processes for modifying national

[1] See below at chapter 7: 'the RRF's governance model has reinforced national ownership and boosted political momentum to deliver on longstanding reform challenges.'

reform and investment measures, responding not only to unanticipated changes in objective circumstances, but also to lessons learned during the implementation process, as foreshadowed in the Commission's guidance on the possibility of modifying Plan commitments in order 'to implement better alternatives' for achieving the original goals. In both respects, a redesigned performance-based financing system could profitably build on the 'diagnostic monitoring' arrangements developed by both private businesses and public industrial policy bodies to govern complex, innovative investment and reform projects under conditions of uncertainty.'

To contrast my view in chapter 9 to chapter 7 by the political scientists, in which Zeitlin et al do not see that national ownership may not have been reinforced or respected (as I argue in chapter 9), lacking, as implementation through the national plans is, of a form of *constitutional guidance*, they equally and coherently do not foresee a path towards reform other than leaving intact both objectives and purposes, thus disabling the potential, constitutional, for generating a form of implementation based on real autonomy on the part of the states through balancing.[2] Therefore, the view held in Chapter 7 I call experimentalism-as-implementation through the NG-EU *without* constitutional guidance.

In his chapter, Steinbach challenges the legal (constitutional) framework around which public goods are governed and re-orders the latter under an economic understanding of cost analysis and specifically of arguments from cost reduction and weighing. In his words:

> The fundamental question that this chapter seeks to address is an old one: how much of the provision of public goods should be the responsibility of the EU rather than that of individual Member States? A question that lawyers typically ask by reference to the subsidiarity principle within the margins of the given allocation of competences. While lawyers do not inquire into this question outside the positivist Treaty framework, economists have more assertively examined the division of mission in federal arrangements beyond a descriptive analysis. To that end, one must address the quandary of determining when the advantages of EU-level provisions outweigh their potential costs, which may incur through the diminution of national sovereignty, the variances across the EU in preferences concerning the nature and extent of public goods, and the increased autonomy of Brussels-based institutions from domestic and local concerns. The inquiry further extends to the potential for reducing these costs through the implementation of suitable institutional arrangements to govern the EU-level provision of public goods – an inquiry to which lawyers can contribute through analysis of the institutional design of the EU legal framework.

Steinbach interestingly and somehow defiantly towards EU law sets aside the legal arguments regarding the EU/Member States' competences and the related

[2] As I argue at chapters 4 and 9.

allocation of powers and instead focuses on economic arguments. This no doubt evidences an 'original sin'[3] consisting of the fact that everywhere else (legislation, reports, in the area of EU crisis governance) there is little attention towards the constitutional dimensions. For example, to refer again to chapter 7, take the notion of *national ownership* as descending from the Commission documents in relation to its unexplored relatedness to what I call constitutional autonomy as I look at it in chapters 4 and 9. The same criticism must apply to the unexplored relatedness of *national ownership* to constitutional equality.

In Chapter 9, I consider the potential of 'experimentalism-as-implementation through the NG-EU', as I describe it, as democratic experimentalism by linking experimentalism to the constitutional dimensions. From this vantage point, political scientists and economic literature point to how power politics operates and engineer a vocabulary that in my view is *'a-constitutional'* due to their not taking into account certain constitutional premises and consequences of the relevant tenets. Hopefully these reflections will help shape a rethinking of political science and economic scholarship on the possible use of key concepts of the EU crisis interventions' tools towards reconciling systemic integration 'needs' and social integration requirements.[4]

[3] To paraphrase Pescatore's view on integration.
[4] I refer to my thoughts at chapter 4 above.

7

Governing the European Union's Recovery and Resilience Facility: National Ownership and Performance-Based Financing in Theory and Practice[1]

JONATHAN ZEITLIN, DAVID BOKHORST AND EDGARS EIHMANIS

1. Introduction

The Recovery and Resilience Facility (RRF), the core of the NextGenerationEU (NG-EU) package adopted in response to the Covid-19 pandemic, has widely been hailed as a breakthrough for European integration. The RRF is remarkable for its massive size (€723bn over six years from 2021 to 2026, of which €577bn has now been taken up),[2] its unprecedented combination of non-repayable grants and loans to Member States, and its financing through common European Union (EU) borrowing. Beyond its quantitative scope, however, the RRF also introduced a series of governance innovations designed to overcome the perceived limitations of previous EU policies seeking to advance the Union's shared objectives by promoting national reforms. First, the RRF is a 'demand-driven' process aimed at fostering 'national ownership' of reform commitments through National Recovery and Resilience Plans (NRRPs) drafted by Member States, in consultation with the European Commission (EC), and adapted to their specific needs. Second, the RRF links structural reforms with complementary investments intended to create political momentum for their implementation by providing positive financial incentives. Third, the RRF is a 'performance-based' instrument, in which periodic payments to Member States are based on the fulfilment of agreed milestones and targets (M&Ts) rather than the reimbursement of eligible costs.[3]

[1] This chapter was previously published as J Zeitlin, D Bokhorst and E Eihmanis, 'Governing the European Union's Recovery and Resilience Facility: National Ownership and Performance-Based Financing in Theory and Practice' (2025) *Regulation & Governance* 19(3) 864–884. https://doi.org/10.1111/rego.12619.

[2] https://ec.europa.eu/economy_finance/recovery-and-resilience-scoreboard/index.html.

[3] For overviews of the financial and governance innovations of the RRF and its significance for European integration, see also F Fabbrini, *EU fiscal capacity: Legal Integration After Covid-19 and the*

The RRF's innovative design has inspired broad debate about its application to other policy areas and its implications for the future of EU governance. Already, the RRF governance framework has been extended through the REPowerEU program, which funds Member States to add new reforms and investments to their NRRPs in response to the energy crisis triggered by the Russian invasion of Ukraine, as well as the Social Climate Fund, which co-finances transitional measures to tackle energy and transport poverty, based on fulfilment of M&Ts embodied in national plans agreed with the Commission.[4] The recently agreed reform of the EU's economic governance framework, in which national medium-term fiscal-structural plans play a central role, likewise draws explicitly on elements of the RRF. There is also ongoing discussion in Brussels about whether the RRF's performance-based financing model should be extended to other programs funded through the Union budget, notably the Cohesion Policy Funds (CPF).[5] These developments, in turn, have spurred prominent scholars to suggest that the RRF may represent a "new method of government' for EU economic policy coordination after the pandemic or even 'a new legal technology' for European governance more generally.[6]

Understanding the effectiveness and legitimacy of the RRF's governance design and operation is thus of utmost importance for scholars and policy makers alike. The RRF's success will ultimately depend on the extent to which the NRRPs fulfil the expectations attached to its governance design by advancing the reform and investment objectives jointly agreed by Member-State governments and the EU institutions. In this study, we analyse how the NRRPs were drafted and are now being implemented, together with how they are being monitored and assessed at both Member State and EU levels, focusing particularly on how 'national ownership' and 'performance-based financing' have worked in practice. Our findings should thus be of broad interest not only to EU specialists, but also to international

War in Ukraine (Oxford, Oxford University Press, 2022); M Buti and S Fabbrini, 'Next Generation EU and the Future of Economic Governance: Towards a Paradigm Change or Just a Big One-off?' (2023) *Journal of European Public Policy* 30(4), 676-695; J Miró, M Natili and W Schelkle, 'Money Makes the World Go Round: How Much Difference do Recovery and Resilience Plans Make to EU Reform Governance?' (2023) *Journal of Common Market Studies*, 1–18, https://doi.org/10.1111/jcms.13558.

[4] European Commission, *Recovery and resilience facility: Two years on. A unique instrument at the heart of the EU's green and digital transformation.* COM (2023) 99 final, 21 February, 5–6; Regulation (EU) 2023/955 of the European Parliament and of the Council of 10 May 2023 establishing a Social Climate Fund and amending Regulation (EU) 2021/100, [2023] OJ L/130.

[5] Regulation (EU) 2024/1263 of the European Parliament and of the Council of 29 April 2024 on the effective coordination of economic policies and on multilateral budgetary surveillance and repealing Council Regulation (EC) No. 1466/97; European Commission, Forging a sustainable future together: Cohesion for a competitive and inclusive Europe. Report of the high-level group on the future of cohesion policy (Luxembourg, Publications Office of the EU, 2024), 38–39; G Sorgi,' EU floats radical change to how it funds poorer members', *PoliticoEU* 27 March 2024, https://www.politico.eu/article/european-commission-propose-change-eu-budget-money-cash/.

[6] C Fasone and N Lupo, 'Learning From the Eurocrisis: A New Method of Government for the European Union's Economic Policy Coordination After the Pandemic',(2024) *International Journal of Constitutional Law (I*CON)*, 1–23, https://doi.org/10.1093/icon/moae064; F. Fabbrini, '*The Recovery and Resilience Facility as a New Legal Technology of European Governance*'. (2023) *Journal of European Integration*, 1–19. https://doi.org/10.1080/07036337.2024.2361830.

and comparative scholars concerned with governance innovations aimed at increasing the performance orientation of public funding and enhancing domestic support for structural reforms.

While the RRF and the NG-EU have attracted widespread attention among academic and policy researchers, few studies to date have sought to tackle these issues empirically based on real-time evidence about the operation of the NRRPs. Most of the literature that has appeared so far focuses either on the political processes leading up to the agreement of the NG-EU package by European and national leaders,[7] or on the policy content and potential impact of the NRRPs.[8] A few pioneering studies have examined the drafting and negotiation of the NRRPs, focusing mainly on individual countries or the inclusion of social actors, while scarcely any academic work has yet investigated the implementation and monitoring phase itself, or examined the practical operation and impact of the RRF's performance-based financing system.[9]

[7] Eg S Ladi and D Tsarouhas, 'EU economic governance and COVID-19: Policy learning and windows of opportunity' (2020) *Journal of European Integration*, 42(8), 1041–1056; C Closa Montero, F González de Leon and G Hernández González, 'Pragmatism and the Limits to the European Parliament's Strategies of Self-empowerment' (2021) *Politics and Governance*, 9(3), 163–174; C de la Porte and MD Jensen, 'The Next Generation EU: An Analysis of the Dimensions of Conflict Behind the Deal' (2021) *Social Policy and Administration*, 55(2), 388–402; M Ferrera, J Miró and S Ronchi, 'Walking the Road Together? EU Polity Maintenance During the COVID-19 Crisis' (2021) *West European Politics*, 44(5–6), 1329–1352; K Armingeon, C de la Porte, E Heins and S Sacchi, 'Voices From the Past: Economic and Political Vulnerabilities in the Making of Next Generation EU' (2022) *Comparative European Politics*, 20, 144–165; S Smeets and D Beach, 'New Institutional Leadership Goes Viral: EU Crisis Reforms and the Coming About of the COVID Recovery Fund' (2023) *European Journal of Political Research*, 62(2), 377–396; S Smeets and F Bekius, 'Coordination and Control in European Council Centered Governance. The Netherlands and the Covid Recovery Fund' (2023) *Journal of Common Market Studies*, 61(2), 486–502.

[8] Eg F Corti, J Nuñez Ferrer, T Ruiz de la Ossa and P Regazzoni, 'Comparing and Assessing Recovery and Resilience Plans: Italy, Germany, Spain, France, Portugal, and Slovakia' (2021) *Centre for European Policy Studies (CEPS)* Recovery and Resilience Reflection, paper no. 5; F Corti, C Morabito, T Ruiz and P Luongo, 'The role of the Recovery and Resilience Facility in Strengthening Childcare Policies' (2022a) Recovery Watch Policy Study, Foundation for European Progressive Studies; F Corti, A Liscai and T Ruiz, 'The Recovery and Resilience Facility: Boosting Investment in Social Infrastructure in Europe?' (2022b) *Italian Labour Law e-Journal*, 15(1s), 15–30.; AM Guillén, M León and E Pavolini, 'Are "Carrots" Better Than "Sticks"? New EU Conditionality and Social Investment Policies in the Aftermath of the COVID-19 Pandemic in Italy and Spain' (2022) *Comparative European Politics*, 20, 220–237; C Hartwell, J Hagemejer, A Pechcińska, G Dragan, M Sass and K Staeher, 'The Added Value of the Recovery and Resilience Facility: A Preliminary Analysis of Plans from Estonia, Hungary, Poland, and Romania' (2022) *European Parliament Economic Governance Support Unit* (EGOV), STU(2022)68951; A Tassinari, 'Labour Market Policy in Italy's Recovery and Resilience Plan. Same Old or a New Departure?' (2022) *Contemporary Italian Politics*, 14(4), 441–457; S Theodoropoulou, M Akgüç and J Wall, 'Balancing Objectives? Just Transition in National Recovery and Resilience Plans' Working Paper 2022.11. European Trade Union Institute (ETUI); B Vanhercke and A Verdun, 'The European Semester as Goldilocks: Macroeconomic Policy Coordination and the Recovery and Resilience Facility' (2022) *Journal of Common Market Studies*, 60(1), 2024–222; P Bocquillon, E Brooks and T Maltby, 'Talkin' bout a Revolution? Institutional Change in the EU Recovery and Resilience Facility: The Case of Climate Policy' (2023) *JCMS: Journal of Common Market Studies*, 1–21. https://doi.org/10.1111/jcms.13536.

[9] For an extensive set of country studies, see E Menegatti and S Rainone (Eds.), 'The NextGenerationEU in Action: Impact on Social and Labour Policies' (2022) *Italian Labour Law e-Journal*, 15(1S). Other comparative studies that examine the drafting, and to a much lesser extent, implementation of the NRRPs include: D Bokhorst and F Corti, 'Governing Europe's Recovery and Resilience Facility: Between

The research presented in this chapter represents the first in-depth comparative analysis of the drafting, implementation, and monitoring of NRRPs across a substantial number of Member States. Our study covers eight countries (Belgium, Croatia, Estonia, Italy, Latvia, Portugal, Slovakia, and Spain), which together account for 62.3% of all RRF funding (52.7% of all grants, 74.2% of all loans).[10] We focused deliberately on southern and eastern Member States, which are the RRF's largest beneficiaries relative to GDP (ranging from 3% for Estonia and 5.6% for Latvia to 11% for Italy and Croatia in 2021), where both the domestic impact of the NRRPs and the EU's potential leverage on their content might be expected to be strongest. Most of these countries also suffer from high levels of public debt, which constrained their ability to carry out large-scale infrastructural and social investments over the decade following the euro crisis, increasing their motivation to treat RRF funding as a transformative opportunity. Among northern Member States, we focused on Belgium, as a heavily indebted country for which RRF funding, though lower than in southern and eastern Europe, might nonetheless be significant for domestic policy actors, and as a highly federalised state, in which regional governments could be expected to play a key role in drafting and implementing the national Plan. By way of contrast, we also looked at the available evidence on the drafting of the NRRPs in three additional northern Member States (Austria, Germany, the Netherlands), where RRF funding was much lower in relation to GDP (less than 1%), though still quite substantial in absolute terms and as a share of total EU grants (just over 10%).[11] Our findings on these 11 cases are summarised in analytical tables in Annex 1, to which we refer in the main text by numbered country codes for each cell (eg BE1, IT7).[12]

Research for this chapter focused primarily on the social dimension of the NRRPs, broadly defined to encompass employment, skills, education, childcare, social inclusion, social protection, health and long-term care. These areas account

Discipline and Discretion' (2023) *Government and Opposition*, 1–17. https://doi.org/10.1017/gov.2023.14; F Corti and P Vesan, 'From Austerity-conditionality Towards a New Investment-led Growth Strategy: Social Europe After the Recovery and Resilience Facility' (2023) *Social Policy and Administration*, 57, 513–548. https://doi.org/10.1111/spol.12906; Miró et al., 'Money Makes the World Go Round'; M Munta, B Pircher and S Bekker, 'Ownership of National Recovery Plans: Next Generation EU and Democratic Legitimacy' (2023) *Journal of European Public Policy*, 1–25. https://doi.org/10.1080/13501763.2023.2248202; N Oellerich and J Simons, 'Supranational Modernization or National Partisanship? Explaining Variation in Recovery and Resilience Plans in Central and Eastern Europe' (2023) *Journal of European Public Policy*, 31, 2636–2662. https://doi.org/10.1080/13501763.2023.2231029.

[10] Own calculations from https://commission.europa.eu/business-economy-euro/economic-recovery/recovery-and-resilience-facility_en.

[11] Own calculations from https://ec.europa.eu/economy_finance/recovery-and-resilience-scoreboard/country_overview.html?lang=en; for details, see Annex 1, Table 1, Column 1, https://onlinelibrary.wiley.com/action/downloadSupplement?doi=10.1111%2Frego.12619&file=rego12619-sup-0001-Supinfo.docx

[12] See https://onlinelibrary.wiley.com/action/downloadSupplement?doi=10.1111%2Frego.12619&file=rego12619-sup-0001-Supinfo.docx. For an earlier and more detailed presentation of our comparative research findings, aimed at a policy audience, see *Governing the RRF: Drafting, Implementing, and Monitoring National Recovery and Resilience Plans as an Interactive Multilevel Process.* Policy Study, Foundation for European Progressive Studies (FEPS), June. https://feps-europe.eu/publication/governing-the-rrf/.

for an average of 28% of planned RRF spending across Member States,[13] as well as 39% of the 2019–2020 Country-Specific Recommendations (CSRs) issued under the European Semester, which the NRRPs need to address.[14] The social field thus represents a very significant share of both RRF investments and reforms, enabling broad conclusions to be drawn about the instrument's governance and effects. In addition, major reforms and investments in other policy fields are investigated, such as the liberalisation of closed professions and water management, where these emerged as especially significant in our country cases.

Alongside extensive documentary and media analysis, our findings are based on 74 semi-structured interviews with 63 separate individuals (some of whom were interviewed multiple times), conducted mainly with national and Commission officials directly involved with the NRRPs, as well as other relevant domestic stakeholders, such as social partners and parliamentarians. The interviews were conducted in three waves, focused respectively on the drafting (2022), implementation (2023), and revision (2024) of national plans. A full but anonymized list of interviews can be found in Annex 2.[15] The interviews are referenced in the text by codes, for which the key appears in this Annex. For reasons of space, only the most essential citations to these sources are provided in the main text. Extensive quotations from interviews and primary documents are provided in the notes to the tables in Annex 1. Wherever possible, we have supplemented our own research findings with information from the secondary literature, which is integrated into the notes to the tables and the main text.

The body of the chapter is structured as follows. The next section sets out the theory that underlies the RRF's 'demand-driven, performance-based' governance model, as elaborated by the EU institutions, as well as how its key features respond to past perceived policy failures. It then goes on to discuss international experience with similar governance approaches elsewhere, highlighting some important limitations of performance-based financing identified by comparative assessments of its operation in other contexts. Section 3 analyses the drafting and negotiation of the NRRPs, focusing on the extent to which governments took ownership of the plans, how far they included other domestic stakeholders, and the role played by the Commission in steering the process. Section 4 analyses the implementation and monitoring of the NRRPs, concentrating on how they have affected domestic policy making, what obstacles have arisen in carrying out planned reforms and investments, and how the Commission assesses fulfilment of the milestones and targets, with particular attention to its interpretive flexibility, administrative load,

[13] https://ec.europa.eu/economy_finance/recovery-and-resilience-scoreboard/country_overview.html?lang=en.

[14] This 39% value is the average of 55% in 2019 and 24% in 2020, where the lower proportion for 2020 is due to Member States receiving a single compound social CSR with more implicit social reform guidance in the recitals (Rainone, 2020).

[15] https://onlinelibrary.wiley.com/action/downloadSupplement?doi=10.1111%2Frego.12619&file=rego12619-sup-0001-Supinfo.docx. All interviews were recorded and transcribed. While we make extensive use in Annex 1 of anonymised quotations from Member State officials and stakeholders, we were not permitted to quote verbatim from interviews with Commission officials.

and responsiveness to unanticipated problems and changes in external circumstances. The chapter concludes by assessing the strengths and weaknesses of the RRF governance model, relating them to theoretical expectations derived from previous international experience, and considering the implications for future EU policy.

Overall, this chapter argues that the RRF's governance model has reinforced national ownership and boosted political momentum to deliver on longstanding reform challenges. Its performance-based financing system, which links investments to reform objectives, incentivises commitment to deliver on policy outputs, thus helping overcome some past implementation obstacles. However, the inflexibility of this system makes it difficult to adjust predetermined milestones and targets in response to unforeseen circumstances, which hampers effectiveness and legitimacy, especially when it comes to more innovative investment projects and complex multi-year reform plans. Within this governance model, the European Commission faces pressure to ensure precise justification of M&T fulfilment, leading to a focus on formal compliance and document verification over substantive implementation – as anticipated by the critical international literature on performance-based financing. Overall, the chapter concludes that while the RRF governance model represents an important innovation in EU economic policy coordination, elements of which are already being extended to other Union policies, addressing these problems would require a redesign of its performance-based financing system. Such a redesign would need to move away from the RRF's complete contracting approach, giving Member States greater flexibility on the means for achieving agreed commitments, as well as for revising them, in collaboration with the Commission, not only in response to unanticipated changes in objective circumstances, but also to lessons learned during the implementation process.

2. The Governance Theory of the RRF and Its Limitations

This section unpacks the governance theory underlying the RRF. By this we mean the theoretical assumptions of its designers about how this novel instrument was expected to work and to advance the objectives for which it was adopted, as well as how its novel features respond to perceived failures of previous EU policies. It then goes on to examine international experience with similar governance approaches elsewhere, drawing attention to some key problems with performance-based financing that emerge from comparative studies of its functioning in other settings. The purpose of this analysis is to provide a framework for assessing how far the practical operation of the RRF has lived up to the expectations of its architects, and how far some of the problems experienced in its implementation could have been anticipated from past experiences with similar governance approaches elsewhere.

The RRF, as the Commission proclaims, is 'a demand-driven, performance-based instrument' that 'supports the implementation of a combination of mutually reinforcing reforms and investments, which are designed together with Member States, and tailored-made to their needs, and provide the adequate incentives to ensure their implementation over the medium term'.[16]

The RRF is demand driven, insofar as Member States draft NRRPs comprising an integrated package of proposed reforms and investments, in consultation with the Commission. As the EC argues, Member States 'have flexibility in designing and implementing the measures in a way that suits their national conditions, which increases their ownership of plans'.[17] Such national ownership of the Plans is expected to enhance their legitimacy as well as their effectiveness, by increasing political commitment and public support agreed reforms and investments. Hence, the RRF Regulation states that in assessing the NRRPs, 'the Commission should fully respect the national ownership of the Plan and should therefore take into account the justifications. . .provided by the Member State concerned'.[18] But the Plans must also meet a series of specific requirements set by the EU. Each Plan should show how it represents 'a comprehensive and adequately balanced response to the economic and social situation of the Member State concerned', while contributing to the recovery and resilience of the Union through support for measures in key policy areas of European relevance.[19] The NRRPs must further devote minimum percentages of expenditure to the green and digital transitions (37% and 20% respectively), and respect the principle of Do No Significant Harm (DNSH) to the EU's environmental objectives. In addition, the plans must demonstrate how they contribute to the implementation of the European Pillar of Social Rights (EPSR), thereby enhancing the Union's economic, social, and territorial cohesion, and effectively address 'all or a significant subset' of challenges identified in the CSRs.[20]

The RRF's combination of investments with reforms is a second key novelty of its governance design. By supporting Member States to address the CSRs, the Commission explains, the RRF creates 'political momentum and financial incentives. . .to deliver on long-standing and newly emerging reform needs'. Although these reforms often do not involve a large budgetary cost, they 'are typically designed to have an enabling effect for both public and private investments' by creating supportive framework conditions and removing absorption bottlenecks, thereby amplifying the domestic impact of EU funding.[21]

[16] European Commission, Report from the Commission to the European Parliament and the Council on the implementation of the recovery and resilience funds: Moving forward, COM (2023) 545 final, September 19, 31.

[17] European Commission, Recovery and resilience facility, 2.

[18] Regulation (EU) 2021/241 of the European Parliament and of the Council of 12 February 2021 establishing the recovery and resilience facility (RRF Regulation). OJ L 57/17. recital 41.

[19] The so-called 'six pillars': green transition; digital transformation; smart, sustainable and inclusive growth; social and territorial cohesion; health and economic, social, and institutional resilience; and policies for the next generation.

[20] RRF Regulation, recital 39, Art. 18.4.

[21] European Commission, Recovery and resilience facility, 2.

Finally, the RRF is performance-based, insofar as payments to Member States depend on the delivery of the agreed reforms and investments, focused on concrete outputs rather than final costs. The RRF Regulation stipulates that the NRRPs 'should set out the detailed set of measures for [their] monitoring and implementation, including targets and milestones', with the periodic disbursement of funds to Member States contingent on their satisfactory fulfilment, as assessed by the Commission and approved by the Council.[22] Here, too, the Commission argues that because these M&Ts 'are designed individually to fit the specific investments and reforms the Member States commit to implement, this gives them full ownership to ensure a successful delivery'.[23]

These demand-driven, incentive-supported, and performance-based features of the RRF's governance design respond directly to critical reflections within the Commission and other EU institutions on the failures of past Union policies to promote national reforms effectively. Such perceived policy failures include the Economic Adjustment Programmes and Memoranda of Understanding (MoU) imposed on bail-out countries during the euro crisis, which were widely considered to have lacked national ownership and legitimacy.[24] They also include the CSRs issued under the European Semester, whose implementation often remained limited according to the Commission's own assessments, despite the possibility of issuing financial sanctions under the Stability and Growth Pact and the Macroeconomic Imbalance Procedure.[25] No less important in inspiring the RRF's governance design

[22] RRF Regulation, recitals 39, 51–52; Arts. 20, 24.

[23] European Commission, Recovery and resilience facility, 1. RRF payments to Member States also depend on compliance with the Rule-of-Law Conditionality Regulation introduced as part of the NG-EU package: see RRF Regulation, Art. 8; Regulation (2020/2092) on a general regime of conditionality for the protection of the Union Budget (16 December 2020); N. Kirst (2023), *Rule of law conditionality*. REBUILD Centre Working Paper 13. Dublin City University, December.

[24] For a conspectus of such criticisms, see S Greer, 'Structural Adjustment Comes to Europe: Lessons for the Eurozone From the Conditionality Debates' (2014) *Global Social Policy*, 14(1), 51–71; W Jacoby and J Hopkin, 'From Lever to Club? Conditionality in the European Union During the Financial Crisis' (2019) *Journal of European Public Policy*, 27(8), 1157–1177. On the critical case of Greece, where the Commission created a parallel Task Force alongside the Troika, aimed at enhancing national ownership by supporting domestic officials to develop their own reform plans within the framework imposed by the MoUs, see M Hamm, 'Les Conditions de l'Europe. Sociologie de l'assistance Technique Européenne dans la Crise Grecque (2011–2015)' (2022) [Unpublished PhD thesis]. Université de Strasbourg.

[25] For representative examples of this view, see Z Darvas and Á Leandro, 'The limitations of policy coordination in the euro area under the European semester' (2015) Bruegel Policy Contribution No. 2015/19. https://www.econstor.eu/handle/10419/126693; K Efstathiou and GB Wolff, 'Is the European semester effective and useful?' (2018) Bruegel Policy Contribution, no. 9, https://www.bruegel.org/policy-brief/european-semester-effective-and-useful. Enhancing national ownership of reforms aimed at advancing common European goals has been a recurrent preoccupation of EU policy coordination since the mid-2000s, figuring prominently both in the relaunch of the Lisbon Strategy under the Barroso Commission, and in the streamlining of the European Semester under the Juncker Commission. See J Zeitlin, 'The Open Method of Coordination and the Governance of the Lisbon Strategy' (2008) *Journal of Common Market Studies*, 46(2), 437–446; J Zeitlin and B Vanhercke, 'Socializing the European Semester: EU Social and Economic Policy Coordination in Crisis and Beyond' (2018) *Journal of European Public Policy*, 25(2), 149–174; P Vanheuverzwijn and A Crespy, 'Macro-economic coordination and elusive ownership in the European Union' (2018) *Public Administration*, 96, 578–593. https://doi.org/10.1111/padm.12413.

was persistent dissatisfaction with the Cohesion Policy Funds, where monitoring and reimbursement are primarily based on financial audits of expenditure against agreed costs rather than on measurable progress towards achieving project objectives, and where successive efforts to introduce ex ante policy conditionalities and a stronger performance orientation are widely believed to have yielded meagre results.[26]

The governance design of the RRF appears to have been taken over directly from the Reform Support Programme (RSP) proposed by the Commission in 2018 and the Budgetary Instrument for Convergence and Competitiveness (BICC) endorsed by the Euro Group in 2019. Both instruments were based on grants to be provided on the basis of 'duly substantiated reform and investment proposals' submitted by Member States, reflecting strategic guidance from the EU through the CSRs, with disbursement of funds contingent on implementation and fulfilment of agreed milestones and targets.[27] The adoption of this template, which can already be found in the July 2020 European Council (EUCO) conclusions, seems to have been driven particularly by the Netherlands, which had been involved in developing the BICC as an alternative to more ambitious proposals for a eurozone fiscal capacity it opposed.[28] Very significantly, however, the financial envelope of both the RSP and the BICC was limited to €25 billion over a six-year period, while the funding available for the RRF is nearly 30 times larger, with obvious implications for the scale of tasks involved in negotiating the plans, monitoring their implementation, and verifying the fulfilment of the M&Ts.

In a longer-term perspective, both the RRF's emphasis on national ownership and its insistence on tying financial assistance to Member States' performance in implementing agreed reforms reflect the influence of changing views within the international financial institutions about the effectiveness of development aid and conditionality-based lending. Thus, the seminal 2005 Paris Declaration on Aid

[26] See for example European Court of Auditors, 'Performance-based Financing in Cohesion Policy: Worthy Ambitions but Obstacles Remained in the 2014–2020 Period' (2021) Special Report 24. Publications Office of the EU. For systematic comparisons between the performance orientations of the CPF and the RRF, see European Court of Auditors, 'EU Financing Through Cohesion Policy and the Recovery and Resilience Facility: A Comparative Analysis' (2023) Publications Office of the EU; J Zeitlin, D Bokhorst and E Eihmanis, 'Revisiting the Governance and Delivery Mode of Cohesion Policy Funds: Is the Recovery and Resilience Facility a Model?' Academic paper commissioned by DG REGIO, European Commission, for the High-Level Group on the Future of Cohesion Policy, November. https://ec.europa.eu/regional_policy/policy/how/future-cohesion-policy_en.

[27] European Commission, Proposal for a regulation of the European Parliament and of the Council on the establishment of the Reform Support Programme, COM (2018) 391 final, 31 May 2018; European Commission, Proposal for a regulation of the European Parliament and of the Council on a governance framework for the budgetary instrument for convergence and competitiveness for the euro area, COM (2019) 354 final, 24 July 2019; Both instruments, in turn, drew on an earlier unsuccessful proposal by the Commission, with political support from Angela Merkel, for a 'Convergence and Competitiveness Instrument' (CCI) involving voluntary 'reform contracts' between individual Member States and the Commission underpinned by EU financial support (*European Commission Towards a deep and genuine EMU: The introduction of a convergence and competitiveness instrument.* COM (2013) 165 final, 20 March).

[28] European Council, Conclusions of the special meeting of the European council (17–21 July 2020). EUCO 10/20 A.19; Smeets and Bekius, 'Coordination and control in European Council centered governance'.

Effectiveness, signed by 150 countries and international organisations including the World Bank and the OECD, committed donors to support national ownership of development strategies by recipient countries in exchange for mutual accountability through a focus on measurable results. Subsequent elaborations of this approach, such as the 2008 Accra Agenda for Action, reiterated the centrality of domestic ownership and results-based management within the emerging aid architecture, while underlining the need for inclusive participation of social and political stakeholders beyond central government in designing and implementing national development strategies.[29] At the same time, international organisations like the OECD, the IMF and the World Bank have devoted considerable efforts over the past two decades to promoting performance-based approaches to financing of public programmes in developed as well as developing countries, including the EU itself, as a vehicle for increasing their effectiveness by tying expenditure more closely to measurable results.[30]

The design of the RRF also appears to have been influenced by the international political economy literature on the effective promotion of structural reforms, which as an ECB review observes, finds positive financial incentives 'to be more persuasive for reform implementation than the mere threat of sanctions', provided that they are based on a clear and transparent set of rules and conditions for funding allocation and performance assessment. Under such conditions, as both ECB and Commission officials have argued, 'financial incentives can be useful to overcome the issue of veto players in the political system that have vested interests and benefit from the status quo'.[31]

[29] For overviews of this shift in international approaches to development aid, see Hamm, 'Les conditions de l'Europe', 164–165; N Dabelstein and MQ Patton, 'The Paris Declaration on Aid Effectiveness: History and Significance' (2013) *Canadian Journal of Program Evaluation*, 27(3), 19–36; Sjöstedt, M. (2013) 'Aid Effectiveness and the Paris Declaration: A Mismatch Between Ownership and Results-based Management?' *Public Administration and Development*, 33, 143–155; M Raffinot, 'L'appropriation (ownership) des Politiques de Développement: De la Théorie à la Pratique' (2010) *Mondes en Développement*, 149, 87–104.

[30] See, for example World Bank. Program-for-results: Two-year review. Operations Policy and Country Services. (2015, March 17); A Banerji, B Barkby, J John, J, T Kinda, S Saksonovs, H Schoelermann and T Wu, 'Building a Better Union: Incentivizing Structural Reforms in the Euro Area' (2015) IMF Working Paper 15/201. International Monetary Fund; R Downes, D Moretti and S Nicol, 'Budgeting and Performance in the European Union: A Review by the OECD in the Context of EU Budget Focused on Results' (2017). *OECD Journal on Budgeting*, 1, 1–62; I Beazley, 'Incentivizing Performance in Public Investment Policies Delivered at National and Subnational Levels: Managing Across Temporal and Institutional Horizons' (2018); OECD; M Wes, 'Anchoring Financing in Results & Reforms: Key Takeaways from World Bank Experience' (2023). Paper prepared for the High-Level Group on the Future of Cohesion Policy. https://ec.europa.eu/regional_policy/sources/policy/how/future-cohesion-policy/WorldBank_230914.pdf. According to Babb and Carruthers, the IMF's principal response to widespread criticisms of the limited impact and legitimacy of its structural adjustment programs has been to make lending conditionality more performance-based, which is considered 'both more effective and more conducive to country ownership'(S Babb and B Carruthers, 'Conditionality: Forms, Function, and History' (2008) *Annual Review of Law and Social Science*, 4, 13–29, 23).

[31] See M Freier, C Grynberg, M O'Connell, M Rodríguez-Vives and N Zorell, 'Next Generation EU: A Euro Area Perspective'. (2022). *European Central Bank Economic Bulletin*, 1, 93–112, 109–110; M Buti, *The Man Inside: A European Journey Through Two Crises* (Bocconi University Press, 2021,ch. 40).

Yet, in designing the governance of the RRF, there appears to have been surprisingly little reflection on practical experience elsewhere with performance-based management of public investment and reforms, whose effectiveness has often been found to be decidedly limited despite its continuing popularity.[32] Thus, for example, the OECD itself acknowledges that despite high-profile efforts to advance substantive goals such as value for money and prioritisation, 'performance budgeting systems are more likely to promote legal/financial compliance than to influence the design of public sector management practices'.[33] Similarly, an authoritative World Bank study found 'a general pattern of disappointment with the results of performance budgeting, balanced by a strong belief in the underlying logic', leaving a persistent 'gap between promise and practice'.[34] More generally, the comparative literature on performance management in the public sector through target setting and financial incentives has documented the frequent incidence of perverse consequences and distortive effects. Examples include 'gaming' the system by deliberately setting unambitious targets that are easy to meet; 'creaming' or 'cherry picking' by concentrating resources on the easiest to serve clients rather those in the greatest need; focusing on short-term targets at the expense of long-term service quality; manipulating reporting systems to present results in a more favourable light; and outright data falsification. But even where agents are operating in good faith, the consequence of such incentive-based performance management systems is often goal displacement, as resources and energy come to be focused on meeting M&Ts, while redirecting attention away from the underlying objectives of the program itself.[35]

Beyond these perverse effects of high-powered financial incentives on agents' behaviour, a central problem with performance-based management systems is their difficulty in coping with unanticipated changes in external conditions and uncertainty about future states of the world more generally. The more innovative

[32] According to Commission sources, there were discussions with experts from the World Bank's Program-for-Results Financing (PforR) group and other international experts about the design of the RRF, as well as with other DGs in the Commission with experience in supporting national reform projects, but none of these discussions seem to have focused on the problems experienced in the implementation of performance-based financing documented in the comparative literature on their practical operation (personal communication from a Commission official, 5 May 2023).

[33] I Beazley, Incentivizing performance in public investment policies delivered at national and subnational levels: Managing across temporal and institutional horizons. OECD (2018), 9, 13

[34] DP Moynihan and I Beazley, *Toward Next-generation Performance Budgeting: Lessons From the Experience of Seven Reforming Countries*, (World Bank, 2016, 2).

[35] For overviews of this literature, see Moynihan and Beazley, *Toward Next Generation Performance Budgeting*, esp. 22–23, 155–156; DP Moynihan, S Fernandez, S Kim, KM LeRoux, SJ Piotrowski, BE Wright and K Yang, 'Performance Regimes Amidst Governance Complexity' (2011) *Journal of Public Administration Research and Theory*, 21, i141–i155; DP Moynihan, 'Through a Glass Darkly: Understanding the Effects of Performance Regimes' (2009) *Public Performance & Management Review*, 32(4), 592–603; M De Vries, J Nemec and D Špaček (Eds.) *Performance-based Budgeting in the Public Sector* (Palgrave Macmillan, 2019).Darvas and Weslau similarly observe that 'a global comparison of experiences with performance-based funding. . .is not encouraging' (Z Darvas and L Weslau, 'First Lessons From the Recovery and Resilience Facility for the EU Economic Governance Framework' (2023, March). Study for the European Parliament, Economic Governance and EMU Scrutiny Unit, IPOL IDA(2023)741748, March, 18).

and complex the project, the less plausible it is that its goals and the intermediate steps to achieve them can be fully specified in advance.

Under such conditions, leading private businesses do not typically use the putatively complete contracting approach underlying the RRF, where compensation for collaborators is tied to the realisation of predetermined milestones and targets, which cannot be modified except in extreme circumstances. Instead, the parties to such 'contracting for innovation', like a biotech firm and a pharmaceutical manufacturer seeking to develop a new drug or vaccine, typically set broad common goals for the project and establish a joint governance framework to oversee it. In this governance framework, while fulfilment of M&Ts – such as regulatory approval or successful completion of a round of clinical trials – may trigger predetermined payments, their primary purpose is to serve as the basis for monitoring the project, assessing whether it is on track, and deliberating about what needs to be done if it is not. Where M&Ts are missed, representatives of both parties jointly analyse the problem, discuss what remedial measures should be adopted, and decide whether to continue or terminate the project. Where the two sides cannot agree, the issue is 'bumped up' to a higher-level body of top leaders from both sides, which has the additional benefit of disincentivising, and if necessary sanctioning, uncooperative behaviour, such as information hoarding, on the part of the lower-level managers directly responsible for the project.[36]

Nor are such governance structures for managing complex, innovative projects under conditions of uncertainty confined to contracting between private businesses. Similar structures and practices also characterise the most successful public industrial policy agencies in both developed and developing countries, such as the US Defense Advanced Research Projects Agency (DARPA) and its energy spinoff (ARPA-E) in the US and the Malaysian Performance Management and Delivery Unit (PEMANDU). Each of these public agencies, despite their differences, sets open-ended goals for innovative projects, ranging from the development of new energy decarbonisation technologies and investment in mass rapid transit systems to taxation and regulatory reforms, and establishes joint committees to monitor and review their performance, using progress against initial milestones and targets as a basis for re-examining and revising where needed both goals and means of achieving them, with termination as an ultimate sanction in case of persistent failure.[37]

[36] RJ Gilson, CF Sabel and R Scott, 'Contracting for Innovation: Vertical Disintegration and Interfirm Collaboration' (2009) *Columbia Law Review*, 109(3), 433–502.

[37] On DARPA and ARPA-E, see MJ Piore, P Colatat and EB Reynolds, 'NSF and DARPA as models for research funding: An institutional analysis', in WB Bonvillian, R van Atta, and P Windham (Eds.), *The DARPA Model for Transformative Technologies: Perspectives on the U.S. Defense Advanced Research Projects Agency*, (Open Book Publishers, 2019), 45–76; CF Sabel and D Victor, *Fixing the Climate: Strategies for an Uncertain World.* (Princeton University Press, 2022, 169–176); on PEMANDU, see CF Sabel and L Jordan, *Doing, Learning, Being: Some Lessons Learned from Malaysia's National Transformation Program* (World Bank, 2015). Like 'contracting for innovation' in the private sector, PEMANDU relies heavily on 'bump-up' mechanisms for resolving coordination failures and disagreements among lower-level project leaders by escalating them to higher-level joint bodies with power to terminate projects and sanction uncooperative behaviour (ibid: esp. pp. 14–16).

Underlying these forms of contracting for innovation in both the public and private sectors is what governance scholar Charles Sabel calls 'diagnostic monitoring': arrangements for ongoing supervision and periodic review by stakeholders of 'problems encountered in realising initial and avowedly provisional plans, with the aim of devising effective methods of implementation when that is possible or revisiting project goals when there is good reason to think it is not'. Such diagnostic monitoring is a response to increasing levels of uncertainty, which undermine the possibility of relying on ex ante plans, whose assumptions will likely prove incorrect or incomplete and need revision during the implementation process. In contrast to standard forms of compliance monitoring aimed at ensuring that agents carry out their principals' instructions, the aim of diagnostic monitoring systems is therefore 'to facilitate and organise problem solving by the actors, not to use the threat of punishment for bad performance as an incentive for good behaviour'.[38] Such mechanisms to ensure flexibility and revisability of national reform and investment projects in the face of uncertainty are conspicuously missing in the RRF's design, which has proved to be a major source of implementation problems, as we will see in section 4 below.

3. Drafting the NRRPs

How has the governance theory of the RRF as a demand-driven, incentive-supported, and performance-based instrument worked out in practice? This section analyses the drafting phase of the NRRPs, focusing on how far national governments took ownership of the Plans and used RRF funding to propose ambitious investment and reform programs; to what extent they involved other domestic stakeholders in their preparation, expanding ownership beyond central government circles; and what role the Commission played in shaping the Plans' content and how this impacted national ownership.

3.1 Ownership and Ambition

Whereas the Commission assessed all plans of Member States covered in our study as contributing sufficiently to addressing a significant subset of CSRs, which was a formal condition for their approval, we found that the level of ambition and national ownership varied considerably. In a number of countries, notably Portugal, Spain, Croatia, and Slovakia, Member States presented ambitious Plans based on a coherent balance between investments and reforms. In each of these

[38] CF Sabel, 'How to Make Smart Specialization Work' (2016, June 1–6). Presentation to Smart Regions Conference, European Commission, DG REGIO, Brussels; E Kutnetsov and CF Sabel, 'Managing self-discovery: Diagnostic monitoring of a portfolio of projects and programs'. In S Radosevic, A Curaj, R Gheorghiu, L Andreescu and I Wade (Eds.), *Advances in the Theory and Practice of Smart Specialization* (Academic Press, 2017, pp. 51–72).

countries, the NRRPs addressed the full set of CSRs, and sometimes went beyond them in the social field, as in the case of pension adequacy, long-term care, and inclusion of people with disabilities in Spain and Croatia.[39] In Italy, which took the full allocation of €191.5bn in RRF grants and loans at the outset and supplemented them with a further €30bn in national funds, the NRRP entails a very extensive program of investment in the modernisation of infrastructure and public services, accompanied by major reforms of public administration, justice, and competition rules. But the Italian Plan leaves significant gaps in addressing CSRs and vulnerabilities in the social field, notably in terms of measures to reduce poverty and enhance inclusion among precarious workers.[40] The Belgian NRRP addresses many but not all of the CSRs, while including some additional measures in fields such as social housing, childcare, and long-term care, but its precision, coherence and level of ambition were criticised by the Commission.[41] Estonia and Latvia, which like Belgium received lower grant allocations relative to GDP than other Member States in our study, were initially reluctant to link investments to reforms, and only agreed to include significant social measures, such as indexation of the minimum income in Latvia or improvements in long-term care in Estonia, at the insistence of the Commission, resulting in a lower level of national ownership for their plans.[42]

In Austria, Germany and the Netherlands, our three northern contrast cases, levels of ambition in the NRRPs were much lower across the board, leaving a substantial set of CSRs wholly or largely unaddressed, including in the social domain. The Netherlands and Germany decided to dedicate all or most (respectively) of their funding to carry out projects that had already been included and budgeted in existing national plans, backdating a substantial portion of spending to 2020 as permitted by the RRF Regulation, thereby minimising the ownership and impact of their Plans within and beyond national administrations.[43]

[39] PT1, ES1, HR1, SK1. See also Corti et al. 'The Recovery and Resilience Facility'; Corti and Vesan, 'From Austerity-conditionality Towards a new Investment-led Growth Strategy'; Bokhorst and Corti, 'Governing Europe's Recovery and Resilience Facility'; Guillén et al., 'Are "Carrots" Better Than "Sticks"?; A Aranguiz, 'National Recovery and Resilience plan: Spain' (2022) *Italian Labour Law e-Journal*, 15(1S), 1–15; AT Ribeiro, 'National Recovery and Resilience Plan: Portugal' (2022) *Italian Labour Law e-Journal*, 15(1S), 1–13; S Laleta, 'National Recovery and Resilience Plan: Croatia' (2022) *Italian Labour Law e-Journal*, 15(1S), 1–15.

[40] IT1. See also Corti et al., 'The Recovery and Resilience facility'; Corti and Vesan, 'From Austerity-conditionality Towards a New Investment-led Growth Strategy; Bokhorst and Corti, 'Governing Europe's Recovery and Resilience Facility'; Tassinari, 'Labour Market Policy in Italy's Recovery and Resilience Plan'; M Barbieri and D Guarascio, 'La Pandemia e la Necessità di Riformare il Sistema Degli Amortizzatori Sociali' (2021) *Politiche Sociali*, 3, 493–510; E Ales, 'National Recovery and Resilience Plan: Italy' (2022) *Italian Labour Law e-Journal*, 15(1S), 1–13.

[41] BE1; see also Corti and Vesan, 'From Austerity-conditionality Towards a New Investment-led Growth Strategy'; P Pecinovsky, 'National Recovery and Resilience Plan: Belgium' (2022) *Italian Labour Law e-Journal*, 15(1S), 1–11.

[42] EE1, LV1; EE-GOV4, LV-GOV1. See also L Romele, 'National Recovery and Resilience Plan: Latvia' (2022) *Italian Labour Law e-Journal*, 15(1S), 1–14.

[43] AT1, DE1, NL1. See also Bokhorst and Corti, 'Governing Europe's Recovery and Resilience Facility'; Corti et al., 'The Recovery and Resilience Facility', 26–27); Corti and Vesan, 'From Austerity-conditionality Towards a New Investment-led Growth Strategy', 8–10.

Comparing these Member States, a number of country-specific factors appear to explain these variations in the levels of ambition and ownership observed in their NRRPs. First, the combination of large RRF funding (relative to GDP) with high fiscal debt constraints encouraged ambitious investment and reform plans in Portugal, Spain, Italy and to a lesser extent Belgium (which combined a high debt constraint with lower RRF funding).[44] In Italy, for example, the NRRP was seen by its drafters as a 'now or never' opportunity to implement long-needed investments blocked by fiscal constraints.[45] This pattern was intensified in Member States such as Spain and Portugal, which had suffered from austerity and reductions in social and labour rights during the decade following the euro crisis, and which had new or recently re-elected left-wing government coalitions.[46] A similar activist pattern can also be observed in less heavily fiscally constrained countries such as Croatia and Slovakia, where newly elected governments were anxious to break with past policies and establish a reform-oriented profile, including in the social domain, taking advantage of high RRF funding.[47] Conversely, a lower relative size of grants, coupled with low fiscal constraints and economically liberal governments and electorates in Latvia and Estonia, led to socially unambitious plans with weak domestic ownership, especially where reform measures demanded ongoing expenditures from the national budget, which could not be financed from the RRF.[48] In Austria, Germany, and the Netherlands, as in the Baltics, low relative RRF grant funding, coupled with weak fiscal constraints, resulted in unambitious plans with limited national ownership, though ideological issues around social policy do not appear to have played a similar limiting role.[49]

3.2 Involvement of Domestic Stakeholders

The RRF governance model was designed first and foremost to promote ownership by Member State governments, which are responsible for proposing the NRRPs and designating a single point of contact with the Commission to oversee their implementation. But national ownership, as a means of enhancing the effectiveness and legitimacy of domestic reform and investment strategies, has been widely understood in the international and European debates discussed in the previous section as extending beyond central government to encompass inclusive participation by other social and political stakeholders in their design and implementation.

[44] In 2021, debt/GDP ratios were 125.5% for Portugal, 118.3% for Spain, 150.3% for Italy, and 109.2% for Belgium, https://ec.europa.eu/eurostat/statistics-explained/index.php?title=Government_finance_statistics#General_government_gross_debt.

[45] IT1. See also Bokhorst and Corti, 'Governing Europe's Recovery and Resilience Facility', 8, 11-12; Corti and Vesan, 'From Austerity-conditionality Towards a New Investment-led Growth Strategy', 10.

[46] ES1, PT1.

[47] HR1, SK1. 2021 debt/GDP ratios were 78.4% for Croatia and 62.2% for Slovakia.

[48] EE-GOV4, LV-GOV1. 2021 debt/GDP ratios were 43.6% for Latvia and 17.6% for Estonia.

[49] AT1, DE1, NE1. 2021 debt/GDP ratios were 82.3% for Austria, 68.6% for Germany, and 52.4% for the Netherlands.

In this vein, for example, a recent comparative study of the NRRPs conceptualises ownership 'as the ability of diverse social actors to (i) participate with national authorities in quality formulation of public policy and (ii) to influence national policy goals and means'.[50]

Both the RRF Regulation and the Commission's guidance on the preparation of the NRRPs are very clear about the need to consult local and regional authorities, social partners, civil society organisations, and other relevant stakeholders, and to report how their input was reflected in the drafting process. At the same time, however, the quality of stakeholder participation in this process did not form part of the formal criteria for the Commission's assessment of the NRRPs.[51] Despite these exhortations, EU-level assessments unanimously concur that stakeholder involvement in drafting the NRRPs was extremely limited, both on the side of local and regional authorities and on that of social partners and civil society.[52] In most Member States national governments typically stuck to the formal requirements to consult stakeholders, but the substantive quality of the process was low. Plans were typically drafted in a highly centralised manner under tight time constraints by small groups attached to Prime Minister's Offices (PMOs) and Ministries of Finance.[53] Exceptions to this pattern among the countries covered in our study include Portugal, where the NRRP built on an earlier National Development Plan, which was based on extensive consultations, while a public discussion of the draft Plan resulted in the addition of two new thematic components; Belgium, where the NRRP was assembled from separate regional plans and consultations with social partners drew on the strong framework for their involvement developed under the European Semester; and Spain, where the drafting of the NRRP was an iterative 'choral exercise' beginning with bottom-up submissions of proposals by line ministries and the autonomous regional communities were consulted on issues falling within their competence through the established system of sectoral confer-

[50] M Munta, B Pircher and S Bekker, 'Ownership of National Recovery Plans: Next Generation EU and Democratic Legitimacy', *Journal of European Public Policy* (2023), 1–25. https://doi.org/10.1080/13501763.2023.2248202, 2. For a similar approach to domestic ownership of the European Semester, distinguishing between governments, administrations, parliaments, and social partners, see P Vanheuverzwijn and A Crespy, A. 'Macro-economic Coordination and Elusive Ownership in the European Union', *Public Administration*, 96 (2018), 578–593. https://doi.org/10.1111/padm.12413.

[51] RRF Regulation: Art 18(4)q, Annex V; European Commission, Guidance to member states on recovery and resilience plans. SWD (2021) 12 final, January 22, 47.

[52] Committee of the Regions, Opinion on the Implementation of the Recovery and Resilience facility. 2022/C 97/05, OJ 97/21; EUROFOUND, *Involvement of Social Partners in the National Recovery and Resilience Plans*, Publications Office of the EU (2022); European Economic and Social Committee, *Involvement of organised civil society in the national recovery and resilience plans—What works and what does not?* European Economic and Social Committee (2021); V Caimi and F. Farrell, *Participation of Civil Society Organisations in the Preparation of the EU National Recovery and Resilience Plans 2020* https://civilsocietyeurope.eu/wp-content/uploads/2021/01/CSE-ECNL-Participation-of-CSOs-in-thepreparation-of-the-EU-NRRPs_spread.pdf.

[53] For details, see Annex 1, Table 1, Column 2, https://onlinelibrary.wiley.com/action/downloadSupplement?doi=10.1111%2Frego.12619&file=rego12619-sup-0001-Supinfo.docx. . Munta et al.'s comparative study of the NRRPs in Croatia, the Netherlands, and Sweden similarly concludes that 'stakeholders were barely involved in all three countries, limiting their impact, while governments had the main responsibility' (Munta et al., 'Ownership of National Recovery Plans', 2).

ences. Conversely, in Italy, where regions also have constitutional responsibilities for specific policy areas, they were nonetheless marginalised in the drafting of the NRRP.[54]

3.3 The Commission's Role in the Drafting Process

The governance design of the RRF gives the Commission a pivotal role in assessing the NRRPs and recommending their approval by the Council. How did the Commission use these powers during the drafting process and how did this impact national ownership of the Plans? In the Member States covered by our study, the Commission's role in the drafting process, which typically involved numerous meetings – 80–90 in countries like Italy, Spain, and Croatia – and intensive negotiations with national officials, seems for the most part to have been closely aligned with the responsibilities assigned to it in the RRF Regulation, namely to ensure the relevance and coherence of the Plans, the effectiveness of coordination and monitoring arrangements, and the operationalisation of milestones and targets, while fully respecting national ownership.[55] In many cases, including Spain, Italy, Portugal, and Croatia, the Commission went beyond this gatekeeper role, serving as an informal consultant to Member States to ensure that their Plans could be effectively implemented, for example by advising national administrations to simplify and reduce the number of M&Ts or to extend the timetable for project completion.[56] The Commission's guidance for the preparation of the NRRPs encouraged Member States to use 'input indicators (eg resources provided, which can be financial, human, administrative). . .or preferably output indicators (eg number of workers trained, numbers of renovated schools)' rather than result or 'impact indicators (eg decrease in the number of unfulfilled vacancies in the IT sector). . .given the unpredictability of such indicators and their dependence on other factors outside the control of the Member State'.[57]

[54] See also S Profeti and B Baldi, 'Le regioni italiane e il PNRR: La (vana) ricerca di canali d'accesso all'agenda', Rivista Italian di Politiche Pubbliche, 3 (2021), 431–458; G Viesti, Riuscirà il PNRR a rilanciare l'Italia? (Donzelli, 2023), 48–56). In most other federal states, including Austria and Germany, regional authorities were consulted more extensively in the drafting of the NRRPs. Interviews AT2; DE2; see also F Corti, D Nigohosyan, C Pancotti and SN Millard, Study supporting the mid-term evaluation of the recovery and resilience facility. Final Report, European Commission (December 2023), 150–151.

[55] For details see Annex 1, Table 1, Column 3, https://onlinelibrary.wiley.com/action/downloadSupplement?doi=10.1111%2Frego.12619&file=rego12619-sup-0001-Supinfo.docx; RRF Regulation, Arts. 19–20.

[56] On the Commission's consultative role, see also Bokhorst and Corti, 'Governing Europe's Recovery and Resilience Facility', 8-9; Miró et al., 'Money Makes the World Go Round, 10.

[57] European Commission, *Guidance to member states on recovery and resilience plans, Pt. I:*, p. 4; Corti et al., *Study supporting the mid-term evaluation of the recovery and resilience facility*, 66–67. A comparative study of NRRPs in six Member States (France, Germany, Italy, the Netherlands, Romania, Spain) confirms that only in two of these (Italy and Romania) did results indicators comprise more than 15% of the total for target fulfilment, with Spain just above 10%, and a negligible share in the other countries (Z Darvas and I. Weslau, *First Lessons from the Recovery and Resilience Facility for the EU Economic Governance Framework*, Study for the European Parliament, Economic Governance and EMU Scrutiny Unit, IPOL IDA(2023)741748, March 2023, 17–21).

Regarding investments, the Commission seems to have been prepared to defer to Member-State preferences in the name of promoting national ownership, even where it was highly critical of the specific choices involved, such as the controversial Pisão Dam project in Portugal or a massive new hospital in the Estonian capital Tallinn.[58] Concerning reforms, the Commission played a stronger role in shaping and steering the drafting of the NRRPs, both in pressing for a balance between reforms and investments where this was initially missing in some national Plans (such as Italy, Croatia, Latvia, and Estonia) and in pushing for measures to address key CSRs, especially where critical vulnerabilities were identified in the Social Scoreboard developed for monitoring the EPSR.[59] The most contentious interactions concerned Member States that combined longstanding resistance to implementing social CSRs with poor performance on the EPSR Social Scoreboard indicators (Latvia and Estonia). There the Commission insisted on inclusion of specific reforms addressing these issues in the NRRPs as a condition of their approval, even though the measures in question could not be financed through the RRF.[60] In most cases, however, the Commission was prepared to defer to domestic policy choices to enhance national ownership of reforms, while ensuring that the specific measures proposed would not run contrary to specific recommendations in the CSRs and that their underlying objective would be addressed through a different route. A striking example of such forbearance is that of pension reforms in Spain and Croatia, where the Commission allowed Member States to index benefits to consumer prices and decouple them from life expectancy in the former and to avoid raising the statutory pensionable age in the latter, in exchange for measures aimed at promoting employment of older workers and increasing the effective retirement age in both countries.[61]

The most important disparities between the Commission's role in the drafting of the NRRPs across Member States in our study concerned the extent to which it pressed them to address the full set of CSRs. While the Commission typically started negotiations with the ambition to see all CSRs addressed as far as possible, in countries that received a low relative amount of grant funding, its leverage to achieve this was often much smaller. Thus, as observed in section 3.1 above, northern Member States such as Belgium, Austria, and the Netherlands were permitted to respond shallowly to a number of CSRs, or as in Germany to leave many almost completely unaddressed.[62] But even among countries that

[58] PT3, EE3; PT-GOV3, EE-GOV3.

[59] IT3, HR3, EU5, EU2, EE-GOV3. On Italy and Croatia, see also Bokhorst and Corti, 'Governing Europe's recovery and resilience facility', 10–11); Miró et al., 'Money makes the world go round', 8. The official criteria for the Commission's assessment of the NRRPs include 'contributing to improving the levels of the indicators of [the] Social Scoreboard' (RRF Regulation, Annex 5, par. 2.3).

[60] EE3, LV3; EU5, LV-GOV3, EU2, EE-GOV3.

[61] ES3, HR3. See also Bokhorst and Corti, 'Governing Europe's Recovery and Resilience Facility', 8–9.

[62] This link between the size of the RRF financial envelope and the extent to which Member States' reform commitments in their NRRPs address the challenges identified the CSRs is confirmed by the independent evaluation study conducted to support the Commission's Mid-Term Review (Corti et al., Study supporting the mid-term evaluation of the recovery and resilience facility,75–76),

received larger relative grant allocations for the RRF, there were considerable variations in how far the Commission insisted that they address the full set of CSR challenges in their NRRPs. In Croatia, for example, the Commission pressed successfully for the NRRP to address all CSRs, while in Latvia and Estonia, as observed above, EC officials insisted that social challenges identified in the CSRs and the EPSR Scoreboard be addressed in the NRRPs, despite their lower level of RRF grant funding.[63] By contrast, in Italy, whose relative RRF funding is similar to Croatia's, the Commission did not require the government to address all CSRs, despite substantial coverage gaps, including vulnerabilities identified as critical in the Social Scoreboard. Commission officials are even reported to have discouraged the Italian authorities from including ambitious reforms of the social shock absorbers, which could not be funded from the RRF because they involved ongoing financial commitments, in the complementary interventions funded from domestic resources, due to concerns for their longer-term budgetary implications.[64] While the evidence we collected does not specifically address the question of how to explain these disparities in the treatment of Member States, it is difficult to avoid the conclusion that country size and other political considerations may have played a contributory role, alongside differences in their fiscal position (eg between high-debt Italy and the low-debt Baltics).

4. Implementing and Monitoring the NRRPs

The novel governance design of the RRF in which payments to Member States are based on fulfilment of pre-agreed M&Ts rather than reimbursement of incurred costs, likewise raises a series of theoretically significant questions about the implementation and monitoring of the NRRPs, which we address sequentially in this section. How has performance-based financing affected domestic policy-making processes within and beyond central government? Does it provide additional leverage for overcoming domestic opposition to controversial reforms, as proposed by the political economy literature? To what extent are problems experienced with the implementation of specific investments and reforms linked to the limited participation of domestic stakeholders in the drafting of the NRRPs, as might be expected from the international debate on broadening ownership of development strategies beyond central government? Does the RRF's performance-based financing model genuinely enhance effective implementation of reforms and investments, or does it result instead in goal displacement and a focus on paper compliance, as anticipated by the critical international literature? How much scope is there for modifying or renegotiating investment and reform commitments in the face of unanticipated

[63] HR3, EE3, LV3; EU5, EELV-GOV3, EE-GOV-2.

[64] IT3; Tassinari, 'Labour Market Policy in Italy's Recovery and Resilience Plan': 8–9, n. 15; Miró et al., 'Money Makes the World Go Round', 8–9.

changes in circumstances, as comparative studies of 'contracting for innovation' and 'diagnostic monitoring' suggest would be necessary?

4.1 Impact of the NRRPs on Domestic Policy Making

The most visible and widespread effect of the NRRPs on domestic policy making has been to reinforce the centralisation of authority and decision making within national governments. Such centralisation is a natural consequence of the RRF's requirements for Member States to establish effective domestic arrangements for implementing and monitoring NRRP commitments and to maintain a single point of contact for verifying the fulfilment of the relevant milestones and targets in support of periodic payment requests. Such effectiveness formed a critical criterion for the Commission's assessment of the NRRPs, which were further elaborated in legally binding Council Implementing Decisions (CIDs) and Operational Arrangements agreed bilaterally with Member states, which include specific indicators for verification of the M&Ts.[65] The countries covered in our study differed in the extent to which they created new bodies to perform the coordination, monitoring, reporting, and auditing functions required for NRRP implementation or assigned them to existing administrative units. But in all cases, the result of these arrangements has been to centralise decision making in the hands of PMOs and Ministries of Finance, albeit with some cross-country variation (lower in Belgium, Portugal, and Spain, where regional authorities and social partners play a larger role in implementation; higher in Croatia, Slovakia, and Italy).[66]

A major attraction of the RRF's performance-based financing model for national governments is the enhanced leverage it provides for overcoming domestic opposition to controversial reforms, while smoothing their passage and amplifying their impact through complementary investments. The tight linkage between fulfilment of M&Ts and approval of payment requests also creates pressures on administrative actors at local and regional as well as central levels to streamline the delivery of investments. In a number of cases, national governments included key elements of their programs in the NRRPs as an explicit strategy of 'hand tying' or '*vincolo esterno*' aimed at using the external constraint of RRF commitments as a critical resource for getting them through the political process. Prominent examples of the effectiveness of this strategy among the countries covered in our

[65] RRF Regulation, Arts. 19–20 and Annex 5.

[66] The independent mid-term evaluation of the RRF concludes that a stronger involvement of Prime Ministers' Offices in NRRP coordination has contributed to smoother implementation 'due to increased political ownership and enhanced capacity to steer internal decision-making processes, especially when it comes to reforms' (Corti et al., 'Study Supporting the Mid-term Evaluation of the Recovery and Resilience Facility', 150). In Italy, the Meloni government, which took over from Draghi in September 2022, further centralised the governance of the NRRP by transferring key coordination tasks, including contacts with the Commission, from the Ministry of Economics and Finance to a new Mission Structure attached to the PMO (IT 4; G Menegus, 'La Riforma della Governance del PNRR', *Osservatorio Constituzionale* 3, 2023, 220–226)

study include the liberalisation of closed professions in Portugal, pension reform in Slovakia, and labour market reform in Spain, all of which were pushed through parliament on the eve of an impending payment request.[67] In some countries, such as Italy and Spain, national officials see the RRF's performance-based financing and monitoring system as a valuable lever for accelerating the implementation of investment projects through the bureaucracy, including at lower levels of government.[68] In others, notably Croatia, Slovakia, and Belgium, interviewees within and beyond central government see the RRF's performance-based management system not only as a source of leverage, but also as an accountability mechanism for ensuring that political commitments are made concrete and visible to the media and the public, with clear deadlines for delivery.[69] At the same time, however, the dependency of RRF payment requests on the timely fulfilment of specific milestones and targets can also backfire, by creating opportunities for hold-ups and side-payment demands by domestic veto players, as in the case of justice reforms in Slovakia.[70] In the longer term, there is a serious risk that as governments change and national ownership of Plan objectives declines, the *vincolo esterno* strategy of tying reform commitments to external constraints will start to yield diminishing or even negative returns, as occurred previously in Italy, where the strategy originated during preparations for euro membership in the 1990s.[71]

4.2 Stakeholder Involvement in NRRP Implementation

In most Member States, as observed in section 3.2 above, involvement of domestic stakeholders such as social partners and local and regional authorities in the drafting of the NRRPs was extremely limited. Recent EU-level studies have found little significant improvement in the involvement of these actors during the implementation phase.[72] In Spain, social partners were actively involved in the negotiation of major reforms of the labour market and pensions, whose design was deliberately left open in the NRRP to leave space for their input.[73] In Croatia, the limited involvement of societal stakeholders in the drafting of the labour market reform

[67] PT4, SK4, ES4; PT-GOV4, SK-GOV2a-b.

[68] IT4, ES4; interviews IT-GOV3, ES GOV-1b-c, ES-GOV2.

[69] HR4, SK4, BE4; interviews HR-GOV4, HR-GOV5, SK-GOV1, SK-GOV4, BE-GOV2c.

[70] SK4.

[71] On the origins and declining effectiveness of the *vincolo esterno* strategy in Italy, see K Dyson and K Featherstone, 'Italy and EMU as a "vincolo esterno": Empowering the Technocrats, Transforming the State' (1996) *South European Politics and Society*, 1(2), 272–299; E Jones, 'Relations with Europe: Beyond the Vincolo Esterno' (2017) *Italian Politics*, 32, 51–69.

[72] See Eurofound, *Involvement of Social in the Implementation of National Recovery and Resilience Plans* (2023) Publications Office of the EU; Committee of the Regions, *Opinion on the Implementation of the Recovery and Resilience Facility*; S Sabato, A Atanasova, L Fiorucci and S Spasova, *Monitoring the Quality of Public Consultation of Social Partners in the Implementation of National Recovery and Resilience Plans* (2023). European Social Observatory/European Trade Union Institute.

[73] ES5. While the labour market reform was agreed by both the trade unions and the main employers' association, the latter refused in the end to support the pension reform (Miró et al. 2023: 11–12).

was corrected during the implementation phase, thereby ensuring support from both unions and employers. In other cases, however, failure to ensure political buy in from domestic stakeholders has created more serious problems in the implementation of promised reforms, as with water management in Croatia, where municipalities who had not been properly consulted in advance were able to delay a proposed reorganisation by taking the government to the Constitutional Court.[74] Regarding investments, the central problem resulting from inadequate involvement of key stakeholders in the drafting process is reduced implementability of the projects themselves. Examples include childcare expansion in Spain, where some regions have complained that the distribution criteria of the funds fail to take account of the existing local mix of public and private providers, and in Italy, where municipalities responsible for implementation lack administrative and financial capacity to cope with tender deadlines and co-funding requirements, resulting in a reduction in the target for nursery places to be created from 265,000 to 150,000.[75]

4.3 Monitoring Milestones and Targets

The Commission's role in monitoring the NRRPs is even greater than during the drafting process, as it must assess whether milestones and targets have been sufficiently fulfilled to warrant periodic payments to Member States. Yet the Commission is not the final decision maker in the approval of NRRP payment requests. As stipulated in the RRF Regulation, the Commission's assessment of the satisfactory fulfilment of the M&Ts underlying these payments is subject to review by the Economic and Financial Committee (EFC), an advisory body to the Council composed of high officials from national finance ministries. The Commission must take account of the EFC's opinion in its final implementing decision on each payment request, which must, in turn, be approved by a comitology committee of national representatives. If one or more Member States disagree with a positive EFC opinion, 'considering that there are serious deviations from the satisfactory fulfilment of the relevant milestones and targets', they may escalate the issue to the EUCO for further discussion, until when (normally a maximum of three months) the decision is suspended.[76] The Commission is thus under considerable pressure to ensure precision in justifying payment requests not only from frugal Member States in the Council, but also from the European Court of Auditors (ECA), which has inserted itself prominently in the process, issuing a series of detailed

[74] HR5; A Kekez and M Munta, 'Compliance as a Component of Policy Design in a Suboptimal Design Space: An Opportunity or a Threat?' [Unpublished paper, 2023], European University Institute.

[75] ES5, IT5. F. Corti, C. Morabito, T. Ruiz, and P Luongo. *The Role of the Recovery and Resilience Facility in Strengthening Childcare Policies* (2022), Recovery Watch Policy Study, Foundation for European Progressive Studies. 23, 32, 38

[76] RRF Regulation, Recital 52, Art. 24. This last step is the so-called 'emergency brake', which has so far never been activated, inserted at the insistence of the Netherlands during the July 2020 EUCO negotiations over the NextGenEU package (Smeets and Bekius, 'Coordination and Control in European Council Centred Governance', 13).

recommendations for tightening up and formalising the procedures for verifying the fulfilment of milestones and targets.[77] At the same time, despite the reinforcement of analytical capacity in its country teams, the Commission's local knowledge and substantive ability to assess national reforms and investments remains inevitably limited compared to that of Member States themselves, especially considering the enormous number of M&Ts in some of the larger Plans (Italy: 527; Spain: 416; Croatia: 372; Portugal: 341).[78]

These structural features of the RRF governance model have given rise to two major practical problems in monitoring and assessing implementation of the NRRPs. First, they have reinforced information asymmetries, allowing for gaming behaviour by Member States, through setting purposely unambitious or ambiguous targets they felt certain of being able to meet, as previously observed in the international literature on performance-based financing discussed in Section 2 above. Thus, for example, the Netherlands set targets for numbers of pig farmers to be bought out in order to reduce nitrogen emissions just below those achieved at the time of RRP submission; had the original program targets been included, they would have been missed by more than one-third.[79] And the Latvian Ministry of Health, building on long experience in managing CPF projects, deliberately set its targets for hospital renovation in elastic terms to accommodate potential difficulties.[80]

Secondly, the RRF performance-based financing system has led to a high level of rigidity in the monitoring and assessment process. Officials from nearly all countries in our study complain about inflexibility in the Commission's assessment of M&T fulfilment, exacerbated by the interventions of the European Court of Auditors, which has been pushing for a more literal and legalistic interpretation of their description in the Council Implementing Decisions. Many Member States that set ambitious targets in their NRRPs warn that they would not do it again, because of the rigid way these have been interpreted.[81] National officials

[77] European Court of Auditors (ECA), Annual report on the implementation of the EU budget for the 2021 financial year (2022), Publications Office of the EU, ch. 10; ECA, The Commission's assessment of national recovery and resilience plans: Overall appropriate but implementation risks remain (Publications Office of the EU, 2022); ECA, Design of the Commission's control system for the RRF (2023), Special Report 07, (Publications Office of the EU, 2023); ECA, Annual report on the implementation of the EU budget for the 2022 Financial Year, (Publications Office of the EU, 2023), ch. 11. Interviewees explained that while frugal Member States in the Council agree that flexibility is a problem, they continue to favour a strict and contractualised approach (interview BE-GOV2c).

[78] Interviews EU5, EU7; https://commission.europa.eu/business-economy-euro/economic-recovery/recovery-and-resilience-facility/country-pages_en.

[79] Council of the EU, Annex to the proposal for a council implementing decision on the approval of the assessment of the recovery and resilience plan for the Netherlands, 12275.22 ADD 1, September 27, 2022,. 8, 22); 'Bijna 300 varkensboeren stoppen door subsidie overheid: minder dan verwacht', *RTLnieuws*, 30 June 2021.

[80] Interview LV-GOV6.

[81] BE6, EE6, ES6, HR6, IT6, LV6, PT6, SK6; interviews EE-GOV3b, LV-GOV1b, BE-GOV1, BE-GOV2c, HR-GOV5, SK-GOV1, SK-GOV3, SK-GOV4, IT-GOV3b, ES-GOV1c. For confirmation of these findings on Member States' complaints about 'lack of sufficient flexibility' and 'the "literal" approach taken by the EC in the assessment of milestones and targets' by the independent mid-term

likewise complain bitterly about the high administrative burden in the verification process, which leads to a loss of ownership and commitment at all levels of governance. Whereas the RRF was supposed to be performance-based, it is now widely perceived as overly bureaucratic, with less flexibility and heavier reporting obligations than the Cohesion Policy Funds, especially since its financial management requirements still oblige Member States to drill down to the level of invoices and receipts in ensuring that the money is being properly spent. But perhaps the worst aspect of the administrative burden created by the RRF monitoring and assessment process is that it does not contribute to improving implementation of the reform and investment projects themselves. While national interviewees gratefully acknowledge the cooperation of Commission officials in helping to find practical solutions to problems in the assessment process, these interactions, which absorb considerable time and human resources on both sides, typically focus on finding workarounds to formal verification issues rather than on improving substantive implementation of reforms and investments, a classic case of goal displacement familiar from the international literature on performance-based financing.[82]

The Commission is aware of this pushback from Member States on the rigidity of the monitoring and assessment process. But as Commission interviewees stressed, the RRF is a new instrument, which is still taking shape through learning by doing, where both parties need to adjust to a changed modus operandi. Rigidity, in their view, is not inherent to the instrument itself, but may stem instead from how monitoring requests are interpreted nationally, how administrations coordinate internally, or how milestones and targets are operationalised, among other teething troubles that may gradually be overcome through pragmatism on both sides. The Commission has also been pushing back against the Court of Auditors' efforts to further rigidify the monitoring process, including by publishing its own framework for assessing M&Ts, which emphasises their broader 'context and purpose' in interpreting Member States obligations.[83] Despite these efforts, however, recent interviews with national officials indicate that the assessment process has become neither more flexible nor less burdensome.[84]

evaluation study, see Corti et al., Study supporting the mid-term evaluation of the recovery and resilience facility, 135. In Belgium, the Commission's pressure on the federal government to demonstrate that a recently adopted pension reform will enhance the system's financial sustainability, as specified by the NRRP in language copied from the coalition agreement with little discussion, has delayed the payment request including this milestone, and risks provoking a backlash against the EC's intervention in domestic political debates reminiscent of similar criticisms during the euro crisis (BE6; interview BE-GOV2b-c).

[82] For an in-depth comparison with the CPF, see Zeitlin et al., 'Revisiting the governance and delivery model of the Cohesion Policy Funds'. Here again, these findings are confirmed by the independent mid-term evaluation study: Corti et al., Study supporting the mid-term evaluation of the recovery and resilience facility, 135–138.

[83] ECA, Annual report on the implementation of the EU budget for 2021,: 269-271, 342-343; ECA, Annual Report on the implementation of the EU budget for 2022: 343-350, 449-455; ECA, The Commission's assessment of national recovery and resilience plans; European Commission, Recovery and resilience facility two years on, Annex 1.

[84] Interviews BE-GOV2c, ES-GOV1c, EE-GOV3b, EE-GOV6b, EE-GOV9, LV-GOV1b, LV-GOV6, LV-GOV7.

4.4 Revisability of Commitments in the Face of Uncertainty

Beyond these issues of interpretive rigidity and administrative burdens in monitoring and assessing milestones and targets, a crucial limitation of the RRF's performance-based financing model is the difficulty of revising Plan commitments in the face of unexpected implementation problems and changes in external circumstances. The RRF Regulation does allow Member States to propose revisions to their NRRPs in the face of unanticipated adverse developments, such as the high levels of inflation following the pandemic and the Russian invasion of Ukraine, as all now done to take advantage of additional funding from the REPowerEU program, as well as in some cases to take up additional loans.[85] But the threshold for such revisions remains very high, since all changes must be justified in terms of 'objective circumstances', levels of ambition for reforms and investments should not be reduced, and the revised Plan must undergo a full new process of approval by the Commission and the Council, taking account of the most recent CSRs.[86] In these revisions, the Commission has displayed some flexibility in applying the 'objective circumstances' requirement, for example by allowing modifications of measures 'to implement better alternatives', for which there is no explicit provision in the RRF Regulation.[87] But most countries nonetheless consider the procedures for modifying the Plans, which typically took about nine months to negotiate, as extremely onerous, with high evidentiary thresholds for justifying changes in M&Ts due to objective circumstances that will deter their future use except where urgently needed.[88]

In this context, several of our study's national interviewees, with long experience in managing complex investment and reform projects, including under the Cohesion Policy Funds, raised principled doubts about the feasibility and effectiveness of maintaining fixed milestones and targets over a six-year period, as envisaged in the NRRPs. There was wide agreement among our national interviewees that any future iteration of the RRF governance model would need to incorporate lighter procedures for monitoring and assessing the fulfilment of milestones and targets, focused more on measures' underlying purpose than on their precise description in legally binding texts. Such a revised governance model, in their view, would likewise need to include more flexible procedures for

[85] See the RRF's country pages for details on updates to the NRRPs: https://commission.europa.eu/business-economy-euro/economic-recovery/recovery-and-resilience-facility/country-pages_en;

[86] RRF Regulation, Arts. 18, 20, 21.

[87] European Commission, Guidance on recovery and resilience plans in the context of REPowerEU., https://commission.europa.eu/publications/guidance-recovery-and-resilience-plans-context-repowereu_en.. The revised Italian Plan makes especially broad use of this possibility, including 43 modifications introduced 'to implement better alternatives' out of 96 amended measures based on objective circumstances (IT7l; European Commission, Proposal for a council implementing decision amending implementing decision (EU) (ST 10160/21; ST 10160/21 ADD1 REV2) of 13 July 2021 on the approval of the recovery and resilience plan for Italy, COM(2023)765 final, recitals 11–16).

[88] BE7, EE7, ES7, HR7, LV7; interviews EE-GOV7, EE-GOV3b, LV-GOV1b, LV-GOV7, ES-GOV1c, HR-GOV5, HR-GOV6. For confirmation, cf. also Corti et al., Study Supporting the Mid-term Evaluation of the Recovery and Resilience Facility, 137.

modifying investment and reform commitments in response not only to unanticipated changes in external circumstances, but also to lessons learned during project implementation itself, like those developed under 'contracting for innovation' and 'diagnostic monitoring' practices elsewhere.[89]

5. Conclusions

The RRF marks a major new departure in EU governance, with significant effects on domestic policy making in Member States, as well as on relations between EU institutions and national governments. Based on in-depth comparative research on the drafting, implementation, and monitoring of NRRPs in eleven countries (eight primary and three shadow cases), as well as on the broader secondary literature, the study discussed in this chapter analysed how the RRF's innovative 'demand-driven, performance-based' governance design has worked in practice, and assessed how far it has contributed to advancing the program's declared goals, identifying both positive and negative effects. In this concluding section, we weigh up the strengths and weaknesses of the RRF's governance model, relate them to the international policy literature on national ownership and performance-based financing reviewed earlier, and briefly consider its implications for future EU policy.

Empirical analysis of the RRF 'in action' clearly shows that its governance design has a number of major *strengths*, as anticipated by the program's architects within the Commission and the Council. Presented synthetically, six *key benefits* stand out. First, the RRF governance design, in which Member-State governments draft recovery and resilience plans addressing both EU and national priorities in return for financial support from the Union budget, reinforces national ownership and commitment to reform and investment objectives, especially within central government. In this respect, the RRF marks a significant advance in terms of legitimacy not only over previous EU policies aimed at promoting national reforms, such as the euro crisis-era Memoranda of Understanding and the European Semester, but also over development aid partnerships between international donors and recipient countries, which as the international policy literature shows have often struggled to sustain domestic ownership and commitment to agreed objectives even within beneficiary governments themselves.[90] Second, it provides direct financial and policy linkages between reforms and investments to amplify their effect, unlike both the European Semester CSRs and the Cohesion Policy Funds.[91] Third, the RRF's performance-based financing system focuses primarily

[89] Annex 1, Table 2, Column 7; see especially interviews IT-GOV1b, IT-GOV3a, LV-GOV1b.

[90] See for example Faust, 'Policy experiments, democratic ownership and development assistance'; Raffinot, 'L'appropriation (ownership) des politiques de développement'.

[91] According to stakeholder consultations conducted with national coordination bodies and EU institutions for the independent mid-term evaluation study, 'support for reforms and the link with investments via the CSRs conditionality is considered the most effective aspect of the RRF', along with 'the high degree of political ownership at national level' (Corti et al., Study Supporting the Mid-term Evaluation of the Recovery and Resilience Facility, 133–135).

on substantive policy outputs (and to a much lesser extent results) rather than on cost-based policy inputs, in partial contrast to the previous EU finding instruments such as the CPF. Fourth, the RRF's requirements for a single point of contact with the Commission and fulfilment of milestones and targets as a condition for periodic payments contribute to improved horizontal and vertical coordination of national policy making, as well as to the development of more effective national and EU arrangements for monitoring domestic reforms and investments funded from the Union budget. Fifth, the RRF governance model enhances transparency and accountability expectations for national governments from their own publics as well as the EU institutions on the fulfilment of agreed commitments. Sixth, the RRF's performance-based financing system increases leverage for national governments in overcoming opposition from domestic veto players to promised reforms, as anticipated by the international political economy literature.

At the same time, however, as our empirical analysis amply demonstrates, the operation of the RRF governance model displays a series of structural weaknesses, many of which could have been predicted from international experience with performance-based financing elsewhere. Here five major *design flaws* stand out. First, the mechanical linkage of payment to fulfilment of fixed milestones and targets often shifts the attention of both national authorities and the Commission away from the underlying objectives and purposes of reforms and investments to verification and documentation procedures, wasting human resources and sapping ownership at all levels of governance. These negative effects have been exacerbated by bureaucratisation and juridification of the monitoring and assessment process under pressure from the European Court of Auditors and frugal Member States in the Council. Second, the inflexibility of the performance-based financing and verification system makes it difficult to adjust predetermined milestones and targets in response to unforeseen or changing circumstances – except through a lengthy and demanding revision of the entire Plan – and leaves insufficient space for improving ongoing projects based on learning from implementation experience.[92] Maintaining fixed M&Ts in managing innovative projects and complex multiyear reform plans is neither practical nor productive. Third, centralisation of NRRP drafting under intensive time pressure made it difficult to involve local and regional authorities in the preparation of measures for whose implementation they are responsible, with negative consequences for both effectiveness and legitimacy, as the international literature on domestic ownership of reform strategies emphasises. Fourth, reinforcement of leverage for implementing agreed commitments by the RRF's performance-based financing system is a double-edged sword. While it can empower governments to push through their programs in the face of political opposition, it can also offer opportunities for hold-up by veto players,

[92] The 'lack of sufficient flexibility' and 'excessive administrative burden' of M&T assessment, along with the cumbersome and difficult procedures for revising the Plans, were considered the least effective features of the RRF by the stakeholder consultations conducted for the mid-term independent evaluation (Corti et al., Study Supporting the Mid-term Evaluation of the Recovery and Resilience Facility, 135–137).

and may yield diminishing returns over time, creating risks of a domestic legitimacy backlash against the EU, as the *vincolo esterno* literature already showed in the Italian case. Fifth, the lack of clear and transparent criteria for ensuring that NRRPs effectively address all or a significant subset of the CSRs creates risks of unequal treatment across Member States, which could call into question the program's legitimacy.

These flaws in the RRF's governance design raise substantial doubts about its fitness of purpose in its current form. A critical question is thus how far these weaknesses could be overcome while retaining the strengths of the current model. Addressing the weaknesses of RRF governance identified in this chapter, while maintaining its benefits in terms of national ownership, linkages between investments and reforms, coordination, transparency, and accountability, would arguably require a further redesign of its performance-based financing system. Such a redesign would need to move away from the RRF's conception of the NRPPs as a putatively complete contract, based on Member States' commitment to implement predetermined reforms and investments, operationalised down to specific documents and verification criteria defined in legally binding texts, in exchange for support from the EU budget. Building on the Commission's own recent guidance, such a redesigned performance-based financing system would need to give Member States greater flexibility on the means for achieving the milestones and targets, while remaining firm on the underlying objectives and purpose of the reforms and investments they represent. Such a system would also require more flexible processes for modifying national reform and investment measures, responding not only to unanticipated changes in objective circumstances, but also to lessons learned during the implementation process, as foreshadowed in the Commission's guidance on the possibility of modifying Plan commitments in order 'to implement better alternatives' for achieving the original goals. In both respects, a redesigned performance-based financing system could profitably build on the 'diagnostic monitoring' arrangements developed by both private businesses and public industrial policy bodies to govern complex, innovative investment and reform projects under conditions of uncertainty.[93]

There are no current signs that the RRF itself will be extended beyond 2026, though debates continue about the need for a central EU fiscal capacity and the

[93] In Zeitlin et al., *Governing the RRF* and 'Revisiting the governance and delivery model of the Cohesion Policy Funds', we develop more elaborate proposals for revising the RRF's performance-based financing system along these lines through the creation of a multitiered system of diagnostic monitoring by national authorities and the Commission. The final report of the Commission's High-Level Group on the Future of Cohesion Policy specifically recommends that 'It should. . .draw inspiration from international best practices in managing innovative investment and complex reform projects, implementing 'diagnostic monitoring' for continuous supervision and periodic review' (European Commission, *Forging a Sustainable Future Together*, 39). Other recommendations for revising the RRF governance model advanced in Zeitlin et al., *Governing the RRF* include making effective inclusion of key domestic stakeholders in the drafting and implementation a binding assessment criterion for the approval of NRRPs and payment requests, and establishing explicit and transparent procedures for ensuring that such Plans address all or a significant subset of CSRs.

form such a capacity might take.[94] But elements of the RRF governance model seem likely nonetheless to become an ongoing component of the EU's policy toolbox. Thus, for example, provisions for disbursement of EU funds to Member States based on 'the achievement of results measured by reference to previously set milestones or through performance indicators' had already been added to the EU Financial Regulation in 2018 as part of the preparations for the proposed Reform Support Programme, one of the RRF's antecedents.[95] In this vein, the Commission is now proposing to extend the RRF's performance-based financing system to the Cohesion Policy Funds, in order to 'accelerate financial implementation, and increase the result orientation of the policy', while encouraging greater involvement of stakeholders and local communities than in the NRRPs.[96] National medium-term fiscal-structural plans, which would oblige Member States seeking an extension of debt-reduction trajectories proposed by the Commission to show how proposed reforms and investments address the CSRs directed to them and operationalise these in binding milestones and targets, likewise figure prominently in the recently agreed revision of the EU's economic and fiscal governance framework.[97] In carrying forward these far-reaching reforms of some of its most prominent policies, it would thus be crucial for the EU to take account of the weaknesses in the RRF governance model analysed in this study, most notably by revising its performance-based financing system.

[94] See for example A Bakker, R Beetsma, and M Buti, 'The Case for a European Public Goods Fund'. Project Syndicate, 4 March 2024. https://www.project-syndicate.org/commentary/public-goods-fund-could-finance-green-transition-and-ensure-fiscalresponsibility-by-age-bakker-et-al-2024-03.

[95] Regulation (EU, Euratom) 2018/1046 of the European Parliament and of the Council on the financial rules applicable to the general budget of the Union (Financial Regulation). Art. 125(1)(ii); P Leino-Sandberg, 'Recovery and Resilience Facility Two Years After – Quo Vadis EU Money?' (2023, September 2023), https://verfassungsblog.de/recovery-and-resilience-facility-two-years-after-quo-vadis-eu/money.

[96] Sorgi , 'EU Floats Radical Change to How it Funds Poorer Members; cf. the recommendations of the HLG on the Future of Cohesion Policy, European Commission, *Forging a sustainable future together,* 38–39.

[97] Regulation (EU) 2024/1263 of the European Parliament and of the Council on the effective coordination of economic policies and on multilateral budgetary surveillance. In assessing these Plans, the Commission is also required to take account of their alignment with the EPSR and 'progress in implementing [its] principles and headline targets, via the social scoreboard and a framework to identify risks to social convergence' (recitals 7, 9, 24; Arts. 3b, 11(c), 13(2-3).

8

European Public Goods: Concept, Identification, and Governance

ARMIN STEINBACH

1. Introduction

The various episodes of crisis that have shaken the EU in the last 20 years have brought an old question to the fore – what should the EU deliver centrally and what should remain in the Member States' hands?[1] crisis-intensive environment frequently propels this discussion in a Jean Monnet sense, which conceptualizes the EU as an entity forged and developed in and through crisis, a perspective that offered the underpinning for classic integration theories, such as neofunctionalism and liberal intergovernmentalism.[2] In fact, each crisis offered an intuitive rationale for the EU to take action rather than leaving each Member State to decide on it alone. The banking crisis laid bare the interconnectedness of financial actors pursuing borderless business across the union, a contagion that led to centralised supervision and resolution mechanism;[3] the debt crisis triggered refinancing issues that practically barred some Member States them from market access, which again due to the currency-based contagion channel became a matter of all euro countries and ushered in various centralised rescue and support schemes, such as the European Stability Mechanism;[4] from the pandemic crisis experience emerged not only EU-centralized vaccine procurement but also the unprecedented debt-based and centrally controlled fund called Next Generation EU (NG-EU);[5] and the migration crisis has fortified the perspective that external border protection is an issue that concerns all Member States, leading towards Frontex as a central

[1] This contribution builds on and draws from A Steinbach, *EU Law and Economics*, Oxford University Press (2025), 201–222; G Claeys and A Steinbach, 'A conceptual framework for the identification and governance of European public goods' Working Paper 14/2024 (Bruegel, 2024); and A Steinbach, European Public Goods, forthcoming in *International Journal of Constitutional Law*, 2026.

[2] F Schimmelfennig, 'Theorising crisis in European integration' in D Dinan, N Nugent, and WE Paterson (Eds), *The European Union in Crisis* (Macmillan, 2017), pp 316–336.

[3] R Lastra, 'Systemic Risk and Macroprudential Supervision' in: N Moloney, E Ferran, and J Payne, *The Oxford Handbook of Financial Regulation* (Oxford University Press, 2015), 309–333.

[4] J Atik, 'From "No Bailout" to the European Stability Mechanism', (2016) 39 *Fordham International Law Journal* 1201.

[5] A Steinbach, 'The Next Generation EU – Are We Having a Hamiltonian Moment?' in: Utrilla/Shabbir, *EU Law in Times of Pandemic – The EU's Legal Response to Covid-19*, 2021, 27.

institution.[6] It appears undisputed that crisis momentum has given the EU instruments that it did not have before, sometimes stretching the Treaty-based competences to their limits.[7]

This anecdotal evidence underpinning the EU's added-value to Member States' course of action has been confronted – partially fuelled by the crises themselves – by a rise of populism that centres its criticism on the EU. This populism stresses the EU inasmuch as its tasks and actions are questioned, which intensifies the self-justification of the EU. With the legitimacy of EU action notoriously challenged and questionned, centralization remains far from self-evident and requires rationalization to secure adherence to centralized power.

The concept of 'European public goods' can offer such a rationalised approach to the various calls for imminent EU action, as evidenced by recent reports such as those of Draghi and Letta.[8] While these reports utilise the term to justify EU (debt)-based financing, it would be too limited to restrict the concept to a single issue concerning the financing of specific projects. The growing literature on European public goods is characterised by an absence of a clear definition of, and an identification framework for, these particular goods, as well as a concept for the governance of their provision within the EU. The fundamental question that this chapter seeks to address is an old one: how much of the provision of public goods should be the responsibility of the EU rather than that of individual Member States? A question that lawyers typically ask by reference to the subsidiarity principle within the margins of the given allocation of competences. While lawyers do not inquire into this question outside the positivist Treaty framework, economists have more assertively examined the division of mission in federal arrangements beyond a descriptive analysis. To that end, one must address the quandary of determining when the advantages of EU-level provisions outweigh their potential costs, which may incur through the diminution of national sovereignty, the variances across the EU in preferences concerning the nature and extent of public goods, and the increased autonomy of Brussels-based institutions from domestic and local concerns. The inquiry further extends to the potential for reducing these costs through the implementation of suitable institutional arrangements to govern the EU-level provision of public goods – an inquiry to which lawyers can contribute through analysis of the institutional design of the EU legal framework.

[6] Y Zhong and H Carrapico, 'The development of Frontex: integration through supranationalism' *European Politics and Society 25* (2023), 233–248.

[7] CJ Bickerton, D Hodson, and U Puetter, 'The new intergovernmentalism: European integration in the post-Maastricht era', 53 *JCMS* (2015), 703–722; see also the discussion on the compatibility of NGEU with EU law, tacitly disputed by the German Constitutional Court and significant parts of the legal literature.

[8] T Breton, 'A Europe that Protects its Citizens, Transforms its Economy, and Projects Itself as a Global Power' (2024) Speech at the European Policy Centre, 10 January 2024; M Draghi, 'The Next Flight of the Bumblebee: The Path to Common Fiscal Policy in the Eurozone' (2023) 15th Annual Martin Feldstein Lecture, 11 July 2023; M Buti, 'When Will the European Union Finally get the Budget it Needs?' (2023) Bruegel, 7 December 2023; E Letta, *Much More than a Market, Report*, European Council, April 2024.

The concept of public goods is typically associated with the question of whether a particular good should be supplied by the private or public sector. The conventional definition of a public good emphasises two key characteristics: non-rivalry, signifying that the consumption of a good by one individual does not diminish the consumption opportunities of others; and non-excludability, implying that the good is accessible to all without restriction. These characteristics are deemed essential, as they prevent the occurrence of free-riding behaviours and ensure adequate provision of the good, thereby validating the need for public intervention.[9]

Public goods can be categorised as either natural, exemplified by clean air, or human-made, such as public health or defence. It is possible to distinguish further between public goods (ie non-rivalrous and non-exclusive in consumption) such as environmental protection or the internal market;[10] common resource goods (non-exclusive but rivalrous in consumption) such as water resources, the use of infrastructure, or central bank liquidity;[11] and club goods (exclusive but non-rivalrous) such as the eurozone or the Schengen space.[12] For the purposes of this analysis, all such goods will be referred to as public goods.[13]

The concept of public goods, as discussed in economics, finds reflection in law in notions of the 'common good' or the 'public interest'. However, both terms have nothing to do with the traditional economic definition of public goods but are closely linked to theoretical debate about the legitimacy of state action. The concept of the common good in legal literature has been associated with the legitimisation of statehood and the exercise of sovereign power.[14] The scholarship devoted to the common good has not produced a sharp definition of what constitutes the common good, nor does a positive law definition exist. For a starter, it can be characterised as forming the basis of statehood, often likened with public interest. As an inherently open and indefinite concept, the common good creates a framework for argumentation for the legitimacy of state or sovereign action.

In capturing the discourse surrounding the legitimacy of the European Union and given the limitations of the economic conception of a pure public good, it appears prudent to adopt a slightly more expansive definition. A public good is hereby defined as a good that is not supplied at an adequate level in the absence of public intervention (that could manifest through various forms, including direct provision, government expenditure, or regulation), owing to any coordination problem (not only non-exclusion/non-rivalry, but also, for instance, network

[9] PA Samuelson, 'The Pure Theory of Public Expenditure' (1954) 36 *The Review of Economics and Statistics* 387.

[10] S Coutts, Supranational public wrongs: The limitations and possibilities of European criminal law and a European community' (2017) CML Rev. 54, 771–800, at 789: 'a collective asset'.

[11] R Berith, European Public Goods in the Neo-Medieval Model of Governance in S Collignon (Ed), *The Governance of European Public Goods* (Palgrave Macmillan, 2017), at 15.

[12] C Fuest and J Pisani-Ferry, 'A Primer on Developing European Public Goods' *EconPol Policy Report 16* (European Network for Economic and Fiscal Policy Research, 2019), at 4.

[13] M Buti, A Coloccia, and M Messori, *European Public Goods* (9 June 2023), https://cepr.org/voxeu/columns/european-public-goods (last visited 20 Feb 2025)

[14] C Calliess, '*Öffentliche Güter im Recht der Europäischen Union* (Bertelsmann Stiftung, 2021), at 7.

effects). This 'extended' notion of public goods concurs with the prevailing approach to public goods, as evidenced by both the academic literature on fiscal federalism and the policy discourse on European public goods.[15] The fiscal federalism theory posits that decentralised provision is the optimal solution when the costs of providing public goods at a lower level are lower than at a higher level. The extant economic literature has conceptualised the answer to this question in the decentralisation theorem, according to which '... in the absence of cost-savings from the centralised provision of a (local public) good and of inter-jurisdictional externalities, the level of welfare will always be at least as high (and typically higher) if Pareto-efficient levels of consumption are provided in each jurisdiction than if any single, uniform level of consumption is maintained across all jurisdictions'.[16]

Accordingly, a European Public Good can be delineated as a good not supplied at the adequate level without public intervention, and which should be provided at the EU level to internalise externalities and reap benefits of scale while ensuring that local preferences are taken into account.

Determining the appropriate governmental level for the organisation and funding of public goods typically involves a trade-off.[17] On one hand, there is potential heterogeneity in preferences across geographical or political entities, which tends to favour the provision of goods at the local level (tailor-made in line with local preferences). On the other hand, there is the potential for improved efficiency through internalising externalities and capitalising on economies of scale, which pushes in the other direction. The optimality of decentralisation is thus contingent on the costs of providing public goods at a lower level being lower than at a higher level. This can be due to no gain related to inter-jurisdictional spillovers or economies of scale, or when these gains are lower than the costs associated with supplying uniform public goods rather than tailor-made public goods to take into account heterogenous preferences. Decentralised provision can also be beneficial due to better knowledge of preferences or higher democratic accountability. Conversely, if the gains/cost relation of central action is positive, fiscal federalism theory would acknowledge a rationale for EU action. In essence, the optimal level of provision of a public good is the one that reaps efficiency gains, while accounting for local preferences.

Where externalities are substantial and public goods and services are shared by large populations, the production and supply of public goods should be dealt with centrally.[18] For the EU, this can be re-phrased by reference to intra-jurisdictional efficiency. The optimal allocation is achieved when the bundle of

[15] I Begg, 'Fiscal federalism, subsidiarity and the EU budget review' *Reports/SIEPS 2009:1* (Swedish Institute for European Policy Studies, 2009), at 8.

[16] WE Oates, *Fiscal Federalism* (Harcourt Brace Jovanovich, 1972) 54.

[17] A Alesina, I Angeloni and L Schuknecht, 'What Does the European Union Do?' (2005) 123 *Public Choice* 275.

[18] RP Inman and DL Rubinfeld, 'Economics of Federalism' in Francesco Parisi (ed), *Oxford Handbook of Law and Economics* (Oxford University Press, 2017) 90.

collective goods supplied satisfies the collective demands of individuals at minimum cost. This cost comprises the costs of producing public services plus the transaction costs of the decision-making process, implementation costs, and agency-related control costs.

2. Dealing with trade-offs

Determining the appropriate level of action in the EU and the funding of public goods typically involves a trade-off.[19] On one side, there are benefits from a larger size and internalisation of spillover; on the other side, there are political costs associated with heterogeneous preferences over public goods and policies. Economies of scale intuitively occur in the provision of public goods, such as a common foreign policy and defence, public health, trans-national infrastructure, or a common monetary system. While the aggregate costs of providing these goods on an EU-wide basis may be rising, their mean cost is declining due to shared fixed expenses. Consequently, economies of scale result in reduced prices per person.[20] Additionally, the internalisation of cross-regional externalities by larger political unions has been demonstrated in the extant literature on political integration and federalism.[21] Within the EU, such internalisation can be achieved through the reduction of Member States' activity, thereby negating negative externalities, or by the extension of Member State activity, thus reaping positive externalities. Nevertheless, the potential benefits of economies of scale and the internalisation of externalities can be counterbalanced by the costs associated with preferences and values across dimensions such as language, culture, religion, and ethnicity. Given that many of these 'costs' are non-economic in nature, it is essential to recognise that economic outcomes and political institutions can be fully understood only when social preferences and attitudes rooted in culture and history are taken into account.[22] This analytical angle can be easily likened – with the emphasis the German Constitutional Court has given to cultural divergences – to factors that could bring the transfer of competences to an halt, because 'the public perception of factual issues and of political leaders remains connected to a considerable extent to patterns of identification related to the nation-state, language,

[19] W E Oates, *Fiscal Federalism* (Harcourt Brace Jovanovich,1972); A Alesina, I Angeloni and L Schuknecht, 'What Does the European Union Do?' (2005) 123 Public Choice 275.

[20] A Alesina and R Wacziarg, 'Openness, Country Size and Government' (1998) 69 *Journal of Public Economics* 305.

[21] W Hauge and T Ellingsen, 'Beyond Environmental Scarcity: Causal Pathways to Conflict' (1998) 35 *Journal of Peace Research* 299; WE Oates, 'An Essay on Fiscal Federalism' (1999) 37 *Journal of Economic Literature* 1120; A Alesina, I Angeloni and F Etro, 'International Unions' (2005) 95 *American Economic Review* 602.

[22] A Alesina and E Spolaore, *The Size of Nations* (The MIT Press 2005).

history and culture'.[23, 24] However, the heterogeneity argument necessitates a more nuanced examination, particularly with respect to the sources of heterogeneity. It is contended that cultural heterogeneity – of traits and preferences– far from being merely costly, has the potential to yield substantial benefits through innovation, specialisation, and learning.[25] In particular, heterogeneity may prove beneficial in contexts that involve the production and exchange of private (ie rival) goods. A society composed of individuals with diverse tastes and preferences in private consumption is likely to function more efficiently and harmoniously than a society in which there is a uniform desire for consumption of the same goods and work schedules. This phenomenon, however, is less evident in the context of public goods. The uniform provision of public goods can result in a discrepancy between policy objectives and individual preferences, leading to discord over issues such as the design of social, family, and foreign and defence policies.[26]

Clearly, the trade-off equation is subject to change over time, with the elements of the trade-off varying depending on the strength of the efficiency case (externalities, scale economies), the occurrence of external factors, the institutional framework, and the evolution of preferences in a society. In particular, preferences emerge as a result of how they are accounted for in an institutional framework of governance, which, if well designed, can lead to reduced political costs from heterogeneity. The hypothesis is that federal institutions are more effective than sub-federal ones in achieving democratic consensus, which may have an impact on regional preferences. In other words, while the benefits of diversity can be maintained, the political costs associated with preference heterogeneity may be reduced by developing inclusive institutions that ensure the consideration of social, political, and economic preferences.[27]

The following two examples demonstrate how the trade-off does not remain constant over time. The Brexit referendum could be interpreted as a case in which the balance between efficiency and heterogeneous preferences has evolved. While positive externalities and economies of scale were a leading motivation for the UK to be part of the EU for a long time, the global reduction in trade barriers made the efficiency case of the EU less visible for the UK. Conversely, the heterogeneity of preferences and the dissatisfaction with the uniformity of EU rules ultimately prevailed over the case for the UK's continued participation in the EU, at least among those who voted in favour of Brexit. This aligns with the literature that underscores the diminution of economic benefits from increased domestic size

[23] VerfGE 123, 267 Lisbon (2009) — Lisbon Treaty, para 251.
[24] BVerfG, Judgment of 30 June 2009 - 2 BvE 2/08 –, para. 249.
[25] A Alesina and E La Ferrara, 'Ethnic Diversity and Economic Performance' (2005) 43 Journal of Economic Literature 762.
[26] E Spolaore, 'The Economic Approach to Political Borders' (2022) CESifo Working Paper No. 10165.
[27] ibid.

due to reduced barriers to international trade, a phenomenon that can potentially lead to political disintegration.[28]

In contrast, the reverse may be true for EU border protection. Border security has long been viewed as sensitive to national sovereignty concerns and thus remained a stronghold of Member States' realm. However, new threats to security have strengthened the case for economies of scale and externality issues (with border security being the weakest link in public goods)[29]. An increasing external threat (eg military or geopolitically) may change attitudes towards joining forces in security and defence affairs and ultimately makes the efficiency gains of scale economies outweigh the trade-offs.[30]

The decision regarding the optimal level of governance, whether centralised or decentralised, is not always clear ex ante, potentially resulting in an inefficient allocation of responsibilities. This is particularly evident in cases where complementary strengths are present. Take financial regulation, where in certain instances, centralised supervision and cross-border integration can be complementary. Centralised supervision can encourage banks to attract foreign funding, while reliance on foreign funding can, in turn, increase cross-border externalities (hence the need for centralised supervision).[31] The conditions that make centralisation beneficial may not be satisfied ex ante, but only ex post. The adequacy of EU-level governance could also lead to changes in preferences over time. The establishment of institutions that represent minority positions (eg the EU level through unanimity in the Council or through an expanded role assigned to the European Committee of the Regions) may serve to overcome scepticism and resistance in Member States regarding centralised EU activity. Furthermore, the provision of compensations to minorities whose preferences and policies diverge significantly from the European median may also serve to modify these preferences. Such compensations could be institutionalised through the establishment of specific rights, such as enhanced regional involvement in the subsidiarity test applied for EU law-making, or through financial compensation mechanisms, including regional and cohesion funds, or individualised EU support schemes. In sum, the assessment of the trade-off should take account of the dynamic effects of external factors as well as internal institutional governance.

[28] A Alesina, E Spolaore and R Wacziarg, 'Economic Integration and Political Disintegration' (2000) 90 American Economic Review 1276; A Alesina, E Spolaore and R Wacziarg, 'Trade, Growth and the Size of Countries' (2005) 1 Handbook of Economic Growth 1499; E Spolaore and R Wacziarg, 'Borders and Growth' (2005) 10 *Journal of Economic Growth* 331.

[29] Weakest-link public good means that all members must invest in the supply of the public good. In the absence of such investment, any state's investment is effectively wasted.

[30] WH Riker, *Federalism: Origin, Operation, Significance* (Little, Brown and Company 1964); E Spolaore, 'Adjustments in Different Government Systems' (2004) 16 *Economics & Politics* 117; 'The Economics of Political Borders' (2012) CESifo Working Paper No. 3854

[31] JE Colliard, 'Optimal Supervisory Architecture and Financial Integration in a Banking Union' (2019) *Review of Finance* 129.

3. Identification of European public goods

For the theoretical approach to become meaningful in offering guidance on the identification of European public goods, we apply a four-step process as an identification strategy.

First, externalities between national jurisdictions must be measured and assessed with view to if and how these externalities can be internalised if the public good is provided at the EU level. There are various methods to do that. A negative externality occurs when the actions of one country have a detrimental impact on the provision of a public good in another country. Security provides an illustrative example. The failure to implement effective border control measures or anti-laundering tools has the potential to undermine security not only in the country concerned, but also in other Member States. In other instances, negative externalities occur when members engage in free-riding behaviour, benefiting from the public good provided by another state without contributing to its provision. In a joint currency area like the euro zone, the public good of economic stability may be at risk. The centralised enforcement of fiscal rules (Article 126 TFEU) is designed to mitigate the phenomenon of free-riding and negative externalities. How could one measure externalities? By looking at the specific public good, the expected contributions and payoffs for each EU country under two scenarios (the status quo and an hypothetical provision at EU level, or vice versa) can be quantified. One can then argue that the level of provision (ie European or national) that leads to a higher correlation between countries' shares in the benefits and costs of the policy is the level that best internalises spillovers.[32]

Secondly, the economies of scale and potential savings that could be achieved by providing the good at the EU level must be measured. Significant scale economies are indicated when fixed costs are too large for a given Member State, and it is necessary to ascertain whether the costs can be supported at the EU level. Examples of this include cost-intensive research, which often requires a sufficiently high level of investment to be successful. This investment must be shared across multiple parties, suggesting that joint action is required for certain risk-prone and expensive research projects (such as Galileo).[33] Procurement of vaccines also contributes to public health, and this can be achieved through the exploitation of scale economies. Various methods exist for estimating economies of scale, including the estimation of slopes of cost or production functions of selected public goods to determine whether economies of scale exist.

Thirdly, notwithstanding the potential for externalities or scale economies, there may still be compelling reasons not to provide a public good at the European level (or at least not exclusively), notably when preferences are too heteregenous.

[32] S Weiss et al., How Europe Can Deliver: Optimising the Division of Competences among the EU and Its Member States, (Bertelsmann Stiftung, 2017).

[33] D Tibor, "EU added value – a categorical imperative for EU action?" in G Moonen and D Meijers (Eds), *Realising European added value* (European Court of Auditors, 2020), pp. 8-18, at 13.

From an economic perspective, preferences are understood as citizens' individual likes and dislikes.[34] Even if there are significant externalities and scale economies that favour centralisation, core public goods such as a European army for joint defence or a centralised taxation competence have remained a prerogative of Member States due to their core sovereignty concerns.[35]

In terms of measurement, heterogeneity of preferences among EU countries must be measured, with two forms of preference heterogeneity being considered: First, preferences on the level of provision of a specific public good (eg defence spending might be more important for Poland than for Ireland), and various instruments could be used to measure this (surveys or current expenditure levels, assuming that the national governance process that has led to these expenditures represent well the preferences of citizens). In view of the foregoing discussion, it is probable that this aspect of preference is endogenous with respect to external events. For instance, the Russian invasion of Ukraine is likely to engender an increased desire for a higher level of provision of this public good, albeit not at the same rate across countries. In some neighbouring countries, the demand for increased defence spending may rise disproportionately (eg in countries neighbouring Russia). While this may lead to an increase in cross-border heterogeneity, there is a shared minimum degree of preference for a certain minimum level of provision of defence as a public good (eg small-scale joint defence activities). Second, it is also necessary to measure at which level of government the good should be provided (eg two countries might have the same defence spending but might prefer that defence is provided only at the national level, because they consider it to be part of national sovereignty). Surveys should be the main tool to measure this. This element of preference is likely to be endogenous to the institutional governance of regional preferences discussed above – the more that a centralised government is able to account for minority rights and local preferences, the higher the likelihood that heterogeneity is reduced.

Finally, a more difficult task is to weigh these three elements to decide if a public good should be provided at the EU level. Indeed, even though there are a few cases that are relatively clear (cross-border infrastructure, external border protection, pandemic health crisis management, research) for which there are homogenous preferences and clear efficiency gains, in most cases, trade-offs arise. This is the case when efficiency gains could be made by providing a good at the EU level, but preferences clearly differ across countries (defence, macroeconomic stability, foreign and security policy). This highlights the necessity for mechanisms that accommodate for differing preferences and addresses them accordingly. The management of these trade-offs can be facilitated by the legal framework of European governance, which is adapted to address the variable trade-offs.

[34] F Parisi, *The Language of Law and Economics* (Cambridge University Press, 2013), at 228.

[35] Conceptually, barriers to transfers of core sovereign rights can be seen as *dis*economies of scale. The deeper and far-reaching integration advances, the higher become the costs of further transfers.

4. Legal options to deliver European Public Goods

European public goods vary in the degree to which they can be characterised as European or national goods. The consequence of this is that there is no 'one size fits all' governance for all EU public goods. The governance of each public good should thus be contingent on its unique characteristics in terms of externalities, economies of scale, and preference heterogeneity, underscoring the pivotal role of the law in this regard. While economics predominates in the identification of public goods, law plays a crucial role in ensuring that the provision of public goods aligns with their economic rationale. Consequently, an interplay emerges between economic and legal analysis, with the objective being to optimise the efficient delivery of European public goods.

A substantial array of institutional and legal instruments, both embedded within the EU treaties and outside them, can be utilised to manage this trade-off, in the sense of optimising efficiency gains to the maximum extent while reflecting preference heterogeneity. These include: decision-making rules in the Council (unanimity versus qualified majority voting); provision of public goods at the level of clubs of Member States with similar preferences (using devices such as 'constructive abstention', 'enhanced cooperation', or intergovernmental treaties); separation of common decision-making from common financing; finding the right mix between common and national financing (fully centralised EU-level funding, EU top-up of national funding, coordinated national financing, or uncoordinated national financing); and compensation of countries or minorities to achieve greater alignment of preferences. The EU's institutional and legal framework offers a diverse range of tools to bring the governance design of public goods in line with the economic rationale for public good provision at the EU level. Specifically, there are different governance design parameters that could be used to address trade-offs related to the provision of public goods in Europe.

4.1 Who holds rule-setting power? Adjusting the scope of competence transfer from Member States to the EU

The most fundamental lever is to allocate the scope of competence between Member States and the EU. There is a spectrum of design in allocating the provision of a public good through the order of competence in the Treaties. On one extreme, competence for public good provision can be at the country level without any involvement of the EU, without institutional or formalised coordination of Member States' policies, and with financial resources entirely supplied at the country level. On the other extreme, the EU can have exclusive competence, legislating and enforcing centrally through EU institutions, and the public intervention can be financed through EU resources (eg monetary policy to deliver the public good of price stability).

The allocation of competence can vary between these two extremes, with legislation and enforcement being centralised, yet allowing Member States leeway if their actions do not pose a risk to the provision of EU public goods (eg competition policy to ensure a competitive and undistorted market). Alternatively, a competence may remain with Member States, but the EU could oblige them to coordinate their domestic policies (eg the European Semester to deliver the public good of macroeconomic stability). The power to legislate is the first level of competence allocation (before implementation or financing), and the degree of competence transfer and the allocation of decision-making power should be adapted to the strength of the economic case for EU level provisions of public goods. It is important to note that, in the absence of a Treaty change, the degree of competences can be shifted only for so-called 'shared competence'. In this area, if the policy actions pass the 'subsidiarity test' under Article 5 para. 3 TEU, centralised action is possible.[36] The legal test requires the policy objective not to be sufficiently achievable at the Member State level, but better achievable at the Union level. This should be the case when spillovers and scale economies suggest action on Union level.[37] However, further transfers of competence are only possible following amendments to the Treaties. In many cases, the current rule-setting power can be maintained through shared competence, as many public goods are often already governed by this mechanism (eg cross-border infrastructure; knowledge through research; external border protection; competitive markets). The subsidiarity principle does not create obstacles to Europeanisation in these cases, due to the strong efficiency case of these public goods.

A shift to EU exclusive competence is desirable when externalities are significant, as is the case in some cases, such as pandemic prevention and crisis management. Indeed, there could be substantial spillovers due to the risk of contagion between countries if there is insufficient prevention and/or insufficient crisis action in one country against a pandemic. In such instances, health emerges as a 'weakest-link' public good, a phenomenon that contrasts with the typically idiosyncratic and path-dependent nature of other health policy elements, which are better suited to remaining within national purview.[38] Consequently, the exercise of EU centralised power should be confined to the prevention of adverse cross-border spillovers and the maximisation of economies of scale. In the context of ex ante EU legislative power, Member States may be obliged to acquire essential

[36] C Calliess, "Öffentliche Güter im Recht der Europäischen Union" (Bertelsmann Stiftung, 2021), at 22; S Weatherill, 'Protecting the Internal Market from the Charter' in S De Vries, U Bernitz and S Weatherill (eds.), *The EU Charter of Fundamental Rights as a Binding Instrument: Five Years Old and Growing* (Hart Publishing, 2016), 136.

[37] C Fuest and J Pisani-Ferry, 'A Primer on Developing European Public Goods', EconPol Policy Report 16 (European Network for Economic and Fiscal Policy Research, 2019); S Naess-Schmidt et al., *Subsidiarity and Proportionality in the Single Market: An EU Fit for Inclusive Growth* (Bertelsmann Stiftung, 2018).

[38] C Wyplosz, 'Which European Public Goods?', In-depth Analysis for the ECON Committee, European Parliament (2024).

medicine and vaccines, or to harmonise vaccine requirements, with a view to ensuring coordination and preventing free-riding behaviour. During health crises, the EU could assume a more significant role in coordinating the response and acting promptly, for example by empowering the Commission to declare an emergency state, as opposed to leaving this decision to the Council.

Conversely, in other areas Member States' competences should be maintained (eg in cultural affairs or primary education) or even re-established. For instance, one of the objectives of the Common Agricultural Policy (CAP) is to contribute to the 'preservation of rural areas'. However, there are no spillovers or economies of scale associated with a country having a 'vibrant rural life'. A similar argument can be made for local infrastructures, which are regarded as public goods and are occasionally funded through the European Regional Development Fund, even in affluent regions of the EU. In such cases, there is no compelling justification for centralisation. At most, the EU could serve as a platform for the dissemination of information, the identification of best practices, and the establishment of benchmarks.

4.2 How is the decision taken? Calibrating decision-making majority in the Council

The heterogeneity of preferences primarily is relevant to determine the appropriate level of public good governance. As such, Member States' preferences should be given variable degrees of representation in the design of decision-making in the Council, ranging from unanimity to qualified-majority voting (QMV). The voting method should reflect the extent to which diverging preferences may impede certain centralising actions (which might be profitable for efficiency reasons). It is important to note that, as a general rule, the more significant efficiency considerations there are – ie the stronger spillovers and scale economies are – the more heterogeneity of preferences could be overruled (and vice-versa). While QMV is the most widely used voting method in the Council today, with 80% of legislation adopted through this method, for certain policy areas unanimity remains the default voting. However, without Treaty changes, decision-making requirements can be adjusted using the 'passerelle clause', which allows for a shift from unanimity to QMV (Article 48 para. 7 TEU). This transition towards QMV may, inter alia, extend in the existing Treaty framework to foreign and security policy (but not military and defence), taxation policy, environmental and energy policy, and social policy. However, passerelle clauses are ambivalent in nature, as they entail a trade-off between democratic legitimacy and alignment with national preferences (through unanimity) on the one hand, and the centralised action required to mitigate efficiency concerns (spillovers and scale economies) on the other. Notwithstanding, passerelle clauses can claim to maintain legitimacy and preference orientation at a high level by enabling national parliaments to contradict and block the transition to QMV if deemed necessary. Consequently, the activation of passerelle clauses should be the prevailing option when there are strong efficiency considerations.

Moreover, preference heterogeneity is also addressed through institutional safeguards aimed at protecting minority and regional rights. These safeguards could be implemented by reinforcing national parliaments within the subsidiarity control mechanism, thereby empowering national parliaments to voice objections to EU actions when they perceive subsidiarity to be compromised. Alternatively, these safeguards could be strengthened by enhancing the role of the Committee of the Regions in EU law-making processes.

In areas with strong efficiency (externality, scale economies) and homogenous preferences, QMV should be the prevailing norm to prevent strategic voting and ineffective bargaining between nations. With regard to the governance of public goods entailing trade-offs, maintaining an unanimity requirement in the Council is essential when the heterogeneity of preferences outweighs the magnitude of spillovers or scale economies. Conversely, if spillovers are considered more significant than heterogeneous preferences, QMV should be sought after to ensure that efficiency cases do not prevail over heterogeneous preferences. Defence is a pertinent example of a public good for which there is a compelling rationale to distinguish voting requirements within the same public good, given the existence of externalities and scale economies. Common procurement of military equipment (with significant scale economies and limited preference heterogeneity) should be governed by QMV, while a joint army should respect unanimity (due to strong preference heterogeneity on core sovereignty issues), at least if it involves the whole EU. Another potential solution to this issue could be to pursue it only with countries that have similar preferences, in which case QMV could be used within this restricted group.

4.3 Who participates? Variable participation in integration: The 'club provision' of public goods

While modifications of the decision-making mode in the Council remain symmetrical in the sense that all Member States participate in the process, instances may arise in which efficiency and heterogeneity of preferences require an asymmetrical approach. This could occur when the efficiency argument does not apply equally to all Member States or when certain countries have notably distinct preferences compared to others. This dynamic can potentially result in the fragmentation of participation, transitioning from a scenario of 'full participation' among all EU members to a 'club cooperation' model. The efficacy of club cooperation in enhancing efficiency and mitigating the under-provision of public goods is evident in scenarios such as the coordination of defence policies among several

EU countries through resource pooling.[39] However, non-participating countries may benefit from the efforts of the club members without making a contribution (eg the commitment to lower emissions by a club would be undermined if non-participating countries benefit from the efforts of the club members without making a contribution because they have no incentive to join the club). In such cases, the feasibility of club goods may be questionable and other instruments – eg compensation of potential losers from centralisation, as discussed below – would be necessary to incentivise participation and avoid free-riding behaviours.

From an institutional perspective, the integration mode typically referred to as 'variable geometry' or 'two-speed Europe' can thus be likened to the provision of 'club' public goods.[40] 'Club cooperation' could take place within the EU institutional and legal framework or outside of the framework. The choice between these options should depend on the economic case. While the passerelle clause (allowing a shift from unanimity to qualified majority voting) does not fragment the participation of Member States either geographically or temporally to achieve a more efficient result in which all Member States participate, 'variable participation' introduces some asymmetry. This could be achieved in three ways. Firstly, in the area of Common Foreign and Security Policy (CFSP), the least intrusive option is through 'constructive abstention' under Article 31 para. 1 TEU, which does not oblige a Member State to implement the decision but to accept that the decision commits the Union. Secondly, 'enhanced cooperation' can be established among a minimum of nine Member States to pursue action within a non-exclusive competence of the Union (Article 20 TEU). While 'enhanced cooperation' is fragmented, it leaves intact the institutions of the EU, allowing non-participating members to easily join the club at a later stage. Thirdly, in instances where 'club integration' is not politically viable within the confines of the Treaty framework, states that are willing may pursue the provision of public goods outside of the Treaty. A notable example of this is the Schengen agreement, which, although initially pioneered by a select few countries, was subsequently adopted by many and integrated as 'enhanced cooperation' into the EU Treaty.[41] Deeper integration in defence, for instance the establishment of joint forces, may be implemented through intergovernmental cooperation.

The evolution of the trade-off between efficiency and preference heterogeneity may be precipitated by club provision, as preferences may gradually converge. Although Schengen was initially inconceivable within the EU institutional and legal framework due to significant differences in preferences, the efficiency case for removing internal border controls (and the absence of significant negative experiences) changed preferences in such a way that Schengen was ultimately integrated

[39] As discussed in eg C Fuest and J Pisani-Ferry, 'A Primer on Developing European Public Goods', *EconPol Policy Report* 16 (European Network for Economic and Fiscal Policy Research, 2019).

[40] DA Kroll and D Leuffen, 'Enhanced Cooperation in Practice: An Analysis of Differentiated Integration in EU Secondary Law', 22 J. *Eur. Public Policy* (2015), 353–373.

[41] B De Witte, 'Using International Law in the Euro Crisis: Causes and Consequences' (ARENA Working Paper Series, 2013), at 2.

into it. A parallel can be drawn with the European Stability Mechanism (ESM), established in 2012 to address the sovereign debt crisis. The initial legal basis for an institutionalised scheme for solvency-securing financial support was not present in the Treaty, prompting the creation of the ESM. It is not integrated into the EU institutional framework and is governed by its own international agreement, yet it was made possible by the amendment of an article in the TFEU. This arrangement, termed 'club integration', operates outside the primary EU Treaties and can be implemented even when the club consists of fewer than nine members, in contrast to 'enhanced cooperation', which necessitates a minimum of nine participants. However, it should be noted that 'club integration' is not well-suited to the provision of all public goods, particularly in cases where non-participating countries could exploit the efforts of club members without contributing. To illustrate this point, consider the example of climate protection: If non-participating countries are able to avoid the costs associated with reducing their emissions, this could undermine the commitment of club members. Similarly, achieving economic security is dependent on all countries participating to a minimum level of Foreign Direct Investment (FDI) screening. This is to avoid any potential weak links that could compromise the overall security standards within the EU. In such cases, the feasibility of club goods might be called into question, and alternative instruments – such as compensation of potential losers from centralisation, as discussed below – would need to be considered to incentivise participation of all countries and avoid free-riding behaviours.

4.4 How deeply is the EU level involved? The centralisation of funding decisions and delivery

In addition to the transfer of competence that entails the shifting of legislative power from Member States to the EU, two further mechanisms exist through which the governance of the European public good (EPG) can be tailored to a specific need: its funding and its delivery. The extent to which all governance levers should be centralised (legislation, funding, delivery) or whether elements of decentralisation should be maintained depends on the specifics of each public good.

The combination of legislation (as previously discussed under 1.), funding, and delivery of public goods can be achieved in several ways. In some cases, it may be sufficient to adhere to a uniform set of regulations (eg to ensure compliance with the single market) while delegating funding and spending decisions to the national level to accommodate national preferences (eg subsidies for cultural goods or industrial policy). In certain instances, a uniform regulatory framework may be adequate to mitigate potential externalities while respecting diverse preferences.

However, in other cases, the provision of an EPG may require both centralised regulation, as well as centralised funding decisions and/or centralised delivery, as public funding and delivery at the national level may fail to account for the potential efficiency gains related to cross-border externalities or scale economies. The

NGEU serves as a case in point, illustrating a centralised funding mechanism (via the issuance of debt) and a uniform rulebook that determines the spending priorities across the EU to deliver several EPGs (climate protection, macroeconomic stability, etc.). Concurrently, in that particular configuration, delivery remained decentralised, leaving the precise project selection to Member States. When decentralised funding proves inefficient, the necessity for full funding at the EU level does not necessarily follow. In such cases, the coordination of spending between countries or the provision of a top-up funding from the EU may often be sufficient to achieve the desired level of provision of the good. This type of top-up funding, for instance, could be adequate to deliver the necessary green investments to achieve climate protection in the future. As previously discussed, this approach has been partially implemented via the NGEU. Another crucial public good that ought to be pursued at the EU level is economic resilience, given the heightened vulnerability to geopolitical shocks exhibited by European countries in recent years. A purely national strategy of 'de-risking' would be inefficient in this regard, as it would not internalise the spillovers from the dependence on specific countries and would also forego scale economies. The solution to this issue lies in centralising instruments to conclude EU trade agreements and to unionise inbound/outbound investment control and promotion of foreign trade and investment, with the clear objective of increasing economic resilience for the EU as a whole. This approach should be complemented by the allocation of additional EU investments to mitigate vulnerabilities associated with reliance on specific countries, particularly in sectors such as innovative technologies.[42]

In certain instances, full budget centralisation or centralised delivery may be imperative, along with the establishment of a uniform legal framework. It is already the norm for centralised funding to be used for subsidies provided to farmers to achieve food security, which are provided centrally through the CAP in the EU budget to avoid negative externalities that this could present on other Member States if subsidies were delivered at the country level. Similarly, external border protection is an example of a 'weakest-link' public good creating externalities because an insufficient border protection of only one EU member can reduce the security for all members. Such impediments may be attributed to a combination of financial constraints and political incapacity. In instances where border protection is deemed inadequate, the EU is empowered to exercise its existing legislative competence in this domain, leveraging Frontex as a centralised entity to deliver effective border protection measures. The centralisation process could be expanded to encompass other policy areas, such as defence procurement (eg large-scale military equipment) or health (eg pandemic prevention and control). High-scale and risky R&D projects that would not be pursued at the country level because they are too expensive should also be funded and delivered at the EU level. Finally, as discussed above, there are also public goods that are

[42] S Tagliapietra, R Veugelers and J Zettelmeyer, 'Rebooting the European Union's Net Zero Industry Act', (2023) Policy Brief 15/2023, Bruegel.

currently financed and/or delivered at the EU level that exhibit neither externalities nor economies of scale: local infrastructures with no cross-border spillovers or the preservation of rural areas. These should be financed and delivered at the national or regional levels.

4.5 How can preferences be accommodated? Compensation to mitigate preference heterogeneity

When efficiency requires either full centralisation or at least broad participation in the provision of public goods, but some countries (or politically influential groups in those countries) would be negatively affected, compensation schemes at the level of EU countries, regions, households, or companies may be a suitable tool to reap efficiency gains that would otherwise be blocked by the losing party, in particular in cases in which club good provision is not desirable (see above). Furthermore, as previously discussed, financial compensation has the capacity to modify preferences, rendering them more homogeneous. Consequently, the proceeds resulting from efficiency gains may need to be utilised, at least in the initial stages, for distributional purposes.

This redistribution may be facilitated through various channels, including the EU allocating budgets to individuals or companies administered by countries or regions, with the aim of mitigating the impact of structural change on individuals (as is already done through the European Globalisation Adjustment Fund).[43] Alternatively, the redistribution may be indirect, through compensation paid to EU countries (eg through the Just Transition Fund, or Structural and Cohesion Funds). The utilisation of these funds and compensation schemes is intended to align local preferences with the efficiency-based necessity for centralisation. For instance, energy security is recognised as a public good of EU relevance, given that national decisions on power plants and renewable energies can have implications for other countries. There is a compelling efficiency argument for the allocation of renewable energy where it can be produced cost-effectively. Consequently, centralised regulatory power should be partially allocated at the central level to unlock efficiency gains that promote energy security. However, it should be noted that this approach may result in significant distributional effects between countries, as certain countries may lack competitive advantages in solar or wind energy. To ensure the participation and influence of all EU countries in shaping their preferences, compensation schemes could be implemented to offset potential losses and mitigate the distributional effects associated with the overall efficiency gains from centralisation. Cohesion policies (eg through the Just Transition Fund) or

[43] See, eg G Claeys and A Sapir, 'The European Globalisation Adjustment Fund: Easing the Pain from Trade?' in L Paganetto (ed), *Capitalism, Global Change and Sustainable Development* (Springer, 2020) 97 (discussing how this fund can compensate potential losers from the EU's trade policies).

policy-specific compensation programmes (eg through the Social Climate Fund) are considered adequate instruments for mitigating this type of distributional effect.

5. Financing European Public Goods

The financing of European public goods should take the particularities of the multilevel governance in the EU and the remaining preferences into account to supply public goods on the national level only. The challenge of bridging the limitation to national taxing power and European public good delivery is further compounded by the absence of genuine taxing power at EU level. The question of how European public goods should be effectively financed is also challenging, given the heterogeneity of the demand for public goods across countries. In a system of multilevel governance characterised by vertical differentiation between the EU and Member States, as well as horizontal distinction between Member States, the financing process becomes increasingly complex if implicit fiscal transfers are to be avoided. Concurrently, our analysis has demonstrated the existence of certain European public goods, thereby highlighting the necessity for a more thorough examination of their financing mechanisms. It is noteworthy that EU law remains silent on the matter of offering guidance on the financing of European public goods. It is evident that the Treaties do not provide a supportive framework for the financing of European public goods through EU revenues, with the exception of specific policy-related rights to levy duties (for instance, in the context of energy policy). The EU's mandate to ensure balanced budgets (Article 310 para. 4 TFEU) has significantly constrained its capacity to incur debt. In terms of public finance, the EU's position is not commensurate with that of a sovereign entity.[44] In this regard, the EU can be seen only as an international organisation that is purely derivative from the sovereign borrowing power of its members. The EU's own resources are constituted exclusively by contributions made voluntarily by Member States, rather than being determined by the discretion or will of the Union institutions.

Given the limited normative guidance offered by EU law, the theory of institutional and fiscal congruence, as introduced by Olson into the field of public finance, can be utilised as a conceptual approach.[45] This theory departs from a political economic point of view by emphasising that the incentive for government spending is stronger when it can externalise the costs for the public good while targeting

[44] S Grund and A Steinbach, *European Union Debt Financing: Leeway and Barriers from a Legal Perspective* (Bruegel, 2023).

[45] M Olson, 'The Principle of "Fiscal Equivalence": The Division of Responsibilities among Different Levels of Government' (1969) 59 The American Economic Review 479; DC Ehmke, *Institutional Congruence the Riddle of Leviathan and Hydra* (Nomos Verlagsgesellschaft 2018) 38.

the benefits at its electorate.[46] This is the traditional common pool problem,[47] and it is obviously one that plays out for the EU too – in the multilevel framework, each Member State seeks to secure the highest share of EU spending distributed among members for their respective constituencies at home. To address this challenge, Olson proposes institutional congruence, defined as the alignment of those who benefit from collective goods with those who finance them.[48] Fiscal congruence, by extension, aims to ensure that those who demand a certain level of public goods provision also contribute financially. In the absence of such alignment, externalities arise, leading to citizens paying for public goods and services they do not favour. The political economy dynamic underpinning Olson's reasoning involves the delivery of public goods to others, which raises the overall demand for the public good to an inefficiently high level because those who demand the public good do not pay the full price for it (eg through taxes). To address this, institutional congruence requires three circles or groups to coincide – the circles of beneficiaries, decision-makers and taxpayers – which brings in alignment risk, return, and control.[49]

This establishes a nexus between fiscal equivalence and fiscal federalism theory. While fiscal federalism delineates the criteria for determining the delivery of public goods at the European or Member State level, fiscal equivalence stipulates the financing mechanisms for such public goods. By anchoring the financing decision to the ultimate beneficiary, fiscal equivalence is contingent on the heterogeneity of preferences that was previously discussed. It is therefore vital to consider citizens' willingness to pay for public goods as a benchmark for the appropriate level of provision. In this regard, the EU should refrain from financing projects that primarily serve local interests, particularly when local taxes can be imposed. The construction of a new bridge in North Rhine-Westphalia, for instance, primarily benefits local residents. When the EU funds projects that are confined to producing local benefits, it may lead to external costs being borne by others. This principle finds application in a range of contexts, including the imposition of user fees to offset the costs of public goods and services, which might otherwise be financed from other sources.[50]

In this regard, the EU unanimity requirement to raise taxes at the EU level is a rational policy. While unanimity increases direct costs through the negotiation

[46] G Jennes, 'Interregional Fiscal Transfers Resulting from Central Government Debt: New Insights and Consequences for Political Economy' (2021) 74 Kyklos 196, 198; PB Anand, 'Financing the Provision of Global Public Goods' (2004) 27 *The World Economy* 215.

[47] M Olson, *The Logic of Collective Action: Public Goods and the Theory of Groups* (Harvard University Press, 1965)

[48] M Olson, 'The Principle of Fiscal Equivalence: The Division of Responsibilities among Different Levels of Government', (1969) 59 *American Economic Review* 483.

[49] CB Blankart, *Öffentliche Finanzen in der Demokratie: Eine Einführung in die Finanzwissenschaft* (Vahlen, 2011); DC Ehmke, *Institutional Congruence the Riddle of Leviathan and Hydra* (Nomos Verlagsgesellschaft, 2018), at 48.

[50] L Epstein and NW Waterbury, 'Judicial Behavior' in William Thompson (ed), *Oxford Research Encyclopedia of Politics* (Oxford University Press, 2020) 16.

process, it also ensures that external costs, such as the externalisation of public expenses to local taxpayers, are minimised.

However, as discussed above, divergent national preferences do not conceptually preclude the EU from public finance power. There is an efficiency case for certain goods to be supplied at EU level, due to positive spillover or economies of scale generated by EU action. By requiring equivalence between those paying and those consuming the goods, we can infer for the European case that what matters is the added value that Member-only action would forego. The foregone efficiency gains represent an argument to tax all EU citizens, because this added value accrues in principle to all EU citizens. With the European case limited to financing the added value of EU supply of public goods, there will be a mixed financing structure shared between Member States and the EU, in particular for domains in which heterogeneous preferences prevail. Consequently, the rules should be crafted in a manner that places both rulemaking and financing in the hands of the EU in instances where EU action generates benefits that are not solely domestic in nature. This implies that in scenarios where Member States express a desire to finance a higher level of public goods, the financial burden should be shouldered by individual Member States.

To illustrate this point, consider a situation in which all Member States concur that joint defence activities are advantageous. However, there may still be a divergence in terms of the extent to which security and defence capabilities are strengthened. Economies of scale should be exploited by the EU, leading to joint actions such as joint military forces, but members retain control and responsibility over other elements of defence to account for their security preferences. Likewise, external border protection may be a sound example for a public good, but members may wish for additional security that they can supply on their own. The EU's provision of supplementary financing can be rationalised as a means of optimising the benefits of public goods, particularly in instances where Member States might otherwise be deficient in their provision. For instance, the EU could assume responsibility for financing additional pandemic medicine, where Member States demonstrate inadequate provision. Fiscal equivalence principles offer a framework for addressing the challenges posed by insufficient alignment of preferences among all Members when it comes to cooperative endeavours. In such scenarios, the financial burden should fall exclusively upon the Member States that are directly involved in the provision of the public good, thereby ensuring that the burden is not shouldered by others.

In terms of specific revenue creation, the question arises of whether the EU should be permitted to tax itself or to rely on contributions from Member States, the latter of which is the prevailing practice. The principle of fiscal congruence suggests that the beneficiaries of EU funding coincide with the decision-makers and taxpayers. The decision-maker for EU public goods is at the EU level, and if the benefits of EU law-making accrue to all citizens, a broad tax base should be established at this level (even if Member States participate through the Council). This approach is consistent with the political economic motivation underpinning fiscal congruence, which aims to ensure that Member States contribute as little as possible and benefit as much as possible from the funding. It is evident that the current EU Treaties do not adequately address the financing of EU public goods.[51]

However, certain elements of the current member contribution to EU do align with the logic of weighted benefits. The Gross National Income (GNI), a residual and pivotal Own Resource, not only supplements other budgetary resources (eg customs duties, ETS revenue) but also constitutes the most substantial contribution to the budget. GNI can be regarded as a credible proxy for the benefits of EU public good provision, at least to the extent that it aligns with a burden sharing approach based on economic strength. However, to the extent that GNI-financed EU implies some externality on net-payers, this should be seen as inevitable in a multilevel union. Perfect institutional congruence would only be perfect (but unrealistic) if each resident is taxed lump-sum. Some residents, regions, or eventually even Member States may benefit over-proportionally, depending on the public good in question.[52]

6. Conclusions

The polycrisis has, at least in some circles, served to strengthen a sense of European solidarity. The continent's exposure to external challenges gives rise to the intuitive perception of the necessity for joint and coordinated responses, thereby rendering the revitalised concept of 'We Europe' a plausible zeitgeist. However, this narrative obscures the fissures that the ascendance of populism has wrought in the European edifice.[53] A European public good perspective is a rational approach to Europe that acknowledges the decline of traditional narratives (eg peace, prosperity, rule of law) and presents a task-oriented perspective on Europe's capacity to deliver. The question 'should public goods be provided at the national or European level?' is not the whole question. The right question is how to find institutional arrangements for public good provision that maximise the benefits of public goods for EU members. In some cases, this will lead to EU decision-making and financing; in others, it will lead to national decision-making and financing, with many possibilities in between. The chapter provides a framework and a set of illustrations that help identify the right arrangements.[54]

Firstly, the determination of whether to offer a public good at the national or EU level, or a blend of both, hinges on the diversity of preferences among Member

[51] C Fasone, 'EU Budget and Spending Powers', in A Hinarejos and R Schütze (eds.), EU Fiscal Federalism (Oxford University Press, 2023) 233, 237.

[52] DC Ehmke, Institutional Congruence the Riddle of Leviathan and Hydra (Nomos Verlagsgesellschaft, 2018), at 51.

[53] R McMahon and W Kaiser, 'Narrative Ju-jitsu: Counter-narratives to European Union', *Journal of Contemporary European Studies* 30 (2021), at 1–9.

[54] For the following see G Claeys and A Steinbach, 'A conceptual framework for the identification and governance of European public goods' Working Paper 14/2024 (Bruegel, 2024).

States and the efficiency argument for EU-level provision. The efficiency rationale may be attributed to economies of scale or the potential for cross-border externalities, both positive and negative. In scenarios where preferences exhibit significant variation and the efficiency argument is negligible, goods should be provided exclusively at the national level. Conversely, when preferences are uniform and the efficiency argument is robust, provision should be at the EU level. However, when preferences are diverse yet the efficiency argument is compelling, a trade-off emerges.

Secondly, a plethora of institutional and legal tools, both within and beyond the EU treaties, can be employed to navigate this trade-off, with the objective being to maximise efficiency gains while accommodating preference heterogeneity or safeguarding minority interests. These tools include decision-making mechanisms in the Council, the provision of public goods at the level of groups of Member States with similar preferences, and the employment of strategies such as 'constructive abstention', 'enhanced cooperation', or intergovernmental treaties. Furthermore, strategies such as the separation of common decision-making from common financing, the balancing of common and national financing, and the compensation of countries or minorities to align preferences could also be employed. Thirdly, both the efficiency argument for European public goods and the distribution of preferences over their provision may evolve over time due to changes in the global context or shifting preferences. This evolution may be driven by external or internal factors, such as institutional or financing practices that persuade dissenting parties that participation in a multi-country arrangement governing public good provision is more beneficial than opting out.

Notwithstanding, it is imperative to acknowledge a salient caveat in this regard. The provision of public goods in this manner has the potential to result in the proliferation of idiosyncratic governance arrangements, contingent on the unique characteristics of each public good. These arrangements would then distribute responsibilities across various governmental levels for different public goods. From a citizen's perspective, this could lead to challenges in comprehending the extent of accountability. Nevertheless, this is arguably the inevitable consequence of not adopting a federal system and placing as much emphasis on subsidiarity as the EU does.

9

Governance Theories 'on Trial': On *A-Constitutionality*: Constitutional Dilemmas in EU Crisis Governance

LEONE NIGLIA

I. Crisis Governance and Theories

In reading the institutional process of crisis governance – the Next Generation EU (NG-EU) and the initiatives regarding the EU public goods[1] – scholarship (political science, economics) proceeds while not considering key EU and comparative constitutional material that, I submit, must be taken into account with a view to really understand the context of the implementation of the NG-EU and the references to public goods.[2] No doubt this is down to the variety of specialisms involved in the analyses of the NG-EU and the need for combining them around the objective of identifying and mapping changes in constitutional structures,[3] which is a key objective of this project.

Specifically, the governance theories regarding EU public goods avoid justifying their arguments against the backdrop of a 'public good' as 'European'; and the governance theories built around the NG-EU, in explaining the NG-EU and its implementation,[4] play down the relevance of the background constitutional relations between the EU legal order and the national legal orders. Despite the talk of 'national ownership' (as constituting a kind of respect for state determinations)[5] the governance theories that focus on the NG-EU do not take note of the normative constitutional materials built over previous decades, which rose out of the conflicts between, on the one hand, the EU governance architecture and, on the other hand, what I would like to call the constitutional essentials of autonomy and equality.[6]

[1] See eg above at chapters 7 and 8.

[2] The data about implementation is not in itself sufficient (see eg https://ec.europa.eu/economy_finance/recovery-and-resilience-scoreboard/index.html): we need conceptual instruments for reading them and redirecting them to the common good (here understood as 'constitutional guidance', see the remainder of this chapter).

[3] See above at L Niglia Ch 1 Prologue.

[4] On implementation of the NG-EU, see Zeitlin et al. in chapter 7 in this book.

[5] See also at chapter 7.

[6] On constitutional essentials see L Niglia, 'Eclipse of the Constitution {*Europe Nouveau Siècle*}'. (2016) *European Law Journal*, 22: 132–156 and L Niglia, *The Structural Transformation of European Private Law. A Critique of Juridical Hermeneutics* (Hart Publishing, 2023).

In so doing, these governance theories, through their readings of the NG-EU (political science) and of the EU initiatives regarding the EU public goods including the NG-EU (economics) run the risk of being unresponsive to the relevant constitutionality requirements (autonomy and equality).[7]

At the same time, one should not underestimate the importance of these governance theories in terms of gaining knowledge on the ground of the implementation of the NG-EU. We can and must learn from these governance theories about what is governance on the ground in terms of their system integration capabilities for crisis resolutions towards the job of integrating further evidence in, and making more effective, the 'social integration' principled approach based on autonomy and equality.[8] This relates to the twin objective of the 'differentiation between theoretical and practical questions' and of the 'transition from non-reflexive (prescientific) to reflexive learning' through filling a gap in legal writings whenever they neglect to take into account political science and economic literature on the NG-EU and on the European public goods.[9]

Similarly to the legalistic position above considered[10] these theories end up portraying what might be labelled crisis governance as *a-constitutional*, that is, as neutral to constitutionalism. The legalistic position, through its resisting the need for policing the redistributive effects of the NG-EU;[11] and, as concerns us in this chapter, the political science and economic positions, through their *neglecting the consideration of, and inclusion of, the range of constitutional essentials* that connote the constitutional relations between the EU legal order and the national legal orders.[12]

This chapter brings to light such constitutional materials towards evidencing the urgent need to re-discuss both positions in their light – for this neglect may endanger, it is submitted, the whole enterprise of the NG-EU in terms of regenerating constitutionally Europe in terms of both effectiveness and legitimation, considering the relevant role played by political science and economic thinking in the organisation and implementation of crisis governance.

One caveat must apply: experimentalism-as-implementation through the NG-EU can be considered to be constitutionally engaged and not a-constitutional

[7] Both theories trespass the realms of the legislative and of the administrative (the NG-EU as legislation and as administrative activity) and are present in the public debates including in the two reports by Draghi and by Letta as inevitable background knowledge around which the reports are built. From this vantage point the two reports can and must be looked at through the critical framework of principled constitutionalism as reflexive governance which also includes a re-reading of the normative arguments that the two reports adopt or imply.

[8] On the need for the double job of the 'differentiation between theoretical and practical questions' and the 'transition from non-reflexive (prescientific) to reflexive learning' see above Niglia at ch 4.

[9] For an essay taking into account public goods as constitutional see the chapter 2 by Petersmann in this book; for essays taking into account the NG-EU in constitutional perspective see the chapter contributions at Parts 1 and 2. On the twin objectives see Ch 4 in this book.

[10] See Ch 4 in this book.

[11] See Ch 4 in this book.

[12] On 'constitutional essentials' see above at fn 6. In this chapter, I consider constitutional autonomy and equality as constitutional essentials regarding the relationship between the EU legal order and the national jurisdictions.

insofar as it is driven by constitutional guidance so that the two governance theories can be redeemed in their constitutional capacity as long as the dimension of constitutional guidance is brought to light and actively deployed. This is one more argument of this chapter.

* * *

Two more points:

The perspective here adopted proposes a new reading of the debate on aspects of federalism concerning crisis – those that see federalism as the solution to Europe's dilemmas as to its ongoing crisis condition – in that the latter discussion tends to be both under-determinative and over- determinative: under-determinative in that it refers to abstract notions of constitutional federalisation whilst neglecting deeper notions coming from the tradition of (federal) constitutionalism such as autonomy and equality as principles; over-determinative in that the federalising positions are presented as if they were capable of crisis resolution by only clinging on a range of abstract-normative arguments yet detached from the constitutional heritage.[13]

The chapters by Zeitlin et al. and by Steinbach are an illustration of how expertise works in crisis governance through EU legislation and the surrounding knowledge that makes the former possible: the reports on the NG-EU and the 2024 reports by Draghi and by Letta are examples of this liaison between expertise and governance that this chapter contributes to explore critically, towards contributing to analysing the role of expertise in crisis governance in the EU[14] from the perspective of crisis governance constitutionalism.

II. A-Constitutionality I: On Political Science Theories Regarding the Implementation of the NG-EU[15]

If the NG-EU corresponds to the description that scholars make of it then it is a-constitutional insofar as it disregards two kinds of constitutional essentials at once: autonomy and equality. Scholarship on the NG-EU tends to disregard these. Their position is characterised in the sense of what we can call a-constitutionality: if we take constitutionality to mean autonomy and equality at once then the converse means that a-constitutionality designates any rendition of governance instruments that justifies them *independently of* these two characterisations. We should work for readings of the NG-EU that go towards making it comply with such requirements

[13] See Niglia, 2016.

[14] Priban at chapter 5 warns us about the need for democratising expertise. See also L Herzog, *Citizen Knowledge: Markets, Experts, and the Infrastructure of Democracy* (New York, NY, Oxford University Press, 2023).

[15] For political science literature see chapter 7 above.

of autonomy and equality, as distribution and recognition,[16] rather than apologetically describing crisis governance as 'good governance', through looking at the actual ways in which the NG-EU is being implemented , that is, at the implementation of the national plans and at the amendments of the national plans.[17]

1. National ownership

A Premise. A central concern in scholarship on the NG-EU pertains to the relationship between, on the one hand, the NG-EU and the national plans and, on the other hand, the so called 'national ownership' that is at the core of the RRF[18] and that the Commission considers central to its agenda. By national ownership is

[16] See above at chapter 4. I consider autonomy and equality coextensively as explained at chapter 4 above.

[17] On the implementation of the national plans see Zeitlin et al. at chapter 7 of this volume; on the amendments of the national plans see S Ladi, D Tsarouhas and P Copeland, 'Negotiating the recovery and resilience facility: the emergence of coordinative conditionality' *Comp Eur Polit* 23, 18–39 (2025). https://doi.org/10.1057/s41295-024-00385-5; S Ladi, L Polverari, 'Reconceptualising the EU-Member States relationship in the age of permanent emergency' *Comp Eur Polit* 23, 1–17 (2025). https://doi.org/10.1057/s41295-024-00384-6.

[18] Whereas 39:

'In order to ensure the national ownership and a focus on relevant reforms and investments, Member States wishing to receive support should submit to the Commission a recovery and resilience plan that is duly reasoned and substantiated. That plan should detail how, taking into account the measures included therein, it represents a comprehensive and adequately balanced response to the economic and social situation of the Member State concerned, thereby contributing appropriately to the six pillars, taking into account the specific challenges of the Member State concerned. The recovery and resilience plan should set out the detailed set of measures for its monitoring and implementation, including targets and milestones and estimated costs, as well as the expected impact of the recovery and resilience plan on growth potential, job creation and economic, social and institutional resilience, including through the promotion of policies for children and the youth, and on the mitigation of the economic and social impact of the COVID-19 crisis, contributing to the implementation of the European Pillar of Social Rights, thereby enhancing the economic, social and territorial cohesion and convergence within the Union. It should also include measures that are relevant for the green transition, including biodiversity, and the digital transition. It should also include an explanation of how it contributes to effectively addressing the relevant country-specific challenges and priorities identified in the context of the European Semester, including fiscal aspects and recommendations made pursuant to Article 6 of Regulation (EU) No 1176/2011 of the European Parliament and of the Council. It should also include an explanation of how the recovery and resilience plan ensures that no measure for the implementation of reforms and investments included in that plan does significant harm to environmental objectives within the meaning of Article 17 of Regulation (EU) 2020/852 (the principle of "do no significant harm")'. Whereas 41:

'The Commission should assess the recovery and resilience plan proposed by each Member State and should act in close cooperation with the Member State concerned. The Commission should fully respect the national ownership of the plan and should therefore take into account the justifications and elements provided by the Member State concerned. The Commission should assess the relevance, effectiveness, efficiency and coherence of the recovery and resilience plan proposed by the Member State, based on the list of criteria set out in this Regulation. The Commission should assess the recovery and resilience plans proposed, and, where applicable, their updates, within two months of the official submission of the recovery and resilience plans. The Member State concerned and the Commission should be able to agree to extend that deadline by a reasonable period if necessary'.

meant, in the words of Zeitlin et al., a notion that entails the combined effects of legitimacy, effectiveness and public commitment, in the sense that:

> The RRF is demand-driven, insofar as Member States draft NRRPs comprising an integrated package of proposed reforms and investments, in consultation with the Commission. As the EC argues, Member States 'have flexibility in designing and implementing the measures in a way that suits their national conditions, which increases their ownership of plans'. Such national ownership of the plans is expected to enhance their legitimacy as well as their effectiveness, by increasing political commitment and public support agreed reforms and investments.

Recall that the RRF Regulation states that in assessing the NRRPs, 'the Commission should fully respect the national ownership of the Plan and should therefore take into account the justifications . . . provided by the Member State concerned' (recital 41). Yet ownership thus understood is problematic in terms of constitutional autonomy and equality.[19]

2. National ownership vs constitutional autonomy and equality.

2.1 The RRF Conditionalities

The Member States, in their drafting and implementing the national plans, are subjected to the RRF conditionalities including with regard to the prescription that:

'The Commission should assess the relevance, effectiveness, efficiency and coherence of the recovery and resilience plan proposed by the Member State, based on the list of criteria set out in this Regulation'.

Recall the conditionalities of the RRF:

First:

> the Plans must also meet a series of specific requirements set by the EU. Each Plan should show how it represents '**a comprehensive and adequately balanced response** to the economic and social situation of the Member State concerned,' while contributing to the recovery and resilience of the Union through support for measures in key policy areas of European relevance.

[19] See my argument below. Note that that this move by the EU towards disciplining the nation state is far from isolated: it is taking place in the case-law of the CJEU where the constitutional architecture of the EU is being changed in that the national level is losing its juridical hermeneutical role of participating in the construction of constitutional Europe which in turn becomes 'heteronomic' and characterised by constitutional 'absorbtion': see for full discussion L Niglia, *The Structural Transformation of European Private Law. A Critique of Juridical Hermeneutics* (Hart Publishing, 2023). Emphasis added in the quotations from chapter 7 and from the RRF Regulation.

Second: 'The NRRPs must further devote minimum percentages of expenditure to the green and digital transitions (37 and 20 per cent, respectively) and respect the principle of Do No Significant Harm to the EU's environmental objectives'. And, third:

> In addition, the plans must demonstrate how they contribute to the implementation of the European Pillar of Social Rights (EPSR), thereby enhancing the Union's economic, social, and territorial cohesion, and effectively address 'all or a significant subset' of challenges identified in the CSRs (RRF Regulation, recital 39, Art. 18.4).

2.2 On National Ownership vs the RRF Conditionalities

One cannot value the extent of 'national ownership' without considering the related conditionalities in that the latter ultimately shape the national plans through their criteria based assessment by the Commission: what the EU Commission say as to the *'flexibility in designing and implementing the measures in a way that suits their national conditions'* is limited by the conditionalities.

The belief that national ownership means that the national plans are made and owned by the state therefore flies in the face of the NG-EU conditionality architecture. The elements identified as national ownership --- the proposed national plans --- are re-determined and re-determinable under the conditionalities including through the country specific recommendations which refer to the RRF as key elements of them.[20]

At a deeper level of analysis, the above co-extensiveness of ownership and conditionalities narrows not just 'ownership' to the limited space left for autonomous decisions by the conditionalities' based interventions[21] but it also restricts constitutional autonomy understood as a degree of self-determination in matters of fiscal power in regimenting the *'liberty to organise national life at will'*.[22]

[20] See eg the country specific recommendation of the European Commission for a Council Recommendation on the economic, social, employment, structural and budgetary policies of Italy of 4 June 2025 European Commission COM 212 2025 with reference to the RRF. Recall the priorities listed in the Regulation, that is, the green transition, which amounts to a minimum of 37 per cent of investments, and digitalisation (at a minimum of 20 per cent).

[21] H. Lokdam and M. A. Wilkinson, 'The European Economic Constitution in Crisis: A Conservative Transformation' in G Grégoire and X Miny (eds) *The Idea of Economic Constitution in Europe*) point out that this approach 'reflects a desire to increase the capacity of the EU level (potentia) to direct economic developments across the Union in a particular direction and gives the Commission significant means for doing so (. . .), thus further narrowing the space for democratic control of economic policy-making decisions (in the sense of potestas)'.

[22] Joerges the economic, at p 793:

The 'liberty to organise national life at will' is a democratic essential. Has this command been overruled by Europeanisation and globalisation? I suggest that we should care about its survival and that a survival is conceivable under a re-conceptualisation of European and international economic law as 'conflicts law'.

As a result, the national plans are not about automatically enhancing 'national ownership' understood as self-determination, as Zeitlin et al argue,[23] but are about implementing the decisions of the Commission as to the national plans through the Commission's approval and its monitoring of the implementation of the national plans.[24]

As this process does not conform to constitutional autonomy, insofar as it prefigures a state that complies in disciplinary mode, it cannot produce 'national ownership' as allegedly implying an exercise of a degree of self-determination that, constitutionally speaking, is not out there.

The national conditions are assessed in the light of the conditionalities' criteria through the Damocles' sword of replacing any nation-based balancing by the Commission's own driven balancing decisions. Not even the European Parliament is really allowed to participate in these balancing acts,[25] let alone the minimal 'participation' of the national parliaments with their ratifying the Own Resources Decision.

And, as experts may and do participate in the NG-EU process,[26] an additional element of lack of national ownership arises when one considers that expertise rather than iterative democratic governance is at work here, as the remainder of this chapter discusses.[27]

We can say that there is a contradiction in the RRF between, on the one hand, the conditionalities and, on the other hand, 'constitutional respect' of the autonomy of national constitutional laws[28] that cannot be resolved by necessarily opting against the state interest; in case of decisions about priorities, or as to any 'non-compliance' as to targets/milestones, or as to any state requested amendment for 'objective circumstances' (Art 21 RRF), the principle of autonomy would require that the Commission adopt the standards of the decision of the CJEU under the principle of solidarity on energy,[29] interpreted in relation to the

[23] See also for a variation on the conception of national ownership the thesis of coordinative conditionality by S Ladi, D Tsarouhas, P Copeland, 'Negotiating the recovery and resilience facility: the emergence of coordinative conditionality' *Comp Eur Polit* 23, 18–39 (2025). https://doi.org/10.1057/s41295-024-00385-5. See M Dawson, 'Europe's expanding coordination space' *European Law Open.* 2024;3(4):746–767. doi:10.1017/elo.2025.8 (coordination space, a negotiation framework where discretion abounds, rules never broken but adjusted).

[24] See the RRF.

[25] Resolution of the EU parliament of 23 July 2020 on the conclusion of the Council of 17–21 July 2020 opposing the RRF for abandoning the methode Communautaire and for opting for intergovernmentalism, requesting to be involved in the ex ante and ex post control of the RRF plan.

[26] See the RRF.

[27] See Ladi et al. on 'cooperative conditionality' in S Ladi, D Tsarouhas, P Copeland, 'Negotiating the recovery and resilience facility: the emergence of coordinative conditionality' *Comp Eur Polit* 23, 18–39 (2025). https://doi.org/10.1057/s41295-024-00385-5.

[28] L Niglia, *The Structural Transformation of European Private Law. A Critique of Juridical Hermeneutics* (Hart Publishing, 2023).

[29] CJEU C-848/19 P *Germany v Poland* ECLI:EU:C:2021:598, see Niglia, Dual Solidarity (manuscript 2026 on file with author).

principles of autonomy and of equality as above explained, whereby the balancing of interests means that the states' interests must be taken into account and not just the conditionalities' criteria as interpreted and applied by the Commission. In the name of European constitutionalism, whenever 'respect of ownership' is at stake, states and any actors legitimated to participate procedurally should take the opportunity to litigate under constitutional autonomy, and equality, including at the implementation stage and at the level of control of action by the EU Commission.

The reading of the NG-EU process as automatically characterised by respect for national ownership is also in stark conflict with experimentalist democratic theories that, in my interpretation of them,[30] do require an element of what I am calling constitutional autonomy (and equality).[31] This is because experimentalist democratic studies have shown that the inputs from the outside are informational but are not held to have to also be decisional.[32] Limiting the inputs from the outside to the informational as opposed to the decisional means preventing 'bureaucratic autonomy', as Downey calls it in a US context, a concept that I would adapt to our European context.[33]

'Bureaucratic autonomy' in my view is an oxymoron in that either one gets autonomy as constitutional self-determination or one gets sheer bureaucratisation without, and shielded from, constitutional autonomy. 'Bureaucratic autonomy' here is a kind of autonomy devoid of the political guidance that is understood as awareness of possible alternatives and decisions being made about them. What is needed instead is specifically 'knowledge of alternatives'[34] as key to ensuring democratic control, a knowledge that must be out there and that must be shown as knowledge that the insiders are aware of. Yet this is what is not out there regarding the NG-EU implementation as described in political science studies.

This is also due to the conditionalities that make the delegator an over-powerful actor and the Member States power-less actors: the Member States have been given the power to draft their national plans but under the yoke of the conditionalities; they do possess the power to implement their plans but, again, under

[30] See also L Downey, *Our Money: Monetary Policy as If Democracy Matters*. Princeton, NJ: Princeton University Press, 2025 at p. 102 arguing at p. 103 that what Sabel and Zeitlin 'do not consider in developing their experimentalist architecture is the need for regular *political* guidance'.

[31] See also L Niglia The Structural Transformation of European Private Law. A Critique of Juridical Hermeneutics, Hart Publishing, 2023.

[32] See Zeitlin et al. See also CF Sabel, J Zeitlin, 'Experimentalism in the EU: Common Ground and Persistent Differences' Regulation & governance 6.3 (2012): 410–426; and CF Sabel, J Zeitlin. *Experimentalist Governance in the European Union: Towards a New Architecture*. Oxford; Oxford University Press, 2010 at ch 1.

[33] Downey *Monetary Policy*, above, at p. 103.

[34] On 'knowledge of alternatives' see Downey, *Monetary Policy*, above, at pp 103–108. On alternatives and the NG-EU (limited to means, not touching on objectives and purposes) see Niglia, Introduction to part 3, in this book.

the yoke of the conditionalities. Therefore, 'not knowing' about alternatives seems to be the key characterisation of the NG-EU in its organisational logic directed at spending funding under the set from above range of conditionalities. I refer to situations in which major choices are being made by the Commission over the states (for example, the case of pension reforms).[35] The criteria of the RRF do constrain the choices of the relevant actors. These choices should be widened under the proposed understanding of the role of balancing.

This is clear in situations in which the opposite might happen that can be taken to be about diverging trends as opposed to the ordinariness of the lack of awareness of alternatives: The contribution by Ladi et al. reports some instances in which it is the states that are allowed to make their own choices as to the funding allocations' priorities. Even from reading Ladi et al. about such reported situations it seems however that only governments sympathetic with the requested (from the Commission) reforms manage to be 'cooperative', and that having a 'reputation' of 'credibility' is relevant in that respect, whilst what may happen with governments that are not sympathetic and/or not well 'reputed' remains an unanswered question, it seems to me.[36] The constitutional benchmark of autonomy requires that a degree of discretion on the part of the state must be respected nevertheless even for the case of governments that are not sympathetic and/or not well 'reputed' as otherwise the underlying asymmetries of power will only rule the day determining the outputs (the actual funding allocations' priorities). This is because the asymmetric relations among the Member States must continue determining the actual decisions as to the implementation of the national plans and their monitoring[37] if

[35] See S Ladi, D Tsarouhas and P Copeland, 'Negotiating the recovery and resilience facility: the emergence of coordinative conditionality', *Comp Eur Polit* 23, 18–39 (2025). https://doi.org/10.1057/s41295-024-00385-5.

[36] See Ladi, S., Tsarouhas, D. & P Copeland, 'Negotiating the recovery and resilience facility: the emergence of coordinative conditionality', *Comp Eur Polit* 23, 18–39 (2025). https://doi.org/10.1057/s41295-024-00385-5.

[37] Contrast Zeitlin et al. Ch 7 in this book and K Nicolaidis '"Once in a Lifetime"? An Immanent Critique of NextGenerationEU' at https://kalypsonicolaidis.com/wp-content/uploads/2022/06/FL-233-3-Nicolaidis.pdf at p. 2:

'The Euro-crisis will be remembered as a moment when EU institutions presided over a radical jump in asymmetric mutual interference allowance under the cover of debt, combining in effect the traditional creditors playbook à la IMF, with the much more far reaching core competences of the EU, which turned the shared polity into the kind of enforcer which hitherto had been a role reserved for externally and temporarily involved agents like the IMF. Against this backdrop, NG-EU on the other hand, can be seen as a shift of the pendulum back to deference, based as it is on a bottom up process of national commitments. In order to access the funds, the Member States need to present ambitious investment programme which integrate the digital and climate transition imperatives. The Commission allocates budgetary envelopes to the Member States which generate their own distribution key between projects. To be sure, EU monitoring and its concurrent emergency break is still part of the equation but linked less to financial solvency than to the contribution to shared purposes.'

only sympathetic or well reputed governments[38] manage to obtain some 'concessions' as opposed to those governments with weaker financial conditions (the debtor states), and therefore with less bargaining power, also considering the limitations descending *externally* given the new stability pact.

Taking the need for experimentalism and regular re-assessment in policymaking coupled by political guidance[39] to mean that the legislature 'iteratively governs the areas of policy it delegates, by knowing and regularly showing its power over the delegated agency',[40] one must admit that not only does the NG-EU lack such political guidance in iterative terms, as the conditionalities are fixed once and for all as stated in the RRF (think of the fixed percentage prescribed for the digital and the ecological aspects of the funding) but also it lacks a deeper form of political guidance – what I would like to call *constitutional* guidance. That is, means of constitutional control that requires that the relevant alternatives should be tested and choices made through the kind of constitutional balancing above indicated under the principled reflexive understanding of governance.[41]

Yet, note instead how just 'competitiveness', as legal constraint, prevails as to attempts of the government to make redistributive trade-offs, as it happened in one major case in which a Supreme Court decided that discretionary decisions of the government in distributing the funds of the NG-EU through the national plans must comply with the principle of competitiveness and that no trade-offs under the NG-EU would be allowed.[42]

Again, not only are the overarching standards fixed once and for all (eg the percentages) and mono-thematically revolving around efficiency objectives rather than acting out of and allowing a full balancing of all relevant considerations (this being a requirement under 'constitutional autonomy'), including those different from and/or alternative to efficiency,[43] but there are rule of law substantive orientations from within national legal traditions that, in judicial form, out-rightly defend just the pursuit of competitiveness. Constitutional guidance should mean that the courts and the administrative bodies act in line with the fuller extent of balancing rather than constraining all under the command of competitiveness.

In a reverse perspective, that is, thinking further about how all should work under the principle of constitutional autonomy, the NG-EU determinations should

[38] S Ladi, D Tsarouhas and P Copeland, 'Negotiating the recovery and resilience facility: the emergence of coordinative conditionality' *Comp Eur Polit* 23, 18–39 (2025). https://doi.org/10.1057/s41295-024-00385-5.

[39] Downey *Monetary Policy*, above, at p. 103 (for whom Sabel and Zeitlin do not consider this aspect).

[40] Ibid at p. 103.

[41] See above and at Ch 4.

[42] Reference is made to a decision of the Spanish Supreme Tribunal decision of 2024 on the NGUE (regions claiming to make trade-offs but the supreme court imposing discipline through competitiveness).

[43] For a genealogy of full balancing as legal and constitutional, and as private law, see L Niglia "A Genealogy of Constitutional Europe" in J Chaisse and O. Stefan (eds.) "ADVANCING THE METHOD AND THE PRACTICE OF TRANSNATIONAL LAW" 2023 (Hart Publishing) and see L Niglia The Structural Transformation of European Private Law. A Critique of Juridical Hermeneutics, Hart Publishing, 2023

be made not only through participation from below, which is both constitutionally possible and necessary, but also as part of the role of the decision-makers and the experts as constitutional actors, considering that a constitutional balance must be made among the relevant conflicting normative considerations if democracy is to work as an open system that adapts to complexity[44] as it emerges from the NG-EU.[45]

The call for 'getting back democracy'[46] as it comes from US scholarship that works on popular participation as democratic,[47] and from scholarship that makes a similar call for the NG-EU,[48] is not to be meant as just about 'getting back democracy' understood as participation but (also) about making the kind of constitutional balancing act that I am arguing about. Typically, as part of this perspective, judicial review should work towards certain objectives such as (with regard to the macro-aspects) the need to protect the interests of the weaker Member States (as 'minorities'); and, (regarding the micro-aspects), the need to protect the interests of those, within states, adversely affected by the relevant decisions (as 'minorities').

At a related level of analysis, how can *learning* work considering that, on the above analysis, constitutional autonomy is not deployed effectively but is constrained by overarching standards that, in turn, prevent context-dependency in decision-making?

Here, I refer to those studies on the need for context-dependency decision-making, namely the arguments that:

> 'This model does not apply well to the present context because the objective itself ('good jobs') is imprecise and multi-dimensional; it needs to be operationalised in a way that is both evolving and context-dependent. Furthermore, creating good jobs depends on a wide array of decisions on investment, technological choice and business organisation, the consequences of which are unknowable ex ante. Technological and operational possibilities are highly uncertain, and neither firms nor government agencies have the information needed to devise concrete behavioural schedules from the outset.'[49]

But the NG-EU fixes targets (the conditionalities) for all states indifferently (despite it being underwritten by the unequal relations) and whilst leaving them to propose their plans it makes an assessment based on the overarching conditionalities including providing for percentage targets and standards – in other words, it is more centralised than decentralised.

[44] Compare DA Innerarity, *A Theory of Complex Democracy* (London, Bloomsbury Academic, 2025).
[45] See above at chapter 4 on crisis and emergency as key to the NG-EU.
[46] Note for this call Downey *Monetary Policy*, above,at p 88.
[47] Ibid.
[48] K Nicolaidis 'Once in a Lifetime'? An Immanent Critique of NextGenerationEU' at https://kalypsonicolaidis.com/wp-content/uploads/2022/06/FL-233-3-Nicolaidis.pdf
[49] https://www.bruegel.org/sites/default/files/private/2023-08/Bruegel%20Blueprint%2033_chapter%203.pdf

Learning presupposes autonomy as context-dependency decision-making otherwise there is no real 'learning' but the mechanical implementation of the conditionalities as technocratic constraints.

The constitutional principles of autonomy and equality 'irritate', hermeneutically speaking,[50] the doings of governance through interrogating the actual decisions made (the NG-EU funding, structural reforms, projects) which in turn revolve around conditionalities as technocratic constraints with no real political guidance understood as choices among alternatives[51] nor constitutional guidance in the principled sense here argued for.

On the one hand fiscal power, as far as the NG-EU funding is concerned, has been given up by the states in condition of necessity[52] and, on the other hand, as far as the NG-EU funding is concerned, no national *ownership* as constitutional autonomy remains in place given that the states are to implement the NG-EU under the conditionalities.[53] What is operational is control and conditioning in a predicament of emergency funding as a matter of the politics of exceptionalism as this has given rise to the NG-EU.

It is here where the argument from balancing that I am proposing steps in with its crucial role of re-aligning the condition of alienation of the relevant fiscal powers as to the NG-EU funding from state to common debt ('debt constitutionalisation').

2.3 Ownership as international vs constitutional autonomy and equality

There is then the issue of the very concept of 'national ownership' under the aspect that it comes from a certain kind of international experience that would, today in contrast to the past, no longer subject states to strict discipline conditional on lending financial aid but would instead recognise a degree of autonomy on the part of the states.[54]

[50] On 'irritants' as hermeneutical see L Niglia The Structural Transformation of European Private Law. A Critique of Juridical Hermeneutics, Hart Publishing, 2023, referring to and re-elaborating on G. *Teubner*, 'Legal *Irritants*: Good Faith in British Law or How Unifying Law Ends up in New Divergences',. 61 *MLR* (1998) 11).

[51] See Downey *Monetary Policy*, above.

[52] On national parliaments acting under necessity see eg Zeitlin et al. Ch 7 in this book ('the liberalisation of closed professions in Portugal, pension reform in Slovakia, and labour market reform in Spain, all of which were pushed through parliament on the eve of an impending payment request').

[53] See eg country specific recommendation of the European Commission for a Council Recommendation on the economic, social, employment, structural and budgetary policies of Italy of 4 June 2025 European Commission COM 212 2025 with reference to the RRF at nn 27 et seq. On the position of the creditor states see the Second Senate of the Federal Constitutional Court that rejected two constitutional complaints directed against the Act Ratifying the EU Own Resources Decision (Eigenmittelbeschluss-Ratifizierungsgesetz – ERatG): Judgment of 6 December 2022 - 2 BvR 547/21, 2 BvR 798/21 and see in English language at https://www.bundesverfassungsgericht.de/SharedDocs/Pressemitteilungen/EN/2022/bvg22-103.html.

[54] Chapter 7 in this book.

As such, this is an argument that does not lend itself to be transposed onto the EU to make intelligible the current relationship between the EU constitutional order and the national constitutional orders in relation to the NG-EU. As a matter of fact, given the underlying unequal relationships between financially strong and weak Member States in the EU, to read the relationship between the EU constitutional order and the national constitutional orders as if it were an administrative practice similar to that which allegedly now presides over the relationships between international organisations and states under 'national ownership' goes against the grain of the logic of the strongest state that in the end in the EU prevails through the NG-EU conditionalities.[55]

Here, the logic of international law applies and not the constitutional logics of European integration, including the elements noted in the previous sections. Here operates an obfuscation of the heritage of constitutionalism in Europe. In other words, 'national ownership' is not just distinct from, but is the opposite of, 'constitutional autonomy'. It is a fancy word to cover the making of discipline through the conditionalities under the NG-EU.

Yet it is equally true that any instances of recovering autonomy within the NG-EU as they may arise out of the implementation process must be looked at carefully to see whether a degree of autonomy is really developing out of the implementation of the NG-EU. Ladi et al. have identified forms of negotiations in which the national level can really exercise influence on the implementation process[56] in contrast to centralisation identified by others as the key feature of the NG-EU.[57] These patterns, in my view, point to forms of governance affected by and made dependent on the principle of equality understood as both recognition and as redistributive and transformative.[58]

Autonomy entails equality in that balancing for the debtor states should mean to allow these states more room for manoeuvre as to the policy choices made regarding redistributing towards those who most need the funds (micro power asymmetries); and, also, in terms of the deadline for using the funds, thus extending it for the debtor states; and, moreover, in terms of enabling on the part of the states any re-prioritisation of the objectives of ecology and of digitisation vis-à-vis those concerning the social, towards addressing the relevant macro

[55] See, on international vs constitutional in regional integration, L. Niglia Regional Integration in Max Plank Encyclopedia of Comparative Constitutional Law (2025) at https://oxcon.ouplaw.com/display/10.1093/law-mpeccol/law-mpeccol-e449. On the power of strong states to shape transnational law see K. Pistor 'From Territorial to Monetary Sovereignty' *Theoretical Inquiries in Law 18 (2):491-517 (2017)* and discussed in P McDougall, '*Global Value Chains, Labor Rights, and the Nature of Transnational Law*', *The American Journal of Comparative Law* 72(1) 2024, 33.

[56] See Ladi, S., Tsarouhas, D. and Copeland, P. Negotiating the recovery and resilience facility: the emergence of coordinative conditionality. *Comp Eur Polit* 23, 18–39 (2025). https://doi.org/10.1057/s41295-024-00385-5.

[57] See H Lokdam and MA Wilkinson, 'The European Economic Constitution in Crisis: A Conservative Transformation?', in G Grégoire and X Miny (eds), The Idea of Economic Constitution in Europe. Genealogy and Overview (Brill Nijhoff, 2022) 458.

[58] See above at chapter 4 on equality and discrimination.

power asymmetries.[59] These 'alternatives' and others are to be taken seriously as part of implementing the principles of autonomy and equality, which in turn must be considered as coextensive principles in the context of crisis governance constitutionalism.

2.4 Ownership vs equality. On the equality of the Member States of the EU

The conditionalities that bind states to certain standards mean that the conditions under which lending takes place are not among equals for they aim at transforming the relationship between the EU constitutional order and the national constitutional orders into an unequal administrative practice similar to that which presides between international organisations and states whenever lending is at stake.

It is true that scholarship discusses a change to a supposedly new system of lending, more cooperative and 'ownership' orientated, yet under the conditionalities the new system must not be different from the previous one.

Constitutional guidance means that both eventual renegotiations and the determinations of the Commission as to the actual decisions under the national plans (the spending and the related reforms) should be subjected to knowledge about the relevant alternatives towards making the decisions fully informed and politically effective.

An Intermediate Conclusion

Coordinative conditionality and experimentalism-as-implementation through the NG-EU, and the thesis of integration seen through the lenses of coordination as negotiations,[60] need to be subjected to the test of constitutionally reflexive governance as compound of the principles of autonomy and equality towards their benchmarking and controlling the relevant determinations. The idea behind this thesis is not just that of formal liberal rule of law limitations on the exercise of power[61] but is the deeper idea of the need for restoring the imbalance produced by 'debt constitutionalisation' towards redeeming the position of state fiscal power in the new landscape of emergency interventions through the novelty of EU fiscal power. This in turn enables the making of reflexive governance, understood as social integration normativities, that limit, constrain and shape the newly designed NG-EU form of fiscal power.

[59] See above Niglia, at chapter 4, for micro- and macro- power asymmetries in relation to the NG-EU.

[60] Dawson 'Europe's expanding coordination space' above.

[61] Notably the NG-EU is seen as being about executive governance under conditionalities in turn linked to the rule of law: see, eg L Fromont Une conditionnalité que ne dit pas son nom: l'état de droit dans la facilité por la reprise et la resilience in Cahiers de droit europe'en 58 2/3 (2022) 523 (on executive management of conditionality linked to rule of law).

III. A-Constitutionality II: Theories regarding the European Public Goods

The theories about public goods convey a strong sense of a shift in the allocation of powers (competences) across the EU and the Member States – holding that the EU is acquiring new powers. Take for example the opinion of Draghi that is representative of this position:[62]

> To maximise productivity, some joint funding for investment in key European public goods, such as breakthrough innovation, will be necessary. At the same time, there are other public goods identified in this report – such as defence spending or cross-border grids – that will be undersupplied without common action. If the political and institutional conditions are met, these projects would also call for common funding.

Yet, the loss of autonomy, of which the literature on public goods speculates in *economic* terms[63] is to be subjected to the argument about the need for the respect of constitutional autonomy. This intercepts, interestingly, Petersmann's thought in his discussion of the *constitutional* question of *competences* as being relevant to the scope of public goods rather than being insulated from that question, which in my view is about going towards meeting this demand. The conundrum is how to combine the position of the economists in their theorising about public goods with those of the lawyers – not as to the classical version of the formal competences attributed to the EU but in the version of reflexivity as crisis governance understood as placing limits on the NG-EU whose competence ambitions under the RRF are notably excessive.[64]

Public goods scholarship and policy reports put together a variety of distinct public goods under the same umbrella without distinguishing the 'identity' of each set of public goods. What would be made of cross-border grids and defence 'homogeneous public goods' is not explained in the constitutional terms here proposed. As a result, such homogeneity, which has dubious undertones in its holistic characterisation, lacks constitutional credibility.

Also, some highly controversial public goods in constitutional terms (competences) are placed on the same level as less controversial public goods.

Here what is prejudiced is constitutional autonomy in that entire sets of decisions as made or to be made by the EU would become legitimated under economic (cost minimisation) arguments applied to the chosen public goods: but the public good presupposes a conception of the community in the singular whilst public goods presuppose a certain economic conception of the plural,[65] so that to justify a supposedly homogenous range of Europe public goods disregards the missing link of the one community whilst, also, rejecting the plural at the same time

[62] M Draghi, https://www.europarl.europa.eu/news/en/press-room/20240913IPR23903/draghi-to-meps-europe-faces-a-choice-between-exit-paralysis-or-integration.

[63] See at Ch 8 above.

[64] See the NG-EU/RRF.

[65] N Walker 'The European Public Good and European Public Goods' in J Komárek (ed.) *European Constitutional Imaginaries: Between Ideology and Utopia* (Oxford, Oxford University Press, 2023) (distinguishing teleocracies from nomocracies).

due to the argument from the presupposed wholeness of the range of European public goods. In other words, what is missing is the autonomy dimension understood as self-determination of a collective. Public goods theories are artificial in that they aim at bettering governance and yet it is in this sense that they are a-constitutional. To give a brief illustration with regard to ecology as conditionality under the RRF: conflicts between social ecologists and free marketeers mean that their own respective definition of public good is incommensurable in that what to the latter is 'alienabile land' is to the former 'humanity's home'.[66]

Equality as principle as discussed above means the need for subjecting European public goods to the argument from redistributive justice as to the power asymmetries.[67] But they are predicated as if insulated from any such consideration which renders them, also in this further sense, a-constitutional.

IV. Conclusion

Not only, as I have held above:

Coordinative conditionality and experimentalism need to be put at the test of constitutionally reflexive governance as compound of the principles of autonomy and equality towards their benchmarking and controlling the relevant determinations. The idea is not just that of formal liberal rule of law limitations on the exercise of power, but is the deeper idea of the need for restoring the imbalance produced by 'debt constitutionalisation' towards redeeming the position of state fiscal power in the new landscape of emergency interventions through the novelty of EU fiscal power. This in turn enables the making of reflexive governance understood as social integration normativities that limits, constrains and shapes fiscal power

but also the theories of public goods are to be reread and rethought of in the light of reflexive governance as compound of the principles of autonomy and equality towards their benchmarking and controlling the relevant determinations.

Crisis governance constitutionalism emerges as structured around legal and political science and economic (this book's contributions) materials. Under the framework of emergency, constitutionalism collapses in a-constitutionality in that it becomes oblivious to a range of constitutional essentials: autonomy and equality. The work of rendering the EU emergency interventions 'constitutional', towards integrating fully a-constitutionalism in the body of crisis governance constitutionalism is ahead of us. *A-constitutional crisis governance* is the predicament of Europe in its devising the EU emergency interventions that calls for corrective thinking. Only an inclusive constitutionalism can ensure the mutual benefits of common funding and of constitutionality un-renounced.

[66] SE Hunt, *We Must Begin with the Land: Seeking Abundance and Liberation through Social Ecology* (London, Zero Books, 2025).

[67] See above.

10

Conclusive Remarks: Between Crisis, Constitutionalism, Governance *and* Democracy

LEONE NIGLIA

As integration crisis is increasingly seen as a crisis of democracy across the EU and the Member States, we need to explore ways in which constitutionalism, and specifically crisis governance constitutionalism, can help reverse such democratic crisis.[1] This book project chooses to look at the constitutionalist structures as the place where the space and time of crisis governance can be intercepted for both describing it and for its normative evaluation.

Yet the power of crisis governance in its legalistic constitutional characterisation, broadly understood as being insulated from concerns about the involvement of the public sphere and about the role of autonomy and equality, is such that it has become a ready-made apparatus for serving any emergency purposes in ways that make of crisis governance an unlimited *qua* unbound area for governance as sheer management. To place this mode of governance under a range of hierarchically constraining values is part of this move. What is missing is to proceed constitutionally under the relevant critical constitutional-normative requirements as these set limits on the one-sided systemic advances of crisis governance as management.

If the above critique as I have proposed it in the above contributions is of any value it is to bring matters on the ground of the constitutional structures towards starting a real reflection on the constitutional shortcoming of acting under exceptional conditions whilst, relatedly, disregarding the very bread and butter of constitutional ordinary materials as known since postwar times.

***

In the light of this book's chapters, we can now return to the two questions posed in the introduction to this book about which I offer my own view which, it goes

[1] We explore further this aspect in the other volumes in the series.

without saying, is not necessarily that of the book's other contributors but is rather my own interpretation:

1. Whether and under which constitutional modalities crisis governance is under constitutional control; whether constitutionalism risks becoming about just managing crisis governance or whether the transformation of crisis governance as new constitutionalism can be combined with preserving the normative-constitutional heritage;
2. Whether we experience a normal or an exceptional mode of crisis governance constitutionalism.

As to question one, I gather that constitutionalism is embedded in crisis governance given the emergence of the triadic 'crisis governance constitutionalism' above analysed in its manifold declinations. We can also say that the perspective of 'crisis governance constitutionalism' obliges us to take note of the risk of constitutionalism being reduced to just managing crisis governance as having materialised yet not integrally: how one deals with that risk towards constitutionally governing new governance depends on the ways in which the said tensions between the conflicting forms of crisis governance constitutionalism as above mapped will unfold. It is at this juncture that we will be able to register, and critically address, the ways in which to proceed constitutionally under the said critical constitutional-normative requirements, as these set limits on the one-sided systemic advances of crisis governance as management.

As to question two, we need to resist the exceptionalism of crisis governance by recovering the value of the said, contingent, constitutional essentials as they characterise the relationships among orders in Europe. There is urgent need for forging a constitutional vocabulary that confers legitimation on the whole thing, at least because the self-legitimation by large bureaucratic organisations is part of the overall remaking of the legitimation process in crisis conjunctures. To restore legitimation, the power holder must call upon other centres of power to make their power effective, one social scientist suggested.[2] Constitutionalism can and must serve this legitimation purpose towards complementing and re-orientating the 'whatever it takes' thinking proper of the ECB crisis interventions and today, we must say, as the further, exceptionalist major intervention of the NG-EU.

Yet I have also argued in the above that a more optimistic and deeper democratic conception must be worked out and put into operation in times of legitimation crisis for governance to justify itself, that is, a conscious participation based on the firm ground of constitutional principles. We will then be able to venture into scrutinizing the ways in which will-formation as participation can set limitations on the one-sided systemic advances of crisis governance as management. What we need to overcome is not just what has been described in political economic

[2] See Arthur Leonard Stinchcombe, *Constructing Social Theories* (University of Chicago Press, 1968): 'A power is legitimate to the degree that, by virtue of the doctrines and norms by which it is justified, the power holder can call upon sufficient centres of power, as reserves in case of need, to make his power effective'.

terms as a conservative transformation[3] and, in political science terms, as lack of demoicracy[4] but a transformation that worryingly, structurally, resists democratisation understood as the reliance on the comparatively relevant crisis resolution constitutional principles above noted (equality, autonomy). For above all what is needed is a new social vision, for as it has been held decades ago, in statements that are needed as to our present problems:

> whilst democracies by their essence not only respect minorities but live by a pluralistic concept of competing forces, their staying power will lastly depend on their continuous ability to impose upon themselves the limitations which are necessary for the preservation of the group unity'.[5]
>
> 'Democratic institutions stand and fall by their belief in discussion before a reasonable public'.[6]

To make another comparative point: one can look at places where governance takes place as 'permissionless innovation' unconstrained by the law[7] and yet the preoccupation of the constitutional scholar, and of the comparativist,[8] must be about whether and to what extent a legitimation that ignores law is capable of democratising the relevant innovative determinations as they take place in the specific locations, looked at and under their own autonomous ways of decision-making labelled as 'non-law'.[9]

Emergency thinking and practice is close to subverting normal constitutionality in that in the EU we note a shifting away from composite constitutionalism and towards a hierarchical ordering of the constitutional relations in Europe.[10] The promise of the thesis of reflexive constitutionalism as here proposed is to point to a new direction: towards a new kind of composite constitutionalism that aims at subjecting to control the doings of power politics in their vigorous embracing, through the EU crisis governance interventions, the mode of exceptionalist governance.

[3] See the thesis of H Lokdam and MA Wilkinson, 'The European Economic Constitution in Crisis: A Conservative Transformation?' in G Grégoire and X Miny (eds), *The Idea of Economic Constitution in Europe. Genealogy and Overview* (Brill Nijhoff, 2022) 458.

[4] See for discussion the chapter by Priban in this book.

[5] S Neumann, *Permanent Revolution: Totalitarianism in the Age of International Civil War*. Third edition. Berlin: LIT, 2023 first ed 1942, at pp 309–310. I leave it another time to discuss what 'group unity' and 'preservation' might mean so as not to conflict with the plural as necessary dimension.

[6] Neumann, *Permanent Revolution*, above, p. 116. Adding that 'such recognition of the masses as responsible participants by necessity limits the sphere of independent leadership in a democracy, already restricted by its institutional character'.

[7] N Stremlau and C Voyvodic Casabó, 'Non-State Law and Technologies' in N Stremlau and C Voyvodic Casabó, eds. *Technology and Governance beyond the State: The Rule of Non-Law* (London, Routledge, Taylor & Francis Group, 2025, at pp 1–3 and 3–17).

[8] L Niglia, *The Structural Transformation of European Private Law. A Critique of Juridical Hermeneutics* (Hart Publishing, 2023); L Niglia, 'Regional Integration' in *Max Plank Encyclopedia of Comparative Constitutional Law 2025* at https://oxcon.ouplaw.com/display/10.1093/law-mpeccol/law-mpeccol-e449.

[9] Stremlau and C Voyvodic Casabó, 'Non-State Law', above.

[10] L Niglia, *The Structural Transformation of European Private Law. A Critique of Juridical Hermeneutics* (Hart Publishing, 2023).

INDEX

www.ingramcontent.com/pod-product-compliance
Ingram Content Group UK Ltd.
Pitfield, Milton Keynes, MK11 3LW, UK
UKHW021826230926
475688UK00003BC/115

9 781509 990016